new york

KU-745-730

a virgin guide

First published in 1999
Virgin Publishing Ltd, London w6 9HA
This edition copyright 2000 © Virgin Publishing Ltd, London
All rights reserved

♫ getting your bearings
[→6–7]

mapping new york's key areas

virgin new york

lower east side & chinatown
[→8–11]

eastern delights
edgy | colourful | hip

tribeca
[→12–14]

hollywood east
quiet | cool | professional

soho
[→15–20]

soho, so chic
glamorous | expensive | busy

nolita & noho
[→21–25]

in the no
young | hip | cute

east village
[→26–31]

village people
wild | funky | creative .

west village
[→32–36]

west side story
quaint | literary | gay

Written by 20 contributors in-the-know, this guide gives the inside take on New York. The focus is on having fun; where to hang out, shop, eat, relax, enjoy and spoil yourself. And there's a selection of the top cultural hot spots...

contents

chelsea & the meatpacking district [→37–41]

go west
gay | clubby | friendly

gramercy park & the flatiron district [→42–45]

all square
pretty | rarefied | calm

midtown [→46–51]

middle ground
full on | workaday | vertical

upper east side [→52–55]

the gold coast
wealthy | gracious | exclusive

upper west side [→56–58]

western hemisphere
affluent | residential | laid-back

harlem [→59–61]

take the a train
urban | vibrant | historic

brooklyn [→62–65]

over the east river
diverse | authentic | emerging

the lowdown on the best shops, restaurants, cafés & bars in each area

getting your bearings
mapping new york's top sights, museums & galleries

[→66–67]

sights, museums & galleries
[→68–82]

big apple highlights
a selection of the best on offer

Manhattan landmarks [→68–70]
one offs [→71–72]
take five [→73–75]
historic houses [→76–77]
melting pot [→77–78]
in the mix [→78–79]
in the picture [→79–81]
gallery seen [→81–82]

spectator sports [→83]
a piece of the action

parks & beaches [→84–85]
turf 'n' surf

children [→86–87]
kids' corner

body & soul [→88–89]
feelgood factor

games & activities [→90–91]
have a blast

getting your bearings
mapping new york's top shopping zones

[→92–93]

shops
[→94–109]

retail therapy
the pick of new york's shops

department stores [→94]
fashion [→95–99]
vintage fashion & discount stores [→100]
shoes [→101]
accessories [→102]
sports gear [→102]
theme stores [→102]
beauty [→103]
interiors [→104–105]
gift & museum stores [→105–106]
books [→106]
electronics [→107]
CDs, records & tapes [→107–108]
food stores [→108–109]
markets [→109]

getting your bearings
mapping new york's night-time hot spots
[→110–111]

restaurants & cafés
[→112–127]

what's where [→112–113]

dine out
70 plus restaurants & cafés to cross town for

timeless classics [→114–116] eat-in delis [→115] big bucks [→116–117] talk of the town [→118–120] diners [→119] bargain gourmet [→120–121] burgers [→120] steaks, grills & bbq [→121] ethnic spice [→122–123] veg out [→123] brunch [→124] romantic rendezvous [→124–125] neighbour-hood standouts [→126]

bars & clubs
[→128–135]

drink up
60 plus bars/pubs to cross town for

club mode [→128] lively sounds [→128–129] the status quo [→129–130] live it up [→130] sports bars [→130] themes & schemes [→131] great dives [→131–132] gay thirst [→132] quiet retreats [→132]

night fever

top venues [→133–134] best nights [→134–135]

entertainment
[→136–146]

that's entertainment
how to get a slice of the action

theatre [→136–137] cabaret [→137–138] comedy [→138] cinema [→139–140] opera & classical music [→140] dance [→141–142] poetry [→142–143] music [→143–144] media [→145] directory [→146] events [→147–148]

hotels
[→149–157]

what's where [→149]

sleep easy
50 of New York's best hotels from the last word in luxury to budget beds

chic boutiques [→150–151] dead famous [→151] last word in luxury [→151–152] designer label [→152–153] home from home [→154] budget beds [→154–155] themes & variations [→155–157] city b & b's [→157]

---

transport [→158–163]

practical information [→164–167]

index & acknowledgements [→168–175]

symbols & key to maps [→176]

subway map [→back cover]

A1 ↑INWOOD

UPPER MANHATTAN

washington heights

W 145TH STREET

hamilton heights

A2 W 125TH STREET (DR MARTIN LUTHER KING BLVD)

morningside heights

Morningside Park

CATHEDRAL PARKWAY

E 110TH STREET

A3

YORKVILLE

upper west side

Central Park

upper east side

MANHATTAN

W 96TH STREET | E 96TH ST

W 57TH STREET

A4

midtown

THEATER DISTRICT

HELL'S KITCHEN

W 42ND ST | 42ND STREET

GARMENT DISTRICT

MURRAY HILL

Bryant Park

LINCOLN TUNNEL

W 29TH ST | E 29TH STREET

FLOWER DISTRICT

A5

FASHION DISTRICT

gramercy park

chelsea

flatiron district

UNION SQUARE

meat-packing district

Washington Square

west village

east village

ALPHABET CITY

noho

E 14TH STREET

EAST HOUSTON STREET

HOLLAND TUNNEL

nolita

soho

WEST HOUSTON STREET

LITTLE ITALY

CANAL STREET

lower east side

A6

tribeca

china-town

CIVIC CENTER

PARK ROW

DELANCEY ST

B6 BOWERY

EAST RIVER

BATTERY PARK CITY

LOWER MANHATTAN

FINANCIAL DISTRICT

BROOKLYN BRIDGE

MANHATTAN BRIDGE

DUMBO

Battery Park

coney island ↓

RED HOOK

BROOKLYN HEIGHTS

ADAMS STREET

Fort Greene Park

fort greene

carroll gardens

BRONX

washington heights

harlem

SEVENTH AVENUE

EIGHTH AVENUE

BROADWAY

AMSTERDAM AVENUE

ST NICHOLAS AVE

SPANISH HARLEM

FIFTH AVENUE

MADISON AVENUE

PARK AVENUE

THIRD AVENUE

FIRST AVENUE

B1 149TH STREET

Mullayly Park

Franz Sigel Park

GRAND CONCOURSE

MAJOR DEEGAN EXPRESSWAY

HARLEM RIVER DRIVE

JACKIE ROBINSON PKWY (MALCOLM X BLVD)

MELROSE AVE

THIRD AVENUE

St Mary's Park

WILLIS AVE

BRUCKNER BOULEVARD

B2 Randalls Island Park

RANDALLS ISLAND

WARDS ISLAND

Wards Island Park

HARLEM RIVER

FRANKLIN D ROOSEVELT DRIVE

B3 Carl Schurz Park

EAST CHANNEL

ROOSEVELT ISLAND

WEST CHANNEL

Rainey Park

LONG ISLAND CITY

QUEENSBORO BRIDGE

Queensbridge Park

B4 E 57TH STREET

VERNON BOULEVARD

QUEENS-MIDTOWN TUNNEL

B5 THIRD AVENUE

EAST RIVER

FRANKLIN D ROOSEVELT DRIVE

WILLIAMSBURG BRIDGE

DELANCEY ST

C6 BROOKLYN

NAVY YARD

FLUSHING AVENUE

McCarren Park

williamsburg

BEDFORD AVENUE

BROOKLYN QUEENS EXPRESSWAY

GRAND STREET

ATLANTIC AVENUE EXT

FLATBUSH AVENUE

Bronx Park

BRONX

EAST RIVER

Flushing Meadows

QUEENS

Central Park

MANHATTAN

NEW JERSEY

BROOKLYN

Prospect Park

UPPER NEW YORK BAY

GRAND CENTRAL PARKWAY

STATEN ISLAND

0 kilometres 4
0 miles 4

QUEENS

Lower East Side & Chinatown [→8–11]

Tribeca [→12–14]

Soho [→15–20]

Nolita & Noho [→21–25]

East Village [→26–31]

West Village [→32–36]

Chelsea District [→37–41]

Gramercy Park & the Flatiron District [→42–45]

Midtown & Hell's Kitchen [→46–51]

Upper East Side [→52–55]

Upper West Side [→56–58]

Harlem & the Heights [→59–61]

Brooklyn [→62–65]

0 kilometres 1
0 miles 1

HENRY HUDSON PARKWAY

HUDSON RIVER

new york's key areas

directory

Alphabet city 🗺B5

Named after Avenues A, B, C, and D, which march from First Avenue to the East River. The mainly Puerto Rican community has been supplemented by an influx of students and yuppies – though the area has always had its artsy-types (like Allen Ginsberg and Iggy Pop).

Brooklyn Heights 🗺B6

This is 'Cosby-country'. With its majestic brownstones, poetically named (Orange, Pineapple, Cranberry etc) tree-lined streets, and the Promenade overlooking the river, the Heights is what the term 'des-res' was invented for.

DUMBO 🗺B6

Down Under the Manhattan Bridge Overpass, the cobbled alleyways are lined with warehouses, which are rapidly being appropriated by escaping Manhattanites. Spectacular skyline views and a thriving art scene herald the area's revival.

Garment District 🗺A4

Delivery trucks and men wheeling racks of cheap clothing clog the streets around Seventh (Fashion) Avenue and 34th Street. Fashion Avenue is a sad misnomer; there is nothing fashionable to be had along the stretch of sweat-shop produced designer rip-offs.

Hell's Kitchen 🗺A4

Once a poor, down-and-out neighbourhood, the area west of the Port Authority Bus terminal is about to 'blow up' according to realtors. Meanwhile, the Cubans have transformed the former Irish enclave around 10th avenue in the 40's with a taste of the homeland. Although the area was rechristened 'Clinton' in 1959, the name never really stuck.

Little Italy 🗺B5

With the ever-expanding Chinatown eating up this tiny neighbourhood, 'little' is an apt description. The tacky restaurants are over-priced, but the cafés are excellent for coffee and desserts; traditional Italian food stores can't fail to please either.

Lower Manhattan 🗺B5–B6

Bustling by day; ghost town by night, the tapered end of the island of Manhattan is home to City Hall [→68], Wall Street and the NY Stock Exchange. New housing developments in Battery Park City [→85] house the movers and shakers living in the shadow of the World Trade Center [→69].

Murray Hill 🗺B4

The constant traffic to and from the Queens–Midtown tunnel has taken something from this once toney neighbourhood south of 42nd Street. But elegant houses and the Morgan Library [→77] raise the zip code's ratings and it's still considered a fashionable address to have.

Museum Mile 🗺B3–B4

Museums abound along Fifth Avenue, from the Frick Collection [→76] on 70th St all the way up to ICP Uptown [→80] on 96th, with the Met [→73–74], Solomon R Guggenheim [→74] and the Cooper-Hewitt [→76] to mention but a few, in between.

Navy Yard 🗺C6

During World War II, 70,000 employees worked here, where the motto was 'Can do'. Today, Navy Yard is still an industrial park but many of its unused buildings are in deep decay, lending it a strange, otherworldly feel. Rumoured to be the location for NY's answer to Hollywood, a plan masterminded by De Niro and co.

Red Hook 🗺B6

Cut off from the rest of Brooklyn by the Brooklyn–Queens Expressway, Red Hook is rather isolated, with Civil War-era warehouses, clapboard cottages, and some of the city's most notorious housing projects. (Red Hook was the setting for Hubert Selby Jr's Last Exit to Brooklyn.) Blessed with extraordinary light, the area is very popular with artists.

Roosevelt Island 🗺B3

Situated in the middle of the East River, the island that used to house a lunatic asylum and a smallpox hospital is now home to a community of 8000. The cable cars across to the island offer some of the best views in town [→70].

Spanish Harlem 🗺B2

East of Fifth Avenue and above 100th Street is a colourful and music-filled neighbourhood (also known as El Barrio), though quite desolate by night. Local landmarks are La Marqueta (the food market on Park Avenue from 110th to 116th Streets), or the Graffitti Hall of Fame at 106th Street between Park and Madison Avenues.

Theater District 🗺A4

Broadway wends its way through Times Square, lined with a profusion of theatres. In New York's sleazy past this was also home to the porn industry – now it's squeaky clean, and Disney has moved in.

Upper Manhattan 🗺A1

With an amazing view of the Hudson River to the west and the Harlem River to the east, the island's narrowest point is an odd mixture of inner city and wilderness. Location of The Cloisters [→78–79], and Inwood Hill Park, which holds the last traces of the island's ancient forest.

Yorkville 🗺B3

Home to the 'old money' of NY: beautiful townhouses, doormen and expensive restaurants define the area from the 70's to 96th Street east of Lexington Avenue. Gracie Mansion – the mayor's official residence, is set in the area's lush Carl Shultz Park.

Bronx 🗺B1

The only NY borough that is not an island. Recent renovations and investment mean it is losing its reputation as a no-go zone and there are several attractions (Bronx Zoo [→86], Botanical Gardens [→75] Yankee stadium [→83]). For the curious, the elevated subway lines provide a safe view of the erstwhile battlegrounds of the South Bronx and will take you through New York's most ethnically diverse communities.

Queens 🗺C3

Visitors to New York will probably only see Queens when journeying to or from its two airports, and truth be told the same can be said for most New Yorkers. But delve deeper and the borough's multicultural makeup has lots to offer. Long Island City houses PS1 – the super-cool studio space and gallery [→81]. Then there's the Greek neighbourhood of Astoria, Irish Woodside, and Indian and South American Jackson Heights. The huge steel 'Unisphere' globe (as seen in Men in Black), is a leftover from the 1964 world fair held in Corona Park.

Staten Island 🗺see locator

The relationship between Staten Islanders and their nte one, with talk of secession baeighbours is a love-handied about over the last few years. Non residents mostly know it for being the site of the largest landfill in the world. But the free ferry service between Manhattan and Staten Island gives one of the best views of Manhattan, and a short trolley ride from the port takes you to the Snug Harbour Cultural Center where there's a gallery, a butterfly house and Opera performances.

getting your bearings

eastern delights

Nowadays, the tenement buildings of the Lower East Side (LES), New York's one-time Jewish ghetto, are more likely to be occupied by Hispanics than bearded men in black hats. But you'll still find some evidence of the district's ancestry: look for its die-hard delis and crumbling synagogues. Recently, a new generation of dream-seekers has moved in – boutique-keepers, bar owners, trust-fund anarchists, and latter-day bohos – migrating from the neighbouring East Village in search of lower rents. As a result, real estate prices here have rocketed, and the LES has been reborn as Hipster Central.

Chinatown, meanwhile, remains irrepressibly Oriental. Bolstered by a continuous stream of Chinese immigration, it teems with authentic markets, restaurants and teahouses (as well as ubiquitous neon signs). But with its proximity to ritzier areas, will it be victim to Downtown's rampant gentrification? It's hard to imagine Chinatown's booming, energetic stronghold will ever be fully repressed.

day

🛍 A mix of bargain shops and cool boutiques (which often open and stay open late); and discount stores and stalls of Chinatown.

👁 Lower East Side Gardens [→85]; Lower East Side Tenement Museum [→76].

night

☆ An eclectic array of groovy bars and live music venues (especially on Ludlow and Orchard Streets).

🍴 Chinatown's excellent restaurants are as busy by night as they are by day.

getting there

Ⓜ B•D•Q to Grand St; F to 2nd Ave, E Broadway or Delancey-Essex Sts; J•M•Z to Canal St, Bowery or Delancey-Essex Sts; A•C•E•N•R•6 to Canal St

🚌 M9 ↔ E Broadway via Essex St & Ave B; M14 ↕ Essex St via Grand St; M15 ↕ St James Pl via Allen St, 1st & 2nd Aves; M21 ↔ Houston St via Ave C; M103 ↔ Bowery via 3rd & Lexington Aves.

shopping

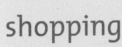

fashion, accessories & interiors

With its Sunday market on Orchard Street and discount stores on Delancey Street, the LES has always been a bargain-hunter's bazaar. But it's no longer just the place to pick up some *schmutter*. New stores open regularly in settings where the aesthetic screams minimalist chic, and the designs are edgy and fresh. **Mary Adams** and *Amy Downs* ✓ are the fashion pioneers of the LES. Mary is mistress of distinctive, feminine party dresses; Amy's forte is hats – always whimsical and themed (like those inspired by NYC locations). But the store that really made the LES happen is *TG-170, thanks to Terri Gillis's gift for finding brilliant new designers. It has ultra-girlie styles at (relatively) affordable prices. Check out United Bamboo, Rubinchappelle and the house label (for basics), along with must-have bags from Pixie Yates and Karen Zoebe. At **Patch 155**, designer Cal Patch's treasure trove of quirky clothes – urban and funky-pretty – includes exclusive labels such as It's

* = featured in the listings section [→92–135]

an Exciting Time to Be Me!. Another tiny shop filled with brilliance is **Fragile**, showcasing a handful of designers including Bill Tournade and Paris-based designer Lamine Kouyaté, whose inspiring pieces often feature the signature multi-textured and multi-coloured patchwork made from recycled materials. Over at **105 Stanton** designers include Min Lee, who specializes in classic clothes with a twist – chic numbers that can be worn all day and night when teamed with tiny evening bags. Alternatively, check out international style trends as perceived by the owners of **Zao**. This lifestyle boutique has the best up-and-coming designers from around the world: fashion, furniture, electronics – plus sexy sounds and happening art shows to boot.

DDC.Lab is an all-white style palace, radiating sophistication and big price tags. The ultimate in hedonism can be obtained in the form of limited-edition Reeboks at a mere $2500! Making quite a splash at the epicentre of the LES, minimal ***Nova USA**, surrounded by a haze of bright lights, carries the basics for men and women that make life worth living. For yet another take on sleek, urban sportswear, there's **Juan Anon**, where the colour palette is neutral to match the low-key vibe. **Recon**, on the other hand, is all camouflage paint and razor wire, selling T-shirts and hi-tech toys – testosterone rules here. Down the street is **Vinnie's Tampon Case**, which oozes oestrogen: devoted to selling the consummate carry-all, Vinnie is so immersed in his products, he's even created a performance piece about them. Satisfy your need for more fun accessories in **Lucky Wang**. If the *tchotchkes* here don't turn you on, stop in at **Toys in Babeland**, a high sex shop with naughty lingerie and toys like the Pocket Rocket for girls home alone.

The LES is a good area for searching out good quality vintage gear. **Las Venus** deals in 20th-century pop culture, focusing on the 50s, 60s and 70s, including some very Valley of the Dolls clothing. Neighbouring ***Timtoum** acts as a magnet for those who attend the owners' club night. Clothing by local designers, utilitarian bags, used garb, and an eclectic selection of vinyl are the lure. ***Cherry** has plenty of top quality 60s collectables and some fun clothes (heavy on glamorous dresses), while ***Foley & Corinna** stock pre-loved vintage clothing, plus their own designs (both clothing and bags) made out of retro fabrics.

chinese emporiums

Discount stalls line Broadway and Canal Street selling fake fashion items. You might get a bargain or you might get ripped off. In the thick of it, the ***Pearl River Mart** – a longtime favourite with beauty editors and stylists – has elegant Chinese clothes at very realistic prices. The top floor stocks a vast assortment of kimonos, silk and embroidered pyjamas and underwear, slippers, cheongsam dresses, and padded jackets. On other floors are kitschy home furnishings, trinkets, Chinese music, videos and food: you're bound to see some celebrity picking through the treasures.

A tip – avoid the rickety elevator and take the stairs! **Oriental Gifts** also has a nice (though smaller) variety of Chinoiserie, from vases to fans, lanterns and woks. If you want your cheongsam custom-made for a fraction of what it would cost you to buy the Dolce & Gabbana version (and it will be nearly as amazing), drop by the **Oriental Dress Company**. You can choose from the shop's own luxurious silks (in a wide variety of colours), or provide your own fabric. Orders take about three weeks, long dresses cost around $280, short ones $250.

eating & drinking

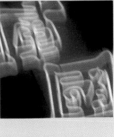

restaurants & cafés

The LES has played host to waves of immigrants from around the world, which is reflected in the choice of restaurants on offer. Only a handful of Jewish eateries remain, including ***Katz's Deli**. Although a bit frayed at the edges, it's still popular with locals and American presidents alike (look for proudly displayed letters from Reagan and Clinton). The glorious pastrami sandwiches are thick enough for two. **Yonah Schimmel's Knishery**, founded in 1910, is a rather decrepit hole-in-the-wall, still beloved for dumpling-like potato knishes and homemade bagels. For more of a DIY snack, check out ***Russ & Daughters** (known locally as the Herring Kings). Among the tasty treats on offer are lox, scallion cream cheese,

superb chopped liver, and chewy bagels to go. **Bereket** is another cheap bet, a bright beacon dispensing fresh Turkish fast food 24 hours a day, while the rather shabby **El Sombrero** is frequented mostly by actors and musicians after performances. Again the (Mexican) food is cheap and pretty basic: the potent margaritas are the real appeal. **Casa Mexicana** is a whole different basket of tortillas: the kitchen puts a more sophisticated spin on Mexican food by marrying non-traditional combinations of ingredients with French culinary techniques. Ambitions are high too at ***71 Clinton Fresh Food**, a small exclusive spot, surprising not only for the incongruous setting but its inventive, reasonably-priced New American cooking. The new, mod LES is epitomized by **Torch**, a swanky lounge and 40s-style supper club. Nightly cabaret acts can be enjoyed along with great cocktails and French/South American-inspired cuisine. For a daytime, boho hang-out, **Lotus Club** has healthy sandwiches and arty magazines to peruse or purchase.

Undeniably, most of the best places to eat in this area are in Chinatown. The most celebrated is ***Joe's Shanghai**, a fragrant, bustling spectacle with a line outside every night. During the day, the Chinese parade to the cavernous **Jing Fong** for dim sum carts loaded with sumptuous tidbits. It's noisy and service might be brusque, but it's also the real McCoy. For a sweet snack, it's hard to beat the **Hong Kong Egg Cake Co** ♩, aka the Egg Cake Lady.

Look for her fading red shack tucked down a side street (11am–5pm Wed–Thu & Sat–Sun), and slip her $1 for a sack of a dozen hot cakes with custard filling. Still hungry? Try **Grand Sichuan**, a bare-bones, spicy Szechuan restaurant. As well as Chinese standards, they serve ethnic specialties you won't find elsewhere. Roasted ducks hang in the window at **New York Noodle Town**, a bright and lively magnet for both Chinese and Westerners. Pan-fried noodles are tossed with poultry, seafood, and vegetables.

Vegetarians are particularly well-served by **Vegetarian Paradise 3**, a friendly, pastel-hued cafeteria with lots of tasty numbers. **New Won-ton Garden**, with lights bright enough to cause sunburn, is good for cheap, quick, quality eats. **Great Shanghai** has a more sleek, dimly-lit ambience; the sweet-and-sour fish and sauteed baby shrimp are excellent. The title for best Vietnamese is held by **Nha Trang**, a rather charm-less abode that pulls in crowds for its gorgeous, glossy platters of sauteed beef, seafood, and delicate vegetables. Another good bet for Southeast Asian fare is the **Thailand Restaurant**, a favoured lunch spot – though the somewhat tacky, wood-panelled room looks better at night. The aroma from these classic dishes is incredible. To perfectly cap off any meal, stop by the **Chinatown Ice Cream Factory** to try exotic flavours like lychee and red bean.

bars & clubs

A star on the Ludlow Street nightlife trail is ***Max Fish**, a long-time hang-out for indie bands that attracts a young mixed crowd. Don't be put off by its bright lighting. For fans of drum 'n' bass and electronica, ***Orchard Bar** (with decor inspired by natural history dioramas) is a required stop. Experimental music collectives regularly spin sounds in this dark, sexy space. Along the block is **Angel** with its low-level lighting, plush seating for slummers and regular rosta of DJs. Equally mellow is the beautiful ***Kush**, one of NY's many neo-Moroccan lounges. Definitely less stylish, but lots of fun is **Welcome to the Johnsons'** a bar fitted out to resemble the typical mid-70s living room, complete with plastic-covered furniture.

The LES has a number of multi-purpose nightspots, including ***Baby Jupiter** and ***Tonic**. Both combine bar and performance spaces,

and the former has a restaurant. Then there's new addition to the scene, ***Slipper Room**, an opulent one-stop venue that's good for catching crazed cabaret acts and sipping exotic cocktails. But the neighbourhood's freakiest theme bar is definitely **Idlewild**, with its lounge designed to look just like an airplane's cabin and lots of regular parties. The highly popular, and much more conventional ***Good World Bar & Grill** is basic but inviting, with laid-back tunes, and a garden. Another unpretentious bar is **169 Bar**, a basic dive with an underground feel that's playing host to exellent, music-orientated parties. A less hetero scene is on offer at **Meow Mix**, a hardcore lesbian dive that features fierce live-music performances. Neighbouring Chinatown's bars remain resolutely Chinese, but for a mix of local flavour and an English-speaking crowd, the place to visit is ***Winnie's**, a raucous karaoke bar.

♫ directory

Amy Downs ♫C1
103 Stanton Street
598-4189

Angel ♫C1
174 Orchard Street
780-0313

Baby Jupiter ♫C1
170 Orchard Street
982-2229 ◖

Bereket ♫A1
187 E Houston Street
475-7700 $

Casa Mexicana ♫C1
133 Ludlow Street
473-4100 $$

Cherry ♫C1
185 Orchard Street
358-7131

Chinatown Ice Cream Factory ♫B3
65 Bayard Street
608-4170 $

DDC.Lab ♫C1
180 Orchard Street
375-1647

El Sombrero ♫C1
108 Stanton Street
254-4188 $

Foley & Corinna ♫C1
108 Stanton Street
529-2338

Fragile ♫C1
189 Orchard Street
334-9166

Good World Bar & Grill ♫C3
3 Orchard Street
925-9975 ◖

Grand Sichuan ♫B3
125 Canal Street
625-9212 $-$$

Great Shanghai ♫B3
27 Division Street
966-7663 $-$$

Hong Kong Egg Cake Co ♫B3
Mott & Mosco Sts $

Idlewild ♫B1
145 E Houston St
477-5005

Jing Fong ♫B3
20 Elizabeth Street
964-5256 $-$$

Joe's Shanghai ♫B3
9 Pell Street
233-8888 $-$$$

Juan Anon ♫C1
193 Orchard Street
529-7795

Katz's Deli ♫C1
205 E Houston Street
254-2246 $

Kush ♫C1
183 Orchard Street
677-7328

Las Venus ♫C1
163 Ludlow Street
982-0608

Lotus Club ♫C1
35 Clinton Street
253-1144 $

Lucky Wang ♫C1
100 Stanton Street
353-2850

Mary Adams ♫C1
159 Ludlow Street
473-0237

Max Fish ♫C1
178 Ludlow Street
529-3959

Meow Mix ♫C1
269 E Houston Street
254-0688 ◖

New Wonton Garden ♫B3
56 Mott Street
966-4886 $

New York Noodle Town ♫B3
28 Bowery
349-0923 $-$$

Nha Trang ♫A3
87 Baxter Street
233-5948 $

Nova USA ♫C1
100 Stanton Street
228-6844

105 Stanton ♫C1
105 Stanton Street
375-0304

169 Bar ♫C3
169 E Broadway
473-8866

Orchard Bar ♫C1
200 Orchard Street
673-5350

Oriental Dress Company ♫B3
38 Mott Street
349-0818

Oriental Gifts ♫B3
96 Bayard Street
608-6670

Patch 155 ♫C1
155 Rivington Street
533-9995

Pearl River Mart ♫A3
277 Canal Street
431-4770

Recon ♫B1
237 Eldridge Street
614-8502

Russ & Daughters ♫B1
179 E Houston Street
475-4880 $

71 Clinton Fresh Food ♫C1
71 Clinton Street
614-6960 $$

The Slipper Room ♫C1
167 Orchard Street
253-7246

TG-170 ♫C1
170 Ludlow Street
995-8660

Thailand Restaurant ♫B3
106 Bayard Street
349-3132 $

Timtoum ♫C1
179 Orchard Street
780-0456

Tonic ♫C1
107 Norfolk Street
358-7504 ◖

Torch ♫C1
137 Ludlow Street
228-5151 $$

Toys in Babeland ♫C1
94 Rivington Street
375-1701

Vegetarian Paradise 3 ♫B3
33 Mott Street
406-6988 $-$$

Vinnie's Tampon Case ♫B1
245 Eldridge Street
228-2273

Winnie's ♫B3
104 Bayard Street
732-2384 ◖

Welcome to the Johnsons' ♫C1
123 Rivington Street
420-9911 ◖

Yonah Schimmel's Knishery ♫B1
137 E Houston Street
477-2858 $

Zao ♫C1
175 Orchard Street
505-0500

lower east side & chinatown

hollywood east

Tribeca (the Triangle Below Canal Street) is fashionable Downtown's most south-westerly outpost. In spite of a prevalence of chic eateries and bars, and a smattering of interesting stores, the area feels positively residential. It's not hard to see why Tribeca, with its availability of cavernous factory and warehouse space, has emerged as the Hollywood of the East Coast – both Robert De Niro's Tribeca Films and Miramax are based here. Starry residents include Bobby himself and Harvey Keitel, who, if you believe the gossip pages can be seen regularly chowing down in the local friendly diners. In reality, you're more likely to encounter bankers and brokers from the neighbouring Financial District, who have also made Tribeca home.

day

🛍 The majority of shops are along West Broadway and its adjacent streets. They sell mostly home furnishings, with a few notable fashion exceptions. Places open late morning and close early evening.

👁 Battery Park [→85]; City Hall [→68]; Ellis Island [→71]; National Museum of the American Indian [→78]; Statue of Liberty [→71–72]; Woolworth Building [→70]; World Trade Center [→70]

night

☆ Great music venues like the Knitting Factory [→143] and Wetlands [→144], as well as the Screening Room [→139] movie house.

🌙 The streets of Tribeca are fairly quiet after dark as the scene is focused on the neighbourhood's restaurants. Bars tend to be calmer than elsewhere in town..

getting there

Ⓜ A•C•E•N•R to Canal St; A•C•1•2•3•9 to Chambers St; 1•9 to Franklin St.

🚌 M6↑ Church St via 6th Ave; M6 ↓ Broadway; M10 ↑ West St via Harrison St, Hudson St & 8th Ave; M10 ↓ Varick St via 7th Ave; M22 ← Chambers St via Madison St.

shopping

home furnishings

Modern, sleek and distinctive defines *TOTEM ✓ (The Objects That Evoke Meaning). From the most fabulous sofas and rugs to loads of frosted plastic accessories, you'll want it all. Over at **Antik,** there's a covetable selection of 20th-century collectables, including lots of Scandinavian ceramics and furniture. But if Hawaiian bamboo furniture is more up your alley, then you will love **Oser**. Here you can sip coffee at the bar, watch an old surf movie, and admire the hot line of own brand swimsuits or the giant shark you've bought to hang on your wall. In the name of over-the-top, quirky glamour, **Anandamali** features bureaux, tables and mirrors decorated (mosaic-style) with antique china. Visit **Orange Chicken** for a more traditional take on furnishing your home.

* = featured in the listings section [→92–135]

fashion & beauty

If you're only going to buy one pair of leather trousers in your life, make sure they're from **Behrle**. And for fetish-inspired pieces that will turn anybody into a sex goddess, try the owner's label World Domination. **Shack Inc**, as much an art gallery as a shop, features ethereal, romantic clothes (all handmade and hand-dyed in situ) plus home furnishings and handbags. Linda St John, the designer behind ***DL Cerney**, freely admits to being obsessed with the 40s, 50s and early 60s, which is reflected in her 'new vintage' clothes – tailored shirts, simple skirts, trousers (for men and women) – and all at reasonable prices. **Working Class** has elevated workwear to a new level of elegance, seen in their vintage jeans with leather pockets, handmade clogs and workboots, and schoolboy satchels – all in bright shades. But for more of a hip, feminine look, **Sorelle Firenze**, run by two Italian sisters, does a fine line in flirty skirts and tops, lacey dresses and delicate accessories.

eating & drinking

restaurants

Dark streets, loading docks, lofts and lots of groovy restaurants define Tribeca. Mr Cool himself, De Niro, is part-owner of ***Nobu** and **Next Door Nobu**, both beautifully designed, innovative Japanese restaurants that regularly attract celebs. Next Door distinguishes itself by offering a range of noodle dishes and a no-reservations policy. Megarestaurateur Drew Nieporent, De Niro's partner, started out in Tribeca with the three-star **Montrachet**, a minimalist bistro serving ravishing nouvelle French cuisine. Then came **Tribeca Grill**, a warehouse-sized restaurant with cross-cultural American food and an award-winning wine list. **Layla** is also part of the empire, an opulent Middle Eastern palace (with bellydancers), featuring mezze, tajines, kebabs and couscous fit for a sultan. There's more razzle dazzle at **Danube**, David Bouley's luxurious downtown tribute to Vienna, offering refined middle European fare in a sumptuous setting at seriously uptown prices (some say it is rather overpriced). But ***The Odeon** continues to be the preferred upscale canteen for the fashion and art scene. Even if you can't get a table, it's fun to observe the action from the bar, or try **Bar Odeon**, its annex across the street, which has its own fair share of celebrity sightings. For a spot of sangria and paella, **Flor de Sol**, reminiscent of a Spanish parador, is an appealing option: its bar serves tapas too. **The Independent** is another local hangout in warm, rustic surroundings. The menu is inspired and moderately priced. Alternatively, give thanks at **Grace**, for another helping of innovative American food and an interesting buzz. The kichen's open 'til 4am, and there's a great bar scene too. ***Spartina** has all the ingredients for success – superb Mediterranean cuisine in a romantic setting, though perhaps one of the most unusual dining choices in Tribeca is the retro-style ***Screening Room**, which provides the perfect one-stop venue for that movie-followed-by-dinner date. The movies are independents and the food is New American.

It is not without good reason that **Chanterelle** is one of NY's top-rated restaurants – creative French cooking in a friendly environment. Another gem is ***Bouley Bakery**, which serves exquisite seasonal new French cuisine, while its bakery holds a myriad delights. Old-guard French food is served in the loft-like space of ***Capsouto Frères**. Big names go there, not only for the elegant food, but also because they're left alone. Even more secluded is ***Rosemarie's**, a posh Italian, specializing in robust-flavoured dishes, while **Pepolino** is much more homey, and even the most basic of pastas won't fail to please.

cafés & diners

For cheap chow try **Kitchenette ↓**, a sweet American roadside stop with hearty country cooking (open 'til 10pm). **Bubby's** is another neighbourhood favourite for unpretentious food like roast chicken, and pancakes: its weekend brunches are terrific. And **Walkers** is a friendly watering hole, serving burgers with beer on tap. Settle in and enjoy the live jazz.

bars & clubs

This area's bars have all the glamour of neighbouring Soho's but mostly without the suffocating crowds. Weekends, however, tend to be packed at the **Ice Bar** – one of the hottest tickets in town, with its all white interior, sexy crowd and wizard DJs. **Dylan Prime** is another recent arrival, where a sophisticated set come to savour excellently-mixed cocktails. (Meaty dining options are also available.) Adding a touch of luxe to Tribeca's Financial District is *Lush, a quietly swank

champagne bar, where you can also indulge in caviar. If you'd rather pop your cork in a crowd, try *Bubble Lounge, located in a considerably more fashionable area. For a more casual, pub-like atmosphere, **S J South & Sons** serves classic British/Irish fare like beef stew and pints of Guinness. **Liquor Store**, another friendly local, features wall-to-wall windows – perfect for people-watching or just settling in with a pint and the paper. For a more rough-and-tumble experience, try the *Nancy

Whiskey Pub, an authentic dive that has steadfastly resisted gentrification. A younger scene can be found at the **Knitting Factory's Tap Bar**, where 18 beers are offered on tap. Free, live music ranges from funk to bizarre, experimental acts (11pm–2am nightly). Meanwhile, DJs spin hip-hop, funk and soul at actor Michael Rapaport's dark and atmospheric bar and club, **Tribeca Blues**. With its large, promoter-driven parties, the club has a secure future.

🔖 directory

Anandamali ♫B2
35 North Moore Street
343-8964

Antik ♫B2
104 Franklin Street
343-0471

Bar Odeon ♫C2
136 West Broadway
285-1155 $$–$$$

Behrle ♫C2
89 Franklin Street
334-5522

Bouley Bakery ♫C2
120 West Broadway
964-2525 $$$

Bubble Lounge ♫C2
228 West Broadway
431-3433

Bubby's ♫B2
120 Hudson Street
219-0666 $–$$

Capsouto Frères ♫A1
451 Washington St
966-4900 $$$

Chanterelle ♫B2
2 Harrison Street
966-6960 $$$

Danube ♫B3
30 Hudson Street
791-3771 $$$

DL Cerney ♫C2
222 West Broadway
941-0530

Dylan Prime ♫B1
62 Laight Street
334-2274

Flor de Sol ♫B2
361 Greenwich Street
334-6411 $$

Grace ♫C2
114 Franklin Street
343-4200 $$–$$$

Ice Bar ♫A1
528 Canal Street
226-2602

The Independent ♫C2
179 West Broadway
219-2010 $$$

Kitchenette ♫B3
80 West Broadway
267-6740 $

Knitting Factory's Tap Bar ♫C2
74 Leonard Street
219-3055

Layla ♫C2
211 West Broadway
431-0700 $$$

Liquor Store ♫C2
235 White Street
226-7121 ◖

Lush ♫C3
110 Duane Street
766-1275

Montrachet ♫C2
239 West Broadway
219-2777 $$$

Nancy Whiskey Pub ♫C1
1 Lispenard Street
226-9943 ◖

Next Door Nobu ♫B2
105 Hudson Street
334-4445 $$$

Nobu ♫B2
105 Hudson Street
219-0500 $$$

The Odeon ♫C2
145 West Broadway
233-0507 $$$

Orange Chicken ♫B2
152 Franklin Street
431-0037

Oser ♫C3
148 Duane Street
571-6737

Pepolino ♫C2
281 West Broadway
966-9983 $$–$$$

Rosemarie's ♫C2
145 Duane Street
285-2610 $$$

Screening Room ♫B1
54 Varick Street
334-2100 $$

Shack Inc ♫C2
137 West Broadway
267-8004

S J South & Sons ♫C2
273 Church Street
219-0640 ◖

Sorelle Firenze ♫C3
139 1/2 Reade Street
571-2720

Spartina ♫B2
355 Greenwich Street
274-9310 $$$

TOTEM ♫C2
71 Franklin Street
925-5506

Tribeca Blues ♫C3
16 Warren Street
766-1070 ◖

Tribeca Grill ♫B2
375 Greenwich Street
941-3900 $$$

Walkers ♫B2
16 North Moore Street
941-0412 $$–$$$

Working Class ♫B3
168 Duane Street
941-1199

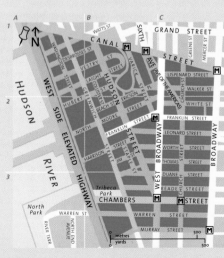

soho, so chic

New York's most conspicuously fashionable neighbourhood is compact to a fault – every big-name designer has a store somewhere in this tiny pocket of intersecting streets. Such a cluster of important shopping venues – alongside swanky commercial art galleries, elegant restaurants and exclusive bars – could only act as a magnet for fashion and media types. Even if you don't run into Gwyneth Paltrow in Miu-Miu, catching sight of some impossibly thin beauty dashing to a shoot at one of the neighbourhood's many photo studios is an everyday occurrence. Despite so many manifest distractions, Soho's magnificent architecture is hard to ignore. The monumental 19th-century buildings are some of the finest and most varied examples of cast iron architecture in the US.

The days when Soho was the epicentre of NY's artistic life have gone, and while there are still plenty of highbrow art galleries (and long-time resident artists, blessed with favourable rents), the cutting-edge art scene has shifted to Chelsea, causing many to observe that Soho's reign as the coolest neighbourhood in NYC could well be over.

day

🏛 Soho is packed with designer boutiques and one-off stores, which tend to open from late morning to 7–8pm – even on Sundays. Swanky galleries are great for browsing.

👁 Soho Guggenheim [→75], the Museum for African Art [→77–78], the New Museum of Contemporary Art [→80], New York Earth Room, and Broken Kilometer (in the Dia Center for Arts) [→80] are close by.

night

☆ NY's premier arthouse cinema, The Angelika [→139], plus Performing Garage theatre [→137], and club-music venue Shine [→133] are all nearby.

🍸 This area is known for its super-stylish restaurants and bars, loungey bar-clubs with strict door policies.

getting there

Ⓜ B•D•F•Q to Broadway-Layfayette St; 7 C•E to Spring St; N•R to Prince St; A•C•E••1•9 to Canal St; 1•9 to Houston St.

🚌 M6 ↑ 6th Ave, ↓ Broadway; M10 ↑ Hudson St, ↓ Varick St; M21 ↔ Houston St.

shopping

women's fashion

*Betsey Johnson ✓, one of the first designers in Soho when it was Nowheresville, makes crazy clothes, and has a dramatic flagship store to match. An eccentric American girl, Betsey's aesthetic is feminine and frilly, with a rock 'n' roll edge. Another designer who consistently whips up the prettiest party dresses and accessories is ***Cynthia Rowley**. In her homey shop, the racks are filled with rich fabrics and plenty of beads and embroidery. Another local lady, **Nicole Miller** has made a name for herself designing wearable evening dresses and chic separates. **Vivienne Tam**'s sleek, exotic clothes – form-fitting, beaded dresses;

* = featured in the listings section [→92–135]

saucy suits; handbags and loungewear with an oriental flair – have become a staple of fashionable gals, including Julia Roberts. Another store with an Asian flavour, **Dosa**, has grown into a cult favourite with It girls. Using classic shapes, it's the special fabrics and interesting details that give these elegant pieces their appeal. For designer **Atsuro Tayama**, however, it's all in the cut: check out his boldly asymmetric, deconstructed garments – but only if you're feeling confident.

Always the Queen of hippy-inspired glamour, *****Anna Sui**'s purple palace is a haven for the young and fabulous. Her leathers are divine, and her accessories – based on vintage designs – adorable. Emerging as America's biggest fashion star is *****Marc Jacobs**, whose airy, minimalist shop is an important stop, even if you can only afford to look. Everything here is the height of sophistication and luxury. Along the block is **Tocca** with its range of very girlie, but eminently wearable designs as well as a pretty range of bed linens. Fashion addicts from all over flock to get their fix of *****Miu Miu**. This more youthful (and less expensive) line from Miuccia Prada is always on the cutting edge of fashion, especially the undeniably fabulous and inventive shoes and bags. While the clothes vary wildly from season to season, the mood is always seductive in a Lolita sort of way. Ethereal and romantic is the theme at *****Morgane Le Fay**, where dresses resembling origami creations conjure up that urban-gypsy look. And at *****Issey Miyake Pleats Please**, there's more designer wizardry, as every piece of clothing folding up like an accordion for a sexy fit with a Far Eastern essence; the store's window glass trickery is equally intriguing. Meanwhile, at *****Vivienne Westwood**, every customer is a star when they step out of their dressing room on to a 'stage' in one of her

Soho's airy spaces vacated by the art world make ideal showcases for swelegant clothes and furnishings.

theatrical creations. More genius clothes (almost upstaged by the architecture) are to be found at **Philosophy di Alberta Ferretti**.

*****Scoop** is an important destination if you're looking for well-selected separates by young names, while *****Kirna Zabete** calls itself 'Shangri-la for swinging style' and boasts a collection of hard-to-find clothing, footwear, and accessory designers from around the world. In addition to the pieces by Joseph Thiminster, Lulu Guinness, Balenciaga et al, this two-storey honeypot also sells beauty products and flowers, and there's even a couple of iMacs to play on for the all-shopped-out. Another fashion pioneer is **Louie**, who also showcases the talents of a small group of burgeoning style-stars, with a unique

collection of accessories. In a similar vein, **Big Drop** houses a colourful collection of clothing, including lots of little sweaters and items by New York Industry or Earl Jean. Best described as a grown-up Urban Outfitters, *****Anthropologie** is the kind of place where labels are less important than the look. Think colourful cowgirl chic, Latin flounces and ruffles, and lots of lovely housewares and furnishings. *****Trufaux**, too has a very definite style: everything is made of *faux* materials – all very PC, but fun! *****Catherine Δ**, is all about creating a lifestyle rather than just getting dressed – sharp, young girl clothes, lots of the designer's signature fedoras, and home furnishings, all in a shop that looks more like an apartment than a store.

men's & women's fashion

Creating luxurious, brightly hued, modern clothes (for both sexes), with bold, graphic shapes is what **Alpana Bawa**, born in New Delhi, does best. Men love her filmy, embroidered shirts in muted hues. If expensive avant-garde is what you crave, *****If Soho New York** has an inspired collection from the fashion stars of today and tomorrow (Dries Van Noten, Veronique Branquino et al).

Check out the Johnny Farah bags – *très* chic, and surprisingly affordable. Artsy but tailored shapes, unexpected fabrics, and fascinating details are responsible for *****Costume National**'s icon status. They also make distinctive, covetable shoes. If you want a mix of styles under one roof, *****Steven Alan** has the best of NYC's up-and-coming designers as well as accessories and watches. Just around the corner is **Steven Alan Menswear**, filled with sharp looks for men. At ***Helmut Lang**, the futuristic 'communications obelisk' is as entrancing as the geometric clothes, while everything in ***Yohji Yamamoto's** amazing gallery-like store is almost too beautiful to wear. How to look fabulous when you're actually doing something more than posing? ***Prada Sport** has filled the obvious gap in the market with its utilitarian designs, while **Polo Sport** goes for an equally casual but more preppy look. For men only, the ***Yves Saint Laurent Rive Gauche** boutique provides daring clothing in that proverbial St Laurent kind of way.

Edgy, trendy, and occasionally kitschy clothes and accessories from around the world are to be found at ***Hotel Venus** (the Soho branch of Patricia Field, Downtown's trendsetting, leading lady for 20 years). This is still the only place in town to get the hugely desirable Courrèges collection and there's even an in-store wig salon. If you're looking for super-cheap clothes more on the casual side, there's plenty to choose from all along Broadway, where discount sportswear stores dominate, including good sneaker outlets. In their midst is ***Canal Jean Co**, a kind of NY institution filled with almost every kind of vintage and new jeans, and cheap T-shirts. A branch of the Spanish chain **Zara International** is

also worth investigating for reasonably priced and stylish separates and shoes. **Stussy** is still the epicentre for upscale skatewear, meant for men but worn by everybody. Definitely

for men only is ***Sean**, a welcome addition to the men's clothing scene, with a mix of well-priced separates, by various designers, that are smart without ever being stuffy.

home furnishings

*Moss has the ultimate in modern, industrial design, and sets the tone for cool furnishings in NYC. All the big names are carried here, displayed museum-style in glass cases. Nearby ***Troy** is becoming increasingly influential: expect bold and interesting small furniture and accessories by new designers. ***Shabby Chic** offers furnishings with a softer edge – their comfortable sofas and 'T-shirt' sheets are legendary. ***Zona** bears a striking resemblance to a lived-in, country home. Vintage and new furniture, jewellery and other *objets* are here, but everybody's favourites are the gorgeous, colour-saturated, hand-dipped candles. ***Jonathan Adler**, known for his entertaining striped pottery (with a 50s accent) has a shop

crammed full of treasures, including some of his own flea market finds that he's willing to pass on to his devoted customers.

Portico Bed & Bath are the lifestyle pioneers in Soho. They offer the finest, most elegant linens and other accessories that will make your home positively scream 'good taste'. ***Ad-Hoc Software** has a wackier edge with great *tchotchkes* for bathrooms, bedrooms and kitchens, plus elegant tablewares and bed linens. For the ultimate in cheap and cheerful, yet well-designed home furnishings, take the stairs up to **Dom** (above Hotel Venus), where you can get colourful home accessories for a song, along with whimsical lighting and inflatable furniture that's easy to store.

accessories & shoes

In the quest to finish your look, start at ***Fragments**, a showcase for 30 or so new jewellery designers working in a range of styles. ***Selima Optique** has the most fabulous eyewear in town, plus an interesting array of hats, scarves and scents. Her nearby lingerie shop, **Le Corset**, is crammed with frilly items from around the world, including some vintage pieces. Everything in **Louis Vuitton** is a heart-stopper, especially the price tags! The traditional LV accessories and luggage are still covetable classics. At the other end of the price scale, ***Steve Madden** is famous for creating on-the-edge and over-the-top shoes and boots. For something more sleek, sharp footwear by an international posse of designers is on offer at ***Otto Tootsi Plohound** whereas the new

*Rockport 'concept' store is a kind of Niketown for the comfy shoe set – they even do made-to-measure.

It's impossible to go anywhere these days without spotting one of ***Kate Spade's** bags on somebody's arm. She makes them saucy, serious, and sublime. Her store also carries cute accessories, like date books or very fem stationery. And to pull the whole outfit together, get yourself a **Casio Baby G-Shock** watch from the store devoted to the eponymous timepieces.

food

The corner of Broadway and Prince sees a stream of folk ducking into the airy ***Dean & Deluca**, which stocks a bounty of flawless produce, appealing prepared foods, and racks packed with goods that are great for gift-giving. ***Gourmet Garage**, with organic fruits, vegetables, and other delicacies. Is more cheap, less chic.

beauty

Soho is a real oasis for beauty seekers. *Bliss Spa is a celebrity favourite, and its boutique has an amazing array of products. *Aveda is a more low-key place to get natural products that really work.

Parisian transplant *Sephora, a make-up superstore, offers an astonishing choice of make-up, bath products, and perfume, from all the best lines, while *Shu Uemera and *M.A.C. are beauty institutions – each have their own loyal following. But for bargains, try *Ricky's, a pharmacy mini-chain where the goods are cheap and plentiful.

eating & drinking

restaurants

Expensive Soho rents mean many restaurants in the historic district are overpriced, catering to tourists, celebrities, and brash Wall Streeters with million-dollar bonuses to blow. The place to check out what the rich-and-famous are eating is the *Mercer Kitchen, where celebrity chef Jean-Georges Vongerichten excels at his unique American-Provençal cooking. The brick-walled, subterranean space in the Mercer Hotel [→157] is the height of glamour. Scene stealer Canteen is just across the street. featuring colourful decor, 60s-style and a very cool crowd. The food ain't bad either – from the rather nostalgic macaroni cheese to the thoroughly modern pumpkin-crusted red snapper – though it is rather overpriced. Katy Sparks at *Quilty's is a much-honoured chef, creating highly innovative seafood, poultry and meat dishes for a sophisticated clientele. The creamy dining room is more homey than intimidating. In contrast, the rather more austere Honmura An has been esteemed for years as one of the city's top Asian restaurants. It's hard to imagine more artful noodle concoctions, and equally hard to imagine paying higher prices.

Places that are big on atmosphere rather than bucks include Penang, a Malaysian outpost that combines an industrial design with hut-like booths and a waterfall. The exotic dishes are flavourful – feast on roti canai and seafood. Coloured lights welcome you into the tiny interior of the Country Café, which is filled to the brim with charming knick-knacks. The French and Moroccan food is richly prepared and served by an affable staff. Alison on Dominick Street is pure romance, a small, out-of-the-way place with straightforward French and new American food. You go there to kiss and share bites, not to be blown away by innovative cuisine. More passion is almost sure to follow after a night at Casa La Femme, a candlelit Middle Eastern casbah, with tented booths and an incredible belly dancer. The food is good but not the point – especially for all the skinny models who slink in. Meigas boasts a handsome, sophisticated, lofty space where chef Luis Angel Bollo seems destined for the same celebrity status enjoyed by Daniel Boulud and David Bouley for their creative take on traditional cuisine – in Bollo's case, that of Spain. Expect refined grilled fish and meat dishes plus options like roast suckling pig with honey and sherry vinegar sauce.

To savour what Soho used to be like, push through the etched-glass doors of Fanelli, a dark-wood corner tavern that opened in 1847. The crowd is interesting, dressed-down and boisterous, and it's a safe bet for burgers, chilli, and chicken pot pie. Further west, the intimate *Blue Ribbon is popular for its wide-ranging menu and cocktails, and dispenses both until 4am, while Lucky Strike is a rollicking bistro that also serves competent (if unexciting) food into the wee hours. It's the ideal place to nibble and drink your way closer to solving the world's problems – or at least your vacation agenda; it's also one of Manhattan's smokers' havens.

Meeting friends for dinner, or looking for new ones? Consider Aquagrill, where singles gather in the brightly decorated front lounge, or at the bar while waiting for a table at this perpetually jammed seafood restaurant. The piscatorially-inclined can also try Ideya ↓, which features a culinary tour of the Caribbean, Central and South America, and a range of potent tropical drinks. Homemade plantain chips and fresh salsa adorn every table at this warm and casual Latin American bistro. Seating is tight at both Jean Claude (classic French cuisine) and Soho Steak (you guessed it), rendering conversation with your neighbour effortless. The simply designed pair are owned by respected restaurateur Jean-Claude Iacovelli, who prides himself on serving quality bistro fare at affordable prices.

cafés & diners

If you'd rather splurge on lavish niceties than costly meals, several affordable possibilities await. The cheap **Brisas del Caribe** ✓ is a ramshackle Cuban luncheonette, which attracts a mixed bag of ragamuffins and cool Soho-ites. Basic breakfasts, rice and beans, and sandwiches provide quick fixes. Every day the **Soup Kiosk** ladles out six steamy seasonal soups to slurp on the move. **Once**

upon a Tart is more up-scale, offering terrific baked goods, crusty sandwiches, and salads in a relaxed café atmosphere. Take a table, spread your newspaper and ease those tired feet. ***Pepe Rosso** is also fantastic for scrumptious focaccia and low-priced pastas. Seating is cramped, so it's prime for take-out. Or there's **Kelley & Ping**, an Asian grocery and noodle shop, and a trendy, modestly priced spot best for the buzz at lunchtimes. The bustling open kitchen, healthy stirfries and vast tea selection are the appeal. Off the beaten track, but worth seeking out, is **Herban Kitchen**, a dimly lit, engaging café, serving uncommonly tasty

organic specialties. **Moondance Diner** is a friendly shack heavy on bygone charm. Satisfy your appetite with hearty soups, big sandwiches and piles of fries. Soho's idea of a modern diner, however, is ***Jerry's**, frequented by rakish arty types and locals. At any time of day or night, the American-Mediterranean fare is appealing, but pricier than any old-school diner.

19

soho

bars & clubs

Soho's once-cozy neighbourhood bar scene has alas, in recent years, fallen prey to velvet ropes and guest lists. As one of the first swank bars to move in, ***Bar 89** set the standard: its high ceilings, bottomless cosmopolitans, and co-ed bathrooms with see-through doors (that turn opaque at the flip of a latch) have yet to be rivalled. Less grand in scale, but equally intimidating, is ***357**, a lounge-bar which has both a rope and a list, and all the right ingredients to perk you up after a hard day – including food. Speaking of tough, the door policy at super-trendy **Veruka** may

be the area's strictest, though women dressed in Gucci and Prada fare well, and models are a shoo-in. Arrive early at **Sway**, a hot Moroccan lounge frequented by musicians and mannequins. Thursday nights are best, but avoid weekends, when the crowd pressing the door is impenetrable. If you can't abandon your posse, head to nearby **Denial**, a dark, sensual sake bar where your social pedigree is, thankfully, irrelevant.

For a taste of Soho's edgier side, pay a visit to ***Void**, a semi-secluded cyber bar that features tables-cum-web browsers, cult-film

screenings and cocktails. Another good option for the attitude-weary is **Café Noir**, a sexy, smoker-friendly, Moroccan themed bar-restaurant.

*Raoul's is one of Soho's remaining old-guard bar-restaurants. Reserve for the dining room, but nothing beats their bar-steak special enjoyed with a glass of cabernet. Jimmy the barman is one of the best in the business. And if all you want is a swift drink before bed, you can hardly do better than the elegant and relaxing ***Grand Bar** in the Soho Grand Hotel [→158].

✄ directory

Ad-Hoc Software ♫C1
136 Wooster Street
925-2652

Alison on Dominick Street ♫A2
38 Dominick Street
727-1188 $$$

Alpana Bawa ♫B2
41 Grand Street
965-0559

Anna Sui ♫C2
113 Greene Street
941-8406

Anthropologie ♫B2
375 W Broadway
343-7070

Aquagrill ♫B2
210 Spring Street
274-0505 $$–$$$

Atsuro Tayama ♫C2
120 Wooster Street
334-6002

Aveda ♫B1
456 W Broadway
473-0280

Bar 89 ♫C2
89 Mercer Street
274-0989 ☾

Betsey Johnson ♫C1
138 Wooster Street
995-5048

Big Drop ♫B2
174 Spring Street
966-4299

Bliss Spa ♫C2
2nd floor
568 Broadway,
219-8970

Blue Ribbon ♫B2
97 Sullivan Street
274-0404 $$–$$$

Brisas del Caribe ♫C3
489 Broadway $

Café Noir ♫B2
32 Grand Street
431-7910 ☾

Canal Jean Co ♫B3
504 Broadway
226-1130

Canteen ♫C2
142 Mercer Street
431-7676 $$–$$$

Casa La Femme ♫C1
150 Wooster Street
505-0005 $$–$$$

Casio Baby G-Shock ♫C2
458 W Broadway
260-4570

Catherine ♫B2
468 Broome Street
925-6765

Le Corset ♫B2
80 Thompson Street
334-4936

Costume National ℬB2
108 Wooster Street
431-1530

Country Café ℬB2
69 Thompson Street
966-5417 $$

Cynthia Rowley ℬB2
112 Wooster Street
334-1144

Dean & Deluca ℬC2
560 Broadway
226-6800

Denial ℬB2
46 Grand Street
925-9449

Dom ℬB2
382 W Broadway
334-5580

Dosa ℬB2
107 Thompson Street
431-1733

Fanelli ℬC2
94 Prince Street
431-5744 $

Fragments ℬC2
107 Greene Street
334-9588

Grand Bar ℬB3
Soho Grand Hotel
310 W Broadway
965-3000

Gourmet Garage ℬB3
453 Broome Street
941-5850

Helmut Lang ℬB2
80 Greene Street
925-7214

Herban Kitchen ℬA2
290 Hudson Street
627-2257 $-$$

Honmura An ℬC2
170 Mercer Street
334-5253 $$$

Hotel Venus ℬB2
382 W Broadway
966-4066

Ideya ℬB2
349 W Broadway
625-1441 $$-$$$

If Soho New York ℬB3
94 Grand Street
334-4964

Issey Miyake Pleats Please ℬB2
128 Wooster Street
226-3600

Jean Claude ℬB1
137 Sullivan Street
475-9232 $$

Jerry's ℬC2
101 Prince Street
966-9464 $$

Jonathan Adler ℬB2
465 Broome Street
941-8950

Kate Spade ℬB2
454 Broome Street
274-1991

Kelley & Ping ℬC2
127 Greene Street
228-1212 $-$$

Kirna Zabete ℬB2
96 Greene Street
941-9656 $$-$$$

Louie ℬB2
68 Thompson Street
274-1599

Louis Vuitton ℬC2
116 Greene Street
274-9090

Lucky Strike ℬB3
59 Grand Street
941-0479 $-$$

M.A.C ℬB2
113 Spring Street
334-4641

Marc Jacobs ℬC2
163 Mercer Street
343-1490

Meigas ℬB2
350 Hudson Street
627-5800 $$-$$$

Mercer Kitchen ℬC2
Mercer Hotel,
147 Mercer Street
966-5454 $$$

Miu Miu ℬC2
100 Prince Street
334-5156

Moondance Diner ℬA2
80 Sixth Avenue
226-1191 $

Morgane Le Fay ℬB2
151 Spring Street
925-0144

Moss ℬC1
146 Greene Street
226-2190

Nicole Miller ℬB2
134 Prince Street
343-1362

Once upon a Tart ℬB1
135 Sullivan Street
387-8869 $

Otto Tootsi Plohound ℬB2
413 W Broadway
925-8931

Penang ℬC2
109 Spring Street
274-8883 $$

Pepe Rosso ℬB1
149 Sullivan Street
677-4555 $

Philosophy di Alberta Ferretti ℬB2
452 W Broadway
460-5500

Polo Sport ℬB2
379 W Broadway
625-1660

Portico Bed & Bath ℬB2
139 Spring Street
941-7722

Prada Sport ℬB2
116 Wooster Street
925-2221

Quilty's ℬB1
177 Prince Street
254-1260 $$$

Raoul's ℬB1
180 Prince Street
966-3518 ◖

Ricky's ℬC2
590 Broadway
226-5552

Rockport ℬB1
465 W Broadway
529-0209

Scoop ℬC2
532 Broadway
925-2886

Sean ℬB1
132 Thompson Street
598-5980

Selima Optique ℬB2
59 Wooster Street
343-9490

Sephora ℬC2
555 Broadway
625-1309

Shabby Chic ℬC2
93 Greene Street
274-9842

Shu Uemura ℬB2
121 Greene Street
979-5500

Soho Steak ℬB2
90 Thompson Street
226-0602 $$

Soup Kiosk ℬC2
Corner of Prince &
Mercer Sts $

Steve Madden ℬC2
540 Broadway
343-1800

Steven Alan ℬB2
women: 60 Wooster St
334-6354
men: 558 Broome St
625-2541

Stussy ℬC2
104 Prince Street
274-8855

Sway ℬA1
305 Spring Street
620-5220 ◖

357 ℬB2
357 W Broadway
965-1491

Tocca ℬC2
161 Mercer Street
343-3912

Troy ℬC2
138 Greene Street
941-4777

Trufaux ℬA3
301 W Broadway
334-4545

Veruka ℬB2
525 Broome Street
625-1717

Vivienne Tam ℬC2
99 Greene Street
966-2398

Vivienne Westwood ℬB2
71 Greene Street
334-5200

Void ℬB3
16 Mercer Street
941-6492

Yohji Yamamoto ℬB3
103 Grand Street
966-9066

Yves Saint Laurent Rive Gauche ℬB2
88 Wooster Street
274-0522

Zara International ℬC2
580 Broadway
343-1725

Zona ℬC2
97 Greene Street
925-6750

in the no

Nolita (north of Little Italy) is another of New York's neighbourhood acronyms created by sharp real estators. It is not just the name that has changed however – over the last few years, the area, formerly known simply as Little Italy, has become so gentrified that it's hard to imagine these were once the mean streets on which Scorsese grew up and Coppola filmed *The Godfather*. Apart from the occasional Italian deli or restaurant along the area's fringes, evidence of the old Little Italy is in extremely short supply. Instead, the characteristic red brick buildings hung with fire escapes are now home to some of the moment's coolest boutiques, cafés and bars (as well as some of the very knowing crowd that frequent them).

Next door Noho (north of Houston) is a tiny enclave which is basically an extension of adjacent Soho. Altogether less populated and more laid-back than its glamorous neighbours, Noho nevertheless holds a smattering of chic attractions, including a few of Downtown's hottest names, in both fashion and food.

day

🛍 Nolita's and Noho's trendy one-of-a-kind boutiques are open from around midday to early evening.

👁 The Children's Museum of the Arts [→86] is in this area.

night

☆ The main entertainment spot here is the Public Theater [→137] and Joe's Pub [→138] but there's also live music at Fez [→143] and poetry readings at Poets House [→142].

🍸 This part of town is packed with ultra-hip bars, restaurants and diners; the occasional lounge for cocktails plus a couple of dive bars.

getting there

Ⓜ B•D•F•Q to Broadway-Lafayette St; J•M to Bowery; N•R to Prince St; 6 to Spring St.

🚌 M5 & M6 ↓ Broadway; M21 ↔ Houston St; M103 ↕ Bowery.

nolita & noho

shopping

fashion

Right on the edge of Noho, ***Antique Boutique**, once a vintage store, now mostly carries cutting-edge pieces from locals Kitty Boots and Stephen Sprouse, and also plays host to the innovative Brit-pack and other hard-to-find European designers. More British designers are favoured at futuristic-looking **Nylon Squid ✔**, where the interesting selection of (men's and women's) streetwear couldn't be any more up-to-date if it tried. Local artists have decorated the walls of the lofty space at **À Détacher**, filled with spare city clothes and housewares to match. One of the few places to find a bargain in this chic

* = featured in the listings section [→92–135]

No shopping neighbourhood is trendier than Nolita which has exploded into a crush of groovy, cosmopolitan, cutting-edge shops.

neighbourhood is *Find Outlet, where designers such as Joseph and Cashmere Studio can be found at up to 80% off the regular price. Sophisticated urban clothes are also the order of the day at Zero, while Built By Wendy, showcases the talents of Wendy Mullen, whose urban cowgirl look continues to prove popular. Another member of fashion's younger generation, Margie Tsai, consistently creates adorable, fun clothes with matching accessories. Initially famous for her custom-made prom and party dresses, *Janet Russo also has pretty frocks for all seasons: her designs often have a floral or ethnic feel. Mayle, the brainchild of ex-model Jane Mayle, features an eclectic selection of retro-inspired clothes for women.

In a cavernous space on trendy Bond Street, *Daryl K does polished rock 'n' roll womenswear, including her much-loved, low-slung hipster trousers, and also her less expensive K189 line. Nearby is hot new name Katayone Adeli, whose art-gallery-style store is a great setting for her innovative yet very wearable designs for downtown girls. Her trousers fit to perfection. *Tracey Feith, also popular with fashionistas (and lots of celebs), has plenty of space to show off his delectable, sexy dresses, a line of menswear, and also Raj, his less expensive and colourful collection of gypsy-hippy clothes for women. Language has a rich and unusual line in higher-priced designer clothes and accessories (including pashmina shawls), while *Calypso St Barths, one of the first outlets to set up shop in Nolita, stocks flirty, feminine, flattering clothes made from fine fabrics. Or across the street, try Hedra Prue, a mixture of groovy

designs for girls from designers from around the world. The accessories are always irresistible.

Dishing out more fashion fabulousness, Hotel of the Rising Star caters for men looking for an eminently wearable, minimalist look. In a more decorative mode, designer Martin Keehn fills his store, Steinberg & Sons, with gorgeous, custom-made shirts worn by celebs as diverse as David Bowie and the late John Kennedy Jr – along with men's essentials inspired by workwear. For the apogee in luxury, Tse Surface, holds ultra-hedonistic four-ply cashmere sweaters and separates (for women) that, unsurprisingly, don't come cheap. At the other end of the seasonal spectrum, Malia Mills stocks the latest and best swimwear which practically guarantee you'll look hot on the beach. If skating is more

your thing, then Supreme has all the necessary hats, baggy pants, T-shirts and other neat stuff that boarders hoard, while X-Large is all about easy and refined streetwear for skate kids who've grown up a bit.

Vintage is always the rage, and this neighbourhood has a fine selection of shops. The star of the vintage pack is *Resurrection. Though expensive, it's worth it for pristine examples of Gucci, Courrèges and Hermès (including some gorgeous Kelly Bags). Lots of famous designers shop here for inspiration. Ditto at *Screaming Mimi's, a NY institution, where there is never a shortage of genius clothes (for men and women), mostly from the 60s, 70s and beyond.

---

accessories, shoes, & one-offs

Modish, elegant shoes, both classic and trendy, have made *Sigerson-Morrison a stop for the terminally fashionable. Selima, owner of *Bond 07, has unerringly excellent taste and carries a focused array of desirable accessories (especially the sunglasses). Exquisite, hand-crafted and totally happening handbags and shoes from Paris in luxe fabrics, makes *Jamin Puech ▲ pure heaven for style devotees. Similarly *Mark Schwartz's very feminine shoes (most with towering heels) are adored by fashion editors and stylists. For jewellery, look no further than *Me & Ro, a design-duo whose oriental-inspired baubles were popular with the likes of Madonna and Gwyneth long before they opened this cute boutique on Elizabeth Street.

With more of a graphic spin, novelty items, from T-shirts to key chains, are decorated with the vibrant work of the late, great artist, Keith Haring at the Pop Shop. So you wanna be a fireman, or just look like one? Then stop in at Firefighter's Friend, the outlet for authorized (and very snappy) NY Fire Dept merchandise, including standard-issue firemen's coats. Far more Zen is the merchandise at *Shi, from the tiny, distinctive tea lights to an engaging collection of ceramics. *Creed is an amazing perfume store where you can buy unique scents specially created for clients like Audrey Hepburn (Spring Flower) and Princess Grace (Fleurissimo) – or go for broke and order your very own!

eating & drinking

restaurants

Little Italy proper is over: the creeping tentacles of Chinatown have strangled the majority of Italian restaurants, essentially leaving tacky tourist spots with gruff service. Say *grazie* then to *Lombardi's for sticking to its roots: this lovable Italian place has checked tablecloths and delicious pizzas baked (since 1905 – when it served America's first) in a coal-fired oven. Another good Italian option is Va Tutto! where the atmosphere is welcoming, the accent is on Tuscan cuisine and there's a pretty garden for the summertime.

Nolita and Noho are now peppered with a wider, more multicultural choice of eateries. **Mexican Radio** has tasty and inventive south-of-the-border dishes as well as potent margaritas. Its new premises are roomier and lit by a myriad of candles and littered with Day of the Dead *tchotchkes*. The intimate **Rice ✓**, true to its name, stirs up a medley of different grains with Asian and Mediterranean toppings. Still in oriental territory, **Clay** is a stylish Korean spot, with steel-wrapped pillars and dramatic lighting. The seafood pancakes are sublime, as are the handmade vegetable dumplings. There's also **MeKong**: its sultry dining room is always filled with the delicious aroma of flavourful Vietnamese soups, pork and seafood dishes; its bar is part of the cool neighbourhood scene. For Malaysian cooking, visit the lively **Nyonya** for a wonderful hodgepodge of fried noodles, exotic casseroles and aromatic seafood preparations – it's

cheap too! And Downunder gets a look in as well, in the guise of **Eight Mile Creek** which brings interesting Aussie treats (including native ingredients like yabbie and kangaroo) to Downtown.

But the biggest draw in the area continues to be *Balthazar, often flanked by a queue of purring limos. This beautiful French bistro actually lives up to its hype, serving dynamically flavoured *brandade* and duck shepherd's pie, as well as an extensive French wine list. *Bond St, a minimalist dream, has the ultra-chic flocking into the restaurant and snazzy basement lounge. The Japanese cuisine is extraordinary, with an equally impressive saké list. The eternally cool Indochine attracts a faithful cadre of raffish musicians and their model girlfriends, who pick at the delicate Vietnamese dishes. *B-Bar & Grill, once thought too hot for its own good, has mellowed, enhanced by good American food, an outdoor patio and swanky cocktails.

*Rialto also has a fantastic back garden, plus a sexy lounge and a good vibe at the bar. Its bistro-style steak and pastas are fine, but nothing's as pleasing as the hamburger (or veggie burger) and fries. Serene, sophisticated parties gather at *Il Buco, which is furnished with antiques, vintage toys and tools. In the afternoon it serves as a wine bar with light meals and snacks, and at night there's a full menu of superb Mediterranean tapas, pasta and meat dishes. Il Buco's former manager has opened a restaurant of

his own nearby, *Acquario, with a similar menu of interesting tapas and Southern European fare (Portuguese fish stew is a highlight). You won't be surrounded by antiques, but it's snug and less costly. The **Astor Restaurant & Lounge**, an art deco brasserie that bears a passing resemblance to Balthazar, attracts a young clientele. The menu is superb (crawfish corn chowder, braised lamb with pistachio couscous), providing ballast for when you retire to the Moroccan-style downstairs lounge for just another cocktail. Another popular spot is **Five Points**. The accomplished American-Mediterranean cooking here is complimented by a beautifully decorated room bisected by a flowing 'creek'; weekend brunches feature eye-opening egg dishes, and irresistible donuts and hot chocolate. **Peasant** is also causing quite a splash. The decor is low-lit and low-key, but the food is as rustic as you'd like. Italian-inspired dishes such as grilled fish and rotisserie-roasted game are cooked over a fire in the open kitchen. For something French, with just a hint of Asian, try the well run, and very civilized, **Kitchen Club**. They do magical things with mushrooms. Check out, too, their adjoining saké bar. **Savoy** is a romantic haven, but perhaps their menu – saltcrust baked duck with braised kale, blood oranges and black olives – is a bit too ambitious. On the other hand, nothing disappoints at *Le Jardin Bistrot, from rich cassoulet to bouillabaisse. The Parisian ambience is engaging and the back garden a treasure.

cafés & diners

Old NYC is epitomized by **Buffa's Delicatessen**, a no-frills hangout, staffed by smart alecks slapping down cheap breakfasts and honest lunch items for its regular actor and director customers (Mon–Fri, closes at 4pm). **Jones Diner** (the genuine free-standing variety) is another favourite for budget breakfasts and cheeseburgers, but shouldn't be confused with **Great Jones Café**, which has also been around for ages – a cramped roadhouse serving Cajun specialities. Rambunctious customers throng the bar, downing cold beers, spicy jalapeño martinis and Bloody Marys, while honky tonk and country plays on the jukebox. Meanwhile, **Café Habana** is a spiffy paean to a Latin luncheonette – the grilled corn-on-the-cob coated in chilli powder and cheese is irresistible. **Café Gitane** is also

immensely popular, with a super-cool crowd often spilling onto the pavement. They come here to smoke, drink coffee, chat, read and occasionally eat low-priced, decent salads and sandwiches.

bars & clubs

Even on off nights, most of Nolita's watering holes are brimming with boozehounds: ranging from beer-soaked dives to the hottest hipster lounges, the area's bars may be the perfect barometer of the Nolita's recent demographic shift. For a taste of the old neighbourhood, visit **Milano's**, a shoebox-sized den where old men start nodding off at 3pm and Jimmy Rosselli tunes remain a jukebox favourite. **Spring Lounge** (aka The Shark Bar) is larger, cleaner and considerably more gentrified, but a few older locals still call it home. *****Mare Chiaro** ✓, on the other hand, clings tenaciously to its past. Photos of visiting celebrities – including Madonna and Ronald Reagan – proudly line the walls, and sawdust is strewn across the floor.

Nolita's younger dive denizens prefer **288** (aka Tom & Jerry's) – great for beer but a martini might disappoint. *****Botanica** is a cozy basement bar especially prized for its DJs who spin drum 'n' bass, dub, and jungle. Excellent DJs are also a fixture at **Double Happiness**, a former Mafia-controlled gay social club transformed into a sleek subterranean lounge. When Double Happiness is packed to the gills, swing by neighbouring *****Sweet & Vicious**, a popular, roomy, local hangout where Turkish raki is the beverage of choice and a sweet garden beckons. If you need space, head straight to **Velvet**, where business has yet to boom and it's easy to get a drink in the restaurant's romantic, antique-furnished lounge bar. Room to move is not an option at **Ñ**, a sexy slip of a tapas bar with potent sangria and at least two people waiting for each seat at the bar. For a slightly less sardine-like experience, head to **M&R**, a neighbourhood staple, and mellow alternative to nearby **Rialto**. This joint is ground-zero for Nolita hipsters. Superb Margaritas served in two-and-a-half glass-sized shakers are a big draw. For a more laid-back vibe, look no further than **Von**, a bar without attitude in a neighbourhood that's renowned for its trendiness. You can actually hear yourself speak in here, the bar staff are all lookers and you almost always get into drunken conversation with some artist dude at the bar.

Noho's nightlife is also thriving, thanks to the addition of **Bond St** and *****Joe's Pub** [→129]. Opened by the owners of Indochine, Bond St's sleek and minimalist basement lounge offers a modified version of the restaurant's menu, sakétinis and young, gorgeous girleens nibbling sushi – if only to have enough strength to continue on to Joe's Pub. Serge Becker's bar is built into one end of the Joseph Papp Public Theater, and has a strangely 80s feel. But if you're in no mood to scream, 'I'm on the guest list!' stop by neighbouring **Fez** – a fun Moroccan-inspired lounge under the trendy Time Café (serving creative American food), where drag acts, and an eclectic roster of musicians (including the Mingus Big Band) perform regularly [→143].

𝄞 directory

Acquario ♪C2
5 Bleecker Street
260-4666 $–$$

À Détacher ♪B3
262 Mott Street
625-3380

Antique Boutique ♪C1
712 Broadway
460-8830

Astor Restaurant & Lounge ♪C2
316 Bowery
253-8644 $$

Balthazar ♪A3
80 Spring Street
965-1414 $$–$$$

B-Bar & Grill ♪C1
40 E 4th Street
475-2220 $$

Bond 07 ♪C2
7 Bond Street
677-8487

Bond St ♪B2
6 Bond Street
777-2500 $$–$$$

Botanica *B2*
47 E Houston St
343-7251

Buffa's Delicatessen *B3*
54 Prince Street
226-0211 $

Built By Wendy *B4*
7 Centre Market Place
925-6538

Café Gitane *B3*
242 Mott Street
334-9552 $

Café Habana *B3*
17 Prince Street
625-2001 $

Calypso St Barths *B3*
280 Mott Street
274-0449

Clay *B4*
202 Mott Street
625-1105 $$

Creed *B2*
242 Lafayette Street
966-0202

Daryl K *C2*
21 Bond Street
777-0713

Double Happiness *B4*
173 Mott Street
941-1282

Eight Mile Creek *B3*
240 Mulberry Street
431-4635 $$–$$$

Fez *C1*
380 Lafayette Street
533-2680

Find Outlet *B3*
229 Mott Street
226-5167

Firefighter's Friend *B3*
263 Lafayette Street
226-3142

Five Points *C2*
31 Great Jones Street
253-5700 $$–$$$

Great Jones Café *C2*
54 Great Jones Street
674-9304 $

Hedra Prue *B3*
281 Mott Street
343-9205

Hotel of the Rising Star *B3*
13 Prince Street
625-9657

Il Buco *C2*
47 Bond Street
533-1932 $–$$$

Indochine *C1*
430 Lafayette Street
505-5111 $$

Janet Russo *B3*
262 Mott Street
625-3297

Jamin Puech *B3*
252 Mott Street
334-9730

Joe's Pub *C1*
425 Lafayette Street
539-8770

Jones Diner *C2*
371 Lafayette Street
673-3577 $

Katayone Adeli *B3*
35 Bond Street
260-3500

Kitchen Club *B3*
30 Prince Street
274-0025 $$

Language *B3*
238 Mulberry Street
431-5566

Le Jardin Bistrot *B3*
25 Cleveland Place
343-9599 $$

Lombardi's *B3*
32 Spring Street
941-7994 $$

Malia Mills *B3*
199 Mulberry Street
625-2311

Mare Chiaro *B4*
176 Mulberry Street
226-9345 ◐

Margie Tsai *C3*
4 Prince Street
334-2540

Mark Schwartz *B3*
45 Spring Street
343-9292

Mayle *B3*
252 Elizabeth Street
625-0406

Me & Ro *C3*
239 Elizabeth Street
632-6376

MeKong *B3*
44 Prince Street
343-8169 $–$$

Mexican Radio *B3*
19 Cleveland Place
343-0140 $$

Milano's *B2*
51 East Houston St ◐

M&R *C3*
264 Elizabeth Street
226-0559

Ñ *A3*
33 Crosby Street
219-8856 $

Nylon Squid *B3*
222 Lafayette Street
334-6554

Nyonya *B4*
194 Grand Street
334-3669 $

Peasant *B3*
194 Elizabeth Street
965-9511 $$–$$$

Pop Shop *B2*
292 Lafayette Street
219-2784

Resurrection *B3*
217 Mott Street
625-1374

Rialto *C3*
265 Elizabeth Street
334-7900 $$

Rice *B3*
227 Mott Street
226-5775 $

Savoy *B3*
70 Prince Street
219-8570 $$$

Screaming Mimi's *C1*
382 Lafayette Street
677-6464

Shi *B3*
233 Elizabeth Street
334-4330

Sigerson-Morrison *B3*
242 Mott Street
219-3893

Spring Lounge *B3*
48 Spring Street
965-1774 ◐

Steinberg & Sons *B3*
229 Elizabeth Street
625-1004

Supreme *B3*
274 Lafayette Street
966-7799

Sweet & Vicious *B3*
5 Spring Street
334-7915

Tracey Feith *B3*
209 Mulberry Street
334-3097

Tse Surface *C3*
226 Elizabeth Street
343-7033

288 *B2*
288 Elizabeth Street
334-8429

Va Tutto! *B3*
23 Cleveland Place
941-0286 $$

Velvet *B3*
223 Mulberry Street
965-0439 $–$$

Von *C2*
3 Bleeker Street
473-3039

X-Large *B3*
267 Lafayette Street
334-4480

Zero *B3*
225 Mott Street
925-3849

ETTES

nolita & noho

village people

east village

Altogether edgier than its West Village neighbour, the East Village has long served as a refuge for the disenchanted and dispossessed. In the early 20th-century, it was Eastern European immigrants who set up shop here; in the 50s, the Beats (including leading light Allen Ginsberg) moved in; in the 60s hippies and free thinkers; then punk rockers in the 70s; and experimental artists and performers during the 80s.

These days, while die-hard bohemians claim the area has lost much of its maverick feel, the East Village still boasts a vibrant energy all of its own. Down-home Eastern European restaurants and the Hispanic hangouts of Alphabet City sit next to funky bistros, trendy boutiques, record stores and thrift shops. Street culture is really what counts here: in spite of the influx of young professionals and the bridge-and-tunnel crowd at weekends, it is possible to pass time ogling the non-stop parade of colourful folk and free spirits who still call East Village home.

day

🛍 East Village is busy with a myriad of funky boutiques – everything opens (and stays open) late.

👁 There are no sights per se, but the Lower East Side Gardens [→85] are a quiet retreat.

night

☆ Lots of Off-Off Broadway theatres [→136–137] around Third Avenue, the indie Anthology Film Archives [→139], live music venues [→143], plenty of bars and poetry readings at joints like the Nuyorican Poet's Café [→142].

🍴 After dark the streets buzz with folks heading for one of the area's diverse restaurants, and hopping from one fun bar to the next.

getting there

Ⓜ L•N•R•4•5•6 to 14th St-Union Sq; L to 1st or 3rd Aves; 6 to Astor Pl.

🚍 M8 → St Mark's Pl, ← 9 St; M9 ↕ E Broadway, Ave B & Essex St; M14 ↔ 14 St; M15 ↑ 1st Ave ↓ 2nd Ave; M21 ↕ Ave C.

shopping

beauty & accessories

*Kiehl's, the cult beauty brand loved by men, women and supermodels alike, has its one-and-only store in East Village. This former pharmacy, on the block since 1851, carries the full range of high-quality Kiehl's products in its signature no-frills packaging. It's busy at weekends but, thankfully, the staff are friendly, and the lotions and potions work wonders on skin and hair. The products at *Demeter will also revive body and soul, and some of the scents available are pretty unique. Dab on some Grass, Holy Water or Dirt, or banish the blues with the Sugar Cookie 'attitude adjustment' lotion.

Of the neighbourhood's accessory mavens, **Jutta Neumann** ✦ stands out. Her artful leather designs are favoured by designers like Marc Jacobs and Anna Sui (who use her handmade bags and shoes in their catwalk shows). Bags at **Manhattan Portage** are more utilitarian but still have lots of fans. For jewellery, don't overlook **Gregg Wolf**, whose excellent silver cufflinks, rings and chains are mainly for men. **Sarah Samoiloff** is another talented local – her silver pieces accented with feathers have a punky edge. For trinkets and T-shirts make your way to **Sears & Robot**, a wacky store specializing in Japanese imports and other kitschery.

fashion

vintage fashion

Given the area's boho edge, it's perhaps not surprising that the East Village is replete with vintage and thrift stores. For barely-worn, designer labels hit *Tokio 7 and Tokyo Joe, two consignment stores offering up last year's Gaultier and Karan at reduced prices. **Metropolis**, a favourite with the NYU set, sells new and used clothing with a funky feel, including never-before-worn utilitarian gear. **Rags a Go Go** is great for cheap vintage togs especially good-quality jeans and good-quality basics. For the highest calibre antique clothing, with price-tags to match, seek out *Resurrection, where the frocks date from the 1890s. Nearby **FAB 208** ✦ is home to a colourful mix of kooky vintage and brand new duds for both sexes. You'll have to look hard to find something worth taking home at **Filth Mart**, a no-frills thrift store, but when you do, it'll definitely be a bargain.

Many of New York's designers started out in the tiny stores of the East Village before going on to bigger and better things. You'll see *Daryl K's first store, which now offers up seriously reduced seconds and sale items, including her famous hipster, boot-cut pants. **Eileen Fisher** also keeps a boutique on in the East Village – her loose-fitting lines in quiet colours are popular with women who want fashion without ostentation.

The neighbourhood is still a breeding ground for up-and-comers touting edgy fashion. **Red Tape** showcases brilliant designer Rebecca Danenberg's bold, graphic pieces for women as well as those of other NYC designers. A block away, **Jill Anderson** has lovely laid-back garb for women – fun dresses and separates in interesting fabrics. On a more experimental note, **Anna** showcases the work of designer Kathy Kemp whose beautifully cut, limited edition

pieces are a hit with downtown girls who appreciate unusual detailing, while **Air Market** is a repository of all things Japanese including clubby asymmetric clothing and Hello Kitty backpacks.

Although they are still far from conventional, you will also find designers here whose work appeals to the dressed-up set. On an entirely feminine trip, **Mark Montana**'s 'couture' suits and frocks are always colourful choice for a party. For the total made-to-measure experience, however, head to **Blue**, presided over by the brilliant Christina Kara. Kara can rustle up a thoroughly modern outfit in weeks. **Blue Skirt** is her ready-to-wear outlet for gals who can't wait to have some Kara style. Nearby, **Selia Yang** makes, and sells, supremely pretty party frocks in diaphanous fabrics. Send your male escort to **Savoia** for a classic 40s-style suit, either off the rack or made-to-measure.

home furnishings

East Village is also a mecca for folks looking for flea market-style finds to dot around your apartment. Ninth Street in particular is clogged with antique and vintage stores including **Cobblestones**, a tiny boutique brimful with *tchotchkes* as well as selection of accessories. **Quilted Corner** also plunders

grandma's attic – this time for stacks of vintage fabric, bedding and linens. **It's a Mod, Mod World** doesn't have vintage per se, but it does carry lamps and clocks recycled from such disposables as cereal boxes. **H**, meanwhile, is home to elegantly modern lamps and furniture as pared down as the store's name.

books & records

The East Village is a haven for bibliophiles who prefer their paperbacks a little dog-eared. The biggest used bookstore in the world, *The Strand, is here, with eight miles of books at all prices points. **Tompkins Square Books** is also a local favourite thanks to its cozy, chaotic feel and late opening hours – there's a good selection of vinyl here too. Fans of comics and sci-fi books, meanwhile, make tracks to

*Forbidden Planet, where the selection of new and used collectables is vast.

St Mark's Place is overrun with decent music stores selling new and used CDs at fair prices. *Kim's Video & Music is the biggest and brightest. This massive, yellow-painted place also sells and rents a huge range of videos. Those in search of dance music have options – Throb carries the latest techno,

house and electronica, likewise the excellent **Temple Records**. *Dance-tracks is a neighbourhood institution – most DJs in the city stop here. On the other hand, **Etherea** has a great selection of alternative, indie and experimental sounds. **Finyl Vinyl** is an endearing place that still refuses to carry CDs, while *Footlight Records is where to find showtunes and old movie soundtracks.

eating & drinking

restaurants

The East Village has gotten so hot as an eating destination that on weekends you'd better have a reservation or expect an hour's wait, especially at *Prune, a tiny, friendly American bistro that serves quirky bar snacks plus a short menu of playful dishes like pastrami duck breast with a rye-flavoured omelette. Also small and equally charming is **Max**. This southern Italian spot with a menu that features flavourful options like 'Mom's meat loaf' and 'Father's style' rigatoni, is guaranteed to make you feel right at home. *Il Bagatto, a dark and jovial Italian trattoria with low-priced, robust dishes is another favourite. For a table here, patrons endure being packed in at the downstairs bar or else spill out onto the street and into its mellow *enoteca* next door. *First is also worth a wait, a fabulous lair with commodious booths, stellar New American cuisine, and expert cocktails. **The Elephant** ✔ is another neighbourhood

magnet, with zesty Asian fusion creations, quirky decor and a constant hubbub at the door from those clamouring to get in.

To get into **Lucien**, a tiny popular French bistro, go early or very late to avoid the crush. Classic dishes are richly seasoned and excellent value, with a smart wine list to match. **Chez Es Saada**, a fashionable upscale casbah, has a cramped dining-room, but there are roomier, candlelit lounges downstairs. Dazzling cocktails and savoury Moroccan-inspired food like chicken *bisteeyah* with saffron lemon sauce come at a price. Another ethnic favourite is **Dok Suni**, a dimly-lit Korean joint, which is usually packed with a noisy, young crowd. Marinated beef, ribs and chicken dishes are high on the spiceometer and skillfully made.

Radio Perfecto is a hopping place, filled with illuminated Bakelite radios, and there's a charming garden at the rear. The

wide-ranging menu mixes anything from Argentine *empanadas* to rotisserie chicken with delicious pesto dipping sauce. **Le Tableau** offers lovely, innovative bistro renditions of wild mushroom casserole, calamari tagine with houmous, and bacon-wrapped monkfish. Live combos make it festive, and sometimes overly loud. A more traditional French bistro is **Jules**, with nightly live jazz in a cozy, very Parisian setting. Salade niçoise, cheesy onion soup and steak *frites* are ace. A former Jules manager opened **Casimir**, a stylish bar-bistro with a French-accented menu and crowd to match. Creative, first-rate seafood is the draw at nautically-themed *Pisces – Avenue A's first upscale restaurant, always busy at dinner and also recommended for weekend brunch. Or there's **Danal**, one of the neighbourhood's sweetest, most romantic restaurants, which has a daily-changing but tantalizing American-Mediterranean menu.

At the other end of the scale, **Two Boots** is a boisterous, child-friendly Italian-Cajun-Creole hangout with big red booths. Pizza is tops – especially the spicy tomato sauce and cornmeal crust. **Mekka** is another comfy, sociable place, with soulful southern Caribbean dishes (you can't beat the fried chicken). The happening bar scene is popular with music-industry types, and great tunes are always spinning.

Accomplished yet 'trashy Southern fixins', like catfish and country ham, are featured at *Old Devil Moon, along with an un-

usual wine and beer list; while Irish expats hang out at **St Dymphna's**, an affable pub, serving beef and Guinness casserole. Its low-key informality has attracted the likes of anti-scenesters Daniel Day Lewis and Ralph Fiennes.

A wave of young Asians has moved into the East Village, leading to a profusion of oriental eateries. One of the best – and most crowded – is *Takahachi, serving both creative and homey Japanese specialities. **Soba-ya** is a clean, stylish environment, with exceptional *udon* and *soba* noodles dishes. Service is

polished, prices are low and the saké list is noteworthy. For a trip back into the 80s, step into the clubby, ink-black **Avenue A Sushi**. Have faith: even though you can't see what you're eating, the Japanese fare is great, and the DJ spins a fun mix nightly. **Holy Basil** is a fine, similarly dark Thai restaurant where it's easier to hold a conversation. Their squid rings are the best, the seafood in general is superb, and the varied wine list is remarkable for a Thai place. **Lucky Cheng's** is a colourful pan-Asian mecca for a mix of gay boys and suits. The average food is theatrically served by cross-dressing waiters, and raunchy drag shows provide entertainment. **Haveli** retains its crown as the king of 6th Street's Indian restaurants. It's a spacious duplex with courtly service and superior dishes; they even have top-notch, though distinctly un-Indian, Belgian beers to cut the spice.

cafés & diners

Probably the best brunch in the neighbourhood (weekends only) belongs to *7A, boho central 24 hours a day. For under $10 you get a judiciously prepared egg dish, crisp roasted potatoes, a juice and endless coffee refills. At other times it's good for burgers and passable Tex-Mex platters. **Yaffa Café** ✓ is another 24-hour dive, whose big plus is its vast back garden. Inside, the screwball decor is diverting, and the fusion food (much of it vegetarian) reasonably healthy. The Italian **Three of Cups**, where Quentin Tarantino once got into a tussle, is great for big salads, hearty pastas and wood-fired pizza. Brunch is under $10 and includes a couple of Bloody Marys. **Dojo's** proximity to NYU makes it a student fixture, and in all kinds of weather they'll take sidewalk tables so they can smoke between courses of wholesome soy burgers and brown rice stir-fries. The hippy spirit of San Fran is also alive and well at pretty *Angelica Kitchen, whose stimulating and nourishing organic veggie dishes prove that macrobiotic fare doesn't have to be boring. **Flor's Kitchen**, on the other hand, is a homey BYOB hole-in-the-wall serving cheap, interesting Venezuelan snacking food.

Totally unhealthy and absolutely addictive is a little nook called **Pommes Frites**, dedicated to paper cones of golden Belgian-style fries. Dozens of inventive sauces are at hand for dipping, and although there are a couple of benches to sit on, most customers just eat on the hoof. Yummy street food is also available at **Habib's Place**, where Habib serves up fresh, cheap and abundant falafels to the sound of Louis Armstrong.

People of all ages love *Second Avenue Deli, an old Jewish kosher favourite. Their *matzoh* ball soup, corned beef and pastrami are legendary – as are the wise-cracking staff. Portions are huge and sharing costs extra, so give up and pig out. **Teresa's**, an authentic Polish diner, may have a new look but still serves the same old-fashioned *kielbasa*, stuffed cabbage and *blintzes*. **Leshko's**, a former no-frills Ukrainian coffee shop is now as sleek and stylish as they come. Indulge in too many of its *pierogis* though and you'll be waving your silhouette goodbye. **Veniero's** *pasticceria*, fabled for towering cakes, rich cheesecake and Italian cookies can also do some serious damage, but it's a sweet place to retire to at the end of a date.

bars & clubs

The East Village's friendly, local bars tend to overrun with out-of-towners and college kids at the weekends, but if you're looking for down-to-earth boozy fun, few neighbourhoods can compare. Even the swank lounges have a laid-back feel, and the old-school dives can't be beat. **Sophie's** and **Mars** remain two of the finest. Each offers the requisite cheap drinks, video games and a good chance of scoring a one-night stand. Sophie's also has a competitive pool table and, to be honest, considerably fewer borderline personalities than Mars, so proceed according to your taste.

DJs define the atmosphere at several East Village bars. *Baraza's Latin nights are always packed thanks, in part, to excellent margaritas, and barbecues in summer. Drinkland is a favourite destination for fans of electronica and breakbeats, while house and drum 'n' bass fills the air at *Alphabet Lounge a lively lounge/club favoured by a cool crew who like to mingle with kindred spirits. An eclectic enthusiastic bunch party down in Guernica's dark basement bar (complete with blue waterfall). It's a happening scene and there's another bar upstairs – plus a restaurant too. More waterworks can be found at *Spa, a glamorous if pricey bar/club, resembling, yes, a spa. Indie-rock stars and rockabilly kids love 2A, a bi-level bar with views onto Avenue A, and a mish-mash of comfy sofas upstairs. The same crowd often frequents the basement *Lei Bar. Decorated like a tiki bar and no bigger than the average East Village studio, Lei Bar serves a delectable array of frozen tropical cocktails, while DJs spin mambo nightly. The cocktails are pretty fine at Black & White too, though this cozy bar/restaurant can get real noisy when the dinner crowd stop by.

Gay bars are also well-represented in this area. *Dick's is one of the diviest,

with dirt-cheap shots, gay porn projected over the entrance, and a serious cruising scene – not to mention a killer jukebox brimming with classic punk and new-wave hits. *The Cock, rivalled only by The Manhole bar in subtle nomenclature, attracts both rock 'n' roll gays and drag queens with its fierce parties, top-notch DJs and hot go-go dancers. The once notoriously sleazy *Wonder Bar has managed to clean up its act without losing its edge, and is one of the city's best bars for groups of gay guys and their female friends.

Groups – either straight or gay – also do well at Odessa, a former Eastern European diner that was transformed into a bar when the owners relocated the diner to a larger space next door. (The bar kitchen still serves diner fare 'til midnight.) If you're intent

on avoiding crowds, *Angel's Share is the place to be. Accessed via a second-floor sushi bar, it strictly enforces a limit on parties of more than four. It's a perfect place for a tryst and, what's more, the cocktails are superb – everyone raves about the lychee daiquiris. Sushi restaurant and saki bar *Decibel is a better bet for those who want both their drink and their friends. Literary types can find plenty of kinship at *KGB ↓, where the walls are lined with commie propaganda and the author readings are top-notch. Country and western aficionados can proceed directly to Joe's Bar. No live music here, but the jukebox could have easily been stolen from a Texas roadhouse. For live music, head to *Lakeside Lounge, where local bands play regularly and its jukebox fills in beautifully when they don't.

♫ directory

Air Market ♫B1
97 Third Avenue
995-5888

Alphabet Lounge ♫E2
104 Avenue C
780-0202

Angelica Kitchen ♫B1
300 E 12th Street
228-2909 $–$$

Anna ♫C3
150 E 3rd Street
358-0195

Avenue A Sushi ♫C2
103 Avenue A
982-8109 $–$$

Baraza ♫E2
133 Avenue C
539-0811

Black & White ♫A1
86 E 10th Street
253-0246

Blue ♫B2
125 St Mark's Place
228-7744

Blue Skirt ♫C1
137 Avenue A
253-6551

Casimir ♫D2
105 Avenue B
358-9683 $–$$

Chez Es Saada ♫D2
42 E 1st Street
777-5617 $$

Cobblestones ♫C2
314 E 9th Street
673-5372

The Cock ♫C1
188 Avenue A
777-6254

Danal ♫A1
90 E 10th Street
982-6930 $$

Dancetracks ♫B3
91 E 3rd Street
260-8729

Daryl K ♫B2
208 E 6th Street
475-1255

Decibel ♫B2
240 E 9th Street
979-2733

Demeter ♫B2
83 Second Avenue
505-1535

Dick's ♫B1
192 Second Avenue
475-2071 ◖

Dojo ♫B2
24 St Mark's Place
674-9821 $

Dok Suni ♫C2
119 First Avenue
477-9506 $–$$

Drinkland ♫D1
339 E 10th Street
228-0123

Eileen Fisher ♫B2
314 E 9th Street
529-5715

The Elephant ♫B3
58 E 1st Street
505-7739 $$

Etherea ♫C2
66 Avenue A
358-1126

FAB 208 ♫B2
77 E 7th Street
673-7581

Filth Mart ♫E1
531 E 13th Street
387-0650

Finyl Vinyl ♪B2
204 E 6th Street
533-8007

First ♪C2
87 First Avenue
674-3823 $$

Flor's Kitchen ♪C2
149 First Avenue
387-8949 $–$$

Footlight Records ♪B1
113 E 12th Street
533-1572

Forbidden Planet ♪A1
840 Broadway
473-1576

Gregg Wolf ♪C2
346 E 9th Street
529-1784

Guernica ♪D3
25 Avenue B
674-0984

H ♪C2
335 E 9th Street
477-2631

Habib's Place ♪C2
438 E 9th Street
979-2243 $

Haveli ♪B2
100 Second Avenue
982-0533 $–$$

Holy Basil ♪B1
149 Second Avenue
460-5557 $–$$

Il Bagatto ♪D3
192 E 2nd Street
228-0977 $

It's a Mod, Mod World ♪C2
85 First Avenue
460-8004

Jill Anderson ♪C2
331 E 9th Street
253-1747

Joe's Bar ♪D2
520 E 6th Street
no phone

Jules ♪B2
65 St Mark's Place
477-5560 $$

Jutta Neumann ♪C2
317 E 9th Street
982-7048

KGB ♪C2
85 E 4th Street
505-3360

Kiehl's ♪C2
109 Third Avenue
677-3171

Kim's Video & Music ♪B2
6 St Mark's Place
598-9985

Lakeside Lounge ♪D1
162–164 Avenue B
529-8463

Lei Bar ♪C2
112 Avenue A
420-9517

Leshko's ♪C2
111 Avenue A
777-2111

Le Tableau ♪D2
511 E 5th Street
260-1333 $$

Lucien ♪C3
14 First Avenue
260-6481 $$

Lucky Cheng's ♪C3
24 First Avenue
473-0516 $$

Manhattan Portage ♪C2
333 E 9th Street
594-7068

Mark Montana ♪C2
434 E 9th Street
505-0325

Mars ♪B3
25 E 1st Street
473-9842

Max ♪D2
51 Avenue B
539-0111 $–$$

Mekka ♪C3
14 Avenue A
475-8500 $–$$

Metropolis ♪B1
43 Third Avenue
358-0795

Odessa ♪C2
117 Avenue A
253-1470 $–$$

Old Devil Moon ♪D1
511 E 12th Street
475-4357 $–$$

Pisces ♪C2
95 Avenue A
260-6660 $–$$

Pommes Frites ♪C2
123 Second Avenue
674-1234 $

Prune ♪B3
54 E 1st Street
677-6221 $$

Quilted Corner ♪A1
120 Fourth Avenue
505-6568

Radio Perfecto ♪D1
190 Avenue B
477-3366 $

Rags a Go Go ♪C2
73 E 7th Street
254-4771
119 St Mark's Place
254 4772

Red Tape ♪B2
E 9th Street
529-8483

Resurrection ♪C2
123 E 7th St
228-0063

St Dymphna's ♪C2
118 St Mark's Place
254-6636 $–$$

Sarah Samoiloff ♪C1
149 Avenue A
460-5392

Savoia ♪B2
125 E 7th Street
358-9182

Sears & Robot ♪B2
120 E 7th Street
253-8719

Second Avenue Deli ♪B1
156 Second Avenue
677-0606 $–$$

Selia Yang ♪C2
328 E 9th Street
777-9776 $

7A ♪C2
109 Avenue A
673-6583 $

Soba-ya ♪B2
229 E 9th Street
533-6966 $

Sophie's ♪D2
507 E 5th Street

Spa ♪A1
76 E 13th Street
388-1060

The Strand ♪A1
828 Broadway
473-1452

Takahachi ♪C2
85 Avenue A
505-6524 $–$$

Temple Records ♪D3
29a Avenue B
475-7552

Teresa's ♪C2
103 First Avenue
228-0604 $

Three of Cups ♪C2
83 First Avenue
388-0059 $

Throb ♪C1
211 E 14th Street
533-2328

Tokio 7 ♪B1
64 E 7th Street
353-8443

Tokyo Joe ♪B1
334 E 11th Street
473-0724

Tompkins Square Books ♪C2
111 E 7th Street
979-8958

2A ♪C3
25 Avenue A
no phone

Two Boots ♪C3
37 Avenue A
505-2276 $–$$

Veniero's ♪C1
342 E 11th Street
674-7070 $

Wonder Bar ♪D2
505 E 6th Street
777-9105

Yaffa Café ♪C2
97 St Mark's Place
674-9302 $

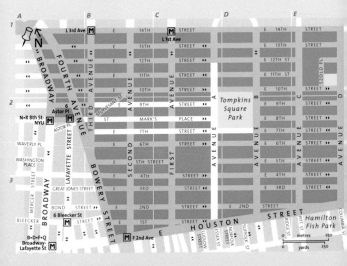

west side story

west village

When Bob Dylan and Joan Baez busked for dimes in Washington Square in the heady days of the early 60s, Greenwich Village must have seemed like the centre of the bohemian universe. And, while associations still persist, the image of the neighbourhood as a haven for musicians, writers, and artists became outdated a good 20 years ago. Today the term West Village has fallen into common use, and although initially a ruse for real estators to extend the area's boundaries, the moniker now also denotes the blocks of tacky, tourist-geared shops and bars in the area's eastern reaches.

The further west you go, the more Manhattan's rigid grid breaks down, giving way to pretty tree-lined streets and beautiful brownstones of legend. Needless to say, this part of town is now home to those who can afford to live in such elegant abodes. The neighbourhood's strong gay identity is still key, though the edgier gay scene has moved to Chelsea. For some residual bohemia, make for Washington Square Park, in the shadow of the NYU buildings, a hang-out for students, skate kids and, to this day, busking Dylan wannabes.

day

🛍 A scattered selection of one-off boutiques and some big-name chain stores along Sixth Avenue. Hours vary, but most places are open till early evening and on Sundays.

👁 No sights per se in the West Village, but plenty of picturesque streets and Washington Square park.

night

☆ West Village entertainment is all about cozy Off-Off Broadway theatres [→137], lots of smoky jazz clubs, and laid-back live music joints like the Bottom Line [→143]. For cinema goers there's always the Film Forum and the Angelika Film Center [→139].

🍽 This area is jammed with excellent restaurants of all varieties, as well as diverse bars and lounges, some with a gay slant.

getting there

🚇 A·C·E·B·D·F·Q to W 4th St-Washington Sq; 1·9 to Houston St or Christopher St- Sheridan Sq.

🚌 M5 ← W Houston St, ↑ 6th Ave; M6 ↑ 6th Ave, ↓ Broadway; M8 ← 9th & Christopher Sts, → 10th & 8th Sts; M10 ↑ Hudson St, ↓ 7th Ave; M21 ↔ W Houston St.

shopping

men's & women's fashion & shoes

While those in search of designer names and cutting-edge fashion should look elsewhere, the West Village does boast a few stand-out boutiques.

Eighth Street (between Broadway and Sixth Avenue) is home to a slew of outlandish clothing and shoe stores. **Patricia Field** ✓ is the best-known of the

bunch, catering to club-kids and drag queens who subscribe to her taste in clingy clothing, 6-inch stilettos and colourful accessories (there's also a

* = featured in the listings section [→92–135]

wig salon). **L'Impasse**
has an equally wild collection of look-at-me garb for
women. At their store next
door, **Beau Gosse**, men can
get into the act with tight
T-shirts and sharp sepa-
rates. For something a little
more sophisticated, make
for *Untitled, where the
racks yield Martin Margiela
(see shopping) and other
hard-to-find designers for
both sexes. Elsewhere,
*Jeannette Lang sells pre-
cious, handmade clothing
for women, with the
emphasis on evening wear.
Good quality, well-priced
vintage frocks, meanwhile,
are the specialty at *Stella
Dallas – Catherine Deneuve
shops here when in town.

Eighth Street is also New
York's shoe central. There
are upwards of 20 shoe
stores here, touting everything from cowboy boots
to platform sneakers.
*Petit Peton stands out
from the crowd thanks
to a good range of
European imports and
the store's own line. Prices
here, as other stores
on the block, are generally
quite reasonable.

accessories & beauty supplies

Christopher Street's main
drag has long been New
York's Rainbow Row, and in
spite of the Mayor's on-
going clean-up campaign,
you still find a residual
number of stores selling
sex toys, leather gear, tight
T-shirts and sleazy underwear. These places tend to
be on the tacky side, so for
more up-scale erotica (this
is New York, yes, there is
such a thing!) make for
Pink Pussycat Boutique,
a neighbourhood institu-
tion that's so unintimidating, the staff might as
well be selling candy bars.
The **Pleasure Chest**,

another erotic boutique, is
as sleek as can be – prices
here are reassuringly
expensive and the window
displays are often wildly
imaginative.

Altogether less shocking
is *Bigelow Pharmacy, one
of the oldest in New York.
Friendly staffers are happy
to make recommendations
from the excellent array of
health and beauty prod-
ucts on offer, including
homeopathic remedies,
topnotch cosmetics,
European imports, and
the store's own brand
of make-up, Alchemy.

one-offs

The **Village Chess Shop** has
been in business since
1972. Folks of all ages come
here for the huge selection
of boards and pieces, or to
pick up a game at one of
the store's small café
tables. Another unique
specialty store is **Kate's
Paperie**, which holds no
fewer than 5000 different
kinds of paper, many of
them handmade.
Beautiful journals, pens
and greeting cards are
also carried. Just as entic-
ing is **Alphaville**, which
yields an amusing selec-
tion of market-style col-
lectibles, including tin
toys, pop novelties and
vintage movie posters in
an all-white setting

The boho 'village' of old can
still be found in the neighbourhood's quaint side streets and
specialty stores.

home furnishings

For excellent home fur-
nishings with a modern
feel and moderate price
tags, look no further than
Christopher Street, where
the owners of the Amal-
gamated company have
two stores. **Amalgamated
Home** is the place for furniture, lamps, and home
accessories, while aesthetic
perfectionists make for
Amalgamated Hardware,
just along the block, which
sells interesting drawer
pulls, door handles, hooks
and other finishing touches.
For funkier flea market-
style finds, the **Lively Set**
has an immaculate collec-

tion of furniture, pottery
and lamps from the 40s
to the 70s.

Don't expect any bargains
when shopping for
antiques in Manhattan.
The stretch of Broadway
just below 14th Street
has a row of antique
stores selling furniture
with price tags that fre-
quently hit six figures.
Many of these are trade-
only, but **Howard Kaplan
Antiques** is an exception;
ditto **Pall Mall Antiques**
on University Place. Both
specialize in 18th- and
19th-century furniture.

food

Less of a deli, more a gastronomic event, legendary *Balducci's holds a mesmerizing selection of foodstuffs from all over the world. Even if you can't justify the high prices, it's worth a visit just for the spectacle of glistening fruits and vegetables, delectable pastries and mouthwatering prepared foods. Expect total sensory overload. Just down the block is another neighbourhood fixture, Jefferson Market; the selection is enormous and prices affordable; the people who work here are without the attitude found in more elitist food venues (like Balducci's).

records & books

Sadly Bleecker Street – once New York's Record Row – now has little to recommend to the avid music shopper. Most of the old stores have closed now, with the exception of the revamped Bleecker Street Records, with its vast selection of vinyl spanning jazz to rock, so scoot around to Carmine Street, where a cluster of decent places have opened. Vinylmania, with its broad ranging collection of techno and electronica, stands out. Elsewhere, look out for Fat Beats, New York's premier hip-hop record outlet, which also has a fine selection of reggae and jazz. Despite its rarefied atmosphere, the West Village has only a small number of bookstores, the best loved of which is *Three Lives & Company. This charming place, with its unmistakable red-painted door, mixes new and used books in an intimate, erudite environment where the regular author readings are always impressive. Nearby, the Oscar Wilde Memorial Bookstore, America's first gay bookshop, has an excellent, if small selection of tomes dedicated to alternative lifestyles.

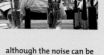

eating & drinking

restaurants

Throughout the West Village's charming tangle of streets are dozens of reasonably-priced restaurants. It is definitely a good place for daytime stops or, if you want an intimate evening, dine in one of its many inviting romantic haunts. One of the most striking exteriors is the one that harbours *Grange Hall. Organic chicken and cranberry-glazed pork chops are typical of the American heartland menu, and the bar is great for whimsical cocktails. The owners behind Home are from the Midwest and proud of it, presenting comfort food, along with alcohol-spiked lemonade. Though tiny, Home, whose motto is 'fine wines, fine ketchup', has a garden.

For a more sophisticated experience, hotshot Italian chef Mario Batali, at *Babbo ✓, tosses together magical pastas, like mint 'love letters' with spicy lamb sausage. He first gained fame at nearby *Pó, serving earthy yet elevated Italian dishes. Loyal disciples have not abandoned the latter, despite Babbo eclipsing its brilliance. But many would say that Batali's latest venture *Lupa is quite possibly NY's best Italian restaurant: kind of casual, with simple but spectacular food. *Bar Pitti is perennially popular for rustic Italian favourites, like mozzarella and tomato salad; the simple dining room is always lively, and fashionistas fill the alfresco tables on warm nights. The Belgian-inspired *Waterloo is just as hot a ticket, with a good-looking crowd, and magnificent pots of mussels and delicious beer-braised seafood.

French Roast stays open 24 hours, 365 days a year, and is good for strong coffee, red wine and a repertoire of well-prepared French classics. The casual milieu is pure Parisian flea market. At Bar Six, French-Moroccan fare is satisfactory for late-night noshing ('til 2am), although the noise can be ear-splitting.

Eating in the intimate, Mediterranean-inspired 'cottage', The Place, is more rewarding than its name implies. Treats such as leek and butternut squash risotto, and curry-crusted leg of lamb are nicely prepared, and 10% of sales go to charity. Picturesque Isla, with its retro decor, smacks of pre-revolutionary Cuba and produces Nuevo Latino dishes that most modern day compañeros could only dream of. The sweet appearance of Casa, an animated and appealing Brazilian spot, could also be used as a movie location. The empanadas and feijoada are homey, and the crowd arresting enough for celluloid. Titou's charms, however, are three-dimensional rather than skin deep: a beautiful, leafy venue, French specialties, and a good deal on wine.

*Gotham Bar & Grill impresses on all fronts,

with a high-ceilinged, high energy, modern room that suits its imaginatively structured American food. Also stylish is *Surya specializing in innovative, spicy seafood dishes based on southern Indian cuisine. It has a happening little lounge, exotic cocktails and a bewitching courtyard. Café Spice is part of the contemporary Indian trend as well: a colourful bistro with vividly flavoured regional specialties. Meanwhile, for Japanese food, you can't go wrong with *Japonica. The dining room is bustling yet peaceful, with the windowed café area prime for people-watching. Noodle hot pots, sushi, sashimi and tempura are all of unimpeachable quality. The sushi at Taka is also superb. What makes this unpretentious townhouse truly unusual is the fact that a woman is the

chef/owner (sushi chefs being overwhelmingly male). Delicious Korean 'dinner guest fare' features on the menu at Jenny Kwak's Do Hwa. Pricier than her hip East Village eatery, Dok Suni, it's still a crowd-pleaser: there's also a late-night film series that's been instituted – Quentin Tarantino's an investor!

The food at Indigo, an unassuming neighbourhood bistro, is also pure poetry. Service is professional, prices modest and the eclectic American cuisine exceptional – especially the wild mushroom strudel. Village (evenings only) is a bit less polished, but this doesn't deter a cool clientele who enjoy its take on French bistro food, with some home-grown dishes thrown in for good measure.

cafés & diners

Since so many West Village places are miniscule, seating is tight at night. That's why it's pleasant to visit adorable *'Ino, a licensed Italian bruschetta and panini stop, in the afternoon. The eccentric *Tea & Sympathy ♪ is also a delightful place to spend a few hours in the day, sampling authentic English fare and various brewed teas. Similarly the engaging Pearl Oyster Bar is also twice as nice in the daytime when there's more space. Crisp Caesar salad and clam chowder with smoked bacon are an ideal combination.

Later on, join the night owls at the Corner Bistro, a dark, old mahogany-stained pub with a television broadcasting sports. During and after drinking bouts, there's nothing like their cheap, messy burgers. If you've got a hankering for Mexican food, Taqueria de Mexico is recommended for roasted tomato and tortilla soup with chipotle chilli, delicious fiery sandwiches, and uncomplicated soft tacos and burritos. It's convenient for take-out but the cheerful dining room is perfectly agreeable. The diminutive Chez Brigitte seats only 11 people at a time. Open for 40 years, Brigitte herself is long gone, but her spirit lives on in hearty, low-priced stews, light omelettes and heavy desserts. Moustache is another tiny treasure, serving tasty Middle Eastern pitzas.

bars & clubs

The area's winding, tree-lined streets and cozy brownstones are home to numerous bars. While still teeming with genial gay and lesbian watering holes, the West Village is now seeing its share of hipster hot-spots and impenetrable guest lists.The owners of Soho's Spy are also behind Moomba. Once past the bouncers with way too much attitude, you can join celebs sipping pricey cocktails. But their numbers are steadily dwindling and many have jumped ship, preferring the shady nooks of the equally expensive lounge-cum-disco-cum-restaurant *Halo. A few notable names also hang out in the West Village institution, Marylou's. This joint is always packed with regulars, and everyone seems to know everyone else.

For a dose of gay glam, head to *Bar d'O, a sexy little boîte where drag legends Joey Arias and Raven-O perform for a mixed crowd of fashionistas and local luminaries, as well as the

occasional bona fide bold-faced name. Those looking for the company of pre- or post-op transsexuals, or even transvestites, need only to visit NowBar, where Gloria Wholesome hosts her popular Trannie Chaser party [→135]. Henrietta Hudson, a neighbourhood girl bar, is more about cruising than boozing, though there's still plenty of the latter.

Quiet drinks for two are the m.o. at Junno's, an intimate Korean-French bar that serves excellent sushi alongside creative house cocktails. If you're out with a group, a more swank vibe can be found at Clementine – resplendent cocktails (and inventive American fusion dishes) are available in the art deco lounge until 3am. For those who'd prefer a decent selection of beer and room to sit with friends, the former speakeasy, Chumley's, is the answer. As a reminder of its past, there is still no sign posted on either of the two 'clandestine' entrances.

♪ directory

Alphaville *♂C3*
226 W Houston Street
675-6850

Amalgamated Home & Hardware *♂C2*
9 & 19 Christopher Street
255-4160 (no. 9)
691-8695 (no. 19)

Babbo *♂C2*
110 Waverly Place
777-0303 $$–$$$

Balducci's *♂C1*
426 Sixth Avenue
673-2600

Bar d'O *♂C3*
29 Bedford Street
627-1580

Bar Pitti *♂C3*
268 Sixth Avenue
982-3300 $$

Bar Six *♂C1*
502 Sixth Avenue
691-1363 $$

Beau Gosse *♂D1*
27 W 8th Street
598-0314

Bigelow Pharmacy *♂C1*
414 Sixth Avenue
533-2700

Bleecker Street Records *♂B2*
239 Bleecker Street
255-7899

Café Spice *♂D1*
72 University Place
253-6999 $$

Casa *♂B2*
72 Bedford Street
366-9410 $$

Chez Brigitte *♂B1*
77 Greenwich Avenue
929-6736 $

Chumley's *♂B2*
86 Bedford Street
675-4449

Clementine *♂D1*
1 Fifth Avenue
253-0003

Corner Bistro *♂B1*
331 W 4th Street
242-9502 $

Do Hwa *♂C3*
55 Carmine Street
414-2815 $$–$$$

Fat Beats *♂C1*
406 Sixth Avenue
673-3883

French Roast *♂C1*
78 W 11th Street
533-2233 $–$$

Gotham Bar & Grill *♂D1*
12 E 12th Street
620-4020 $$$

Grange Hall *♂B2*
50 Commerce Street
924-5246 $$–$$$

Halo *♂C2*
49 Grove Street
243-8885

Henrietta Hudson *♂B3*
438 Hudson St
924-3347

Home *♂C2*
20 Cornelia Street
243-9579 $$

Howard Kaplan Antiques *♂E1*
827 Broadway
674-1000

L'Impasse *♂D1*
29 W 8th Street
533-3255

Indigo *♂C2*
142 W 10th Street
691-7757 $$

'Ino *♂C3*
21 Bedford Street
989-5769 $

Isla *♂C2*
39 Downing Street
352-2822 $$–$$$

Japonica *♂D1*
100 University Place
243-7752 $$

Jeannette Lang *♂D3*
171 Sullivan Street
254-5676

Jefferson Market *♂C1*
450 Sixth Avenue
533-3377 $

Junno's *♂C3*
64 Downing Street
627-7995 $$

Kate's Paperie *♂D1*
8 W 13th Street
633-0570

Lively Set *♂C3*
33 Bedford Street
807-8417

Lupa *♂D3*
170 Thompson Street
982-5089 $$

Marylou's *♂D1*
21 W 9th Street
533-0012

Moomba *♂C1*
133 Seventh Avenue S
989-1414

Moustache *♂B2*
90 Bedford Street
229-2220 $

NowBar *♂C3*
22 Seventh Avenue S
293-0323 ₵

Oscar Wilde Memorial Bookstore *♂C1*
15 Christopher Street
255-8097

Pall Mall Antiques *♂D1*
99 University Place
677-5544

Patricia Field *♂D1*
10 E 8th Street
254-1699

Pearl Oyster Bar *♂C2*
18 Cornelia Street
691-8211 $–$$

Petit Peton *♂D1*
27 W 8th Street
677-8730

Pink Pussycat Boutique *♂C1*
167 W 4th Street
243-0077

The Place *♂B1*
310 W 4th Street
924-2711 $$

Pleasure Chest *♂B1*
156 Seventh Avenue S
242-2158

Pó *♂C2*
31 Cornelia Street
645-2189 $$

Stella Dallas *♂D2*
218 Thompson Street
674-0447

Surya *♂B2*
302 Bleecker Street
807-7770 $–$$

Taka *♂B2*
61 Grove Street
242-3699 $$

Taqueria de Mexico *♂B1*
93 Greenwich Avenue
255-5212 $–$$

Tea & Sympathy *♂B1*
108 Greenwich Ave
807-8329 $–$$

Three Lives & Company *♂C1*
154 W 10th Street
741-2069

Titou *♂B1*
259 W 4th Street
691-9359 $$

Untitled *♂D1*
26 W 8th Street
505-9725

Village *♂C1*
62 West 9th Street
505-3355 $$–$$$

Village Chess Shop *♂D2*
230 Thompson Street
475-8130

Vinylmania *♂C3*
60 Carmine Street
924-7223

Waterloo *♂A2*
145 Charles Street
352-1119 $$$

go west

Chelsea's concentration of tenements, warehouses and brownstones has experienced a major regeneration over the last decade. Thanks largely to the defection of Manhattan's gay scene from West Village, and the relocation of influential art dealers from Soho, Chelsea has exploded with cute cafés, fab boutiques, hip bars and restaurants, and major contemporary art spaces: these places, along with a cluster of big-deal nightclubs, means that the area acts like a magnet for the city's cool and queer crowd.

The southernmost edges of Chelsea are where you'll find the former factories of the Meatpacking District, where white-hot art galleries and hangouts are opening at a great pace, making this as good a place as any to witness a very cool scene that's yet to pass its sell-by date. But Chelsea's new image still has a place for the enduring Chelsea Hotel – where Sid Vicious killed his girlfriend Nancy Spungen in 1978 – adding to the area's somewhat seedy, artsy fascination.

day

🛍 Big-name chain stores along Sixth Avenue, trendy one-off boutiques and the weekend flea market.

👁 Dia Center for the Arts [→80] & numerous commercial galleries, especially around Tenth Avenue [→81–82]. For details on the Art Shuttle, a bus linking Soho galleries with those of Chelsea and beyond ☎ 769-8100.

night

🍽 Lots of bustling restaurants and gay-slanted bars on Seventh and Eighth Aves.

☆ The megaclubs of the far west side (sometimes called WeChe), and the Meatpacking District. A few Off-Off Broadway theatres like The Irish Rep [→137].

getting there

Ⓜ A•C•E•F•1•2•3•9 to 14th St; C•E•F to 23rd St; 1•9 to 18th, 23rd or 28th Sts; L to 8th Ave.

🚌 M5, M6 & M7 ↑ 6th Ave; M10 ↑ 8th Ave; M10 ↓ 7th Ave; M11 ← 15th St via 10th Ave; M11 ↓ 9th Ave; M14 ↔ 14th St; M23 ↔ 23rd St.

chelsea & the meatpacking district

shopping

fashion & accessories

The shopping opportunities here are nothing short of diverse. One-off boutiques keep company with trendy sportswear outlets, major chain stores hog the main drag of Sixth Avenue, the city's biggest flea market brings out the weekend hordes, and that's before you've taken in some art

at one of the many commercial art galleries.

The opening of *Comme des Garçons ✓ gave Chelsea its first blast of 'serious' (and expensive) fashion – its avant garde creations wouldn't look out of place in one of the nearby art spaces. Besides

Comme, the look on offer at the area's many boutiques tends towards the clubby, sportswear-inspired gear favoured by Chelsea's gay male residents (affectionately known as 'Chelsea boys'). **Tom of Finland** is just one such place, offering a smarter take on the

* = featured in the listings section [→92–135]

chelsea & the meatpacking district

theme, with fashion-forward clothes for men who aren't afraid to stand out in the crowd. **Raymond Dragon** goes all-out with stretchy, second-skin numbers and swimwear for men that requires regular trips to the gym. The truly outrageous, however, head to **Lee's Mardi Gras** for the large-size dresses, beard-covering make-up, costume-jewellery and size-15 pumps beloved of drag queens and trannies.

There are plenty of stores on a grand scale in the area. The brainchild of the former shoe buyer at Barney's, ***Jeffrey** is a brand-new fashion department store, which gives this area its second shot of serious fashion chic. **Barney's Co-Op** is a branch of the midtown store but focuses on more casual lines of clothes (Daryl K, Maharishi etc) reflecting the tastes of the local residents and young edgy crowd who love to shop there. It also has shoes, cosmetics and plenty of accessories. Meanwhile, on Sixth Avenue, big-name chains include ***Old Navy**, a kind of poor man's Gap, which specializes in inexpensive, basic clothing and accessories for all. More basic basics can be snapped up at **Dave's New York**, a tiny, 30-year old jeans outlet with a great selection of utilitarian workwear (Levis, Hanes, Schott, Carhartt) at excellent prices. The staff really know their stuff, making this a good alternative to the massive Canal Jean Co in Soho. For a more conservative look, make for ***Loehmann's**, the giant discount store. Women's everyday separates are sold at ridiculously reduced prices – best bets are shoes and accessories.

lifestyle stores

La Maison Moderne, a tiny, cluttered shop, has plenty of precious accessories, such as vintage silver knives and beaded lampshades. The latter would look equally at home in **Apartment 48**, a store laid out to resemble the pad of some clever interior decorator. The overall feel is traditional-casual chic, with a mixture of flea market finds, designer knick-knacks and useful kitchen implements. ***Auto**, on the other hand, reflects a very different mindset. The displays of furniture and home accessories are perfectly considered, resembling a look-but-don't-touch kind of home, though the tactile leather cushions, wool throws and smooth lines of ceramics and glassware are hard to resist. The ***Housing Works Thrift Shop ✓** (all proceeds go to homeless people living with HIV) receives a constant stream of donations, which means the inventory of clothes, furniture, ceramics and paintings is vast. This is one of the few thrift stores in town where you're likely to get a real bargain. In contrast, **Eclectic Home ✓**, offers a sleek, post-modern aesthetic; its lamps, clocks and other accessories have a colourful, kooky edge. In a similar mode, the store that nobody can pronounce, **Mxyplyzyk**, carries lots of highly designed items to make every aspect of your home utterly groovy. And the **Chelsea Garden Store** specializes in essential tools and interesting gifts for the green-fingered.

Of the chain stores, **Hold Everything** does just that – stocking containers, dividers and racks for all your wordly possessions. ***Williams-Sonoma**, a division of the popular Pottery Barn chain, is slightly more upscale than its sister stores, with the focus on snazzy kitchen items and stylish tablewear.

Not surprisingly, the city's biggest gay, lesbian and trans-gender book and record store, ***A Different Light**, is located in Chelsea. This multi-storey outlet holds books on all aspects of gay interest, plus CDs, as well as a café and gift store. Nightly readings, meetings and events have turned this place into a veritable community centre. Home-from-home for vinyl jazz buffs is the ***Jazz Record Center**, whose collection (including Blue Note label treats) just can't be beat.

markets

The ***Annex Flea Market** is a quintessential New York experience. Every weekend, over 500 vendors set up around 26th Street. Precious antique pieces and outright junk can be found in equal measure, but don't expect any real bargains. Also clustered around 26th Street are several indoor antique 'malls' which hold higher-end furniture, jewellery and unusual objects. Nearby, along 28th Street, the weekday Flower District offers the chance to snag big bunches of blossoms at prices that can't be bettered – come early.

For a bit of DIY foodery, the ***Chelsea Market**, a mini-mall open daily for gourmets, offers a mouthwatering array of international delicacies: Amy's Bread, Thai and Italian import goods, an exclusive wine store, and incredible ice-cream from Ronnybrook Farm Dairy.

Hot on the heels of art galleries relocating to the neighbourhood came scores of restaurants and bars catering to all, especially the local gay crowd.

eating & drinking

restaurants

The opening of the 24-hour ultra-mod *Cafeteria was so explosive that the food and service suffered under the crush of young style experts begging to be seen. Proceedings are now more under control, and American favourites like fried chicken and macaroni cheese score every time. Red firehouse doors conceal the formerly super-hot Restaurant 147 ✓. The fire may have burnt itself out, but it's still a groovy setting for caviar, crab cakes – and a spot of live jazz.

Two places very much in the spotlight are *Pastis and *Fressen. The former is a slightly-hard-to-find bistro owned by Keith 'Balthazar' McNally that serves a decent fish and chips (well, frites), plus robust dishes like glazed belly pork with lentils and superb salads. In addition, the fetching pre-war Paris decor and the no reservations policy ensures the place is thronged (lunches and breakfasts might be less of a crush). Drinks at the bar are right on the mark too. Fressen is also a gorgeous Meatpacking District spot albeit much more 'high design', so beautiful people and celebs find it a fitting backdrop. Its name means 'pig out' in Yiddish and the mostly organic, creative American fare means that more often than not, you will. Not hungry? Drink in the scene at the popular bar.

Bottino is a spare, attractive Tuscan restaurant with a wonderful back garden, luring a cool art and publishing crowd. Pasta dishes and fish are straightforward, and the adjacent take-out shop sells panini and other prepared foods during the day. Try the Amero-Mediterranean food at the Red Cat (open evenings only) and you'll leave grinning like a Cheshire puss. Not only is the menu sorely tempting – a sweet pea risotto cake with oysters and a champagne cream, perfect chicken and mash, and grown up desserts like caramelized banana tart – but the prices aren't bad either. The Tonic is a fashionable (read: pricey) enterprise, featuring sumptuous new American cuisine. If you want to say you've been there but don't want to pay top dollar, their handsome bar next door (the Tavern) serves a full menu including Yankee pot roast and fish and chips.

Date-places abound for gays and straights alike. Promising an illicit evening, is the speakeasy entrance to Alley's End. The candlelit dining room facing a picture-perfect garden is sure to seduce, and the American bistro menu and boutique wine list crackle with creativity. La Lunchonette feels like a French version of a frontier saloon, a lively, red-hued affair with richly-flavoured Gallic classics. El Rey del Sol, a dark, belowstairs hideaway, entices with an excess of tacky Mexican souvenirs and a back garden dappled with multi-coloured lights. Sangria and margaritas by the pitcher are the prelude to respectable enchiladas, fajitas and the like. Much sangria is also consumed in El Cid, a frumpy yet cherished tapas joint attracting vivacious groups. Alternatively feast to a reggae beat on Jamaican chicken and roti bread at Negril. Swaying plants, beachside murals and an aquarium behind the bar give you that island feel.

For a quick bite or a (relatively) quiet drink, stop by *Florent. This French diner is infamous for its annual Bastille Day celebration (complete with guillotine), and message-board advertising the best parties in the neighbourhood. At weekends, it hits peak traffic around 4am – just when all the clubs begin to close and its tables are quickly claimed by ravenous nightcrawlers. The Meatpacking District's Markt gained an immediate following upon opening. A bona fide reproduction of a stylish Belgian brasserie, its kettles of mussels and beer-braised seafood are superb – especially when washed down with world-class Belgian brews.

cafés

The old, authentically retro *Empire Diner, once home to late-night clubbers and drag queens, has become a haven for artists (paint-stained clothes and grubby fingernails), as well as gallery-goers (spotless attire and manicures). Updated

chelsea & the meatpacking district

comfort food and blue-plate specials are dished up 24 hours a day. Snug little ***Joe Jr's** gets no points for epicurean talents, yet it's a genuine treat to huddle in one of its booths for diner staples like a grilled tuna melt. **Le Gamin**, in a charming brick townhouse, attracts an artsy crowd, serving French crepes, interesting salads and big bowls of coffee. Service is leisurely, and the atmosphere especially magnetic at weekend brunch. While Le Gamin is languid, the Belgian **Petite Abeille** is brisk and cheerful, and adorned with Tintin posters. Omelettes, gourmet sandwiches, and beefy carbonade offer sturdy daytime refuelling. Belgian-style fries (fried twice to ensure maximum soft-on-the-inside crispness) are served at **F&B**, the answer to every fast-food connoisseur's dream; wash down your Danish frankfurters and Swedish meatballs with mini bottles of Pommery champagne.

*O Padeiro exudes the spirit of Portugal. Their Portuguese loaves build exceptional sandwiches, as well as providing the base for the curious açorda, thick bread soup.

Southwestern cooking meets the Far East at **Bright Food Shop**, a cute spot open all day. The staff are welcoming and the prices pocket-friendly. **Rocking Horse Café Mexicano ♪** is perpetually jammed with a varied crowd, who sup ambrosial libations and eat very fresh Mexican comidas in colourful, contemporary surroundings. Day and night, **Big Cup** is a fundamentally gay hangout, serving (yes) big cups of coffee along with muffins, pastries and sandwiches. The decor is droll and the atmosphere conducive to comfortable – and sober – cruising.

bars & clubs

Many of Chelsea's most welcoming nightspots are its gay bars. Once groundzero for trannie clubs and prostitution, the Meatpacking District is seeing more suits and ties than ever before. The result? A schizophrenic bar and club scene equally dominated by late-night joints and ultra-trendy hang-outs.

G is the place for serious gay cruising. The lounge's circular bar aids mass flirtation, and DJs spin sounds several nights a week. Plus, boys on the wagon can take advantage of the fully-stocked juice bar. ***Hell** attracts gay and straight alike. Lively parties and nightly DJs inspire some dancing, but most simply lounge around the bar, or table-hop. A resolutely straight meat market, good for late-night boozing, is **Hogs & Heifers**. Ostensibly a biker bar with men in leather vests arriving on Harley-Davidsons, the scene is more kitsch than threatening, and it also attracts a fair number of bright young media moguls. The bar is most notorious for its collection of bras displayed behind the bar – Drew Barrymore once whipped off her brassiere here. A wild, raucous night is guaranteed.

If you're looking more for a bar to call home, swing by the **Village Idiot**. With a jukebox that plays Country & Western music, patrons who spontaneously two-step, and some of the cheapest beer in town, it feels more like Nashville than 14th Street. Alternatively, ***Ciel Rouge's** yards of red velvet and chiffon is sure to bring out the romantic in you. Ponder the extensive and exceptional drinks list while being soothed by the torch singers crooning at the piano. **Serena** is another atmospheric spot, a popular Moroccan-themed boîte in the basement of the famed Chelsea hotel. Skip the front bar and head straight to the back bar for a warmer welcome. **Bongo's** style is bobby sock's retro, a paean to the 50s/60s and popular with Chelsea's arty types, as well as cocktail addicts. A seafood menu is also available. **Restaurant 147's** basement lounge (designed by Christopher Ciccone, Madonna's brother) has returned some of the heat to this former hot spot – another place to go for a pretty cocktail. **Lot 61** has certainly helped boost nightlife in West Chelsea. Located in a giant converted industrial space, it serves an array of cocktails and international tapas. Visit after gallery openings when local artists stop by to toast their new opuses. Similarly roomy, **Rhône** focuses more on wine: no less than 26 wines are available by the glass and surprise, surprise, come from the Rhône valley. Relaxed and stylishy slick.

✈ directory

Alley's End *C3*
311 W 17th Street
627-8899 $$–$$$

Annex Flea Market *E1*
Sixth Ave at 26th St

Apartment 48 *E3*
48 W 17th Street
807-1391

Auto *B4*
805 Washington St
229-2292

Barney's Co-Op *C2*
236 W 18th Street
826-8900

Big Cup *C2*
228 Eighth Avenue
206-0059 $

Bongo *B1*
299 10th Avenue
947-3654

Bottino *B1*
246 Tenth Avenue
206-6766 $$

Bright Food Shop *C2*
216 Eighth Avenue
243-4433 $–$$

Cafeteria *D3*
119 Seventh Avenue
414-1717 $–$$

Chelsea Garden Store *C3*
207 Ninth Avenue
741-6052

Chelsea Market *C3*
75 Ninth Avenue
243-5678

Ciel Rouge *D2*
176 Seventh Avenue
929-5542

Comme des Garçons *B2*
520 W 22nd Street
604-9200

Dave's New York *E1*
779 Sixth Avenue
989-6444

A Different Light *D2*
151 W 19th Street
989-4850

Eclectic Home *C2*
224 Eighth Avenue
255-2373

El Cid *C3*
322 W 15th Street
929-9332 $–$$

El Rey del Sol *D3*
232 W 14th Street
229-0733 $–$$

Empire Diner *B2*
210 Tenth Avenue
243-2736 $–$$

F&B *D2*
269 W 23rd Street
486-4441 $

Florent *C4*
69 Gansevoort Street
989-5779 $–$$

Fressen *B3*
421 W 13th Street
645-7775 $$–$$$

G *D2*
225 W 19th Street
929-1085

Hell *C4*
59 Gansevoort Street
727-1666

Hogs & Heifers *B3*
859 Washington St
929-0655

Hold Everything *C4*
104 Seventh Avenue
633-1674

Housing Works Thrift Shop *D3*
143 W 17th Street
366-0820

Jazz Record Center *D1*
8th flr, 236 W 26th St
675-4480

Jeffrey *C2*
449 W 14th Street
206-1272

Joe Jr's *E4*
482 Sixth Avenue
924-5220 $

La Lunchonette *B3*
130 Tenth Avenue
675-0342 $$

La Maison Moderne *D2*
144 W 19th Street
691-9603

Lee's Mardi Gras *C3*
400 W 14th Street
645-1888

Le Gamin *C2*
183 Ninth Avenue
243-8864 $–$$$

Loehmann's *D3*
101 Seventh Avenue
352-0856

Lot 61 *B2*
550 W 21st Street
243-6555

Markt *C3*
401 W 14th Street
727-3314 $$–$$$

Mxyplyzyk *C4*
125 Greenwich
Avenue
989-4300

Negril *C3*
362 W 23rd Street
807-6411 $–$$

Old Navy *E3*
610 Sixth Avenue
645-0663

O Padeiro *E2*
641 Sixth Avenue
414-9661 $–$$

Pastis *C4*
9–11 Little West 12th
Street
929-4844 $$

Petite Abeille *E3*
107 W 18th Street
604-9350 $

Raymond Dragon *D3*
130 Seventh Avenue
727-0368

Red Cat *B4*
227 Tenth Avenue
242-1122 $$

Restaurant 147 *D3*
147 W 15th Street
929-5000 $$–$$$

Rhône *C4*
63 Gansevoort St
367-8440

Rocking Horse Café Mexicano *C2*
182 Eighth Avenue
463-9511 $$

Serena *D2*
222 W 23rd Street
255-4646

Tom of Finland *C2*
261 W 19th Street
229-1375

The Tonic *E3*
108–110 W 18th Street
929-9755 $$–$$$

Village Idiot *C3*
355 W 14th Street
989-7334 ₵

Williams-Sonoma *D3*
110 Seventh Avenue
633-2203

chelsea & the meatpacking district

all square

gramercy park & the flatiron district

Straddling eternally hip Downtown and bustling, workaday Midtown, the section of Manhattan encompassing Gramercy Park, Union Square, the Flatiron District and Madison Square Park has experienced a reversal of fortune in recent years. The height of fashion in the 19th century, when it was home to the likes of Edith Wharton and the Roosevelts, the area was gradually abandoned by the rich who migrated uptown, leaving its lovely buildings to fall into disrepair and its pretty parks to become squalid.

Now, city clean-ups, renovations and the arrival of publishing, new media and advertising companies, have rejuvenated the area, which holds manifest treats for those in search of fine dining (especially around Union Square and Gramercy Park) and historic architecture. Shoppers also fare well, particularly for home furnishings around the Flatiron District with its striking namesake which appears to sail up Fifth Avenue.

day

🛍️ There are plenty of big-names and big-name chains all long Fifth Avenue, and home furnishing stores in the Flatiron District.

👁 All the Midtown sights are within walking distance, and the Flatiron Building [→68] is central to the area.

night

☆ Top bands play at Madison Square Gardens and Irving Plaza [→143]. There are a few cinemas in the area too.

🍴 There are superb and often expensive restaurants in Gramercy Park, all around Union Square and on Park Avenue, but good bars are few and far between.

getting there

Ⓜ F to 14th or 23rd Sts; L•4•5•6 to 14 St-Union Sq; 6 to 23rd or 28th Sts; N•R to 14 St-Union Sq, 23rd or 28th Sts.

🚌 M1 & M2 ↑ Park Ave S; M1 ↓ Park Ave, M2 & M3 ↓ 5th Ave; M14 ↔ 14th St; M15 ↑ 1st Ave, ↓ 2nd Ave; M101, M102 ↑ 3rd Ave; M101, M102 ↓ Lexington Ave .

shopping

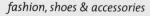

fashion, shoes & accessories

A retail wasteland not that long ago, lower Fifth Avenue has turned itself into quite a stylish shopping zone. At *Paul Smith, expect men's classics (suits, shirts); fancy underwear and socks; accessories; and stylish objects for the home – all with a little English eccentricity.

Further North, *Emporio Armani offers sleek and glossy Italian fashion (less pricey than the Armani Collection Uptown) and there's even an in-store café for a classy pit stop. Isabel Toledo Lab overlooks the city from its fifth-floor vantage point, and is the showcase for the Cuban-

born designer. Check out her feminine yet architectural clothes for women; her capsule collection for men; pieces for the home; and pen-and-ink drawings by her artist husband, Ruben. Still in fabulous mode Intermix, which offers innovative clothes from a group of rarely-

* = featured in the listings section [→92–135]

found international designers, could be your next stop. For a similar look on the cheap, try **Club Monaco**. Once the well-kept secret of fashion editors, now everybody has found out that this great chain does the trendiest sportswear, in edgy colours, at excellent prices. Another chain that is bringing high fashion to the younger crowd is **Bebe**. You can find lots of suits, dresses, separates and coats here in current styles and hues: the accent is always on sexy. *****J Crew** (a more expensive and conservative version of Gap) remains the perfect outpost for locating just the right T-shirt, sweater or plain chinos, while *****Banana Republic** (with separate stores for men and women) is a bit more upscale – their home furnishings (in the women's store) follow suit.

Serious bargain-hunters can hit the jackpot at *****Daffy's** discount superstore. However, be prepared to pick through a lot of dross to find what you want; best bets are children's clothes, sleepwear and men's suits. The women's department can be very hit or miss, but the deeper you dig, the better the chance of lucking out. If you're stuck on the styles of yesteryear, hotfoot it to 19th Street, where **The Fan Club ↗**, has OTT glamorous garb (some of it donated by celebrities) from the 20s to the 90s. All proceeds go to charity. On a mission to outdo Imelda Marcos? Stop by *****Kenneth Cole**, who has made his fortune by offering derivative versions of expensive, designer footwear for men and women at fairly affordable prices. He's also branched out into slick, mainly black, separates, bags, leather clothing and accessories.

interiors, sport, books & music

Whether you're buying or browsing, don't miss the utterly unique *****ABC Carpet & Home** – a gigantic, six-storey palace (on both sides of the street), crammed with a fantastic selection of housewares. On the same street, you can let loose the purse strings at *****Fishs Eddy**, which features all sorts of cute, vintage crockery. Campagna, one of city's chic Italian restaurants, has spawned its own **Campagna Home Shop**, which is full of imported painted porcelain, pots and pans too gorgeous to actually cook with, and other snazzy objects.

*****Paragon** has been providing the best in sportsgear for nearly 100 years. Good for quality but no real bargains, unlike **Circuit City**, which is filled with great deals on everything you've ever wanted that plugs in, has an on button or takes a picture.

For book buyers and browsers *****Barnes & Noble's** flagship store is on Fifth Avenue: you can't beat this chain for selection and value. But those seeking bargains on CDs and vinyl should head for *****Academy CDs & Records**: that sells mainly used, classical and jazz sounds.

eating & drinking

restaurants

The visionary restaurateur Danny Meyer first dared to take a chance on the emerging Union Square area in 85, opening the hospitable *****Union Square Café**. Chef Michael Romano's resourceful American dishes with a melting pot of accents employ nearby Greenmarket produce, and the wine list is extraordinary. Meyer next helped revitalize Gramercy Park with *****Gramercy Tavern**, a gently lit, active spot, whose eclectic American menu is matched by an interesting assortment of wines. Meyer has since opened two more exciting restaurants, side-by-side in the same art deco building: *****Eleven Madison Park** – New York cuisine with a French slant – and *****Tabla** – contemporary American with Indian spices. Both are beautiful, dramatically designed showplaces that have lured back the upper-echelon types who used to populate Madison Park 100 years ago.

Another pioneer in the area was Bobby Flay, who opened *****Mesa Grill** in 91. The pop-style, dynamic atmosphere is the right setting for bold Southwestern flavours and top-notch Margaritas. Around the corner, the **Blue Water Grill** is a sophisticated seafood restaurant with a great raw bar, fresh lobster, and grilled wild striped bass, plus a fab outdoor terrace.

For a colourful culinary experience, try Douglas Rodriguez's Nuevo Latino cooking (he invented the genre) at his new restaurant *****Chicama**. The food and atmosphere here positively thrill. His former Nuevo Latino venture, *Patria, now helmed by chef Andrew DiCataldo, is still an exciting place to eat and the high-energy in the Gaudi-inspired dining room is infectious. Equally buzzy, the super-chic Commune is proving a favourite with movie premiere parties and other special events. Presided over by Matthew Kenney (of Canteen fame), the restaurant serves up satisfactory American-inspired dishes, although you're more likely to be here to be seen, rather than to eat. At *Union Pacific the daring global creations, such as sauteed foie gras with green papaya and tamarind, give jaded palates a seismic jolt, and the dining room is just as breathtaking. Hands down, Periyali features the most stupendous Greek seafood in town, served in a peaceful, civilized atmosphere, while Puglia's cuisine gets top billing at I Trulli, a gracious, exquisite spot with an enchanting *enoteca* (wine bar) attached. Joanie's, with bordello-red walls and whimsical décor, is also prime for romance. The food is expensive but worth it for originality and flavour, such as blue crab chowder, and apple-curry pasta with seafood.

Hidden in the basement of a picturesque townhouse is Yama, which dishes up plentiful sushi at decent prices served in the ambience of a Japanese living room. Another gorgeous townhouse holds *Verbena, run by owner/chef Diane Forley, one of New York's few women restaurateurs who has risen to the top. She offers a riveting organic take on American cuisine like wild Columbia River sturgeon with celery root, leek and chard. The garden is beautiful.

Fronting modern Union Square, *Zen Palate is cherished for its creative Asian vegan dishes and serene decor. Downstairs is cheaper and more casual, and upstairs more medita-

tive (and expensive). Also on the pricey side is *Veritas known for its showy dishes and awesome wine list. Singles hang out at Candela, as dark and gothic as a medieval castle. Along with a hyper bar scene is surprisingly thoughtful food, such as an abundant seafood platter, and asparagus, goats' cheese and basil purée. Lola possesses a more assured sexiness, serving an inventive mix of American, Mediterranean and Asian cuisines; the live gospel music at Sunday brunch is especially rousing. If you're into jazz, head for 27 Standard (performances downstairs). The cavernous dining room offers superb eclectic dishes like pecan-crusted pork, and tuna sashimi wrapped in *nori*.

cafés & diners

Keeping pace with the wide number of local businesses, lunchtime stops have multiplied. The slick City Bakery has huge cookies and other mouth-watering sweets, plus a line-up of fresh soups, sandwiches and prepared foods – to go or eat-in at several small tables (closes 6pm). Flavors, an illustrious catering company, has a market/café outpost selling assorted breakfast and lunch items, as well as a fantastic salad bar and beautiful desserts (closes 6.30pm). For the ultimate salad fix, head for Tossed ∆ where you can choose from eight types of lettuce, and vegetable toss-ins with dressings such as champagne-raspberry (closes 10pm).

If you've maxed out on shopping, take a tranquil break at the ABC Parlour Café at the back of this magical furniture store. Or, the Coffee Shop is a stylish canteen, with an amazing S-shaped bar, that pulses until 6am. What it lacks in service it makes up for in robust Brazilian dishes including a *feijoada* brunch. Republic is the consummate Pan-Asian cafeteria: minimalist, capacious and cool. Brothy noodle soups and curried duck noodles are tasty and modestly priced.

The airy diner Mayrose is popular for turkey burgers, milkshakes and big breakfasts (served at any time). The food isn't amazing but it's abundant and popular with pre- and post-cinema goers. Curry in a Hurry in the part of Lexington Avenue known as Little India resembles an Indian McDonald's. *Masala dosa* – vegetarian pancakes stuffed with potatoes and peas – are the best item, and it's BYOB which makes it super-cheap. The rather dowdy Eisenberg Sandwich Shop (closes at 5pm) has been open since 1929, and one hopes it'll last forever. Thank the counterman for your chocolate shake and cheap, thick tuna sandwich and he'll respond, 'My pleasure, darling.' How often do you hear that in New York?

bars

While both Gramercy Park and the Flatiron District boast a slew of restaurants, neither offers much in the way of a bar scene. **The Galaxy** is a bar and a fusion restaurant. The house cocktails – much like its planetarium-chic decor – are both imaginative and palatable, and it makes an ideal stop en route to or from a concert at Irving Plaza [→143]. For a more down-to-earth experience head to **Pete's Tavern**. Boasting original tin ceilings, an ancient oak bar and, in some cases, what look like original bartenders, this friendly neighbourhood institution is still going strong after a century of business.

Expect old-fashioned cocktails and classic pub grub.

The boy-bar scene is considerably more lively in nearby Chelsea, but if you just can't get there, try **Splash**, which offers two floors of boozing and cruising, as well as DJs and dancing. Sin City lives.

directory

ABC Carpet & Home *♭B2–B3*
888 Broadway
473-3000

ABC Parlour Café *♭B2*
38 E 19th Street
677-2233 $–$$

Academy CDs & Records *♭A3*
10 W 18th Street
242-4848

Banana Republic *♭A3 & A3*
89 & 122 Fifth Avenue
366-4630/366-4691

Barnes & Noble *♭A3*
105 Fifth Avenue
807-0099

Bebe *♭A3*
100 Fifth Avenue
675-2323

Blue Water Grill *♭B3*
31 Union Square W
675-9500 $$–$$$

Campagna Home *♭B3*
29 E 21st Street
420-1600

Candela *♭B3*
116 E 16th Street
254-1600 $$

Chicama *♭B3*
35 E 18th Street
505-2233 $$$

Circuit City *♭B3*
52 E 14th Street
387-0730

City Bakery *♭A3*
22 E 17th Street
366-1414 $

Club Monaco *♭A2*
160 Fifth Avenue
352-0936

Coffee Shop *♭B3*
29 Union Square W
243-7969 $–$$

Commune *♭B2*
12 E 22nd Street
777-2600 $$–$$$

Curry in a Hurry *♭B1*
119 Lexington Avenue
683-0900 $

Daffy's *♭A3*
111 Fifth Avenue
529-4477

Eisenberg Sandwich Shop *♭A2*
174 Fifth Avenue
675-5096 $

Eleven Madison Park *♭B2*
11 Madison Avenue
889-0905 $$–$$$

Emporio Armani *♭A3*
110 Fifth Avenue
727-3240

The Fan Club *♭A2*
22 W 19th Street
929-3349

Fishs Eddy *♭B2*
889 Broadway
420-9020

Flavors *♭A3*
8 W 18th Street
647-1234 $

The Galaxy *♭B3*
15 Irving Place
777-3631 ◐ $

Gramercy Tavern *♭B2*
42 E 20th Street
477-0777 $$$

I Trulli *♭B1*
122 E 27th Street
481-7372 $$$

Intermix *♭A3*
125 Fifth Avenue
533-9720

Isabel Toledo Lab *♭A1*
277 Fifth Avenue
685-0948

J Crew *♭A3*
91 Fifth Avenue
255-4848

Joanie's *♭B1*
126 E 28th Street
689-5656 $$$

Kenneth Cole *♭A3*
95 Fifth Avenue
675-2550

Lola *♭A2*
30 W 22nd Street
675-6700 $$$

Mayrose *♭B2*
920 Broadway
533-3663 $

Mesa Grill *♭A3*
102 Fifth Avenue
807-7400 $$–$$$

Paragon *♭B3*
867 Broadway
255-8036

Patria *♭B2*
250 Park Avenue S
777-6211 $$$

Paul Smith *♭A3*
108 Fifth Avenue
627-9770

Periyali *♭A2*
35 W 20th Street
463-7890 $$$

Pete's Tavern *♭B3*
129 E 18th Street
473-7676 ◐ $–$$$

Republic *♭B3*
37 Union Square W
627-7172 $

Splash *♭A3*
50 W 17th Street
691-0073

Tabla *♭B1*
11 Madison Avenue
889-0667 $$$

Tossed *♭B2*
295 Park Avenue S
674-6700 $

27 Standard *♭B1*
116 E 27th Street
447-7733 $$$

Union Pacific *♭B2*
111 E 22nd Street
995-8500 $$$

Union Square Café *♭B3*
21 E 16th Street
243-4020 $$$

Verbena *♭B3*
53 Irving Place
260-5454 $$$

Veritas *♭B2*
43 E 20th Street
353-3700 $$$

Yama *♭B3*
122 East 17th Street
475-0969 $$$

Zen Palate *♭B3*
34 Union Square E
614-9291 $–$$

gramercy park & the flatiron district

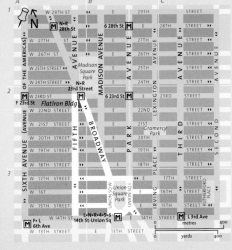

middle ground

For many New Yorkers office-heavy Midtown means one thing: work. But to the visitor, Manhattan's central segment is as exciting and intense as any place on earth. This is where you'll find vertigo-inducing skyscrapers, world-famous hotels, fancy stores, and some of NYC's most expensive restaurants. Midtown's dramatic hub is Times Square [→70]. The stretch of Broadway which cuts through this dazzling neon morass is of course, *the* Broadway, with its slew of legendary venues in the Theater District. Also cutting through Times Square is 42nd Street, the city's former red light district. Theme stores and renovated theatres have now replaced most of the sex shops.

West of Times Square, Hell's Kitchen – formerly the stamping ground of Irish and Hispanic immigrants – is a fully gentrified neighbourhood. Directly south is the busy, work-a-day Garment District, home to clothing manufacturers and textile wholesalers. Glamorous Fifth Avenue, which, to many, epitomises New York, lies directly east, and its vista of historic skyscrapers and landmarks can truly take the breath away.

day

🛍 Check out theme and flagship stores around Times Square, and historic shops along Fifth Avenue.

👁 American Craft Museum [→78]; Bryant Park [→85]; Chrysler Building [→68]; Empire State Building [→68]; Grand Central Station [→68]; ICP (Midtown) [→80]; Intrepid Sea Air Space Museum [→86-87]; MetLife Building [→69]; MoMA [→74]; NY Public Library [→71]; Morgan Library [→77]; Radio City Music Hall [→69]; Rockefeller Center [→69]; St Patrick's Cathedral [→69]; Trump Tower [→70]; UN Building [→70].

night

☆ Make for the bright lights of the Broadway theatres and Times Square.

🍴 Dine out in the Theater District and along Ninth Avenue.

getting there

Ⓜ Nearly all lines stop at various Midtown stations: major hubs are Times Sq-42nd St, 34th St-Herald Square, Grand Central-42nd St & 47–50th Sts-Rockefeller Ctr.

🚌 Similarly, several buses travel along 5th, 6th, & 7th Aves, Madison & Broadway; there are regular cross-street services too.

shopping

department stores

Midtown is a hive of shopping activity. The famous, stretch of Fifth Avenue is home to a host of glossy shops, including several of the city's legendary department stores. The venerable

*Bergdorf Goodman is a hedonistic shopping experience for those with one eye on the cutting edge. While it still has old-world elegance, it is also trendy Fashion Central, offering

the top designers, excellent accessories and unique homewares. Across the street, Bergdorf Men is a newer addition. ***Saks Fifth Avenue** is another NY institution – an old-fash-

* = featured in the listings section [→92–135]

ioned department store (with excellent service) that also carries the top designers (for more designer-label street cred), while *Macy's, the 'biggest department store in the world', has just about everything. **Henri Bendel** is a real jewel of a store filled with good things, especially if you're after a sweater (with a myriad colour options), or fabulous make-up brands with staff on hand to give you some top tips.

*Takashimaya (from Japan) and *Felissimo ✏ are two quasi-department stores which sell gorgeous clothes, accessories and homewares – all displayed and wrapped with great aesthetic flair.

flagship stores

Flagship super-emporiums are a dime a dozen in this area. On one block of 57th Street (heading east from Fifth Avenue), the luxury stores abound – Versace, **Chanel, Hermès, Burberry,** and more. If hard-core fashion is what you crave, get your fix at the *Prada store. Behind the glass and marble storefront are Muiccia's genius clothes for men and women. Nearby is *Gucci, a stop for career fashion (and shoe) lovers. Along with high fashion for men and women, check out Tom Ford's beautiful handbags. More perfect tailoring comes in the shape of **Christian Dior.**

There is nothing more American than *Gap, and the biggest and best of them all can be found here, offering affordable sportswear with a few extra, upscale surprises, like the luxury baby boutique. A recent import, the Swedish chain *H&M has opened its first US megastore on Fifth Avenue. On day one queues formed around the block, and it still continues to attract the crowds, who are drawn here by seemingly endless supplies of super-cheap, fashion knock offs.

megastores

The theme stores have arrived, packed with tempting licensed merchandise. There's plenty to see at *Sony Style ►, including a glimpse of the future of entertainment, high-tech toys and music machines – all of which keep the cash tills whirring. Few people leave New York without a visit to the ultimate megastore, *Niketown. Five floors of gear with the 'swoosh' in a suitably futuristic interior, and a huge screen showing Nike commercials. *Warner Bros Studio Store is also good fun, with some imaginative toys, while at the NBA Store, which holds a full-range of merchandise from every NBA basketball team, you can get kitted out just like

Shaq. If Mickey, Minnie and Co are more up your street, swing by the *Disney Store. And *FAO Schwarz is just plain toy nirvana [→87].

Right on Times Square, the giant *Virgin Megastore must surely have the biggest selection of music in town (plus great quantities of videos and books): *HMV (with very helpful and knowledgeable staff) and *Tower Records are not as cavernous, but offer more of the same.

home furnishings, books & food

The famous Chicago home furnishings outpost, **Crate & Barrel,** has a beautiful and spacious NY store. On offer are high quality yet functional and chic furniture, dishwares, and other home accessories – all at affordable prices. To add to your book collection, it's worth visiting **Coliseum Books,** which has an enormous selection with lots of discounts. *Rizzoli has an equally impressive selection, particularly on art, design and architecture, displayed in a historic and utterly beautiful store.

All shopped out and need something sweet to give you a boost? Don't settle for anything less than the very best chocolate. Empyreal French delicacies almost too exquisite to eat can be found at **Richart,** while **Godiva Chocolatier** from Belgium and **Teuscher** from Switzerland are two other divine choices to keep you going.

accessories & shoes

British-based *Manolo Blahník displays his fabulous footwear in a townhouse store. No price tags here – but if you need to ask... Another Brit import, *Jimmy Choo, has made a real splash with his unusual and very luxe collection, giving new meaning to well-heeled. For a bag on the cheap, sneak into **Suarez ►** which makes look-alike Hermès, Chanel and more. Or take a peek at the edgy, of-the-moment bags by Karl Lagerfeld at **Fendi,** where the clothes are also wonderful.

There is no better place for fine jewellery than **Tiffany's.** The famous blue boxes decadently scream 'I've just spent a pile of money and don't give a damn!'. Nearby **Cartier,** purveyor of movie star jewellery offers equally extravagant retail therapy.

eating & drinking

restaurants

In Midtown's asphalt jungle, it's easy to feel confounded when it's time to eat. Mediocre tourist traps abound but you won't feel cheated at any of these...

Surrounded by glitzy new high-rises, a little piece of New York's cultural history is still alive at the **'21' Club**, marked by a line of colourful, miniature jockeys. It's outrageously expensive but incredibly charming and old-world, and the American classics are genuinely good. **Keens Steakhouse** has been around since 1885. The bygone tavern decor is glorious and the dry-aged steaks and mutton chops legendary. Prices are steep but the brief bar menu is more affordable (closed Sun). Another landmark restaurant has only recently reopened after five years of shut doors (and an extensive renovation to the tune of $20 million). The **Russian Tea Room**'s OTT decor includes Tiffany stained-glass ceiling and mirrored walls. The food is hardly the lure, so head for the upstairs lounge where you can sup on caviar and cocktails. **The Brasserie** has also re-opened after a massive makeover. Its new super-cool interior and upscale bistro food are a big draw at all hours (open 'til 1 am). The restored and at times bustling ***Oyster Bar ✓** in Grand Central Station is a lark for its antiquated setting, and serves well-nigh every type of fish in the sea – and, of course, oysters. Sit at the counter for chowder and beer, or choose the dark saloon for a more leisurely affair.

Upstairs, overlooking the main concourse, basketball superstar ***Michael Jordan's The Steakhouse** offers an awe-inspiring panorama of the commuter hubbub below and a canopy of illuminated stars above. The tables are ringed around the mezzanine and the steak-oriented menu is superb. Another impressive backdrop is beautiful Bryant Park (behind the Public Library) where **Bryant Park Grill & Café** offers a retreat from the hustle of Midtown. The Café wins hands down in the summer with an ample supply of alfresco seating (singles flock here on Thursday evenings), while the classy Grill serves top-notch New American food and has huge windows affording a great view. The ***Trattoria dell' Arte**, near Carnegie Hall, also possesses an attractive grandeur.

Big-name publishing and movie personalities frequent it, not only for the scene but also for its splendid Italian cuisine.

The trendy, attitude-heavy scene at **Asia de Cuba** can be over the top, so it's not for everybody. If, however, you want to lounge in a creamy boudoir, share punchbowl-sized tropical drinks and sample exotic, expensive Asian-Latin fusion dishes, step right up. Pretensions are wonderfully absent at **Don Giovanni**, a Theater District favourite adorned with vintage actors' photos and straw-covered Chianti bottles. The terrific brick-oven pizzas are better than the pastas. **Esca**, Mario Batali's new Southern Italian seafood-themed restaurant is another Midtown hit. Convenient to Broadway's theatres, it's a classy, but not a stuffy affair. Red-checked tablecloths and a quaint French bistro ambience have made ***La Bonne Soupe ✓** appealing for decades. Besides hearty Gallic classics, the soups are meals in themselves and the price includes a salad, dessert and glass of wine. At **Virgil's Real BBQ**, goodwill towards all – even children – reigns. It's big, fun and rambunctious.

An unusual pre-theatre choice is **Lakruwana**, an opulent Sri Lankan restaurant embellished with brass, crushed velvet curtains and wooden sculptures. Dishes are spicy, there's a good vegetarian selection, and it's BYOB. Exceptional vegetarian choices are found at two of Koreatown's best restaurants: ***Cho Dang Gol** are the tofu specialists, though carnivores will also be happy with their barbecued prime beef ribs. The other is **Hangawi**, an enchanting, serene temple devoted exclusively to vegetarianism. Wear good socks as shoes are left at the door.

For something truly international, book a table at the **UN Delegates' Dining**

> Midtown eateries dish it out to the lunchtime work crowd, early evening theatre-going set and night owls alike.

Room. Expect an extravagant buffet and a room full of dignitaries with stunning river vistas (11.30am–2.30pm Mon–Fri). Allow 15 minutes to pass security (photo ID and jackets required).

The city's top Scandinavian restaurant is *Aquavit, occupying the ground level of a mansion formerly owned by the Rockefellers. The tranquil main dining room offers an innovative menu while the upstairs, less formal café serves traditional herring, gravlax and Swedish meatballs. For the most fabulous French seafood creations in an elegant setting, *Le Bernardin is a heavenly experience. You'll pay through the nose but not regret it. *Lespinasse evokes the Palace of Versailles, with prices ($35 appetizers) that could start a revolution. If money is no object, the French cuisine is breathtaking and memorable, the service faultless. Even if you're unimpressed with the bistro food at **Guastavino's** (simple, pricey, yet kind of tasty) you'd still want to experience Terence Conran's first New York venture simply for the spectacular setting. Conran has revamped the cavernous Bridgemarket, a former farmer's market under the 59th Street Bridge. Next door there's a food hall and the Conran Shop.

cafés

Don't let the varnished panelling and tacky chandeliers dissuade you from stopping in at *Ess-a-Bagel for arguably the best and biggest bagels in town. There are also smoked fish platters and a range of calorie-laden desserts. Service might be strict and prices rather high, but the soups at **Soup Kitchen International** (from which the famous 'Soup Nazi' *Seinfeld* episode was derived) are celestial (12–6pm Mon–Fri).

Within the Rockefeller Center [→69] is a busy Italian marketplace called **Tuscan Square**. The downstairs self-service café dishes up tasty prepared foods, delicious soups and has a great salad bar (closes at 8pm). Takashimaya, the fancy Japanese department store, has a calming, minimalist café, **The Tea Box**, which serves bite-sized sandwiches, elegant bento boxes and lovely afternoon tea (11am–6pm). Another fine spot is **Mezze**, a sunny, casual Mediterranean café near Grand Central Station. Breakfast coffee can be savoured with rich pastries, and at lunch there are quality, pre-cooked meat, seafood and vegetable selections (closes at 5pm).

If you want something good and fast before a Broadway show, bypass the traditional options on 48th Street's 'Restaurant Row' and head for Ninth Avenue, which has recently been rejuvenated by an influx of new restaurants. **Vynl Diner** ✒ in Hell's Kitchen is super-friendly, with mosaic tabletops and camp decor. In addition to American staples like grilled cheese and meatloaf, there are Thai-accented curries and stir-fries. Great burgers and milkshakes (but no fries) are found at *Island Burgers & Shakes, a relaxed, crowded nook that's especially popular at lunchtimes. They also make bang-up grilled chicken sandwiches with lots of toppings. Los Dos Rancheros **Mexicanos** has some of the most authentic Mexican *moles*, *tamales* and *chiles rellenos* in New York. It's a funky cafeteria with few gringos so you know it must be the real thing.

bars

While Midtown proper is dominated by tourist traps and theme restaurants, Hell's Kitchen is home to a number of fantastic dive bars. *Rudy's Bar & Grill is one of the few original to survive the Mayor's efforts to sanitize the neighbourhood. Free hot dogs at the bar, a great happy hour and heaps of authenticity add to its appeal. Several newer bars also offer a taste of that bygone scene. Two blocks away from the Port Authority, **Bellevue Bar** is a good place to fortify yourself with a beer. Its subterranean sister bar *Siberia is another favourite. Tucked in a corner of the Downtown 1•9 subway station, it never fails to entertain – especially if you've sampled a few shots of chilled Soomskaya vodka. Vodka is just about the only

thing you can drink at ***The Russian Samovar ►**, a swank Theater District bar and restaurant boasting dozens of house vodkas infused with everything from plums to horseradish. But for some of the best Margaritas in NYC, check out ***Chase**, an upscale gay bar, which draws an after work crowd. When the suits head home, the fashionistas also flock here for late night cocktails.

After the show, head to **Xth Ave Lounge** and mix with budding thespians, writers and other rent-challenged types. ***Swine on Nine**, a watering hole billing itself as Manhattan's only theme dive bar, could easily lay claim to the nation's largest assemblage of porcine paraphernalia. To jump-start their own collections, ladies get a free piggy bank as a souvenir.

If being so close to Broadway makes you want to belt out a few tunes of your own, head to **Japas 55**. Part bar, part sushi restaurant, Japas features private karaoke booths where you can humiliate yourself in front of up to

20 friends, or do a duet in a space for two. Singing around a piano is still a lively tradition at ***Regents**. An older, mostly gay clientele regularly gathers at this casually elegant brownstone for drinks, dinner and a few rounds of standards. Singers of a different stripe meet at **O'Reilley's Pub**, where young Irish expats – and anyone fond of whisky and beer – sing along with the jukebox, seduce local lasses and generally have a raucous good time.

Too much whiskey is a phrase that could aptly describe the interests of Rande Gerber, Cindy Crawford's husband. The latest NY annexes to the bar impresario's empire are **Whiskey Blue** and **Whiskey Park**. The latter is housed in the Trump Parc building, and that is all you need to know. The former, located in the W New York hotel [→153], attracts more of a bar-to-boudoir crowd, (especially on Thursdays), along with plenty of Hamptons-haunting ladies and wealthy sugar daddies. But the latest bar venture from Gerber is the **Wet Bar**, a roomy, red-walled place with a velvet rope

and private nooks for getting up to no good in. No wonder it's gained a reputation as a pick-up spot. If you prefer to watch the world go by, try **Metrazur**, on the East Balcony of Grand Central Station's main hall. Besides a fantastic view onto the commuters below, Metrazur offers cocktails and very classy bar snacks such as lobster spring rolls. If you're looking for an old New York hotel bar, the ***Blue Bar** is a quiet retreat, while ***Top of The Tower**, a 26th-floor art deco gem, offers breathtaking views of Manhattan, a tinkling piano, and dapper old waiters serving classic cocktails. The art-deco-inspired **One 51** is altogether more chic and drinks are appropriately pricey. There's a dancefloor at the back, but the upstairs lounge provides a haven for those who like to talk rather than get their groove on.

🎵 directory

Aquavit *♫E2*
13 W 54th Street
307-7311 $$$

Asia de Cuba *♫F6*
Morgans Hotel,
237 Madison Avenue
726-7755 $$$

Bellevue Bar *♫B6*
538 Ninth Avenue
695-5507 ◐

Bergdorf Goodman *♫E1*
754 Fifth Avenue
753-7300

Blue Bar *♫E5*
59 W 44th Street
840-6800 ◐

Bryant Park Grill & Café *♫E6*
25 W 40th Street
840-6500 $$–$$$

Burberry *♫E2*
9 E 57th Street
371-5010

Cartier *♫E3*
653 Fifth Avenue
753-0111

Chanel *♫E2*
15 E 57th Street
355-5050

Chase *♫C2*
255 W 55th Street
333-3400

Cho Dang Gol *♫E7*
55 W 35th Street
695-8222 $–$$

Christian Dior *♫E2*
703 Fifth Avenue
931-2950

Coliseum Books *♫C2*
1771 Broadway
757-8381

Crate & Barrel *♫F1*
650 Madison Avenue
308-0011

Disney Store *♫E2*
711 Fifth Avenue
702-0702

Don Giovanni *♫B5*
358 W 44th Street
581-4939 $–$$

Esca *♫B5*
402 W 43rd Street
564-7272 $$–$$$

Ess-a-Bagel *♫G3*
831 Third Avenue
980-1010 $

FAO Schwarz *♫E1*
767 Fifth Avenue
644-9400

Felissimo *♫E2*
10 W 56th Street
247-5656

Fendi *♫E2*
720 Fifth Avenue
767-0100

Gap *♫D7*
60 34th Street
643-8960

Godiva Chocolatier *♫E2*
701 Fifth Avenue
593-2845

Gucci *♫E2*
10 W 57th Street
826-2600

Guastavino's *♫J1*
409 E 59th Street
980-2455 $$–$$$

Hangawi *♫E8*
12 E 32nd Street
213-0077 $$–$$$

H&M *♫E3*
640 Fifth Avenue
480-8777

Henri Bendel *♫X2*
712 Fifth Avenue
247-1100

Hermès *♫E1*
11 E 57th Street
751-3151

HMV *♫D7*
57 W 34th Street
629-0900

Island Burgers & Shakes *♫B3*
766 Ninth Avenue
307-7934 $

Japas 55 *♫B2*
253 W 55th Street
765-1210 $–$$

Jimmy Choo *♫E3*
645 Fifth Avenue
593-0800

Keens Steakhouse *♫E7*
72 W 36th Street
947-3636 $$$

La Bonne Soupe *♫E2*
48 W 55th Street
586-7650 $–$$

Lakruwana *B5*
358 W 44th Street
957-4480 $$

Le Bernardin *D3*
155 W 51st Street
489-1515 $$$

Lespinasse *E2*
St Regis Hotel
2 E 55th Street
339-6719 $$$

Los Dos Rancheros Mexicanos *A6*
507 Ninth Avenue
868-7780 $

Macy's *D7*
151 W 34th Street
695-4400

Manolo Blahnik *E2*
31 W 54th Street
582-3007

Mezze *E5*
10 E 44th Street
697-6644 $–$$

Metrazur *F5*
Grand Central Station
42nd Street
687-4600

Michael Jordan's The Steakhouse *F5*
Grand Central Station
42nd Street
655-2300 $$–$$$

NBA Store *E3*
666 Fifth Avenue
515-6221

Niketown *E2*
6 E 57th Street
891-6453

One 51 *G3*
151 E 51st Street
753-1144

O'Reilley's Pub *D8*
56 W 31st Street
684-4244 ℂ

Oyster Bar *F5*
lower level, Grand Central Station, 42nd Street
490-6650 $–$$$

Prada *E2*
724 Fifth Avenue
664-0010

Regents *H3*
317 E 53rd Street
593-3091 ℂ $$

Richart *E2*
7 E 55th Street
371-9369

Rizzoli *D2*
31 W 57th Street
759-2424

Rudy's Bar & Grill *A5*
627 Ninth Avenue
974-9169 ℂ

The Russian Samovar *C3*
56 W 52nd Street
757-0168 ℂ

Russian Tea Room *D2*
150 W 57th Street
974-2111 $$–$$$

Saks Fifth Avenue *E4*
611 Fifth Avenue
753-4000

Siberia *C3*
Downtown 1·9 subway station,
1627 Broadway
333-4141 ℂ

Sony Style *E2*
550 Madison Avenue
833-8800

Soup Kitchen International *C2*
259a W 55th Street
757-7730 $–$$

Suarez *F2*
450 Park Avenue
753-3758

Swine on Nine *A4*
693 Ninth Avenue
397-8356 ℂ

Takashimaya *E2*
693 Fifth Avenue
350-0100

The Tea Box *E2*
693 Fifth Avenue
350-0180 $–$$

Teuscher *E3*
620 Fifth Avenue
246-4416

Tiffany's *E2*
727 Fifth Avenue
755-8000

Top of the Tower *J4*
Beekman Tower Hotel
3 Mitchell Place
355-7300

Tower Records *E2*
Garden level, Trump Tower, Fifth Avenue
838-8110

Trattoria dell'Arte *C2*
900 Seventh Avenue
245-9800 $$–$$$

Tuscan Square *E3*
16 W 51st Street
977-7777 $–$$

'21' Club *E3*
21 W 52nd Street
582-7200 $$$

UN Delegates' Dining Room *J4*
45th Street (at First Avenue)
963-7626 $$

Versace *E2*
647 Fifth Avenue
317-0224

Virgil's Real BBQ *D5*
152 W 44th Street
921-9494 $$

Virgin Megastore *C5*
1540 Broadway
921-1020

Vynl Diner *B2*
824 Ninth Avenue
974-2003 $

Warner Bros Studio Store *E2*
1 E 57th Street
754-0305

Wet Bar *G6*
W Court Hotel
130 E 39th Street
726-9500

Whiskey Blue *F4*
W New York
541 Lexington Avenue
407-2947

Whiskey Park *D1*
Trump Parc
100 Central Park S
307-9222

Xth Ave Lounge *A5*
642 Tenth Avenue
245-9088

the gold coast

The UES is the stomping ground of New York's financial aristocracy, and every inch of this privileged enclave, from the designer stores of Madison Avenue to the magnificent museums along the edge of Central Park, screams big money. Fifth Avenue is punctuated by 19th-century mansion houses built by some of America's legendary millionaires, and now home to the city's premier museums. The magnificent townhouses, apartments and exclusive clubs of New York's fabulously rich line the adjacent streets of Fifth, Madison and Park Avenues. Madison Avenue is, of course, New York's most important shopping address, with its flagship stores and commercial art galleries. East of Lexington Avenue, the prevailing atmosphere becomes more neighbourly and family oriented but it's still far from edgy.

day

🛍 Madison Avenue is the only address that counts for designer shopping.

👁 Central Park [→84]; Cooper-Hewitt, National Design Museum [→76]; El Museo del Barrio [→77]; Frick Collection [→76]; International Center of Photography (Uptown) [→80]; Jewish Museum [→77]; Metropolitan Museum of Art [→73–74]; Solomon R Guggenheim Museum [→74]; Whitney Museum of American Art [→75].

night

☆ The area is distinctly lacking in attractions after dark, though there are some toney bars.

🍴 Dining out at one of the area's many upscale restaurants is the main event.

getting there

Ⓜ 6 to 77th, 86th, 96th, 103rd or 110th Sts; 4·5 to 86th St.

🚌 M1, M2, M3, M4 ↑ Madison Ave, ↓ 5th Ave; M15 ↑ 1st Ave, ↓ 2nd Ave; M31 ↕ York Ave; M66 ↔ 67th St, → 68th St; M72 ↔ 72nd St; M79 ↔ 79th St; M86 ↔ 86th St; M96 ↔ 96th St; M101, M102, M103 ↑ 3rd Ave, ↓ Lexington Ave.

shopping

fashion

If you're off to shop on the UES, chances are you're heading for Madison Avenue. Every inch of this strip is devoted to selling luxuries: expect to pay high prices, encounter snooty staff, and rub shoulders with the fake-tan-and-fur-coat brigade.

There are a couple of top department stores in the area: *Bloomingdale's [→94] is a revered NY institution, and much more old school than *Barney's [→94], every upwardly-mobile New Yorker's style barometer. Its fantastically talented buy-

ers consistently discover the most exciting, unique and interesting designs. Nearby, *Shanghai Tang ⬆ is an altogether wackier affair. The richly decorated space is filled with owner Alan Tang's modern take on the traditional Chinese aesthetic: coolie jackets in

* = featured in the listings section [→92–135]

acid colours and beautifully tailored cheongsams.

The fashion heavyweights are all shoulder to shoulder on Madison Avenue, and the fashion-hungry flock here for the lastest creations. American überdesigner **Calvin Klein**'s five-floor flagship is filled with the entire range of Klein's signature understatements, from evening wear to underwear. Opposite is the city's first *DKNY store, stocked with Donna's rather glamorous take on streetwear. A few blocks north you'll find Giorgio Armani's more reserved flagship, *Emporio Armani, showcasing every aspect of the designer's work, including his cheaper diffusion lines, all against a minimalist backdrop. In contrast, the *Versace store is out-and-out exuberant. Although the late designer's flagship is located in Midtown, this smaller store is just a little less intimidating (and replete with Donnatella's wild designs). Whimsical and pricey fashion (for men and women) is the order of the day at **Moschino**, although there is a cheaper line for those who can't afford the four-figure price tags. Vying with Moschino for the most irreverent designer is Brit-star Alexander McQueen, who reigns at

Givenchy. His genius couture is a marvel of tailoring and innovation. **Chloé** has recently opened its first American store on Madison to house the feminine womenswear by another British star, Stella McCartney.

The list of big names continues with **Valentino**. His elegant emporium is beloved of the neighbourhood's fur-coat-brigade. And few stores can rival the magnificent *Polo Ralph Lauren flagship. Housed in a former mansion, and decked out to resemble an English stately home, it's filled with the designer's collection of classically influenced clothing. Across the street is the **Polo Sport** store, which carries Lauren's sportier creations.

Italians *Dolce & Gabbana have two enormous stores on Madison, one to house their less expensive D&G line. Fabulous sweaters and leather goods from Italy can also be found at **Etro**, or pop into **Emilio Pucci**, for clothing, swimwear, undies, and home accessories featuring retro-style psychedelic swirls. *Prada's also in the nabe – its biggest outlet stocks a large range of menswear, while *Diesel's trendy superstore has jeans and stylish sporty

clothes that don't cost a bundle. Yet another Latin-born designer, **Roberto Cavalli**, has recently made inroads on Madison Avenue. This is his only boutique in North America, providing a home for his *outré*, multimedia designs for women and men.

British favourite **Joseph** has two stores on Madison, one for his perfect-fit pants and the other for luscious knitwear. The British invasion continues at **Nicole Farhi**, who has opened a store (across the road from Barney's) for her elegant easy-to-wear clothing that also accomodates a stylish, in-store restaurant, Nicoles.

Searle is an exclusive UES affair, which has no fewer than four stores on Madison. They specialize in clean-lined coats, sportswear and covetable knitwear. Cashmere is the *raison d'être* at **TSE**, where brilliant designer Hussein Chalayan spins the soft stuff into coats and sweaters. **Missoni** also excels in unusual and sensuous knits in gem-like colours.

one-offs

Although most of the neighbourhood's street-level real estate is given over to designer stores, there are still a few unique and unusual places to be discovered. **Chrome Hearts**, a mecca for leather fans, is hidden away in an unmarked brownstone. The look here is biker-chic-meets-rockstar. More sedate fare is to be found at **Nocturne**, which, as the name might suggest, specializes in sleep wear. It's also one of the only places in town to stock up on cult favourite Lily Pulitzer's flowered frocks and separates. Hard to believe, but one of the

biggest thrift stores, *Out of the Closet, is in the UES. The merchandise is pristine and varied, and thanks to wealthy neighbourhood types who regularly donate their unwanted treasures, bargains are likely.

There are plenty of chichi home furnishing stores on the UES, but the enormous *Gracious Home, which takes up nearly two blocks, can't be beat in terms of price, range or service. Get a key cut, spend hundreds of dollars on linens, or shop for state-of-the art kitchen equipment: this place covers all the bases.

beauty, shoes & accessories

Fresh is a welcome addition to the NY beauty scene. Imported cosmetics, as well as the store's own line, are displayed in an all-white setting. To follow in the footsteps of Madison's well-heeled, make straight for *Stéphane Kélian ↓: the French shoemaker creates luxe and inventive fashion-forward footwear. If you want high heels, but can't take the pain, you should join the many members of the *Christian Louboutin fan club. He's renowned for his comfortable, elegant and innovative designs, but such a combination does not, of course, come cheap.

The popularity of shoe-maker *Tod's shows no sign of abating. His version of the driving shoe (part loafer, part moccasin) is the slipper of choice for celebrity summers. Hair stylist Frédéric

Fekkai has seen his fair share of famous clients. Drop by his in-salon boutique to pick up polished hair accessories and treatment products as well as bags and purses.

eating & drinking

restaurants

Epicentre of the social register, UES is filled with chic, clubby restaurants which, not surprisingly, are run by some of the most celebrated chefs in New York. The affable, well-known Daniel Boulud is at the stove at *Daniel, a supremely grand Renaissance-style restaurant with seasonal French cuisine. His smaller and more informal (but still expensive) *Café Boulud serves global cuisine alongside traditional and seasonal Gallic classics. The room is comfortable and inviting, the clientele cultured, and service impeccable. As if Boulud doesn't have enough on his plate, he also co-owns the dreamy *Payard Patisserie & Bistro. Rapturous desserts and savoury items are featured in the patisserie; at the back is a deluxe French bistro on two floors.

Another titan of the food world, Jean-Georges Vongerichten, is behind JoJo, a jewel box of a townhouse restaurant. The crowd is refined, the staff unfailingly pleasant, with inventive French cooking the speciality – the $28 prix-fixe lunch is a bargain. The Lenox Room is another genteel option, with a great raw bar and exceptional new American food. The polished dining room attracts affluent, mature types until 9pm, when a

younger crowd arrives for drinks and elevated snacks. Deluxe French seafood is the order of the day at Cello, one of the toughest (and most expensive) tickets in the UES.

A more homey neighbourhood place is Miss Saigon, serving tasty, delicately prepared Vietnamese dishes at pocket-friendly prices. The whimsical architecture evokes a village hut, its walls adorned with Asian artefacts. For old-fashioned Sicilian food (veal parmigiana, chicken marsala) in a charming, bygone atmosphere, Carino will warm your heart – especially knowing that octogenarian Mama Carino is in the kitchen.

cafés & diners

The welcome mat is always out at *Comfort Diner ♪: classic American favourites at affordable prices in an atmosphere to match, complete with a gleaming soda fountain. For a real old-fashioned soda fountain, the Lexington Candy Shop is the business; grab one of their amazing flavoured seltzers. You'll feel like you're in an episode of Friends at DT-UT (Down-Town-UpTown), a mellow coffeehouse (they have

beer and wine too) with comfy chairs for reading. Bolt into the uptown branch of Jackson Hole for an energy-enhancing hamburger or one of their blue-plate specials. But for the best hot dog/shake combo around, try Papaya King: the hot dogs are delicious and the shakes freshly made (unsurprisingly papaya is the specialty here). For good quality fare and fast service, the ultra-clean First Wok scores pretty high. The Chinese dishes are ample, but the real incentive is their free, unlimited house wine.

bars

This simply isn't the neighbourhood to visit for a wild night on the town, though for a taste of NY's toniest bars, look no further. Of all the UES institutions, *Elaine's may be the most famous. Frequented by literati, glitterati, and anyone who aspires to socializing with them, it can be intimidating. Act like you belong and you'll do just fine. Understated designer clothing and a generous credit line are also boons at *Harry Cipriani, the New York relative of Harry's Bar in Venice, and home of the famous Bellini, made of prosecco and peach purée.

Cabaret queens won't want to miss **Café Carlyle**, where Eartha Kitt and other legends perform regularly. Just down the hall, another Carlyle Hotel classic, **Bemelman's Bar** offers all the swank of Café Carlyle without the steep tab. Hotel guests tend to prefer Bemelman's, where piano players perform nightly. Torch Song Trilogy star Michael Feinstein recently opened the self-titled *boîte*, ***Feinstein's at the Regency**, a cabaret-bar serving up an eclectic range of performers and fine cocktails. If you can't muster the energy to put on a tie, head to **Subway Inn**, easily one of UES's most beloved theme bars. The booze is cheap and everybody is welcome.

☂ directory

Barney's ♫A7
660 Madison Avenue
826-8900

Bemelman's Bar ♫A4
Carlyle Hotel
981 Madison Avenue
744-1600 ◖

Bloomingdale's ♫B7
1000 Third Ave
705-2000

Café Boulud ♫B4
20 E 76th Street
772-6400 $$$

Café Carlyle ♫A4
Carlyle Hotel
981 Madison Avenue
744-1600

Calvin Klein ♫A7
654 Madison Avenue
292-9000

Carino ♫C2
1710 Second Avenue
860-0566 $$

Cello ♫A4
53 E 77th Street
517-1200 $$$

Chloé ♫A5
850 Madison Avenue
717-8220

Christian Louboutin ♫A4
941 Madison Ave
☎ 396-1884

Chrome Hearts ♫B6
159 E 64th Street
327-0707

Comfort Diner ♫B2
142 E 86th Street
426-8600 $–$$

Daniel ♫B6
60 E 65th Street
288-0033 $$$

Diesel ♫B7
770 Lexington Avenue
308-0055

DKNY ♫A7
665 Madison Avenue
223-3569

Dolce & Gabbana ♫A5
825 Madison Avenue
249-4100

DT-UT ♫C2
1626 Second Avenue
327-1327 $

Elaine's ♫C2
1703 Second Avenue
534-8103

Emilio Pucci ♫A6
24 E 64th Street
752-4777

Emporio Armani ♫A6
760 Madison Avenue
988-9191

Etro ♫A6
720 Madison Avenue
317-9096

Feinstein's at the Regency ♫A7
Regency Hotel
540 Park Avenue
759-4100

First Wok ♫B2
1570 Third Avenue
410-7747 $

Frédéric Fekkai ♫A5
874 Madison Avenue
583-3300

Fresh ♫A3
1061 Madison Avenue
396-0344

Givenchy ♫A4
954 Madison Avenue
772-1040

Gracious Home ♫B5
1217 & 1220 Third Ave
517-6300

Harry Cipriani ♫A7
781 Fifth Avenue
753-5566 ◖

Jackson Hole ♫A1
1270 Madison Avenue
427-2820 $

JoJo ♫B6
160 E 64th Street
223-5656 $$$

Joseph ♫A6
804 Madison Avenue
570-0077

Lenox Room ♫B4
1278 Third Avenue
772-0404 $$$

Lexington Candy Shop ♫B4
1226 Lexington Avenue
288-0057

Missoni ♫A5
1009 Madison Avenue
517-9339 $$

Miss Saigon ♫C3
1425 Third Avenue
988-8828 $–$$

Moschino ♫A6
803 Madison Avenue
639-9600

Nicole Farhi ♫A7
14 E 60th Street
421-7720

Nocturne ♫A6
698 Madison Avenue
750-2951

Out of the Closet ♫B3
220 E 81st Street
472-3573

Papaya King ♫B2
179 E 86th Street
369-0648 $

Payard Patisserie & Bistro ♫B4
1032 Lexington Ave
717-5252 $–$$$

Polo Ralph Lauren ♫A5
867 Madison Avenue
606-2100

Polo Sport ♫A5
888 Madison Avenue
434-8000

Prada ♫A5
841 Madison Avenue
327-4200

Roberto Cavalli ♫A7
711 Madison Avenue
840-5110

Searle ♫A3
1035 Madison Avenue
717-4022

Shanghai Tang ♫A7
714 Madison Avenue
888-0111

Stéphane Kélian ♫A6
910 Madison Avenue
980-1919

Subway Inn ♫B7
143 E 60th Street
223-8929 ◖

Tod's ♫A7
650 Madison Avenue
644-5945

TSE ♫A5
827 Madison Avenue
472-7790

Valentino ♫A5
747 Madison Avenue
772-6969

Versace ♫A5
815 Madison Avenue
744-6868

western hemisphere

upper west side

Characterized by its spacious avenues, landmark apartment buildings and proximity to Central Park, the UWS has the feel of a genuine, residential neighbourhood, albeit a very rarefied one. Celebrity sightings are plentiful and if you're lucky, you might even run into Upper West Siders like Woody Allen at Zabar's deli or Jerry Seinfeld at the Reebok gym. More likely you'll just stumble over the baby strollers of the many well-to-do families who live here. Without the distraction of happening nightspots or cutting-edge stores, residents take pride in two of the city's most important cultural institutions – the Lincoln Center and the American Museum of Natural History – plus a healthy sprinkling of dining options.

day

▣ Big-name chains, one-off boutiques & great deli's along the Avenues.

◉ American Museum of Natural History [→73]; Central Park [→84]; Children's Museum of Manhattan [→86]; Dakota Building [→69]; Museum of American Folk Art [→79]; New-York Historical Society [→79]; Strawberry Fields [→69].

night

☆ Nightly performances at the Lincoln Center's various halls [→137–144].

♂ Nightlife is limited: most people eat out – bars are scarce and clubs non-existent.

getting there

Ⓜ A•B•C•D•1•9 to Columbus Circle-59th St; 1•9 to 66th St-Lincoln Center; B•C•1•2•3•9 to 72nd or 96th Sts; 1•9 to 79th, 86th or 103rd Sts; B•C to 81st St-Museum of Natural History.

🚌 M7 ↑ via Sixth & Amsterdam Aves, ↓ via Columbus Ave & Broadway; M11 ↑ via 10th St & Amsterdam Ave, ↓ via Columbus & 9th Ave; M104 ↕ via Broadway & 8th Ave; M66 ↔ via E 67th & W 66th Sts, → via W 65th & E 68th Sts; M72 ↔ via 72nd St & 65th St transverse; M79 ↔ 79th St; M86 ↔ 86th St; M96 ↔ 96th St.

shopping

fashion, beauty & accessories

The UWS has always been something of a shopping wasteland, so unless your preference is limited to the preppy staples offered up by The Gap and Banana Republic, you'll probably look elsewhere. There are some boutiques worth making a detour for, however. *Olive & Bette's continues to bring downtown style Uptown. This entirely girlish boutique carries hot young designers like Daryl K and Vivienne Tam, as well as fun T-shirts, cute bags and witty jewellery. Another neighbourhood duo, Allan & Suzi ✓, fill their racks with a riot of barely-worn and vintage couture. Versace and Gaultier are the designers of preference, and although you can find jeans, they'll probably be studded with rhinestones. With a less ostentatious vibe, Only Hearts showcases the store's own line of dreamy cotton-lycra lingerie. The rest of the store is replete with great PJs, dressing gowns and gift-items, most of which are heart-shaped. Naughty & Nice, on the other hand, is the neighbourhood's friendly sex store – the sign outside says 'Romance Boutique'. Inside are sex toys, naughty lingerie and erotic videos. This being the Upper West Side, it is only slightly tacky.

* = featured in the listings section [→94–135]

Face Stockholm's largest NY store offers a new look at a reasonable price. A favourite with make-up artists and those in-the-know, it offers an intoxicating array of all-natural beauty products, cosmetics in unique and seductive colours as well as cool make-up bags. And for looking good when you work out, the members-only **Reebok Sports Club**, New York's most prestigious gym, carries requisite sweats and cycle shorts at the in-house store.

food

Zabar's is a New York legend with good reason. This marvellous deli has been supplying locals with bagels, freshly ground coffee and cold-cuts since 1943. The upstairs kitchen supply store is a superb resource for culinary equipment. **Fairways** is another UWS deli that wows foodies, and is open 24 hours

one-offs

The question most often asked at **Maxilla & Mandible** is 'are they real?'. 'They' refers to the human bones for sale at this extraordinary place, and the answer is 'yes'. If dem bones aren't your thing, the store also has fascinating fossils, sea-shells, bugs, butterflies and other natural history-related phenomena.

eating & drinking

restaurants & cafés

Until recently the UWS was disparaged for its scarcity of fine or trendy establishments but that is rapidly changing. Jean-Georges Vongerichten's signature showplace, *Jean Georges astonishes palates with new French flavour combinations and has managed to silence UWS restaurant sceptics. The tasteful, subdued dining-room has an air of privilege, with sky-high prices to match. **Nougatine**, its adjacent café, is slightly more affordable. The time-honoured *Café des Artistes cleaves to classic French cuisine in a formal, old-world setting – lush with flowers and paintings of frolicking nudes, it's a romantic sight to behold.

More modest budgets are accommodated at *Pampa, a lively South American spot that satisfies from start to finish. Steaks, spit-roasted chicken and fish are all made (and consumed) with gusto. **Rain** is also a fun place for spicy and aromatic Thai-Vietnamese dishes. Golden hues, exposed brick and tropical plants evoke a colonial feel.

Alternatively, pan-Latino flavours are featured at *Calle Ocho ✓, a magically-designed place, with warm colours, where chef Alex Garcia packs a punch with shrimp chowder and Cuban steak with yuca fries.

At any time of the day, **Avenue**, a French country charmer with brick walls and dark wooden tables, delivers quality food at moderate prices, including a cornucopia of delicious baked goods. **Josie's**, an attractive, 'earth-friendly' hangout, is the place to be after dusk. Do your body a favour and feast on the myriad fresh juices, free-range meats and innovative vegan choices. Or do the opposite and grab some cholesterol from *Artie's New York Delicatessen. This Jewish-style deli is new for its breed, but attracts all sorts of New Yorkers with its fine pastrami and garlicky frankfurters.

A beloved deli that's been around forever and feels straight out of *Seinfeld*, *Barney Greengrass is a veritable Jewish general store. Its few tables are completely packed for weekend brunches, so stop in during the week for bagels, pickled herring, and knishes (closes 6pm, and all day Mon). Meanwhile the pretty, European-style **Café Lalo** is an ideal date place which has a full coffee and liquor menu as well as light salads and sandwiches – make sure you save room for their luscious desserts. **Drip** is another place to meet your match. This cafe-com-bar has a noticeboard, where, for a small fee, you can display your lonely heart details. **Café con Leche** is a more casual hang, cramped and colourful, with great coffee, Cuban-style rice and beans, crispy chicken and roast pork. Their early-bird special (4–7pm Mon–Thu) offers a full dinner for around $8. **Gabriela's**, with its Guadalajara-style home cooking, is highly popular for low-priced, massively portioned enchiladas, tamales and roast chicken. The atmosphere is old luncheonette crossed with a Mexican fiesta. More of a dive, the 24-hour *Big Nick's Burger serves gargantuan, juicy hamburgers.

bars

There's a reason Seinfeld always met his buddies at the local diner – he lived in the UWS which, unlike most of Manhattan, has limited nightlife options. Apart from junior yuppie watering holes and Ivy League meat markets, unlimited coffee refills are your main option. Just across from the American Museum of Natural History are a couple of upscale options. **Evelyn Lounge** is a labyrinthine bar-lounge with a door policy, comfy sofas, a separate cigar bar and a smoky, low-lit atmos-phere. **Potion Lounge** also feels more downtown than uptown, and is known for its coloured. layered 'potion' cocktails. Rather less swanky is **Saints**, a hetero-friendly gay bar frequented by Columbia University students and anyone wishing to cruise them. Columbia students can also be found slamming shots at **Smoke** and **Night Café**. The former, a smoky jazz dive, tends to attract a mellower crowd, while the latter is a favourite of the edgier UWS set. Expect a competitive pool table, and a number of Nietzsche fans. Escape from Engels, Marx and talk of marginalized peoples at **Dive Bar**. Located a safe 20 blocks south of Columbia, this is one of the few tolerable neighbourhood joints – if you don't mind the cigar smoke. A heartier, happier haunt is the swell Irish **Malachy's Donegal Inn**. Loud, local sports fans gather round the big-screen TV for games, and their shouting is only rivalled by the jukebox. Perfect for a wolfing down a burger and swilling a beer or two.

directory

Allan & Suzi *A6*
416 Amsterdam Ave
724-7445

Artie's New York Delicatessen *A6*
2290 Broadway
579-5959 $$

Avenue *B6*
520 Columbus Avenue
579-3194 $$

Barney Greengrass *B5*
541 Amsterdam Ave
724-4707 $–$$

Big Nick's Burger *A7*
2175 Broadway
362-9238 $

Café con Leche *A6*
424 Amsterdam Ave
595-7000 $

Café des Artistes *C9*
1 W 67th Street
877-3500 $$$

Café Lalo *A6*
201 W 83rd Street
496-6031 $

Calle Ocho *B6*
446 Columbus Avenue
873-5025 $$–$$$

Dive Bar *B3*
732 Amsterdam Ave
749-4358 ◐

Drip *B6*
489 Amsterdam Ave
875-1032 ◐

Evelyn Lounge *B1*
380 Columbus Ave
724-5145

Face Stockholm *B7*
226 Columbus Avenue
769-1420

Fairways *A7*
2127 Broadway
595-1888

Gabriela's *B4*
685 Amsterdam Ave
961-0574 $–$$

Jean Georges *C10*
Trump International
Hotel, 1 Central Park W
299-3900 $$$

Josie's *B8*
300 Amsterdam Ave
769-1212 $$

Malachy's Donegal Inn *B8*
103 W 72nd Street
874-4268 ◐ $

Maxilla & Mandible *B6*
451 Columbus Avenue
724-6173

Naughty & Nice *A7*
212 W 80th Street
787-1212

Night Café *B2*
938 Amsterdam Ave
864-8889 ◐

Nougatine *C10*
Trump International
Hotel, 1 Central Park W
299-3900 $$

Olive & Bette's *B8*
252 Columbus Ave
579-2178

Only Hearts *B7*
386 Columbus Ave
724-5608

Pampa *B3*
768 Amsterdam Ave
865-2929 $–$$

Potion Lounge *B7*
370 Columbus Ave
721-4386

Rain *B6*
100 W 82nd Street
501-0776 $$

Reebok Sports Club *B9*
160 Columbus Ave
595-1480

Saints *B1*
992 Amsterdam Ave
222-2431

Smoke *A2*
2751 Broadway
316-3737

Zabar's *A5*
2245 Broadway
787-2000

take the a train

Harlem holds an essential place in African-American history: the great jazz musicians lived here in the 20s; in the 60s this was the centre for black activism; and in the 80s the first rappers honed their skills on its mean streets. Although still predominantly black in population, more and more young New Yorkers are fleeing Downtown's steep rents and making the move Uptown. While you still see the signs of urban decay which gave Harlem a bad rap, counteract that with rows of beautiful brownstones, cheap eateries and the colourful chaos of 125th Street. Just south, the neighbourhood of Morningside Heights is home to Columbia University, so the streets are flooded with students and lined with bookstores and cafés.

harlem & the heights

day

🏛 125th Street, Harlem's main drag, is lined with stores selling bargain sportswear, ethnic goods and eats at the local markets. Going to church on Sunday is an event in itself.

👁 Central Park [→84]; The Cloisters [→78–79]; Morris-Jumel Mansion Museum [→76–77]; St John the Divine [→69]; Schomburg Center for Research in Black Culture [→81]; Studio Museum of Harlem [→81].

night

🍴 Harlem's colourful eateries are big on African and soul food.

☆ Lots of venues for jazz and contemporary music, including the Apollo Theatre [→144] although you'll have to factor in the cost of a cab home again.

getting there

Ⓜ A to 125th or 145th St; B•C to Cathedral Pkwy, 116th, 125th, 135th or 145th Sts; 1•9 to Cathedral Pkwy, 116th St-Columbia University, 125th, 137th or 145th Sts; 2•3 to Central Pk N, 116th, 125th, or 135th Sts; 3 to 145th St or Harlem-148th St.

🚌 M1 ↓ 5th Ave; M2 ← Central Pk N; M3 ↔ Central Pk N via St Nicholas Ave; M4 ↔ Central Pk N via Broadway; M7 ↕ Lenox Ave; M10 ↕ Central Pk W; M11 ↕ Amsterdam Ave; M60, M100 & M101 ↔ 125th St; M102 ↕ Lenox Ave; M104 ↕ Broadway; M116 ↔ 116th St.

shopping

fashion, accessories & interiors

Although Harlem is changing, the neighbourhood stores are still very local. The heart of the district, 125th Street, offers everything from slick, Italian sportswear to all things Afrocentric, both inexpensive and pricey.

The younger generation of urban homeboys contin-ues its mad love affair with classic/preppy casual chic. **Scheme**, a major fashion outpost in the neighbourhood, carries lots of labels like Iceberg and Moschino plus a wide array of edgy trainers and must-have boots. There's also a fashion-forward selection of leather jackets. If you're thinking local instead of global, then **The Harlem Collective** ⬇ is the right place to be. It features clothes for men and women, accessories, jewellery, art, books and small pieces of furniture; many of the artisans and designers are locals, and much of the merch is ethnic. A showcase for all things African – garments,

* = featured in the listings section [→92–135]

home furnishings, art, and tie-dye – **African Paradise** is just that. And if you're really into making a total statement, you'll need an 'ear spear' by designer Lavalais of **Bamboozle Studio**. These heavy but elegant carved earrings are in both artistic and tribal styles. Looking for a trendy name necklace? Have yours made where the fashion pack get there's at **Home Boy of Harlem**. This den of glinting gold jewellery has plenty of bargains and a custom service for initial rings and name pendants. At the centre of Harlem is the Studio Museum [→81], devoted to modern African-American culture. The **Studio Museum Gift Shop** stocks all manner of related goodies – books, posters and decorative objects. If a visit here inspires you to create your own African-style outfit, then head over to **Kaarta Imports**, the place for all kinds of African fabrics and almost all of it 100% cotton.

markets

Across the street from the legendary Apollo Theatre [→144], sits the aptly-named **Mart 125**. All under one roof are many different outlets for African food, clothes, fabrics, music and more. Open daily, the market is very much the local shopping hub. The outdoor version, with an even grander selection of merchandise, is the *Malcom Shabazz Harlem Market**, in its new, $3.1 million headquarters.

eating & drinking

restaurants & cafés

For a fun night out in Harlem, head up to *Copeland's** – especially on Saturdays when live jazz plays all night. Good Southern-style soul food and spicy Louisiana specialties are served in a faded, genteel dining room. Homey *Sylvia's** (the 'queen of soul food') attracts bus loads of tourists so the food is not as carefully prepared. Still, the Sunday gospel brunch is enjoyable. **Africa** is very authentic, a mellow Senegalese restaurant adorned with African fabrics and chairs carved with animal figures. Look out for grilled fish, couscous and lamb stew with peanut butter. In Morningside Heights at the top of an elegant residential building is **The Terrace**, a pricey French restaurant with breathtaking views of the city, even if its interior resembles that of a cruise ship.

*Tom's Restaurant** is the diner immortalized by Seinfeld and, while you'd think it would be overrun with tourists by now, it's still filled with neighbourhood sitcom types. It's great for cheap and reliable diner fare (24 hours Thu–Sat; to 1.30am Sun–Wed). Across the street from the Cathedral of St John the Divine [→69], the **Hungarian Pastry Shop** is an old, softly-lit café with pastries and great coffee. You can sit here long enough to write a book without anyone bothering you. Further north is **Obaa Koryoe**, a friendly, relaxed nook attached to a shop stocked with unique *tchotchkes*. Specializing in exotic West African cuisine, people flood in on Sundays for the great value all-you-can-eat buffet brunch. **Slice of Harlem** ✓ is a more boisterous scene, with a huge mural of black history and pop culture – just the ticket for cheesy pizza by the slice, garlic knots and sausage rolls. Owned by the same guy, **Bayou** dishes out Creole food at its best; the New Orleans chef makes a sinful *pain perdu* (New-Orleans-style french toast). And for dessert, you must try one of **Krispy Kreme's** light glazed donuts from its outpost near the Apollo Theatre – one taste and you'll be hooked.

bars

The city-wide drop in crime, combined with increasingly high downtown rents, has spurred a nightlife renaissance in the upper reaches of Harlem and neighbouring Washington Heights. True to the neighbourhood's history, jazz bars continue to be favourite haunts in Harlem, and shoebox-sized **St Nick's Pub** is one of the oldest. Jazz musicians perform here all week, and Monday nights feature saxophonist Patience Higgins jamming with the Sugar Hill Jazz Quartet. **Lenox Lounge**, another Harlem institution, is beginning to attract a younger crowd thanks to aggressive party promoters, DJs and superb live jazz. While St Nick's and Lenox Lounge start filling up at 11pm, **Café Largo**, a much newer bar and restaurant, caters to an early-evening crowd, with live jazz performances starting at 8pm, and lazy jazz brunches served on Sundays. **Londel's** is a friendly, unintimidating joint that draws a healthy mix of the old school locals as well as new additions to the neighbourhood. Catch some live jazz on weekends.

Head to Washington Heights and Sugar Hill, farther north, where Latin bars are key. One of the most popular is **Zapatas Manoletas**, a fantastic bar filled with bull-fighting posters and glittery tropical murals. Patrons are partial to salsa and the

crowd tends to be older. Poets and rappers take the stage at **Sugar Shack**, a homey soul-food restaurant with open-mic nights, while sporty types flock to *Coogan's, a spacious Irish sports bar. Large-screen TVs make it a local favourite during any play-offs.

♫ directory

Africa ♫B9
247 W 116th Street
666-9400 $

African Paradise ♫C8
27 W 125th Street
410-5294

Bamboozle Studio ♫B9
171 E 118th Street
360-6848

Bayou ♫C2
308 Lenox Avenue
426-3800 $$

Café Largo ♫A6
3387 Broadway
862-8142 ◑ $–$$

Coogan's ♫A1
4015 Broadway
928-1234 ◑

Copeland's ♫A5
547 W 145th Street
234-2357 $–$$$

The Harlem Collective ♫B8
2533 Eighth Avenue
368-0520

Home Boy of Harlem ♫B8
166 W 125th Street
316-1320

Hungarian Pastry Shop ♫A10
1030 Amsterdam Ave
866-4230 $

Kaarta Imports ♫C8
121 W 125th Street
866-4062

Krispy Kreme's ♫B8
280 W 125th Street
531-0111 $

Lenox Lounge ♫C8
288 Lenox Avenue
427-0253 ◑

Londel's ♫B6
2620 Eighth Avenue
234-6114

Malcolm Shabazz Harlem Market ♫C9
Lenox Avenue
987-8131

Mart 125 ♫B8
260 W 125th Street
316-3340

Obaa Koryoe ♫A8
3143 Broadway
316-2950 $

St Nick's Pub ♫A4
773 St Nicolas Avenue
283-9728 ◑

Scheme ♫B8
201–303 W 125th Street
678-2146

Slice of Harlem ♫B6
2527 Eighth Avenue
862-4089 $

Studio Museum Gift Shop ♫B8
144 W 125th Street
864-0014

Sugar Shack ♫B6
2611 Eighth Avenue
491-4422 ◑ $–$$

Sylvia's ♫C8
328 Lenox Avenue
996-0660 $–$$

Tom's Restaurant ♫A10
2880 Broadway
864-6137 $

The Terrace ♫A9
400 W 119th Street
666-9490 $$$

Zapatas Manoletas ♫A1
1218 St Nicholas Ave
923-9769 ◑

over the east river

brooklyn

As Manhattan rents continue to skyrocket, Brooklyn, the biggest of NY's five boroughs, is becoming an increasingly appealing alternative for those who want to live with light and space without paying a fortune. Generations of immigrants have settled here over the last 150 years, and many long-term residents still mourn the defection of legendary local baseball team, The Dodgers, in 57. Thanks to the huge diversity of Brooklynites, the neighbourhoods vary wildly, from up-and-coming Fort Greene, artsy Williamsburg, and quietly elegant Brooklyn Heights, to the irresistibly tacky Coney Island and the atmospheric Russian enclave of Brighton Beach. Recently gentrified neighbourhoods may provide the requisite cool cafés, boutiques and restaurants to meet the needs of new residents, but the borough remains forever Brooklyn. Those black-clad figures are just as likely to be Hassidim as fashionable bohos.

day

Williamsburg: shops and cafés get going around noon. The local gallery scene is ad-hoc, so pick up the *Waterfront Week* to check what's on, especially at the Williamsburg Art & Historical Center (also has shows, events, movies and concerts ☎ 1-718-486-7372). **Fort Greene:** pretty laid back by day, except at weekends. UrbanGlass opens its glass-blowing studios to the public one Sunday each month ☎ 1-718-625-3685. **Cobble Hill & Carroll Gardens:** great to wander around in the day, though the new boutiques only open around noon. **Coney Island & Brighton Beach:** in summer crowds throng the seaside attractions, including the world-famous funfair [→90]. Off season, the area's much quieter, but not without a certain charm.

👁 Brooklyn Botanical Gardens [→85]; Brooklyn Museum of Art [→79]; Prospect Park [→85].

night

Williamsburg: buzzy bars and eateries. Galapagos hosts events and screens art-house movies on Sundays ☎ 1-718-388-8713. **Fort Greene:** the Brooklyn Academy of Music (BAM) [→142] has a concert, dance and movie programme; nearby restaurants stay open late. **Carroll Gardens:** serious restaurants are open, but not much else. **Brighton Beach:** wild partying in Russian nightclubs and restaurants; at Coney Island little stirs.

❶ Wherever you are, it's best to avoid deserted-looking blocks at night.

getting there

Ⓜ Williamsburg: L to Bedford Ave; J•M•Z to Marcy Ave. Fort Greene: D•Q•N•R•M to De-kalb Ave; D•G•2•3•4•5 to Atlantic Ave; A•C to Lafayette Ave. Carroll Gardens: F•G to Carroll St. Coney Island/Brighton Beach: B• D•F to Stillwell Ave; D•Q to Brighton Beach.

williamsburg

Along Williamsburg's gritty streets, which are traditionally home to Hispanics and Hassidic Jews, groovy *boîtes* sit alongside die-hard bodegas and Polish bakeries. The cool zone is really quite small: running along Bedford Avenue and the parallel Berry Street between N 5th to N 12th Streets.

shopping

Right on Bedford, you can't miss **Ugly Luggage**, which is crammed with trading cards, ashtrays, lunchboxes, and assorted memorabilia. **Max & Roebling** sells arty, interesting clothes from local designers, as well as leather bags and beaded dresses from India, while **Ear Wax** has an eclectic mix of CDs and some LPs. On Wythe Avenue, there's a row of great bric-a-brac and furniture stores: **R** is a good, if pricey, source of covetable post-World War II furniture (in good condition), and at **Junk**, you'll find that Depression-era glass candy dish, or electric beer sign. Up and down Bedford there are used-clothing places, but it's worth going a little further afield to the legendary

Domsey's Warehouse Outlet a megastore for the thrifty, with racks and racks of used clothing and housewares, for literally next-to-nothing.

eating & drinking

The best known and established restaurant in the area is the century-old *Peter Luger's, generally considered to have the best steaks in town. Family owned and run, it serves up juicy and tender hunks of cow; you'd have to be crazy (or vegetarian) to order anything else. The neighbourhood's most relaxed places for casual food are the **L Café** (good sandwiches and salads, mismatched tables and chairs), and **Kasia's** (tasty Polish and diner grub in a log-cabinesque setting). For more attitude, try **Oznot's Dish ✓**, where quirky decor meets Middle Eastern cuisine (and there's a garden), **Plan-eat Thailand** (excellent Thai food), and **Diner**, which serves vaguely French cuisine in an actual chrome-and-tile diner. The closest place to a club – tiny, peppy **Vera Cruz** – dishes up Mexican food, Margaritas and, on Monday nights, mambo dancing. **Teddy's** is the mellowest local hang-out – a perennial favourite with its majestic wooden bar and big windows that are opened in good weather. The **Brooklyn Ale House** has a parade of serious beer including some made

at the local Brooklyn Brewery, while hip tavern *Pour House** is a new found favourite with local types. Sip a brew, rub shoulders with artists and old-timers, or play a round of darts. The extremely partisan Williamsburgian bar pack all agree – the *Stinger Club** is a hit. Off the beaten Bedford Avenue track, this place is an appropriately seedy home to cheap beer, live bands and red lights. At the gritty North end of Williamsburg on the edge of Greenpoint, is **Enid's**, a drinking outpost worth the trek. This bar is huge, with well-priced brews, comfy furniture, good Southern food, a pinball machine and a knowing crowd.

Brooklyn Ale House
103 Berry Street (at N 8th St)
☎ 1-718-302-9811 ◖

Diner
85 Broadway (at Berry St)
☎ 1-718-486-3077 $–$$

Domsey's Warehouse Outlet
431 Kent Avenue
(bet. S 9th & S 10th Sts)
☎ 1-718-384-6000

Ear Wax
204 Bedford Avenue
(bet. N 5th & N 6th Sts)
☎ 1-718-218-9608

Enid's
560 Manhattan Avenue (bet. W 123rd & W 124th Sts)
☎ 1-718-349-3859

Junk
324 Wythe Avenue
(bet. Grand & S 1st Sts)
☎ 1-718-388-8580

Kasia's
146 Bedford Ave (at N 9th St)
☎ 1-718-387-8780 $

L Café
189 Bedford Avenue
(bet. N 6th & N 7th Sts)
☎ 1-718-388-6762 $–$$

Max & Roebling
189 Bedford Avenue
(bet. N 6th & N 7th Sts)
☎ 1-718-387-0045

Oznot's Dish
79 Berry Street (at N 9th Street) ☎ 1-718-599-6596 $$

Peter Luger Steak House
178 Broadway (bet. Bedford & Driggs Aves)
☎ 1-718-387-7400 $$–$$$

Plan-eat Thailand
141 N 7th Street
(bet. Bedford Ave & Berry St)
☎ 1-718-599-5758 $

Pour House
790 Metropolitan Avenue
(at Humboldt St)
☎ 1-718-599-0697

R
326 Wythe Avenue
(bet. Grand & S 1st Sts)
☎ 1-718-599-4385

Stinger Club
241 Grand Street (bet. Driggs & Roebling Sts)
☎ 1-718-218-6662

Teddy's
96 Berry Street (at N 8th St)
☎ 1-718-384-9787 ◖

Ugly Luggage
214 Bedford Avenue
(bet. N 5th & N 6th Sts)
☎ 1-718-384-0724

Vera Cruz
195 Bedford Avenue
(bet. N 6th & N 7th Sts)
☎ 1-718-599-7914 $–$$

brooklyn

fort greene

Tranquil Fort Greene is booming: apartments in beautiful brownstones are being snapped up and the area's become the focus of an African-American artistic renaissance that's brought artists, writers and interesting stores to its gracious, tree-lined streets.

shopping

While you'll find antique shops for browsing on Fulton Street, the real retail thrill here is clothes. At **Moshood**, they're bold and simple, urban and African (and on weekends you'll see live mannequins mod-

elling in the window). **4W Circle of Art** features more traditional African wear (by neighbourhood designers) as well as jewellery, candles and cards. The collection at **Courtney Washington** is simply exquisite: flowing, clean-lined clothes in scrunchy natural fabrics, dubbed 'ethnic-European' and made on site, while **Exodus Industrial Sport** is a small place that carries more somber, chic, clothes.

eating & drinking

The stylish **New City Bar & Grill** offers French-American bistro food in a

cool, airy setting. Also with an American menu, this time with African accents, is **Lucian Blue**, a spacious bar-restaurant that wouldn't look out of place in Soho. At the charming **SEA Cambodian** (NY's only Cambodian restaurant), the fragrant, spicy food is great value, while **Miss Ann's**, a true hole-in-the-wall, serves sublime Southern dishes – but only to 12 people at a time. Or, at the popular **Keur 'n' Dye**, you'll get Senegalese cooking in a pleasant, calming environment. There's a livelier scene at the intimate **Brooklyn Moon Café**, where the chatty crowd gets big at the Friday open-mic sessions [→143]. **Tillie's of Brooklyn** is an arty coffee bar with jazz on the weekends (and occasional sightings of Rosie Perez who lives locally), and the laid-back **Butta Cup Lounge** features hip-hop, a comfy lounge upstairs and African statuettes dotted around.

Brooklyn Moon Café
745 Fulton Street (bet. S Portland & S Elliot Sts)
☎ 1-718-243-0424

Butta Cup Lounge
271 Adelphi St (at De Kalb Ave)
☎ 1-718-522-1669

Courtney Washington
674 Fulton Street (bet. S Portland and S Elliott Sts)
☎ 1-718-852-1464

Exodus Industrial Sport
771 Fulton Street (bet. S Oxford & S Portland Sts)
☎ 1-718-246-0321

4W Circle of Art
704 Fulton Street (bet. S Portland and S Oxford Sts)
☎ 1-718-875-6500

Keur 'n' Dye
737 Fulton Street (bet. S Elliott & S Portland Sts)
☎ 1-718-875-4937 $–$$

Lucian Blue
63 Lafayette Avenue (at Fulton St)
☎ 1-718-422-0093 $$

Miss Ann's
86 Portland Avenue (bet. Hanson Pl & Lafayette Ave)
☎ 1-718-858-6997 $

Moshood
698 Fulton Street (bet. S Portland & S Oxford Sts)
☎ 1-718-243-9433

New City Bar & Grill
25 Lafayette Avenue (bet. Flatbush Ave and Ashland Pl)
☎ 1-718-875-7197 $–$$

SEA Cambodian
87 S Elliott Place (bet. Fulton Pl & Lafayette Ave)
☎ 1- 718-858-3262 $–$$

Tillie's of Brooklyn
248 DeKalb Avenue (at Vanderbilt Ave)
☎ 1-718-783-6140 $

carroll gardens

This quiet old Italian neighbourhood, with its tree-lined streets and predominance of young families, has chic little stores in among its delis, bakeries and front-yard shrines.

shopping

Smith Street is where the action is. **Refinery** has stylish, one-off bags made of vintage and recycled materials. **Frida's Closet** (inspired by Frida Kahlo) is a pristine space with racks of classic handmade women's clothes and jewellery. And at **Stacia New York**, the adorably feminine clothes are made by the owner, who used to work for Cynthia Rowley. Satisfy your schlock-horror movie-poster needs at **Main Street Ephemera/Paper Collectibles**, while homewares (cocktail shakers, clunky lamps and spindly dinette sets) can be found at the all-retro **Astroturf**.

eating & drinking

The most atmospheric local saloon is **PJ Hanley's** – a dark, comfy 100-year-old place with an ornate bar, frequented by plumbers and bond-traders alike. Brooklyn's true bohemians are more likely to be in the **Fall Café** – a haven of big sofas, little tables, cool music, art on the walls, and artistic types dawdling over chilli, sandwiches and coffee.

Respectable bagels (12 kinds), plus knishes and burritos, are available at the low-key **Bagels by the Park**, but lunch at **Vinny's of Carroll Gardens** if you want to soak up the sound of some authentic 'Brooklynese'. Whether you choose the clam spaghetti or the tortellini *en brodo*, portions are huge. **Helen's Place** is another old-fashioned Italian joint, with white tablecloths, a linoleum floor, and atmosphere courtesy of the radio and memory. Top off any lunch with Italian pastries or ices from long-standing **Monteleone's**, (the delicate lemon ice is a winner), or exquisite soufflé cakes, madeleines, and fruit tarts from the more recently arrived **Sweet Melissa**.

In the evenings, **Patois**, a French-American bistro, is jammed; fortunately, its waiting area (out back, under casbah-like drapes) is beguiling. The absolutely unique **Halcyon**, founded by three DJs, is a record store and coffee shop hybrid where you can also shop for flea market finds; weekly events feature DJs and local artists. Another addition to Smith Street's burgeoning restaurant row is **The Grocery**, which features a minimalist decor and food inspired by the seasons; the desserts are particularly delicious. Just along from Patois, and run by the same folk, is **Uncle Pho**, a delectable French-Vietnamese eaterie where the imaginative decor is matched by the menu. Try the coconut bouillabaise. More Soho than Smith Street is **Quench**, a new lounge-bar with a super-slick look, an impressive wine list, beers on tap, and nicely inventive cocktails. For organic steaks and Argentinian specialties, try rowdy, friendly **Sur**.

Astroturf
290 Smith Street (bet. Union & Sackett Sts)
☎ 1-718-522-6182

Bagels by the Park
323 Smith St (at President St)
☎ 1-718-246-1321 $

Fall Café
307 Smith Street (bet. President & Union Sts)
☎ 1-718-403-0230 $

Frida's Closet
296 Smith Street (bet. Union & Sackett Sts) ☎ 1-718-855-0311

The Grocery
288 Smith Street (bet. Union & Sackett Sts)
☎ 1-718-596-3335 $$–$$$

Halcyon
227 Smith Street (bet. Butter & Douglass Sts)
☎ 1-718-260-9299

Helen's Place
396 Court Street (bet. 1st Pl & Carroll Street)
☎ 1-718-855-9128 $–$$

Main Street Ephemera/ Paper Collectibles
272 Smith Street (bet. Sackett & DeGraw Sts)
☎ 1-718-858-6541

Monteleone's
355 Court Street (bet. President & Union Sts)
☎ 1-718-624-9253 $

Patois
255 Smith Street (bet. DeGraw & Douglass Sts)
☎ 1-718-855-1535 $$

PJ Hanley's
449 Court Street (at 4th Pl)
☎ 1-718-834-8223

Quench
282 Smith St (at Sackett St)
☎ 1-718-875-1500

Refinery
254 Smith Street
(bet. DeGraw & Douglass Sts)
☎ 1-718-643-7861

Stacia New York
267 Smith St (at DeGraw St)
☎ 1-718-237-0078

Sur
232 Smith Street
(bet. Douglass & Butler Sts)
☎ 1-718-875-1716 $–$$

Sweet Melissa
276 Court Street
(bet. Douglass & Butler Sts)
☎ 1-718-855-3410 $

Uncle Pho
263 Smith Street
(at DeGrow Street)
☎ 1-718-855-8737 $$–$$$

Vinny's of Carroll Gardens
295 Smith Street
(bet. Union & Sackett Streets)
☎ 1-718-875-5600 $–$$

65

coney island & brighton beach

Even during the rather desolate winter months, Coney Island – tattered and faded – has a unique mix of people, a swathe of boardwalk, an atmospheric funfair (closed in winter), an expanse of beach, and a lingering feeling of good times gone by. In neighbouring Brighton Beach, the Russian language prevails, giving rise to its nickname 'Little Odessa by the Sea'.

shopping

People don't come here to shop, but it's hard to avoid the temptation of **Philip's Candy Store** in the Coney Island subway station. It's been selling made-on-the-premises candies for over 40 years. Off Surf Avenue, underneath the elevated subway tracks, is an eccentric, if rather sad, flea market: more of a curiosity than a place for real bargains.

Brighton Beach, just a short stroll along, has America's largest concentration of Russian emigrés. And they love food, from serious smoked fish to gooey cakes, all abundantly displayed in the many delis and shops. Good bargains (like salmon caviar for about $16 per pound) can be easily found. The chaotic **M&I** is *the* serious gourmet store, but be persistent to get anyone to wait on you. For an easier shopping experience, try the **Sea Lane Bakery** or the elegant **Odessa**, which offers fancy foods like duck legs with apples and *coubiliac* of salmon. Far less showy is the great (if little) **Mrs Stahl's Knishery**, making cheap, rib-sticking snacks to go, in flavours like mushroom and potato or blueberry. **Isay's Leather** is crammed with interesting items from the former USSR: amber jewellery, dolls, hand-painted

boxes, and leather goods; it is the area's only non-food shop worth mentioning.

eating, drinking & clubbing

Forget healthy, be gone wholesome! The essential Coney Island dining experience is **Nathan's Famous Restaurant**, serving the best hot dog in the universe (together with sublime fries and sauerkraut) in basic surroundings. Up on the boardwalk, **Ruby's Old Thyme Bar** (open summer only) is a reliquary with a liquor licence. Cluttered with memorabilia, everything in it – including much of the clientele – harks back to Coney's glory days.

If your tastes run to cigarettes and vodka, the Russian cafés off Brighton Beach will delight. Whatever the weather, or time of day, you'll find hardy fur-clad locals sitting outside among the seagulls at the **Tatiana Café** (elegant) or the **Café Restaurant Volna** (more basic), slugging down the Stoli and inhaling deeply. Brighton Beach's nightclubs are legendary and keep going into the wee hours nightly, with a truly OTT party atmosphere at weekends. From the outside, the clubs look like funeral parlours or KGB headquarters. Inside, they're huge, glitzy places where you eat a heavy, multi-course meal surrounded by Russians in sequins and shantung, hell-bent on partying. These places are said to be associated with the Russian mob, so be nice. Knock back the vodka, watch Vegas-type acts and dance under a mirrored ball. The veteran **Primorski** has the best

food and the smallest dance floor; **Rasputin** is the most glamorous (book way in advance); while the **Winter Garden** offers a winning combination of location (on the Boardwalk), excellent food (cherry dumplings, breast of duck), and a 'groovy' floorshow (perfumed smoke, glamour, and 70s sounds). Call to book, wear all your jewellery, go in a rowdy group (if you can), and call a car to get home.

Café Restaurant Volna
3145 B 4th St (bet. Brighton Beach Ave & Boardwalk)
☎ 1-718-332-0341 $

Isay's Leather
292 Brighton Beach Avenue
(at 3rd St) ☎ 1-718-769-8775

M&I
249 Brighton Beach Avenue
(bet. 2nd & 3rd St)
☎ 1-718-615-1011

Mrs Stahl's Knishery
1001 Brighton Beach Avenue
(at Coney Island Ave)
☎ 1-718-648-0210 $

Nathan's Famous Restaurant
1310 Surf Ave (at Stillwell Ave)
☎ 1-718-946-2202 $

Odessa
1113 Brighton Beach Avenue
(bet. B 13th & B 14th Sts)
☎ 1-718-332-3223

Philip's Candy Store
1237 Surf Avenue (in Stillwell Ave-Coney Island station)
☎ 1-718-372-8783

Primorski
282B Brighton Beach Avenue
(at B 3rd St)
☎ 1-718-891-3111 $

Rasputin
2670 Coney Island Avenue
(at Avenue X)
☎ 1-718-332-9187 $

Ruby's Old Thyme Bar
1213 Boardwalk (at W 12th St)
☎ 1-718-748-7636

Sea Lane Bakery
615 Brighton Beach Avenue
(bet. 6th & 7th Sts)
☎ 1-718-934-8877

Tatiana Café
3145 B 4th Street
(bet. Brighton Beach Ave & the Boardwalk)
☎ 1-718-646-7630 $–$$

Winter Garden
3152 B 6th Street (bet. Brighton Beach Ave & the Boardwalk) ☎ 1-718-934-6666 $–$$

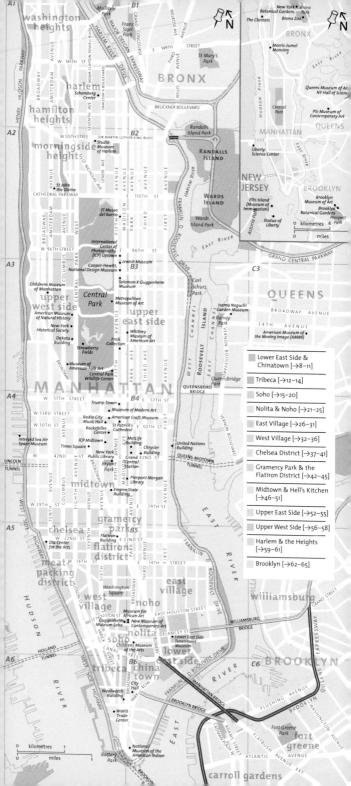

A1

washington
heights

Mullaly
Park

B1

Franz
Sigel
Park

MELROSE AVE

149TH   STREET

BRONX

St Mary's
Park

New York
Botanical Gardens

The Cloisters

Bronx
Park

Bronx Zoo

N

Morris-Jumel
Mansion

145TH ST

harlem

Schomberg
Center

BRUCKNER BOULEVARD

Queens Museum of Ar
NY Hall of Science

hamilton
heights

Randalls
Island Park

PS1 Museum of
Contemporary Art

QUEENS

A2

W 125TH STREE
(DR MARTIN LUTHER KING BLVD)

morningside
heights

Studio
Museum
of Harlem

B2

Randalls
Island

MANHATTAN

Central
Park

St John
the Divine

CATHEDRAL PARKWAY

El Museo
del Barrio

110TH ST

Wards
Island

NEW
JERSEY

Liberty
Science Center

BROOKLYN

Brooklyn
Museum of Art

Wards
Island Park

Ellis Island
(Museum of
Immigration)

Brooklyn
Botanical Gardens

Prospect
Park

A3

W 96TH STREET

Childrens Museum
of Manhattan

upper
west side

American Museum
of Natural History

New-York
Historical Society

Dakota
Building

International
Center of
Photography
(ICP) Uptown

Cooper-Hewitt,
National Design Museum

B3

96TH ST

Jewish Museum

Solomon R Guggenheim
Museum

Central
Park

Metropolitan
Museum of Art

Statue of
Liberty

kilometres

miles

C3

QUEENS

BROADWAY   AVENUE

Carl
Schurz
Park

Isamu Noguchi
Garden Museum

34TH   AVENUE

American Museum of
the Moving Image (AMMI)

upper
east side

Whitney
Museum of
American Art

Frick
Collection

Strawberry
Fields

Museum of
American Folk Art

Central Park
Wildlife Center

MANHATTAN

B4

E 57TH ST

Rainey
Park

Queensbridge

QUEENSBORO
BRIDGE

A4

W 57TH STREET

Trump Tower

Museum of Modern Art

W 53RD STREET

American Craft Museum

Radio City
Music Hall

St Patrick's
Cathedral

W 50TH STREET

Rockefeller
Center

MetLife
Building

midtown

Times Square

Chrysler
Building

Intrepid Sea Air
Space Museum

W   42ND   STREET

New York
Public Library

Grand
Central
Station

United Nations
Building

LINCOLN
TUNNEL

Bryant
Park

Pierpont Morgan
Library

QUEENS-MIDTOWN
TUNNEL

W 29TH STREET

Empire State
Building

E 29TH ST

gramercy
park

B5

EAST
RIVER

chelsea

flatiron
district

Dia Center
for the Arts

W 22ND ST

Flatiron
Building

E 22ND ST

14TH   STREET

meat
packing
district

Washington
Square

east
village

williamsburg

HUDSON

west
village

noho

Museum for
African Art

WEST HOUSTON ST

EAST HOUSTON STREET

Guggenheim
Museum Soho

New Museum of
Contemporary Art

WILLIAMSBURG
BRIDGE

soho

Childrens Museum
of the Arts

CANAL   STREET

nolita

lower
east side

Lower East Side
Tenement
Museum

DELANCEY ST

HOLLAND
TUNNEL

tribeca

china
town

Woolworth
Building

City
Hall

B6

MANHATTAN BRIDGE

C6

BROOKLYN

World Trade
Center

BROOKLYN BRIDGE

Fort Greene
Park

fort
greene

kilometres

miles

A6

Battery
Park

National
Museum of the
American Indian

EAST   RIVER

ATLANTIC   AVENUE

carroll gardens

Lower East Side &
Chinatown [→8–11]

Tribeca [→12–14]

Soho [→15–20]

Nolita & Noho [→21–25]

East Village [→26–31]

West Village [→32–36]

Chelsea District [→37–41]

Gramercy Park &
the Flatiron District [→42–45]

Midtown & Hell's Kitchen
[→46–51]

Upper East Side [→52–55]

Upper West Side [→56–58]

Harlem & the Heights
[→59–61]

Brooklyn [→62–65]

new york's top sights, museums & galleries

directory

American Craft Museum *A4* [→78]
American Museum of the Moving Image *C3* [→75]
American Museum of Natural History *A3* [→73]
Battery Park *A6–B6* [→85]
Bronx Zoo *see locator* [→86]
Brooklyn Botanical Garden *see locator* [→85]
Brooklyn Bridge *B6* [→68]
Brooklyn Museum of Art *see locator* [→79]
Bryant Park *A4* [→85]
Central Park *A2–A3* [→84]
Central Park Wildlife Center *A3* [→86]
Children's Museum of the Arts *A5* [→86]
Children's Museum of Manhattan *A3* [→86]
Chrysler Building *B4* [→68]
City Hall *B6* [→68]
The Cloisters *see locator* [→78–79]
Cooper-Hewitt, National Design Museum *B3* [→76]
Dakota Building *A3* [→69]
Dia Center for the Arts *A5* [→80]
Ellis Island (Museum of Immigration) *see locator* [→71]
El Museo del Barrio *B2* [→77]
Empire State Building *B4* [→72]
Flatiron Building *B5* [→68]

Frick Collection *B3* [→76]
Grand Central Station *B4* [→72]
Guggenheim Museum Soho *B5* [→75]
International Center of Photography (ICP) Midtown *A4* [→80]
International Center of Photography (ICP) Uptown *B2* [→80]
Intrepid Sea Air Space Museum *A4* [→86–87]
Isamu Noguchi Garden Museum *B3* [→80]
Jewish Museum *B3* [→77]
Liberty Science Center *see locator* [→87]
Lower East Side Tenement Museum *B5* [→76]
MetLife Building *B4* [→69]
Metropolitan Museum of Art *A3* [→73–74]
Morgan Library *A4* [→77]
Morris-Jumel Mansion Museum *see locator* [→76–77]
Museum of American Folk Art *A3* [→76]
Museum of Modern Art *A4* [→74]
Museum for African Art *B5* [→77–78]
National Museum of the American Indian *B6* [→78]
New Museum of Contemporary Art *B5* [→80]

New-York Historical Society *A3* [→79]
New York Public Library *A4* [→71]
NY Botanical Gardens *see locator* [→75]
NY Hall of Science *see locator* [→75]
Prospect Park *see locator* [→91]
PS1 Museum of Contemporary Art *C4* [→81]
Queens Museum of Art *see locator* [→75]
Radio City Music Hall *A4* [→69]
Rockefeller Center *A4* [→69]
St John the Divine *A2* [→69]
St Patrick's Cathedral *B4* [→69]
Schomberg Center for Research in Black Culture *A1* [→81]
Solomon R Guggenheim Museum *B3* [→74]
Statue of Liberty *see locator* [→71–72]
Strawberry Fields *A3* [→69]
Studio Museum of Harlem *A2* [→81]
Times Square *A4* [→69]
Trump Tower *B4* [→69]
UN Building *B4* [→69]
Whitney Museum of American Art *B3* [→75–76]
Woolworth Building *B6* [→69]
World Trade Center *A6* [→69]

tours

boat tours
Circle Line at Pier 83
☎ 563-3200
Ⓜ A•C•E to 42nd St ⌖ $24
◑ Apr–Nov: 3-hr trip; Jun–Aug: 2-hr evening cruise. Other tours also available.

bus tours
Gray Line
☎ 397-2600
ⓦ www.graylinenewyork.com
⌖ $17–$49 ◑ 7.45am–8pm daily. Choose from more than 20 different tours.

Gateway Bus Tours Inc.
☎ 967-6008 ⌖ $15–$25 (hop on-hop off; ticket valid for 10 days. ◑ 9.15am–4pm daily, every 30 min–1 hr.

Harlem Spirituals
☎ 391-0900
ⓦ www.harlemspirituals.com
⌖ $35–$85 ◑ vary. Tours of the Bronx, Manhattan, Brooklyn, and Harlem, including gospel tours. Also walking tours.

Hassidic New York
4-hr tour of Williamsburg & Crown Heights, Brooklyn. Bus meets by the lion sculptures in front of the New York Public Library [→71] ☎ 1-718-953-5244 to book ⓦ www.jewishtours.com ⌖ $36 ◑ 9.30am Sun.

Helicopter tours
Liberty Helicopters
Midtown Heliport (at Twelfth Ave & 30th St) ☎ 967-4550
Downtown Heliport (at Wall Street/Pier 6) ☎ 487-4777
⌖ Mon–Fri $48 for 4¹/₂ min, $83 for 10 min and $155 for 15 min; Sat–Sun $52 for 4¹/₂ min, $104 for 10 min and $180 for 15 min.
◑ 8.45am–8.45pm daily; every 10 min. Private tours available.

walking tours
Big Apple Greeter
☎ 669-2896
ⓦ www.bigapplegreeter.org
⌖ free ◑ 9.30am–5pm Mon–Fri. A volunteer friend shows you around your choice of neighbourhood. Book 3–4 days ahead.

Big Onion Walking Tours
☎ 439-1090 ⓦ www.bigonion.com ⌖ $10 ◑ vary. Specializes in ethnic and historic neighbourhood tours.

Street Smarts
☎ 969-8262 ⌖ $10 ◑ 2-hr tours Sat–Sun. Specializes in walks around the oldest parts of town.

Citypass
Save 50% on admission costs, and avoid queues with this pass (valid for nine days), that covers the Metropolitan Museum of Art, Empire State Building, Museum of Modern Art, American Museum of Natural History, Intrepid Sea Air Space Museum and the World Trade Center. The cost for adults is $26.75, and the pass is available at any of the above attractions.

big apple highlights

Immigrants from all over the world have contributed to the palimpsest that is New York: a heritage exemplified by the city's mosaic of museums and cultural institutions.

↓ manhattan landmarks

Brooklyn Bridge

When this 1596-ft bridge (the first to employ steel-wire suspension) was unveiled in 1883, it was the world's longest. The Williamsburg Bridge beat it by 4ft 20 years later, but the walkway of one of New York's most visible landmarks still commands unrivaled views. Catch the Brooklyn Bridge live camera at www.romdog.com/bridge/brooklyn.html.

Chrysler Building | Lexington Ave | Midtown

Unmistakable in the midtown skyline, the 77-storey art deco skyscraper was built as a celebration of the motor car's rise to success in the 1930s. Exterior details are based on car motifs like the gargoyles modelled on hood ornaments; inside, Edward Trumball's ceiling mural glows above the red marble lobby.

City Hall | City Hall Park | Lower Manhattan

A prime example of Federal architecture, this has been home to the mayor and seat of NYC government since 1812. It's also the traditional finishing point of tickertape parades along Broadway. The apple trees in the park opposite were used as gallows by the British before Independence.

Empire State Building | Fifth Ave | Midtown

Recognisable from its role in the film classic *King Kong*, the 1250-ft high building is visible from almost anywhere in NY. The coloured lights illuminating the top floors mark special occasions: pink for Gay Pride Day, orange for Halloween, red for Memorial Day...

Flatiron Building | Broadway | Flatiron District

NYC's first skyscraper, this building got its shape and name from its plot at the intersection of Broadway, Fifth Avenue and 23rd Street. The site was a favourite with turn-of-the-century voyeurs as swirling drafts raised women's skirts: policemen who chased them away gave rise to the expression '23 skidoo'.

Grand Central Station | 42nd St | Midtown

Opened in 1913, this beaux arts belle was officially recognized as a landmark sight in 1978. It's most impressive for its cathedral-like concourse and ingenious design which separates train, car and pedestrian traffic; outside, statues of Mercury, Hercules and Minerva hover around its famous clock [→72].

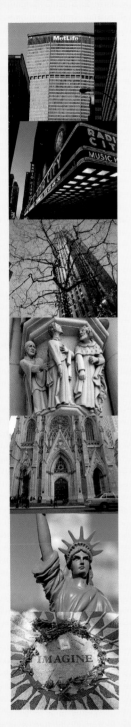

The MetLife Building | Park Ave | Midtown
Built for Pan Am in 1963 by a team of architects which included Bauhaus founder Walter Gropius, and now owned by Metropolitan Life Insurance Company, this may well be most hated building in the city. Not only does it block the Fifth Avenue view, but it glowers over Grand Central Station.

Radio City Music Hall | Sixth Ave | Midtown
Part of the Rockefeller Center, and resplendent in its art deco finery, cascading chandeliers (the world's largest) and sweeping staircases, Radio City defines the opulence of 1930's New York. As well as the resident Rockettes, acts as varied as Barry Manilow and Riverdance have shared the stage in its vast auditorium.

Rockefeller Center | Sixth Ave | Midtown
JD Rockefeller Jr, the benevolent billionaire, created many jobs during the Depression with the construction of this monument to business – a gift to his city. Mitsubishi is now the major shareholder of the complex, which boasts 19 buildings, 40 restaurants, and one of NYC's best seasonal ice rinks.

St John the Divine | Amsterdam Ave | Harlem
Begun in 1892 – and still unfinished. If it is ever completed, this cathedral church will be the largest in the world (work in progress can be seen in the stoneyard). The annual October 'animal blessing' sees a parade of New Yorkers and their pets, in line for benediction.

St Patrick's Cathedral | Fifth Ave | Midtown
Once set in rolling hills, the largest Roman Catholic church in the USA, and the seat of the archdiocese of New York, now resides in the shadows of Midtown's skyscrapers. The relief-figure on the central doors is Anne Seton – the first American-born saint.

Statue of Liberty | Liberty Island
Representations of Lady Liberty – modelled on the sculptor Bartholdi's mother, and the quintessential symbol of freedom – abound. The real McCoy stands proud guarding the tip of lower Manhattan [→71–72].

Strawberry Fields & the Dakota Building
Central Park West | Upper West Side
Tucked in Central Park, a leafy shrine commemorates the life of John Lennon who was killed outside his home in the Dakota building opposite. NYC's first luxury apartments (built in 1884) were so far from the city that 'society' named them Dakota after Indian territory in the Wild West.

sights, museums & galleries

Times Square

Once the heart of NY's Theater District, after the Depression this area declined and became the epitome of sleaze. Beneath the trademark neon signs of this now spruced-up part of town, gawping out-of-towners shuffle by the fast-disappearing strip clubs. *The* place to be on New Year's Eve in the Big Apple.

Trump Tower | Fifth Ave | Midtown

Often called gauche, tacky and over-the-top, Donald Trump's erection stands tall; a tribute to the days when *Dallas* was considered chic. Above the atrium's shiny brass and pink marble five-storey waterfall are 20 floors of offices and ritzy apartments – most worth well over one million dollars.

UN Building | First Ave | Midtown

Overlooking the East River, the three buildings (greatly influenced by Le Corbusier's design philosophy) that make up the UN's head-quarters are flanked by the flags of its 180-member nations. The site is actually an inter-national zone and not part of US territory.

Woolworth Building | Broadway | Lower Manhattan

Until the sad demise of 'Woolies' in 1997, the 60-storey 'cathedral of commerce' was the headquarters of the five-and-dime store empire. A comical sculpture inside the building shows founder, Frank Woolworth counting the coins that made his fortune.

World Trade Center | West St | Lower Manhattan

Some 50,000 workers occupy 12 million sq ft of office space in the five buildings of the WTC. Its two stainless steel and glass towers, a quarter of a mile high, have transformed the Manhattan skyline. In 1993, six people died in a terrorist bombing that shook more than just the foundations of the building.

At street level the city seems a crazy maze of concrete and steel, but you can rise above it all...

↓ uplift yourself

Brooklyn Heights Promenade
Ⓜ 2•3 to Clark St; N•R to Court St

Empire State Building
350 Fifth Ave (at W 34th St)
🎫 $6 🕐 9.30am–midnight daily. ☎ 736-3100 Ⓜ B•D•F•N• Q•R to 34th St-Herald Sq

Riverside Church Observatory
490 Riverside Dr (at W 120th St)
☎ 870-6700 🎫 $2 🕐 11am–4pm Tue–Sat; 12.30–4pm Sun.
Ⓜ 1•9 to 116th St-Columbia Uni

Rooftop Sculpture Garden
Metropolitan Museum of Art, 1000 Fifth Ave (at E 82nd St)
☎ 535-7710 🎫 suggested $8
🕐 May–Nov: 10am–5.15pm

Tue–Sun (to 8.30pm Fri & Sat).
Ⓜ 4•5•6 86th St

Roosevelt Island Tramway
Second Ave & E 60th St
☎ 832-4543 🎫 $1.50
🕐 6–2am daily (to 3.30am Fri–Sat). Ⓜ 4•5•6 to 59th St

Staten Island Ferry
Battery Park ☎ 1-800-573-7469
🎫 free 🕐 24 hrs daily.
Ⓜ 1•9 to Whitehall St

Subway
B•D•Q across the East River

World Trade Center Observation Deck
2 World Trade Center, West St
☎ 323-2340 🎫 $8 🕐 9.30am –9.30pm daily (to 11.30pm Jul–Aug). N C•E to World Trade

Center; 1•9 to Cortlandt St
See also the Greatest Bar on Earth [→129]

↓ consume with a view

The Rainbow Room
30 Rockefeller Plaza, W 50th Sts (bet. 5th & 6th Aves) ☎ 632 -5000 Ⓜ B•D•F•Q to 47th-50th Sts-Rockefeller Center

Top of the Tower
Beekman Tower, 3 Mitchell Pl (bet. Beekman Pl & First Ave)
☎ 355-7300 Ⓜ 6 to 51st St [→130]

The View Lounge
Marriot Marquis, 1700 Broadway (at W 44th St)
☎ 398-1900 Ⓜ N•R•S• 1•2•3• 7•9• to Times Sq-42nd St

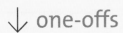

Ellis Island (Museum of Immigration)

Ellis Island stands as a testament to the millions of European immigrants who dared to venture into the 'new world', forced from their homes because of famine and political unrest. By 1892, the number of immigrants had reached such a phenomenal level – one million a day at its peak – that a huge complex was built on Ellis Island, comprising dormitories, a baggage room, a registration room and a hospital. Over the next 60 years, the station processed 17 million successful immigrants, mainly from Ireland, Germany, southern Italy and the old Russian empire.

Some people say that recent renovations have resulted in an overly sanitized atmosphere. But seeing the personal testimonies, belongings and photographs, and hearing voice-recordings of some immigrants, you can go some way to imagining their anguish and hope. It is even more poignant if you remember that just under half of all US citizens have ancestors who were registered at Ellis Island. The highlight is the beautiful Registry Hall, where each new arrival waited anxiously for medical and legal processing. If you can bear the rather corny tone of the 30-min documentary film *Island of Hope, Island of Tears* (shown continuously in two theatres), you can glean some fascinating insights.

☎ 363-3200; 269-5755 (ferry information)
🚇 4•5 to Bowling Green; 1•9 to South Ferry
🚊 $7 return ferry ticket – from Castle Clinton, Battery Park – includes entrance to Ellis Island Museum and Liberty Island. 🚌 none
◑ 8.30am–3.45pm, every 30 min, daily (may change in winter). ♿ 🎧
❶ Bring provisions. Queues get incredibly long in summer when it can be so crowded that it's hard to appreciate the atmosphere; going early in the day helps.

New York Public Library

The lions 'Patience' and 'Fortitude' sit majestically either side of the white marble-columned entrance to this stunning beaux-arts building, and the steps outside are a popular meeting place and impromptu picnic spot for both visitors and locals. Its cool rooms and ice-cold marble floors are reason enough to visit in summer, and the hushed tones throughout the building are incredibly soothing. The public reading room is a must-see, its beautiful ceiling restored to reveal a vibrantly painted blue sky with scudding clouds; the bronze reading lamps and rows of polished tables are in immaculate condition. Around twelve million manuscripts, three million pictures and six million books, as well as some real literary treasures are housed here. Among them are original manuscripts of TS Eliot's *The Wasteland*, the diaries of Virginia Woolf, Charlotte Brontë's writing desk and even the original stuffed animals on which AA Milne based his *Winnie the Pooh* stories. There are frequent free exhibitions in the library's long corridors – always excellently researched if a little understated. Imaginative and varied exhibitions are held in the Gottesman Hall.

Fifth Avenue (at 42nd St)
☎ 930-0800 📠 869-8089 🚇 B•D•F•Q to 42nd St 🚊 free ◑ 11am–7.30pm Tue–Wed; 10am–6pm Thu–Sat. ♿
❶ Free internet access on 24 computer terminals in the Bill Blass Public Catalog Room.

Statue of Liberty

So thoroughly has Lady Liberty come to symbolize America and the values upheld by the American Constitution that it is easy to forget her European origins. A gift from the French people in 1886, the 151-ft-high statue was designed by sculptor Frédéric Auguste Bartholdi, together with Gustave Eiffel. The latter was the brain behind designing Liberty's flexible 'skeleton', which allows the statue some give during high winds. The separately designed pedestal – a formidable structure in its own right at 89 ft – now houses the museum and elevator (taking visitors as high as Liberty's feet). The climb to the top of the crown (the narrow, steep route up the torch is now prohibited for safety reasons) is

sights, museums & attractions

Grand Central Station ↓

the equivalent of a 22-storey trek, and is not for those who are claustrophobic or prone to vertigo. In her right hand Liberty carries a burning torch, metaphorically lighting the way for millions of immigrants whose first sight of America was her awesome silhouette. The tablet in her left hand is inscribed with the date of Independence Day, 4 July 1776, and the broken shackles at her feet represent the end of slavery and escape from tyranny. To modern visitors, her comparatively diminutive size (now that she is dominated by the skyscrapers of Manhattan) may well be a little disappointing.

☎ 363-3200; 269-5755 (ferry information) Ⓜ 4•5 to Bowling Green; 1•9 to South Ferry Ⓢ $7 return ferry ticket – from Castle Clinton, Battery Park – includes entrance to Liberty Island and Ellis Island Museum. �} none ◑ 9.30am–3.15pm, every 30 min, daily (may change in winter). Informative tours are given by the National Park Service Rangers; call in advance for group bookings ☎ 363-7620 ♿

❶ 1| In the summer months waiting times to climb to the crown can exceed 3 hours, and access to the crown is limited. Come early. 2| There is still an excellent view from the top of the pedestal which you can reach by elevator. 3| If you're going on to Ellis Island, don't delay – visiting both sites can easily take all day.

Empire State Building

Probably the best-known stack of bricks, cement and glass in New York. Aside from being the city's second highest building at 1450 ft, the Empire State Building holds a special place in the heart of New York: it was the secret meeting spot for a highly romantic rendezvous in *An Affair to Remember*, Spiderman used to climb it at the beginning of every episode, and King Kong hung from the point at the top. Spectacular panoramic views – as far as 80 miles on a clear day – can be seen from two observatories: an outdoor one on the 86th floor and an enclosed glass one on the 102nd floor. There are no extra gimmicks, frills or thrills, though if that's what you crave, the Skyride on the 2nd floor simulates a flight over the city.

350 Fifth Avenue ☎ 736-3100 Ⓜ B•D•F•N•Q•R to 34th St-Herald Sq; 6 to 33rd St E $6 ◑ 9.30am–midnight, daily. �} none ♿ (Skyride: ☎ 279-9777 Ⓢ $11.50 ◑ 10am–10pm daily)

❶ 102nd floor observatory is closed at weekends.

Even New Yorkers are blown away by the transformation of Grand Central Station (officially Grand Central Terminal) following its recent facelift. The marble interior is now so clean it's almost translucent. Huge, sparkling chandeliers and 2500 lights – representing the constellations of a winter sky and set in the vaulted ceiling – light the main concourse. The vast wall of windows, recognizable from so many of Hollywood's best black-and-whites, lets the sun stream into the main hall in dusty shafts of light, illuminating the clock in the centre of the hall – *the* place to meet. Original brass fixtures and wrought-iron ticket-booth window grates have been put back in place with the same attention to detail that has evidently gone into the whole restoration process. The downside with the renovation is that parts of the station have been transformed into a shopping mall.

Two new restaurants overlook the main concourse, but they are tastefully kitted out and don't detract from the grandeur of the space. For the authentic Grand Central encounter, however, descend through the confusing maze of tunnels to the lower concourse. Down here, directly outside the Oyster Bar [→125], the 'Whispering Gallery' phenomenon takes effect – acoustics are so fine-tuned that murmured secrets don't stay secret for long.

E 42nd Street (at Park Ave) ☎ 340-2583 Ⓜ 4•5•6•7 to Grand Central-42nd St Ⓢ free ◑ 5.30–1.30am daily. ☞ The Municipal Arts Society's free tours take you through the common areas, lower level passageways & behind the wall of windows (12pm Wed) ♿

↓ take five

American Museum of Natural History ⌐

Visitors here are greeted by a soaring skeletal tableau of a three-storey-high *Barosaurus* protecting its frightened young from the attack of a ferocious *Allosaurus*. If any of this makes sense to you, then you will probably want to head up to the top floor for more prehistoric skeletons, from mammoth and sabre-toothed tiger to the Mike Tyson of the dinosaur world, the flesh-devouring *Tyrannosaurus Rex*. This is undeniably one of the top museums in the world; the American Museum of Natural History (abbreviated to the barely pronounceable AMNH) has been working on its presentation since 1869, and it's time that has been well spent.

With a mission to study all of mankind, civilizations around the globe and the complete history of the earth – oh, and the celestial universe as well – it will come as no surprise that the museum's five sprawling floors are crammed with one fantastic, in-your-face display after another. That said, it does have its more serene corners, such as the dark but quietly dazzling Hall of Minerals, which glitters with polished rocks and crystals. A super-big-screen IMAX theatre is on the first floor, with hourly screenings of nature films all day, and 3D laser shows accompanied by rock music on Friday and Saturday nights. Even the Ocean Life Café in the basement is set amidst stuffed walruses and seals, with a 100-ft model of a blue whale suspended overhead.

Just in time to welcome the new millenium, the AMNH recently unveiled the Rose Center for Earth and Space. This state-of-the-art centre, a museum in its own right, houses interactive permanent exhibits and presents absorbing space shows in a revamped Hayden Planetarium that looks like a giant dinosaur's egg trapped in a steel and glass scaffold.

73

Lasers and sound effects speed you on your galactic journey or you can amble along the Heilbrunn Cosmic Pathway to get to grips with different orders of scale in the universe.

👁 The Star of India, the world's biggest blue sapphire (ground flr); the 16-ft cross-section of a Giant Sequoia trunk (1st floor). Central Park W (at 79th St), Upper West Side ☎ 769-5000 🖷 769-5100 **w** www.amnh.org Ⓜ B•C to 81st St-Museum of Natural History 💲 $10 suggested donation; $19 combination ticket (Museum, Rose Center, Hayden Planetarium Space Show) 🚇 AE/MC/V ◑ *10am–5.45pm daily (to 8.45pm Fri–Sat).* ♿ ☞ 🎧 ♨ ♉ 🛍 ❶ 1| Visit 5–8.45pm on a Friday or Saturday when crowds are minimal. If you only want a quick look, the museum offers free admission for the last hour of opening each day. 2| To avoid queuing at the Hayden Planetarium, you can purchase the tickets for the Space Show either on line on the Museum's web site or by calling 769-5200

Metropolitan Museum of Art ⌐

The Met is New York's cultural behemoth. Its list of galleries and departments reads like the artistic equivalent of a Roman banquet: Assyrian sculpture, the classical art of the Greek empire, galleries packed with African, Asian and Islamic treasures, Roman sculpture, a pre-Columbian gold treasury, early Flemish and Netherlandish paintings, a succession of 19th- and

sights, museums & attractions

20th-century galleries and much, much more besides. Museums simply don't get any better than this, and each of the 22 curatorial departments has its own stunning highlight, whether it be the polished steel of arms and armour or the dandyish delights of Tiffany and La Farge (the latter displayed in a lovely garden setting). The Temple of Dendur stands in timeless repose on its own plinth in the Egyptian wing and, in the summertime, the huge rooftop garden provides its own attraction as a place to drink coffee, view a changing selection of sculpture and breathe in the spectacular treetop views over Central Park.

👁 The Temple of Dendur, Roof Garden. 1000 Fifth Avenue (at 82nd St), Upper East Side ☎ 570-3951 📠 535-7710 w www.metmuseum.org Ⓜ 4·5·6 to 86th St 🎫 $8 suggested donation 🍴 none 🕐 9.30am–5.30pm Tue–Sun (to 9pm Fri–Sat). ♿ ☞ 🎧 🎵 ✎ 🛍 ❶ Evenings, especially Fridays and Saturdays are quieter times to visit popular exhibitions. No pushchairs allowed on Sundays.

Museum of Modern Art (MoMA)

The pre-eminent modern art museum in the US, if not the world, MoMA has more than 100,000 art works in its permanent collection, with only about 12% on view at any one time. This is the holy writ of modernism told the American way. Through its holdings, MoMA presents a resolutely triumphalist view of the progress of modern art, beginning in France with the Impressionists and Post-Impressionists, and opening a new chapter with Picasso, before making the giant leap across the Atlantic to Pollock, Rothko, Newman and Reinhardt.

Special exhibitions of painting, sculpture, prints, drawings, photography and architecture regularly rewrite art history – or at least scribble a few important notes in the margin. High up in the fourth floor's atrium a dangling helicopter lets you know you've hit the design department. The bright enclave of the sculpture garden exemplifies the aesthetic links between the pleasures of classicism and modernism, whilst also providing a fine location for refreshments in the summertime. In the basement the museum has a movie theatre with an extensive alternative film programme, which is great if you want a rest.

👁 Rousseau's The Dream, Gauguin's The Moon and the Earth, Picasso's Les Demoiselles d'Avignon, Monet's Waterlilies and Van Gogh's Starry Night. 11 W 53rd Street (bet. Fifth & Sixth Aves), Midtown ☎ 708-9400 w www.moma.org Ⓜ E·F to Fifth Ave 🎫 $9.50 🍴 none 🕐 10.30am–5.45pm Thu–Tue (to 8.15pm Fri). ♿ ☞ 🎧 🎵 ✎ 🛍 ❶ 1| Admission is by donation 4.30–8.30pm Fri – pay as much as you wish. 2| Lunchtime lectures are usually on Tuesdays and Thursdays, while there's live jazz in the garden on Friday nights (in the café in winter).

Solomon R Guggenheim Museum ⚓

Though never quite as sharp or pristine as it appears in photographs, the spiralling rotunda of Frank Lloyd Wright's final work, the Guggenheim Museum, is one of the great architectural achievements of the 20th century; fortunately, the collection of modern and contemporary art housed here is equal to its home. Works from the permanent collection (Chagall, Picasso, Brancusi, Kandinsky and Gauguin are all represented), are mostly hung in the tower, which was added to the back of the building in the 1990's. There's a small selection of impressionist, post-impressionist and early modernist works in the small rotunda. The rotunda is the counterbalance to the main spiral, which is the focus for all temporary exhibitions. There are two ways to view the temporary shows – by a spiralling ascent on foot or heading straight to the elevator and making your way down this cultural helter-skelter (less tiring!); whichever you choose, you are bound to spend as much time looking at the building as the art. The museum shop is packed with books and Gugg memorabilia, including ceramic mugs inspired by the building's distinctive shape.

👁 Picasso's voluptuous sleeping Woman with Yellow Hair and Kandinsky's vibrant Dominant Curve. 1071 fifth Avenue (at 89th St), Upper East Side ☎ 423-3500 w www.guggenheim.org Ⓜ 4·5·6 to 86th St 🎫 $12 💳 AE/MC/V 🕐 9am–6pm Fri–Wed (to 8pm Fri–Sat). ♿ ☞ 🎧 🎵 ✎ 🛍 ❶ Admission is by donation 6–8pm Fri.

Guggenheim Museum Soho

Far from Fifth Avenue's museum mile is the downtown Guggenheim – established in 1992 on the first two floors of a cavernous brick loft building on Broadway. The museum makes good use of the extensive Guggenheim collection: the temporary exhibitions tend to flit between the historical and the contemporary, and it may be that this lack of a clear agenda has contributed to the gallery's rumoured financial problems. This aside, the curators always have some interesting, and occasionally irreverent ideas up their sleeves, and the separate museum store is one of the coolest in town. Who could resist a Guggenheim snow-shaker?

575 Broadway (at Prince St), Soho ☎ 423-3500 **w** www.guggenheim.org Ⓜ N•R to Prince St; B•D•F•Q to Broadway-Layfayette St ⑤ $8 AE/MC/V ◑ 11am–6pm Wed–Sun (to 8pm Sat). ⓘ ☞ ⌂ 🎧 🛍
❶ Admission is by donation 6–8pm Sat.

Whitney Museum of American Art

Founded in 1930 in the studio of Gertrude Vanderbilt Whitney, and now occupying a wonderful Bauhaus-designed building, this is *the* leading collection of American art in the world. A selection from its permanent collection (including works by Edward Hopper, Jasper Johns, Georgia O'Keeffe and Andy Warhol) is usually on show alongside temporary exhibitions, or its famed biennials of contemporary American art – US national pride writ large in paint on canvas. Anachronism or barometer? You decide.

Until recently, it seemed that the Whitney loved to make trouble. The 1993 biennial, for instance, had a 40-ft-long replica of a toy firetruck parked out front, two artists dressed like natives in a cage in the basement, and the world's largest puddle of plastic vomit on the floor upstairs. Bad press and low attendance curtailed such amusing artistic tantrums, and the museum is now better-mannered, garnering praise for its retrospectives (recently of restrained abstract painters such as Mark Rothko, Richard Diebenkorn and the like) and other grand-scale exhibits.

945 Madison Avenue (at 75th St), Upper East Side ☎ 570-3676 **w** www.whitney.org Ⓜ 6 to 77th St ⑤ $10 AE/MC/V ◑ 11am–6pm Tue–Wed & Fri–Sun; 1–9pm Thu. ⓘ ☞ book in advance 🎧 🛍
❶ 'Thursdays with a twist' offers cocktails in the sculpture court and you pay as much as you wish (though $10 is suggested) 6–9pm.

sights, museums & attractions

↓ off manhattan

American Museum of the Moving Image (AMMI)
American Spielbergs can experiment with sound effects and editing techniques.

35th Ave (bet. 36th & 37th Sts), Astoria, Queens ☎ 1-718-784-0077 Ⓜ R to Steinway St ⑤ $8.50 ◑ 12–5pm Tue–Fri; 11am–6pm Sat–Sun. ⓘ ☞ 3pm Mon–Fri 🎥 ⓘ
❶ make your own video flip book

NY Botanical Gardens
A blooming 250-acre urban oasis (based on London's Kew Gardens), spectacular at any time of the year.
Southern Boulevard (at 200th St), Bronx

☎ 1-718-817-8700 Ⓜ C•D•4 to Bedford Park, then Bx26 bus ⑤ $10 adults ◑ Apr–Oct: 10am–6pm Tue–Sun. 🎥 ⓘ
❶ free admission 10am–6pm Wed & 10am–12pm Sat

NY Hall of Science
Science is made fun with lots of exciting, hands-on exhibits.

4701 11th St (at 48th Ave), Flushing Meadows, Corona Park, Queens

☎ 1-718-699-0005 Ⓜ 7 to 111th St ⑤ $6 ◑ Sep–Jun: 9.30am–2pm daily (to 5pm Thu–Sun); Jul–Aug: 9.30am–5pm daily (to 2pm Mon).

Queens Museum of Art
Best known for its amazing Panorama – an incredibly detailed scale model of NYC.

New York City Building, Flushing Meadows, Corona Park, Queens

☎ 1-718-592-9700 x223 Ⓜ 7 to 111th St ⑤ $5 (suggested voluntary donation) ◑ 10am–5pm Wed–Fri; 12–5pm Sat–Sun. ⓘ 🎧 ⓘ

Cooper-Hewitt, National Design Museum

This museum – the only one in the US devoted entirely to design – is housed within the dark, wood-panelled walls, of a mansion that was built for the super-rich and highly philanthropic steel magnate Andrew Carnegie.

The opulent atmosphere provides a strange background to some of the more adventurous short-term exhibitions, such as the one of Latino culture in Los Angeles, but such juxtapositions are all part of this museum's attraction. The focus of other temporary exhibitions have ranged from Huguenot silverware to the classically modern furniture of Charles and Ray Eames. Every three years, the Cooper-Hewitt hosts the National Design Triennial, which lasts for four months and offers an overview of the issues and ideas animating design in the States. The museum's collection of over 250,000 items – including one-off and mass-produced prints, textiles and furniture – is available for personal study, but only by prior appointment.

2 E 91st Street (at Fifth Ave), Upper East Side ☎ 849-8400 w www.si.edu/ndm 🚇 4·5·6 to 86th St 💲 $8 🚪 none ⏰ 10am–5pm Tue–Sat (to 9pm Tue); 12–5pm Sun. ♿ ☞ 🐕 🛗 ❶ 1| Admission is free 5–9pm Tue. 2| School groups tend to visit in the mornings. 3| The next opportunity to see the National Design Triennial is in Spring 2003.

Frick Collection

If the Cooper-Hewitt has whet your appetite for leisurely strolls through echoing halls and sumptuous rooms, then head for the Frick Collection on Fifth Avenue. This mansion was the home of a steel industrialist of a more acquisitive kind, Henry Clay Frick. In the few years he spent here before his death in 1919, he covered the walls with European art, carpeted the floors in oriental rugs, and adorned the 18th-century French furniture with porcelain and other fanciful objets d'art to indulge his decorative whims.

Today, the Frick is perhaps the most elegant small museum in the country. It features some 20 rooms filled with about 175 paintings by masters ranging from Gainsborough to Vermeer

and El Greco, plus a music room for concerts and a new basement gallery for temporary exhibitions. The acutely observant may notice traces of similarity between this mansion and the NY Public Library, for the two buildings share a common architect – Thomas Hastings. His design for the indoor courtyard provides a light and serene haven in the midst of the city. 👁 Bellini's St Francis in the Desert, Rembrandt's monumental, great last Self Portrait, Goya's dark and muscular The Forge, Vermeer's light-strewn Officer and A Laughing Girl and two rooms of lovely rococo romance – Fragonard's six-painting cycle The Progress of Love and Boucher's eight-painting decorative scheme The Arts and Sciences.

1 E 70th Street (at Fifth Ave), Upper East Side ☎ 288-0700 w www.frick.org 🚇 4·5·6 to 68th St Hunter College 💲 $7 🚪 none ⏰ 10am–6pm Tue-Sat; 1–6pm Sun. ♿ 🎧 🛗 ❶ No children under 10.

Lower East Side Tenement Museum ✓

Tenement blocks are integral to the character and history of New York. These were the buildings that were thrown up all across town in the 19th century to house the swelling tides of immigrants landing upon the eastern shore of America. Often built without plumbing or running water, such expeditious and economical construction was necessary to meet the demands of this expanding city-port.

The tenement at No. 97 Orchard Street was built in 1864, and its useful life was just 70 years – the building being sealed due to its unsafe condition in 1935. During its short lifespan, however, it was home to an estimated 10,000 people from 20 countries. The building stood idle for 52 years until 1987, when, with the process of gentrification transforming many of the former poor, run down and slum neighbourhoods, this tenement was selected to become a testament to the urban poor who built the multi-ethnic, tough-talking character of New York that the city still trades on today. The Tenement Museum preserves three apartments as they once were – homes to German, Italian and Lithuanian families – complete with furnishings and

personal effects. The museum can be visited only by joining a guided tour. There is also a more lighthearted tour (designed for kids) where the guide plays the part of an Italian matron of 1916, welcoming relatives to the new country, while dispensing advice and admonitions in equal measure to her young charges.
👁 The scale model of the building on the ground floor for a bird's eye view.

90 Orchard Street (at Broome St), Lower East Side ☎ 431-0233 w www.wnet.org/ tenement 🚇 F·J·M·Z to Delancey St-Essex St; B·D·Q to Grand St. 💲 $8 💳 AE/MC/V ⏰ 12–5pm Tue–Sun (to 11am Sat–Sun). ☞ compulsory 🐕 🛗 ❶ Tours around the tenement are limited to 15 people – call ahead to book tickets. If you do have to queue, there's a video to watch.

Morris-Jumel Mansion Museum

Said to be the oldest existing house in New York, this classical mansion's white façade now looks a little frayed, though still remains an amazing landmark. This lavishly-proportioned summer villa, built in 1765 for one Lt. Col Roger Morris, stands on the island's northeast corner in a neighbourhood that has clearly seen better days. George Washington lived here during the Revolutionary War while he drew up battle plans, but the house's most infamous resident was Madame Eliza Jumel, a scandalous and wealthy widow who resided here in the 1830's (a former prostitute, apparently she allowed her rich husband to bleed to death so she could inherit his fortune). The mansion opened as a museum in 1907, and to this day you can admire the interior decor which includes period wallpaper, stained-glass roundels and many items from the time of Eliza's occupation including her

mesmerizing obituary, which details her raucous life.
👁 Eliza's bed (said to have once belonged to Napoleon), the octagonal sitting room, George Washington's study.

65 Jumel Terrace (bet. 160th & 162nd Sts), Harlem ☎ 923-8008
Ⓜ C to 163rd St-Amsterdam Ave
🎟 $3 📇 MC/V ⏱ 10am–4pm Wed–Sun. ♿ limited ☞ pre-book a month in advance 🔊 🏛
❶ If there are no groups on Mondays & Tuesdays, the museum opens to individuals – phone ahead to check.

Morgan Library ✓

This gorgeous 1902 library houses one of the finest collections of manuscripts in the world. It was built as a library and study for the financier and avid manuscript collector, JP Morgan, whose son (JP Morgan Jr) bequeathed the building and its collection to the city in 1924. Temporary exhibits change regularly: you might get a glimpse at such delights as Mozart's multicoloured music script for a horn concerto, John

Tenniel's illustrations for Lewis Carroll's *Alice*, or recent acquisitions from 20th century literature (in December, an original of Dicken's *Christmas Carrol* is always on show). After you've taken in the current displays in the annexed exhibition space, explore the two sumptuous rooms of the actual library and study, lavishly decorated with Italian motifs and heavy with furniture and paintings. But if the wealth of edifying visual material makes you a little weary, there is a light and airy courtyard café in which to take a breather

and boost your reserves. The museum's shop is has a particularly lovely selection of books and gifts.
👁 Old Master drawings, ancient Near Eastern cylinder seals.

29 E 36th Street (bet. Madison & Park Aves), Midtown
☎ 685-0610 Ⓜ 6 to 33rd St
🎟 $7 📇 none ⏱ 10.30am–5pm Tue–Sat (to 8pm Fri; 6pm Sat); 12–6pm Sun. ♿ ☞ 🔊 🎧 🏛

↓ melting pot

Jewish Museum

It seems only appropriate that the biggest collection of Jewish artifacts outside Israel can be found in New York. In spite of a wealth of Jewish history to draw upon – 4000 years to be precise – the Jewish Museum has always been something of an avant-garde pioneer, staging exhibitions that explore the twin strands of minimal and conceptual art. Its curators consistently hazard shows on such controversial subjects as the Arab-Israeli conflict, as well as mounting retrospectives of crowd-pleasers such as Mark Chagall, Camille Pissarro and Chaim Soutine on two of the museum's four magnificent floors. In the remaining space is the permanent collection, where you can see Canaanite cult idols from 800 BC (the kind of things that got Moses' flock into such trouble), sling-shot ammo (clay balls capable of slaying a Goliath) and one of the earliest surviving tax records on a 4th-century Babylonian cuneiform tablet – as now, so then, death and taxes are life's only certainties.

1105 Fifth Avenue (at 92nd St), Upper East Side ☎ 423-3200
🌐 www.thejewishmuseum.org
Ⓜ 4·5·6 to 96th St 🎟 $8
🍴 none ⏱ 11am–5.45pm Sun–Thu (to 8pm Tue). ♿ ☞ 🎧 🔊 🏛
🏛 ❶ admission free 5–8pm Tue.

El Museo del Barrio

El Museo has become *the* place to see frequently vibrant and life-affirming exhibitions chronicling the art that stems, either geographically or socio-politically, from the Caribbean and Latin America. It was founded in 1969 by a Puerto Rican community group as a cultural focus for East Harlem's Spanish-speaking 'el barrio', a low-rent neighbourhood that is still home to immigrants and the descendants of immigrants from Latin America and the Caribbean (particularly Puerto Rico). Some of the exhibitions explore and document the folklore and history of the Latin American peoples, but much is contemporary and tackles varied and universal issues. The museum's temporary shows are always worth a look, and recently gallery space has been given over to investigations of Afro-Caribbean Sacred Spaces and the perennial Search for Miracles. The small gift shop specializes in unusual examples of folk art, supplied locally or imported from Mexico and South America.

1230 Fifth Avenue (at 104th St), Spanish Harlem ☎ 831-7272
🌐 www.elmuseo.org Ⓜ 6 to 103rd St 🎟 $4 (suggested donation) ⏱ 11am–5pm Wed–Sun (Jun–Sep: to 8pm Thu). ♿ ☞ 🔊 🏛

Museum for African Art

This relatively young museum, founded in an Upper East Side townhouse in 1984 and moved to Soho in 1992, occupies two cosy floors of galleries designed by Maya Lin, whose previous work includes the National Vietnam Veterans Memorial in Washington, DC. Until recently the museum has specialized in exhibitions of classical African art, whether focusing on surveys of artefacts made by individual peoples, or the broader-based holdings of collectors. However, under new director Elsie Crum McCabe, the Museum for African Art is widening its remit into contemporary African social and political issues. This is borne out in recent and up-and-coming shows, which cover broad-ranging subjects such as political machinations of the Congo in the post-colonial era, the art emerging from South Africa since the end of apartheid and a serious look at style through the Language of Hair in African Art and Culture. A regular series of gallery talks and discussions contributes to the sense of analysis and debate. As well as a fair selection of books on African art, the museum shop, which occupies the lobby area, also sells jewellery, textiles, crafts and even furniture.

593 Broadway (bet. Houston & Prince Sts), Soho ☎ 966-1313 **w** www.africanart.org Ⓜ N·R to Prince St; B·D·F·Q to Broadway-Lafayette St 🚇 $5 🈯 AE/MC/V ◑ 10.30am–5.30pm Tue–Fri; 12–6pm Sat–Sun. ❺ ☞ ✆ 🛈 ❶ Free admission on Sundays in February.

National Museum of the American Indian ✓

At the southern end of Manhattan Island, between the green tip of Battery Park and a bronze statue of a charging bull, is the Alexander Hamilton US Customs House. Built in 1890 on the site of the colonial-era Fort Amsterdam, the Customs House is a marvel of limestone and multicoloured marble, its façade ornamented with a dozen faux Corinthian columns and four massive allegorical figure groups representing the continents. This astonishing beaux-arts structure is home to one of New York's newest museums (opened in 1994), the George Gustav Heye Center of the National Museum of the American Indian (to give it its full, illustrious title).

The museum presents its wares within a rigorously educational context, complete with high-tech touch-screen video stations, dioramas and installations. Though such window-dressing is often unnecessary (and even tacky) the incredible beauty of the artefacts shines through regardless. Huron moccasins decorated with moose hair and porcupine quills, a 19th-century ledger with drawings of Lakota chiefs on horseback by Red Dog, an Algonquin duck decoy made of woven reeds – all such items can be found in the museum's two permanent installations; All Roads Are Good: Native Voices on Life, and Culture and Creation's Journey: Masterworks of Native American Identity and Belief. Temporary exhibitions frequently showcase contemporary art by Native Americans living in the US as well as the traditional art and artefacts of indians from around the world. The museum shop has a wealth of books, jewellery, textiles and crafts for sale, while a second shop is devoted to things for kids. Among its offerings is a 'talking

feather', which is held by the speaker at a powwow while everyone else must remain silent (at $3.50 this could be an inexpensive way to settle traditional family hostilities).

George Gustave Heye Center, US Custom House, 1 Bowling Green (bet. State & Whitehall Sts) ☎ 514-3700 Ⓜ 1·9 to South Ferry; N·R to Whitehall St 🚇 free ◑ 10am–5pm daily. ❺ ☞ 🛈

↓ in the mix

American Craft Museum

The applied arts at their most exotic and imaginative are found in the American Craft Museum. The museum has done pioneering work as a centre and clearinghouse for information on traditional crafts, and gone further to explore that strange twilight world between craft and art. There are ceramics of every shape and size, blown and cast glass, contemporary fibre art and quirky quilts, bizarre furniture, stained jewellery and much more besides. Located across the street from the Museum of Modern Art in ground-level galleries in Deutsche Bank's high-rise headquarters, the museum has something of a showroom ambience, filled as it is with fancy home furnishings. But the exhibitions are consistently entrancing: In addition to theme exhibitions, which often cover historical material (art nouveau porcelain, for instance), the museum also mounts retrospective surveys of work by the leading lights of contemporary crafts. Like so many American museums in this era of dwindling government support, the museum shop fills the lobby and offers sleek high-end wares from artisans.

20 W 53rd Street (bet. Fifth & Sixth Aves), Midtown ☎ 956-3535 Ⓜ E·F to 5th Ave 🚇 $5 🈯 AE/MC/V ◑ 10am–6pm Tue–Sun (to 8pm Thu). ❺ ☞ 🛈 ❶ Admission is by donation 6–8pm Thursday – pay as much as you wish.

The Cloisters ✓

If you make only one trip to a museum beyond Museum Mile make this the one. Located at the northern tip of Manhattan in Fort Tryon Park, The Cloisters is the branch of the Metropolitan Museum devoted to the art and architecture of medieval Europe. Not only is the museum itself an absolute treasure-trove of delights, but the location – within a wild and rocky 56-acre preserve – will show you an entirely different side to New York from the adrenalin-fired life of Downtown.

The Cloisters is a 20th-century recreation of a medieval monastic complex that incorporates genuine architectural features pillaged from Europe, such as the secluded central cloister with its 12th-century Romanesque arcade. In fact, the whole building is a wonderful hodge-podge of sections taken from five Romanesque and Gothic cloisters that originated in

France. This fabulous place was the brainchild of John D Rockefeller, who not only donated much of the money to buy the buildings in 1925, but provided the land, an endowment and the bulk of the collection, which numbers about 4000 items.

There are incredible examples of polychrome sculpture, stained glass, Spanish lustre-ware and carved oak furniture, as well as a handful of pieces that deserve special mention: the *Belles Heures de Jean, Duc de Berry* (a staggeringly intricate and beautiful illuminated manuscript); Robert Campin's small but perfectly formed Merode Altarpiece (*Triptych of the Annunciation*); and the freshly conserved and presented Unicorn Tapestries from Brussels, made in around 1500 AD.

The Bonnefont and Trie cloisters enclose gardens containing hundreds of plants and herbs used in the Middle Ages, either medicinally or for culinary purposes. The shop offers up a pretty good selection of reproduction jewellery and other medieval-style keepsakes, as well as tapes and CDs of monks humming their ecclesiastical medleys – very relaxing.

Unicorn Tapestries, Fuentidueña chapel with its fresco of the Virgin and Child

Fort Tryon Park, Inwood 923-3700 w www.metmuseum.org M A to 190th St, then M4 bus $8 (suggested donation) none *Mar–Oct: 9.30am–5.15pm Tue–Sun (Nov–Feb: to 4.45pm).* limited
Ticket also valid for Metropolitan Museum.

Museum of American Folk Art

'We all have little obsessive concerns,' wrote Robert Penn Warren in an essay about folk art, the umbrella term for the imaginative and heartfelt artefacts and crafts produced by untutored, often rural people as a part of their everyday lives. Recently, folk art has come to overlap with 'outsider art', which tends to describe art made by untrained artists and those in institutions. The permanent collection includes duck decoys, religious art, woven coverlets and quilts, painted trays and boxes, weathervanes, dolls and devotional figures, carvings and paintings – a small, jewel-like selection is always on show in a special gallery. Though the facility has something of the feel of a commercial mall, its three galleries devoted to two temporary exhibitions do justice to the fascinating works of art.

2 Lincoln Square, Columbus Avenue (bet. 65th & 66th Sts), Upper East Side 595-9533 w www.folkartmuse.org M 1•9 to 66th St-Lincoln Center $3 (suggested donation) *11.30am–7.30pm Tue–Sun.*

New-York Historical Society

Where else but in the strange world of the New-York Historical Society could you find three centuries of New York restaurant menus, a sample of George Washington's hair, and more Tiffany lamps than you could shake a stick at. Founded in 1804, the society – complete with the archaic hyphen in New-York – is often referred to as the city's attic, a description that suggests a musty storehouse filled with junk that no one in the family really wants. To be fair, although the Historical Society was hit by scandalous revelations in the early 1990's over mismanagement and neglect, its multifarious acquisitions could never be described as junk. Now brought back from the brink of fiscal disaster, the museum has become widely recognized as a source of artefacts in which resides the physical presence of New York (and US) history. Not only does it hold the nation's largest collection of Tiffany lamps (113 in all) and the 431 original watercolours for Audubon's Birds of America, but it is also home to the five-part series *The Course of Empire* painted by Thomas Cole, founder of the Hudson River School, and has more than 500,000 19th- and 20th-century American photographs. The society stages temporary exhibitions as well as its permanent collection on subjects such as how Manhattan was purchased from the indigenous population for a mere $24 and a handful of beads.

2 W 77th Street (at Central Park W), Upper West Side 873-3400 w www.nyhistory.org M B•C to 81st St $5 none *11am–5pm Tue–Sun.* *1pm & 3pm daily*

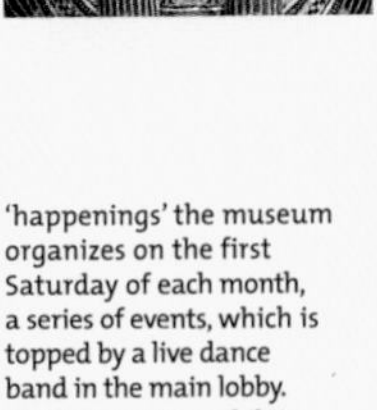

↓ in the picture

Brooklyn Museum of Art ✓

This is a browser's pleasure palace – the delightful epitome of a provincial museum, that brings together a miscellany of exhibits from Rodin sculptures to full-scale Dutch farmhouses of the 18th century. It was founded approximately 175 years ago as the Brooklyn Museum, and only recently added the 'of Art' to its name. Apparently, visitors didn't realize quite what it was about and kept asking to see the dinosaurs!

The museum's encyclopedic collection, spread through a spacious five-storey building, includes assemblages of both African and Egyptian art that have few matches in the US. The first floor has a gallery dedicated to temporary shows, and a small space for contemporary art, often devoted to showing work by members of Brooklyn's burgeoning artist population. Asian art is on two – look for an elegant Chinese wine jar with a cobalt blue design of fish and waterplants on white ceramic from the Yuan dynasty – while Egyptology takes up a fair slice of the third floor. The Dutch farmhouses are on the fourth floor, which gives some indication of the size of the museum, nestled alongside 28 period rooms – Brooklyn was the first museum to present this kind of exhibit. Among the American and European paintings on the fifth floor is a selection of 58 works by Rodin. Brooklyn- ites (and others, of course) flock to the 'happenings' the museum organizes on the first Saturday of each month, a series of events, which is topped by a live dance band in the main lobby.
The Egyptian exhibits include a brilliantly painted mummy cartonnage (a type of elaborately decorated coffin) of Nespenetjerenpare, as well as the gilded coffin for an ibis. On the first floor, be sure to check out the Haida totem poles and the 2000-year-old, richly embroidered Paracas Textile from Peru.

200 Eastern Parkway, Brooklyn 1-718-638-5000 w www.brooklynart.org M 2•3 to Eastern Parkway-Brooklyn Museum $ free *10am–5pm Wed–Fri; 11am–6pm Sat–Sun.*

① 1| On the first Saturday of each month there's a special free programme (including a band and Latin dancing) 5pm–11pm. **2|** Don't forget the adjacent Brooklyn Botanical Garden [→85].

Dia Center for the Arts

Located since 1987 in a 40,000-sq-ft warehouse in Chelsea, Dia specializes in lavish, long-term exhibitions of works by contemporary artists from around the world, ranging from Francesco Clemente and Alighiero e Boetti to Jenny Holzer, Andy Warhol and Richard Serra. Launched in the 1970's, Dia was part of a visionary scheme to provide long-term or permanent installations of major works by a select handful of primarily Minimalist and Conceptual artists.

One work by Dan Graham and two by Walter de Maria are still maintained in New York. One of Graham's trademark glass pavilions is permanently sited on the roof and is a good spot to watch the sun set over the Hudson. The Walter de Maria pieces are in the Soho district and are worth a special visit: the New York Earth Room takes up a floor of a loft at 141 Wooster, where soil 2 ft deep has been spread throughout the gallery; viewers stand at the door, behind a perspex sheet which holds back the earth, taking in the dank smell and pointing out the occasional sprouting of grass. The second work, the Broken Kilometer at 393 West Broadway, is composed of 1066 yards of solid brass rod, divided into 500 upended lengths arranged in a formation that subtly plays with your sense of perspective. 548 W 22nd Street (bet. Tenth & Eleventh Aves), Chelsea ☎ 989-5566 w www.diacenter.org Ⓜ C·E to 23rd St 💲 $6 🚫 AE/MC/V ◑ 16 Sep–18 Jun: 12–6pm Wed–Sun. ♿ ✆ 🛍
① Don't forget to visit the space across the street from the main gallery. Check Dia's calendar for poetry readings, lectures and performances.

International Center of Photography

New York's only museum dedicated solely to photography was established in 1974 by photojournalist Cornell Capa, brother of the late war photographer Robert. Due to its distinctive heritage, the ICP regularly shows work with a journalistic slant, as opposed to oeuvres of artist-photographers. The museum's headquarters are located Uptown on Museum Mile, where there are two floors of intimate gallery space within an imposing early 20th-century brick building that previously housed the National Audubon Society. A second two-storey facility, grey-carpeted in corporate style, is located a block away from Times Square. Regular and multiple exhibitions draw on the ICP's extensive archive and include a recent Robert Capa retrospective as well as other displays of the masters of this fascinating art form. The shop is a great resource for photo books.
1130 Fifth Ave (at 94th St), Upper East Side ☎ 860-1777 w www.icp.org Ⓜ 6 to 96th St-Lexington Ave 💲 $6 🚫 none ◑ 10am–5pm Tue–Sun (8pm Fri; 6pm Sat–Sun). 🛍 ✆

1133 Sixth Ave (at 43rd St), Midtown ☎ 768-4682 w www.icp.org Ⓜ B·D·F·Q to 42nd St 💲 $6 🚫 none ◑ 10am–5pm Tue–Sun (to 8pm Fri; 6pm Sat–Sun). ♿ 🛍 ✆
① Admission is by donation 6–8pm Fri – pay as much as you wish.

Isamu Noguchi Garden Museum ⸙

The minimalism of high modernism meets the traditions of Zen Buddhism in this stylishly asymmetrical, one-storey museum, designed by the Japanese– American sculptor Isamu Noguchi (1904–1988) and dedicated in 1985. This is one of the most serene spaces in all of the city, and it houses more than 250 of his works, spread throughout 13 galleries.

Noguchi made a virtue of creating simple abstract forms that became part of the everyday environment – sculptures in stone and metal, models for public art projects, playground sculptures and dance sets (including 20 sets for Martha Graham). The museum includes one of the artist's small, meditative gardens (closed during winter months), with weeping cherry trees, bamboo, juniper and ivy, as well as major granite and basalt sculptures. One of the large cubes also functions as a tranquil fountain that gently bubbles its water supply. The museum shop offers a complete line of Noguchi's Akari lamps – light-sculptures inspired by classical Japanese lanterns of bamboo and pleated paper. A programme of films on Noguchi's life and work runs continuously.
👁 The artist's unusual musical weatherwane, as well as his biomorphic glass-topped coffee table, a design which has been sold by Herman Miller since 1949.

32–37 Vernon Boulevard, Long Island City, Queens ☎ 1-718-721-1932 w www.noguchi.org Ⓜ N to Broadway (Queens) 💲 $4 (suggested donation only) 🚫 AE/MC/V ◑ 10am–5pm Wed–Fri; 11am–6pm Sat–Sun. ♿ limited ✆ 🛍
① **1|** $5 round trip by shuttlebus, hourly at weekends from the Asia Society, E 70th Street (at Park Ave). **2|** Check out the Socrates Sculpture Park in nearby Rainey Park.

New Museum of Contemporary Art

With its recently renovated, three-storey facility and new director – former Whitney curator Lisa Phillips – the New Museum is poised to take on the art of the new millennium. The museum doesn't have a permanent collection, but can be counted on each year for a dozen or so challenging temporary exhibitions of new art from around the globe. Much of it is likely to be political, community-based and funky, as it endeavours to catch the best artists of our times on the way up. Previous exhibitions have showcased Jeff Koons and Christian Boltanski.
583 Broadway (bet. Houston & Prince Sts) ☎ 219-1222 w www.newmuseum.org Ⓜ 6 to Spring St or Bleecker St; N·R to Prince St; B·D·F·Q to Broadway-Lafayette St 💲 $6 🚫 AE/MC/V ◑ 12–6pm Wed–Sun (to 8pm Thu–Sat). ♿ ✆ 🛍
① Admission is free 6–8pm Thu.

PS1 Museum of Contemporary Art

Out amid the industrial units of Queens is a unique New York art institution that captures the lively spirit of contemporary art – PS1. A ramshackle, four-storey, red-brick school that was converted into an art centre over 20 years ago, PS1 combines exhibition galleries with artists' studios. In 1998, with the help of an $8 million grant from the city, the museum got a new brutalist courtyard designed by architect Frederick Fischer, and spruced up its galleries considerably, though it still has a refreshing informality.

What makes the place seem particularly energetic are the long-term special projects by artists all around the building, from the Robert Ryman painting bolted to the wall next to the furnace in the basement, to the picnic table on the roof decorated by Julian Schnabel (where you can also take in a dramatic view of the Manhattan skyline and the Queensboro Bridge). There's a tiny, sexy video by Pipilotti Rist embedded in the hallway floor and a perplexing neon sculpture installed by Keith Sonnier in the airshaft above the foyer. All this is in addition to the major temporary exhibitions (check the listings magazines for current shows) and the artists-in-residence programme that opens up the studios for public inspections once in a while.

22–25 Jackson Avenue, Long Island City, Queens ☎ 1-718-784-2084 **w** www.ps1.org Ⓜ E•F 23rd St (Ely Ave) 💲 $5 suggested donation ◑ 12–6pm Wed–Sun.♿ ☞ �æ ⚲ ᵖ
❶ Be sure to wait till dusk and see *Meeting by James Turrell*, the leading US master of inflecting space with colour. It's in Room 306, in the south wing, a carpeted space ringed with wooden seating, artfully lit and open to the sky – the effect of light and hue is phenomenal.

Schomburg Center for Research in Black Culture

This lodestone of African American learning is the biggest resource of its kind in America. Home to a massive collection of books, artworks, artifacts and documents (5 million at the last count), the Schomburg is actually a branch of the New York Public Library [→71] and as such it continues to elucidate and inform. The centre was named after the Puerto Rican-born black scholar and bibliophile, Arturo Alfonso Schomburg, who was once told there was no such thing as black history and decided to prove otherwise. He added his personal collection to the library's Division of Negro Literature, History and Prints in 1926 and served as the collection's curator from 1932 until his death in 1938, and in 1940 it was renamed in Schomburg's honour. The collection includes publications in over 200 indigenous African and Creole languages and dialects, and more than 300,000 photographs and prints, ranging from 18th-century graphics to contemporary works, all serving to document the history and culture of peoples of African descent worldwide. Schomburg's red-brick, modernist facility, located in the heart of Harlem, is also home to a lively community centre with two exhibition spaces and a theatre – there's always something going on, whether it be concerts, jazz performances or readings. There are several New York-oriented exhibition mounted in the library each year.

515 Lenox Ave (at 135th St), Harlem ☎ 491-2200 **w** www.nypl.org Ⓜ 2•3 to 135th St 💲 free ◑ 12–8pm Mon–Wed; 10am–6pm Thu–Sat; 1–5pm Sun. ♿ ☞ by appointment 🛈
❶ Saturdays after 3pm are a quiet time to visit. Phone for details of concerts and special programmes. An appointment is required to view the library's extensive holdings of art objects, rare books and manuscripts.

Studio Museum of Harlem

Founded in 1967 by a group that included abstract painter William T Williams, and some staffers from the Museum of Modern Art, the Studio Museum in Harlem grew out of the Black Art movement of the 1960's and is now the linchpin of the Upper Manhattan art scene. Its special quality comes from the constant involvement of artists – indeed, of its four or five exhibitions each year, one is always dedicated to work by the three yearly participants in the museum's artists-in-residence programme. To commemorate the museum's 30th anniversary, construction has started on new (in fact, the first ever) galleries for the permanent collection, Bearden, Elizabeth Catlett, Robert Colescott and Jacob Lawrence. Among the offerings in the museum shop are exhibition catalogues for 30 years of exhibitions at the museum, plus African jewellery, textiles and woven containers.

144 W 125th Street (bet Seventh & Lenox Ave), Harlem ☎ 864-4500 **w** www.studio museuminharlem.org Ⓜ 2•3 to 125th Street 💲 Suggested donation 🍴 none ◑ 10am–5pm Wed–Fri; 1–6pm Sat–Sun. ♿ ☞ �æ ᵖ
❶ Free admission on the first Saturday of the month.

sights, museums & attractions

↓ gallery seen

downtown

The Lower East Side, Nolita and East Village have a smattering of shop front art showcases, but the hub of the downtown art scene is around Soho and Chelsea. With its super-high rents, the former's galleries are dominated by power dealers. Larry Gagosian alternates museum-quality shows of high moderns like Andy Warhol with the newest works of established contemporaries like Anselm Kiefer, while Deitch Projects exhibits a wide range of hot young artists from around the world. Yet more avant-garde is to be had at American Fine Arts, specializing in 'institutional critique' by young artists. For photos, visit Janet Borden – the wares range from the sharp-focus landscapes of Lee Friedlander to surreal post-apocalyptic visions by Oliver Wasow. No visit to Soho would be complete without looking in at Phyllis Kind, the veteran Chicago dealer who specializes in Outsider art. Nearby is the Tony Shafrazi Gallery, with an emphasis on graffiti art by Jean-Michel Basquiat, and work by Keith Haring and Kenny Scharf. More on the area's fringes is Ace Gallery, easily New York's grandest gallery space. Look for monolithic minimalism, mural-sized painting and anything else that's massive in scale.
In Chelsea and the Meatpacking district, a burgeoning commercial gallery scene has emerged west of Tenth Avenue, concentrated on 22nd and 24th Streets. These blocks are home to a

complex known as 'MGM' – **Metro Pictures, Barbara Gladstone and Matthew Marks Gallery** – a compulsory stop for viewing what's new and what's hot. Metro grew famous for showing feminist postmodernists such as Cindy Sherman, while next door at Gladstone you can find works by Richard Prince who first made his mark with rephotographed images of the Marlboro Man. The suave young newcomer, Matthew Marks, has two galleries where he shows mature blue chips such as Ellsworth Kelly and Brice Marden, while also establishing a market for fashionable and collectable new artists like Gary Hume and Katharina Fritsch. Of note among the 22nd Street galleries are **Pat Hearn**, who specializes in poetic paintings filled with colour and light, and **303 Gallery**, a video gallery showing work by – among others – Doug Aitken and angry feminist painter Sue Williams. Two veteran dealers who have set up shop in the area include **Paula Cooper**, whose grand space brings out the most of Cooper's eclectic stable ranging from minimalist sculptor Sol LeWitt to transgressive photographer

Andres Serrano. **John Weber**, who made a name for himself in the 70s as the home of process-oriented art, now has a gallery on the second floor of a 10-storey building housing more than a dozen galleries large and small, and is still very strong on conceptual art.

Ace Gallery
275 Hudson Street
255-5599

American Fine Arts
22 Wooster Street
941-0401

Barbara Gladstone
515 W 24th Street
206-9300

Deitch Projects
76 Grand Street
343-7300

Janet Borden
560 Broadway
431-0166

John Weber
529 W 20th Street
691-5711

Larry Gagosian
136 Wooster Street
228-2828

Matthew Marks Gallery
522 W 22nd Street
243-1650
523 W 24th Street
243-0200

Marlborough Gallery
40 W 57th Street
541-4900

Metro Pictures
519 W 24th Street
206-7100

Pat Hearn
530 W 22nd Street
727-7366

Paula Cooper
534 W 21st Street
255-1105

Phyllis Kind
136 Greene Street
925-1200

303 Gallery
525 W 22nd Street
255-1121

Tony Shafrazi Gallery
119 Wooster Street
274-9300

uptown

In the upper floors of the buildings lining 57th Street are some of NY's toniest galleries. **PaceWildenstein** is one of the city's most successful contemporary spaces. Look for work by Photorealist Chuck Close, Minimalist Agnes Martin, feminist body artist Kiki Smith, Neo-expressionist superstar Julian Schnabel, and sculptor Henry Moore – to name just a few. The **Kennedy Galleries** have dozens of contemporary artists' work, as well as a huge collection of exclusively American paintings and prints dating from the 18th century, while the international **Marlborough Gallery** specializes in 'pop figuration' and has recently taken on neon artist Keith Sonnier. It is a while since **Mary Boone** fled the boutiquification of Soho and moved Uptown – but the queen of the 80s art boom is still making new art stars. New talent also abounds in the dozen or so galleries located in the glorious art deco Fuller Building. Of particular note is **Robert Miller**, who features an eclectic assortment of modernist photography, classic Modernist painters (like

David Hockney) and cutting-edge Contemporaries (such as Walter Niedermayr). Moving further Uptown, the Upper East Side is home to some of the oldest and best galleries in the city. **Wildenstein & Co**, founded in Paris over 120 years ago, has assembled an inventory of old masters and impressionists which is the envy of the international art world. **C & M Gallery**, meanwhile, specializes in museum-quality exhibitions of classic moderns – sculpture by Maillol and portraits by Picasso. **Gagosian Gallery** houses an assortment of works from the stars of the 80s art explosion, including Eric Fischl and David Salle, while over at **Hirschl & Adler**, Impressionists and American Modernists are kept downstairs and the contemporary artists upstairs. Next door is **Knoedler & Company**, which specializes in sturdy Modernists such as Frank Stella and Helen Frankenthaler. **Salander-O'Reilly**, however, mixes shows of contemporary artists like Elaine de Kooning with retrospectives of work by Courbet and Ralph Albert Blakelock.

C & M Gallery
45 E 78th Street
861-0020

Gagosian Gallery
980 Madison Ave
744-2313

Hirschl & Adler
21 E 70th Street
535-8810

Kennedy Galleries
2nd flr 730 Fifth Ave
541-9600

Knoedler & Co
19 E 70th Street
794-0550

Mary Boone
745 Fifth Avenue 752-2929

PaceWildenstein
32 E 57th Street
421-3292

Robert Miller
41 E 57th Street
980-5454

Salander-O'Reilly
20 E 79th Street
879-6606

Wildenstein & Co
19 E 64th Street
879-0500

Whether you're itching for action on the hardwood or want to take in some hot dogs and sun at the ballpark, NY's got all the bases covered.

↓ a piece of the action

American football

This is a game of testosterone and touchdowns. NY has two teams, the Jets and the Giants, both based at Meadowlands Sports Complex, and each with its own rabid fan base. Tickets are hard to come by for either team. Season: Sep–Dec with the Superbowl played on the 3rd Sun in Jan.

Baseball

Touted as the most American of sports, baseball maintains a strong tradition. New York has two teams, the Yankees and the Mets. The Yankees are the most recognized franchise name in baseball and the Mets (based at the Shea Stadium) are the often the most maligned. Tickets are easy to get and nothing beats the combination of summer sun, beer and baseball. Season: Apr–Oct.

Basketball

Fast and furious, basketball is exciting to watch even if you're not so hot on all the rules. The two men's professional teams in the New York area are the NY Knicker-bockers (Knicks), who play at Madison Square Garden and the New Jersey Nets (based at the Meadowlands Sports Complex). Tickets are expensive and difficult to get hold of. Season: Nov–Jun. Alternatively, go to a women's basketball league game. Tickets for NY Liberty (who play at Madison Square Garden) are reasonably priced, easily available (though book ahead for good seats) and fun. Season: Jun–Sep.

Boxing

A few of the mega-money, bloody bouts take place at Madison Square Garden each year. The Golden Gloves, a NY tradition and amateur boxing's biggest event, takes place every April. Call for ticket prices of individual fights.

Ice hockey

'Went to the fight and a hockey game broke out' is a common description of a night at the rink. Despite the frequent pummellings, hockey is an incredibly swift and often graceful game to watch – if you can keep up with the puck. The three area teams are the New York Rangers (Madison Square Garden), New York Islanders (Nassau Coliseum) and the New Jersey Devils (Meadowlands Sports Complex). It's a popular game and tickets may not be easily available if the team has done well in past seasons. Plan ahead. Season: Oct–Apr.

Tennis

The US Open is the USA's top tennis event and held at the Arthur Ashe Stadium at the end of August or early September. Tickets go on sale from May 31, but are incredibly difficult to get for the big matches. Chance a scalper or try your luck at the Will Call window for corporate tickets that are returned. Madison Square Garden also boasts elite women's international tennis matches (the Chase Championships) held in November. Tickets on sale in April.

Arthur Ashe Stadium
USTA Tennis Center, Flushing, Queens
☎ 1-718-760-6200
Ⓜ 7 to Willets Point-Shea Stadium ▭ $30–$65 ♿

sport

Meadowlands Sports Complex
50 Route 120 N, East Rutherford, New Jersey
☎ 1-201-935-9000
▯ from Port Authority Bus Terminal 42nd St & 8th Ave
American Football: Jets & Giants ▭ $20–$65 ♿
Basketball: Nets ▭ $10–$500 ♿
Ice Hockey: Devils ▭ $20–$65 ♿

Madison Square Garden
W 33rd St & Seventh Ave
☎ 465-6741 Ⓜ A·C·E·1·2·3·9 to 34th St-Penn Station
Basketball: Knicks ▭ $22–$220 ♿ ; Liberty ▭ $8–$55 ♿
Boxing: ▭ $15–$35 for Golden Gloves
Tennis: ▭ $15–$45 ♿
Ice Hockey: Rangers ▭ $22–$65 ♿

Nassau Coliseum
Hempstead Turnpike, Uniondale ☎ 1-516-794-9300
Ⓜ LIRR from Penn Station to Hempstead, then bus N70, N71 or N72 from Hempstead bus terminal (one block away) **Ice Hockey:** Islanders ▭ $19–$60 ♿

Shea Stadium
126th St (at Roosevelt Ave), Queens ☎ 1-718-507-8499
Ⓜ 7 to Willets Point-Shea Stadium ▭ $9–$24 ♿

Yankee Stadium
161st St & River Ave, Bronx
☎ 1-718-293-6000
Ⓜ C·D·4 to 161st St-Yankee Stadium ▭ $12–$23 ♿

Websites
(all preceded by www.)

baseball: sports.excite.com/mlb/
basketball: nba.com (men's) & wnba.com (women's)
boxing and all other Madison Square Garden events: thegarden.com
football nfl.com
horse racing: sports.excite.com/rah/
ice hockey nhl.com
soccer: sports.excite.com/mls/
tennis: sports.excite.com/ten/

booking tickets & what's on

Sports are very popular with the locals so it's best to get tickets as early as possible. Most events can be booked ahead in person, by phone or online with a credit card and collected at the gate. First try the stadium's box office, then call **Ticketmaster** ☎ 307-7171. When all else fails, you can call a ticketing agency such as **Soldout. com** ☎ 1-800-765-3688. Scalping (buying a ticket from an individual, usually on the day of the event outside the arena at an inflated price) is illegal, risky and subject to police crackdowns on the day. If you come up empty handed, simply catch the action on TV or if you'd like some company try one of the sports bars [→130].

The *Daily News*, *NY Post* and *NY Times* all give in-depth coverage and listings of sports as do the local TV newscasts. WFAN radio (660 AM) broadcasts sports talk and play around the clock. For schedule, ticket and seating info look in the front of the *Manhattan Yellow Pages* or go to any team's website through the listed league sites.

↓ turf 'n' surf

When the 24-hour pace gets tough, take a hike into the great urban outdoors: whether it's the planned expanse of Central Park or the ad-hoc gardens of Alphabet City, New Yorkers have an unexpected sense of pastoral pride.

Central Park

Completely man-made, Central Park (lush in summer, bleak in winter) is the quintessential city park. Designed in 1858, with a view to preserve a green space in the heart of Manhattan, it stretches for about 50 blocks, and contains woodland, lawns, bridle trails, plants and ponds – all kept in impressive shapeby the ever present City Parks folk. Cars are allowed on the East and West Drives (just inside the park's periphery): but not between 10am–3pm and 7–10pm Mon–Fri; 7pm Fri–6am Mon, or from 7pm the night before until 6am the day after a public holiday. Distinctive areas, from Strawberry Fields to The Mall, as well as popular landmarks such as the Hans Christian Andersen and Alice in Wonderland statues, are part of the park's unique appeal. Vast and fascinating to explore, it's easy to lose your bearings and so worth remembering the old New Yorker navigation-trick: look at the numbers on the lampposts – they indicate the equivalent street outside the park. (Addresses within the park are given as street coordinates.)

1| Belvedere Lake and Castle
A mock medieval creation at the park's highest point – home of the Park Rangers' HQ and the Meteorological Observatory's weather centre.
2| The Ramble
Scary after dark, but romantic by day. Officially the paths and groves are good for bird watching; but they're also the place for a gay pick up.
3| Strawberry Fields
Yoko Ono's tribute to her late husband who was murdered nearby [→69].
4| The Mall
Ever since amplified sound was welcomed at this spot, it has been a performance mayhem of drummers, mime artists and trick-skaters.
5| Sheep Meadow
In summer, hacky-sack, frisbee and general posing are the order of the day – some even sunbathe topless (now legal in NY State).
6| Rumsey Playfield
Music, spoken word and dance acts take place throughout humid summer months [→137].

🛼 Roller Disco between The Mall & Sheep Meadow.
🎠 The Carousel 64th St at mid park
☎ 879-0244 💲 90¢ ⏲ 10.30am–5pm Mon–Fri; 10.30am–6pm Sat–Sun.
⛸ Wollman Rink [→91].
✗ Loeb boathouse: Fifth Ave & E 74th St
☎ 517-4723 Bike rentals 💲 from $8 per hr. Rowboat & gondola 💲 $10 per hr (plus $30 deposit).
⏲ 10am–5pm daily (summer only).
🐴 Claremont Riding Academy: 175 W 89th St
☎ 724-5100 ⏲ 6.30am–10pm Mon–Fri; 6am–5pm Sat–Sun 💲 $40 per hr (exp. riders only).
☕ Park View at the Boathouse [→124];
Leaping Frog Café.

☎ **Useful Numbers**
Central Park Information: ☎ 360-3444
Central Park Police Precinct: ☎ 570-4820
Visitor centres: The Dairy ☎ 794-6564;
Belvedere Castle ☎ 772-0210 and The Charles A Dana Discovery Center ☎ 860-1370 The Urban Park Rangers offer walking tours, general and emergency assistance in all major Manhattan parks ☎ 628-2345

Battery Park

Battery Park proper occupies the southern tip of Manhattan, and contains the Civil War-era Castle Clinton (now essentially the ticket office for ferries to Liberty and Ellis Islands). Adjoining it, and flanking the Hudson River, is Battery Park City, a former wasteland, today revamped and teeming with life. It encompasses lush grassy areas, an esplanade that is popular for post-brunch strolls, the Museum of Jewish Heritage and, for gawpers, a dock housing millionaires' yachts, on-board helicopters and all.
♫ Gorgeous sunsets; outdoor jazz and blues in the summer.

Battery Place & State St
☎ 797-3143/3133 Ⓜ 4·5 to Bowling Green; 1·9 to South Ferry Ⓢ basketball; cycling, fishing; softball; rollerblading etc

Brooklyn Botanical Gardens

Set back from the sprawling Prospect Park, the Botanical Gardens is a place out of time. In spring the Cherry Orchard, with a variety of cherry trees unmatched outside of Japan, and the Herb Garden with its 300 kinds of fragrant plants, perfume the air. In the winter months the conservatory is a treat; the Tropical Pavilion includes plants from the Amazon basin while the Bonsai Museum has trees over a century in the growing.
♫ The Osbourne Garden's kaleidoscope of colour; the Shakespeare Garden with over 80 species mentioned by the great bard.

900 Washington Ave at E Parkway, Brooklyn
☎ 1-718-623-7200 Ⓜ D·Q to Prospect Park; 2·3 to Eastern Parkway-Brooklyn Museum
💲 $3 adults Ⓞ Apr–Sep: 8am–6pm Tue–Sun (10am Sat–Sun); Oct–Mar: 8am–4.30pm Tue–Sun (10am Sat–Sun).
☞ 1pm Sat–Sun ⚲

Ⓞ free all day Tuesday & 10am–12pm Saturday.

Bryant Park

Being the only open space in this section of Midtown, Bryant Park is very popular with the lunchtime crowd – 'brown-bagging it' as a workers' picnic is known. Its large lawn is enclosed by overflowing flowerbeds and trees; green garden chairs are scattered throughout, and two small concession stands sell over-priced beverages when the weather is good. In the summer the park takes on a life of its own with a boisterous, boozy singles scene at the Bryant Park Grill & Café [→48], and the occasional classical or rock concert. Sitting in the park, surrounded on all sides by skyscrapers, it's amazing to think that less than 180 years ago the site was just a potter's field.
♫ Free movies every Monday night in summer.

Sixth Avenue (at 42nd St), Midtown ☎ 983-4142
Ⓜ N·R·1·2·3·7·9 to 42nd St-Times Sq Ⓞ 24 hours daily. ⚲

Lower East Side Gardens

Birdsong, frog-burps and butterflies – common sights and sounds on a summer's day in the Big Apple? The gardens of Alphabet City defy the cliché of what used to be one of the dodgiest areas in Manhattan. Proudly maintained by the local community groups, there's a garden on almost every block: ponds, stone chess tables and weeping willows offer shady relief from the blaring salsa of the Puerto Rican neighbourhood and heat of the summer.

East Village ☎439-1090
Ⓜ F to 2nd Ave; L·N·R·4·5·6 to 14th St-Union Sq Ⓞ 8am–sundown Sat–Sun. ☞ Big Onion Walking Tours

Prospect Park

Landscaped by the architects who designed Central Park, Brooklyn's Prospect Park has some of the same features – a boating lake, an ice-rink, woodland areas and miles of pedestrian footpaths – but it

also has attributes all of its own. The less manicured fields give it a much more rural feel; there's a stream that runs through a small valley; and areas that can make you feel like an explorer stumbling on uncharted territory. In summer the local neighbourhood residents pour into the park in droves – the BBQ areas are teeming with families of all ethnic diversities and kiteflying, games of soccer and volleyball are open to anyone.
♫ A summer music programme – for details, see listings mags.

Flatbush Ave (at Grand Army Plaza), Brooklyn
☎ 1-718-965-8999 (events hotline) Ⓜ 2·3 to Grand Army Plaza 💲 free Ⓞ dawn–dusk.
Ⓢ soccer, volleyball, etc

beaches

Brighton Beach & Coney Island Beach [→65]

Packed during the summer, but worth it for a juicy slice of Brooklyn life.

Ⓜ B·D·F to Brighton Beach or Stillwell Ave-Coney Island
Ⓞ year round.

Jones Beach

When buying your train ticket, ask for the 'special', which includes the bus ride (approx 15 min) to the beach. The beach bus makes three stops; the first is best for families, the second is more youth-oriented, and the third is less crowded and leads to the gay beach farther down.

Ⓜ LIRR from Penn Station to Freeport, then bus.
Ⓞ Memorial Day–Labor Day.

Robert Moses State Park

The extra 30 min or so on the journey is well worth it to experience the white sands and untouched dunes of Fire Island. It's always pretty mellow, even in the height of summer – and the water is cleaner too.

Ⓜ LIRR from Penn Station to Babylon, then bus to the beach (again, ask for the special).
Ⓞ Memorial Day–Labor Day.

Rockaway Beach

This seven-mile stretch of beach is not necessarily the most beautiful you'll ever see, but it's close to the city and is used mainly by locals.

Ⓜ A·S to any stop along the beach, from Rockaway Park Beach 116th St to Beach 25th St
Ⓞ year round.

Always intense and exciting – from the roar of an urban zoo to the intrigue of a futuristic science centre – NYC is cool for kids. Go have some fun.

↓ kids' corner

kids' eats

Ellen's Stardust Diner

Owned by Ellen Hart, Miss Subway 1959, this vintage subway car-shaped diner with a dinnertime show was made for kids. The food is standard American with cleverly named kids' dishes, inspired by hugely popular kids' TV channel Nickelodeon.

1650 Broadway (at 51st Street), Midtown ☎ 956-5151 🚇 1·9 to 50th St ⏰ 7.30am–midnight Sun–Thu; 7.30–1am Fri–Sat. 🚼 all ages

Two Boots

This is a very family-friendly, funky, eclectic pizzeria with a strong Cajun influence. All kids get colouring books and, depending on age, can even drink from boot-shaped mugs. Specialties include kid-size personalized pizzas, little-tot-size ravioli and the ubiquitous chicken fingers.

37 Avenue A (at 2nd Street), East Village ☎ 505-2276 🚇 F to 2nd Ave ⏰ 12pm–midnight daily. 🚼 all ages

Cowgirl Hall of Fame

Round up those kiddies and bring them to this Western wonderland of cowhide, lassos and steer horns. The full kids' menu with a Tex-Mex, Southern feel, and there's a great room in the back for romping around with other kids, which is stocked with toys and games. Crayons and colouring materials are also available.

519 Hudson Street (at 10th St), West Village ☎ 633-1133 🚇 A·C· E to 14th St; 1·9 to Christopher St ⏰ 12–11pm Sun–Thu; 12pm–midnight Fri–Sat. 🚼 all ages

Serendipity 3

Kids are wild about their dreamy 'frozen hot chocolate', fountain sodas and ice-cream sundaes. The whimsically nostalgic setting also houses a general toy store out front. They serve standard American lunches and dinners, but leave plenty of room for their famously outrageous desserts.

225 E 60th Street (bet. Second & Third Aves), UES ☎ 838-3531 🚇 4·5·6 to 59th St ⏰ 11.30am–midnight daily. 🚼 all ages

animal adventures

Bronx Zoo

This is the largest urban zoo in America with a special children's zoo where kids can try out the exhilarating 'spider web' rope climb and see life underground in the 'prairie dog burrow'. The World of Darkness, full of bats, should also prove a big hit. There are camel rides – and trams, buses, and a monorail offering a narrated journey through Wild Asia make it easy to get around, but it's a big place and may become too much for kids under four.

Bronx River Parkway, Fordham Road, Bronx ☎ 1-718-367-1010 w www.wcs.org 🚇 2 to East Tremont ⏰ $9 adults; $5 2–12 yrs (Wed free); monorail $2 ⏰ 10am–5pm daily (to 5.30pm Sat–Sun). 🚼 all ages ♿

Central Park Wildlife Center

Children can get up close and personal with the wild things at the Petting Zoo in this, the biggest of Manhattan's parks [→84]. They can also look at, but not touch, penguins, puffins, sea lions and monkeys through eye-level Plexiglas. Divided into three zones: the Polar Circle, Temperate Territory and Tropical Zone, the centre's intimate atmosphere and convenient locale make it a fun outdoor fun for some outdoor fun.

Entrance at Fifth Ave & 64th St ☎ 861-6030 w www.central park.org 🚇 N·R to 5th Ave; 6 to 68th St ⏰ $3.50 adults; 50¢ 3–12 yrs ⏰ 10am–5pm Mon–Fri; 10.30am–5.30pm Sat–Sun & Public holidays. 🚼 all ages ♿

New York Aquarium

Kids get the feel of smaller sea-life in the touch pool or marvel at sea-mammal shows held several times daily at the open-air amphitheatre. There are over 10,000 specimens, including such favourites as Beluga whales and dolphins, and interactive displays aimed at kids. The aquarium is situated near the famous Coney Island boardwalk and amusement park – a fascinating slice of Americana – which is an ideal distraction for older children and teens.

W 8th St (at Surf Ave), Coney Island, Brooklyn ☎ 1-718-265-3474 w www.wcs.org/zoos /aquarium 🚇 B·D·F·N to Stillwell Ave, Coney Island ⏰ $9.75 adults; $6 2–12 yrs ⏰ 10am–6pm daily. 🚼 2 & up ♿ 🚼

kid culture

Children's Museum of the Arts

A true celebration of the art of play, this museum allows kids to get to grips with painting, sculpture, theatre, music and even graphic design. Sessions are tailored to match attention-spans and allow children to roam from one interest to the next. There's also an additional infant playroom.

182 Lafayette St (bet. Broome & Grand Sts), Nolita ☎ 941-9198 🚇 6 to Spring St ⏰ $5 (under 12 months free) ⏰ 12–5pm Wed–Sun (to 7pm Wed). 🚼 10 & under 🚼

Children's Museum of Manhattan ⚑

Another interactive museum where children run free and explore myriad make-believe worlds. They can cook green eggs and ham in the area dedicated to Dr Seuss, shoot down an artery in the Body Odyssey or produce their own TV show in the Media Center. With the Winnie the Pooh playland, added attractions for the under fours, storytelling, face painting and theatre, it all makes for an enjoyably full schedule.

212 W 83rd St (bet. Broadway & Amsterdam Ave), UWS ☎ 721-1234 w www.cmoc.org 🚇 1·9 to 86th St ⏰ $5 (under 12 months free) ⏰ 10am–5pm Wed–Sun. 🚼 all ages 🚼

Intrepid Sea Air Space Museum

A 900-ft former aircraft carrier, the Intrepid is the centrepiece of this engrossing

interactive museum, which also features a submarine, helicopters, lunar-landing modules, and simulators. It's packed with displays and models, and anecdotes from retired sea-dogs spice up your visit even more.

Pier 86, W 46th St and 12th Ave ☎ 245-2533 Ⓜ A•C•E to 42nd St. Then M42 bus. 🚇 $10 adults; $7.50 12–17 yrs; $5 6–11 yrs; $1 2–5 yrs. ◑ Apr–Sep 10am–5pm Mon–Fri (6pm Sat–Sun); Oct–Mar 10am–5pm Wed–Sun. 👶 all ages ⓢ 🍴

gifts & goodies

Books of Wonder

This store claims to be the oldest and biggest independent children's bookstore in New York and a real Aladdin's cave it is too. The vast stock of children's literature even includes a foreign language section, and while kids check out their favourites, parents can take a nostalgia trip and peruse the selection of rare and collectible children's books. The store also regularly hosts readings.

16 W 18th St (bet. 5th and 6th Aves), Flatiron District ☎ 989-3270 w www.booksofwonder.com Ⓜ 1•9 to 18th St; 4•5•6•L•N•R to Union Square ◑ 10am–7pm Mon–Sat; 12–6pm Sun. 👶 all ages

Enchanted Forest

Toys Я Art rather than Toys Я Us. Handmade stuffed animals, puppets, masks and instruments are discreetly displayed in the branches of this shop's mock forest. Highly recommended for beautiful, top-quality, one-of-a-kind toys.

85 Mercer St (bet. Spring & Broome Sts), Soho ☎ 925-6677 Ⓜ 6 to Spring St ◑ 11am–7pm Mon–Sat; 12–6 Sun.

FAO Schwarz

The larger-than-life stuffed animals, huge music box-cum-clock and extensive train set will have you and the kids marvelling at this, the grand-daddy of all toy stores. Highly commercial, it has everything a child could want.

767 Fifth Ave (at 58th St), Midtown ☎ 644 9400 Ⓜ E•F•N•R to 5th St ◑ 10am–6pm Mon–Sat (from 11 am Sun).

Penny Whistle Toys

An uptown treasure-trove of time-tested toys for newborns through to teens. Parents will love their high-quality, educational aspects, while the bubble-blowing bears outside and the satisfying toys inside keep the children happy.

448 Columbus Ave (at 81st St), UWS ☎ 873-9090 Ⓜ B•C to 81st St; 1•9 to 79th St ◑ 10am–7pm Mon–Fri (to 6pm Sat); 11am–5pm Sun.

new frontiers

Liberty Science Center

Here, more than 250 scientific exhibits offer kids a chance to touch and test the physical world. Large-scale displays include a geodesic dome, a lighthouse, a solar telescope and a fully-equipped ambulance. Informative staff encourage participation. The museum also houses the largest domed IMAX cinema in the USA. The centre's observation deck offers a pleasant café and great views of Lady Liberty and the city skyline.

251 Philip Street, Jersey City ☎ 1-201-200-1000 w www.lsc.org ⛴ NY Waterway ferry (1-800-533-3779) from World Financial Center to Colgate Piers, then free shuttle bus 🚇 $9.50 adults; $7.50 2–12 yrs; (OMNI) IMAX cinema $2 ◑ 9.30am–5.30pm daily (Sep–Mar closed Mon). 👶 2 & up ⓢ 🍴

Sony Wonder Technology Lab ⓘ

Four floors of hi-tech tinkering, with numerous interactive gadgets from robots to ultrasound scanners. Everyone gets a card-key imprinted with their image, name and voice, which personalizes each of the exhibits when used. Printouts of the experience provide a permanent memento. ◑ Midtown is littered with theme stores and restaurants (Disney, Warner, Niketown, Planet Hollywood et al). Big on razzle dazzle and long lines, they are real black holes of merchandising, but if you can say 'no', the interactive exhibits can be great fun.

550 Madison Ave (at 56th St), Midtown ☎ 833-8100 w www.wondertechlab.com Ⓜ E•F to 5th Ave 🚇 free ◑ 10am–6pm Tue–Sat (to 8pm Thu); 12–6pm Sun. 👶 8 and up ⓢ 🍴

children (sidebar)

show time

Central Park [→84] is packed with free performances during the summer. You can count on both the Crowtations puppet show at Bethesda Fountain, and storytelling at the Hans Christian Andersen statue. For details of all park events call ☎ 794-6564 or 360-3444. The **Swedish Marionette Theater** has year-round indoor shows. If you are looking for big-screen entertainment, Manhattan has two **IMAX** cinemas. Other notable venues include the New **Victory Theater**, with everything from opera for kids to circus; the **Grove Street Playhouse**, which does great adaptations of children's classics; and **Theatreworks/**

USA for wild and witty musicals. For a wide variety of shows from The Wiz to Shakespeare, check out the **New York Youth Theater** and **Here**. Call for showtimes, age recommendations and prices.

Grove Street Playhouse

39 Grove Street (bet. Seventh Ave & Bleecker St) ☎ 741-6436

Here

145 Sixth Avenue (at Spring St) ☎ 647-0202

IMAX

Sony Theater, Broadway (at 68th St) ☎ 336-5000 Naturemax (IMAX), American Museum of Natural History, Central Park West (at 79th St) ☎ 769-5100

New Victory Theater

209 W 42nd Street (bet. Broadway & Eighth Aves) ☎ 382-4000

New York Youth Theater

Central Presbyterian Church, 593 Park Avenue (at 64th St) ☎ 888-0696

Swedish Marionette Theater

Central Park (at 81st St on westside) ☎ 988-9093

Theatreworks/USA

The auditorium at the Equitable Centre, 787 7th Avenue (bet. 51st & 52nd Sts) ◑ Oct–April) ☎ 647-1100

NYC is famous for a lot of things and being peaceful just ain't one of 'em. If you find yourself in need of some pampering, tranquillity, or a place to let it all sweat out, these are some of the best Gotham City has to offer.

↓ feelgood factor

spas & baths

The Avon Center

Given that Avon is a rather old-fashioned name, this place is surprisingly chic – with make-up lessons ($85), applications ($50), and a hair salon. You can get made up for free if you buy a product or have a facial. The whole range of treatments is covered, from half leg wax ($35) to paraffin body wrap ($150).

725 Fifth Avenue (bet. 56th & 57th Sts) ☎ 755-2866 Ⓜ N·R to Lexington Ave; 4·5·6 to 59th St Ⓘ 9am–6pm Mon–Sat (to 8pm Thu). 🚭 AE/MC/V ♿

Bliss ✓

When Uma Thurman, Winona Ryder and Gwyneth Paltrow crave R&R, they hit Bliss, the city's most talked-about and hottest day-spa for men and women. From the buffet of champagne and chocolates, and the lavish boutique of beauty products, to the menu of ultra-luxurious treatments ($50–$225), such as a facial exfoliation with micro-crystals, a 2-hour rub down with crushed ginger and oils, a hot almond-milk pedicure and a mint body mask, the Bliss mantra is simple: indulge! Book anything from 2 weeks to 2 months ahead.

568 Broadway (bet. W Houston & Prince Sts) ☎ 219-8970 w www.blissspa.com Ⓜ N·R to Prince St Ⓘ 9.30am–8.30pm Mon–Sat (to 6.30pm Sat). 🚭 AE/MC/V ♿

Carapan

This is an intimate, sage-scented haven, decked out with rustic furnishings, which aims to heal the body (men's and women's) inside and out. Their specialties are massage, aromatherapy, reflexology and cranio-sacral work ($95 per session).

5 W 16th Street (bet. Fifth & Sixth Aves) ☎ 633-6220 Ⓜ L·N·R·4·5·6 to 14th St; Union Sq Ⓘ 10am–10pm daily. 🚭 AE/MC/V

La Casa de Vida Natural

Shake off your world-weariness and take time out in this exotic day spa's 'rainforest' setting. On top of basic treatments – massage ($70),

body wrap ($75), non-surgical face lift ($75) – you can enjoy flotation ($50 or $25 with any other treatment) or, for something more radical, try flossage, which cleverly combines the benefits of massage and flotation ($65 per hour).

41 E 20th Street (bet. Park Ave S & Fifth Ave) ☎ 673-2272 w www.lacasaspa.com Ⓜ 6 to 23rd St Ⓘ 10am–8pm daily (to 5pm Sat–Mon). 🚭 AE/MC/V

Soho Sanctuary

This women-only day-spa is so tranquil, you'll feel transported. They offer massages and facials (both $95 for one hour), body treatments, yoga and meditation ($20 per class), and perhaps the best steamroom in town (mosaic tiles and delicious herbal scents).

119 Mercer Street (bet. Prince & Spring Sts) ☎ 334-5550 Ⓜ N·R to Prince St; 6 to Spring St Ⓘ 10am–9pm Tue & Thu; 9am–9pm Wed & Fri; 10am–6pm Sat; 12–6pm Sun. 🚭 AE/MC/V ♿

Tenth Street Baths & Health Club

These old Russian baths are the perfect place to flush out all those impurities and toxins. After a session in the traditional steam baths and a plunge in the cool-pool ($20), there's a choice of rigorous massages ($45 per hour), Dead Sea mud treatments or even a spot of flagellation with genuine dried oak branches (call to check prices). No pain no gain, as they say. Mixed most days or for the full frontal experience, ladies' day is on Wednesdays, and men's day on Sundays.

268 E 10th Street (bet. Ave A & First Ave) ☎ 473-8806 Ⓜ L to 1st Ave Ⓘ 10am–10pm daily. 🚭 MC/V

fitness & dance

Crunch

These gyms are known for their 'no judgements' policy, so leave your self-consciousness behind. At the Lafayette Street locale, which is by far the biggest, there are 2 floors of cardio equipment, a boxing ring, tanning facilities and

fun classes like firefighter training (a real firefighter has you lugging hoses and dragging bodies). It's $22 per day whatever you choose to do, but don't sweat at the price, they have state-of-the-art machinery to make the most of your work-out.

404 Lafayette Street (bet. E 4th St & Astor Pl) ☎ 614-0120 Ⓜ 6 to Astor Pl Ⓘ 24 hours Mon–Fri; closes 9pm Sat; 8am–9pm Sun. 🚭 all ♿

162 W 83rd Street (bet. Amsterdam & Columbus Aves) ☎ 875-1902 Ⓜ 1·9 to 86th St Ⓘ 6am–11pm Mon–Thu (to 10pm Fri); 8am–9pm Sat–Sun. 🚭 all ♿

Fred Astaire Dance Studio

To pick up some smooth moves – swing, ballroom, Latin, waltz, tango, foxtrot, rumba or cha-cha-cha – you'll need to take a few lessons ($25 each). Call ahead to fit into a programme of classes or, for more instant success, a private session ($88). Don't expect a grand setting – facilities are basic.

666 Broadway (bet. Bond & Bleecker Sts) ☎ 475-7776 Ⓜ 6 to Bleecker St Ⓘ 1–10.30pm Mon–Fri; 12.30–6pm Sat. 🚭 AE/MC/V

697 E 43rd Street (at Second Ave) ☎ 697-6535 Ⓜ 4·5·6·7 to Grand Central–42nd St Ⓘ 1.30–10.30pm Mon–Fri; 11am–5pm Sat. 🚭 AE/MC/V

Power Pilates

The business of stretching the body and releasing toxins and fluids is really hot, and Pilates is one of the latest ways for the supermodels and celebs to get fit. The rigorous mat-based classes last an hour ($15) or you can have a semi-private (3 people) machine session for $40, or a one-to-one for $65–$100.

49 W 23rd St, 10th floor (bet. Fifth & Sixth Aves) ☎ 627-5852 Ⓜ N•R•6 to 23rd St ◑ 7am–9pm Mon–Fri (to 8pm Thu); 9am–3pm Sat; 10am–4pm Sun. 🚫 MC/V

Revolution

Sans frills and fancy stuff, Revolution is exactly what a gym is supposed to be – a place to sweat. Classes range from spinning (static cycling), boxing and body-conditioning to the more eclectic holistic self-defence, Thai kickboxing, and strength and alignment sessions. Just pay by the class ($15). And if you're looking for some personal attention, they have some of the most educated and bodily aware trainers in the business.

❶ BYOT (towel)!

104 W 14th Street (bet. Sixth & Seventh Aves) ☎ 206-8785 Ⓜ L•N•R•4•5•6 to 14th St-Union Sq ◑ 6am–10pm Mon–Fri; 8am–4pm Sat–Sun. 🚫 all ♿

alternative therapies

Jivamukti

Anyone hooked on yoga will dig this huge centre ($15 for any class, including astanga, and their unique jivamukti yoga). The peaceful setting is complete with a waterfall, pastel-painted rooms, each with an incense-laden altar, and a boutique dedicated to satisfying your spiritual needs – incense, books, clothes, music etc. Keep your eyes peeled – you might be contorting next to Sting.

404 Lafayette Street, 3rd floor (at E 4th St) ☎ 353-0214 Ⓜ B•D•F•Q to Broadway-Lafayette St; 6 to Astor Pl ◑ 6.45am–10pm daily. 🚫 all ♿

Open Center

This is a serene oasis in which to learn the arts of belly-dancing, yoga, tai chi, martial arts, astrology and more at the centre's lectures, seminars and cool classes. There's also a free meditation room (donations welcome).

83 Spring Street (bet. Crosby St & Broadway) ☎ 219-2527 Ⓜ N•R to Prince St; 6 to Spring St ◑ 10am–10pm daily (to 6pm Sun). 🚫 AE/MC/V ♿

Osaka Health Center

One of the best remedies for an achy body is a shiatsu massage. The approach of this parlour is pretty intense – there are ropes above the tables for therapists to hold on to while they walk on your back and dig their toes into your pressure points – but it's worth it ($50–$100, including hot and cold tub, and sauna).

50 W 56th Street (bet. Fifth & Sixth Aves) ☎ 956-3422 Ⓜ N•R to 57th St ◑ 10am–midnight daily. 🚫 AE/MC/V

beauty treatments

J Sisters

Famous for their pedicures (for $55 they'll even dig and get rid of in-grown toe-nails), and bikini wax service ($45), this glam venue has professionals who'll go places your partner wouldn't!

35 W 57th Street (bet. Fifth & Sixth Aves) ☎ 750-2485 Ⓜ B•N•Q•R to 57th St ◑ 9am–5.30pm Tue–Sat (to 7.30pm Wed–Thu). 🚫 MC/V ♿

Ling

The shape of your brows can make or break your face. Ling's got the best eyebrow 'designers' in town. They do all the models and actors and know how to sculpt the perfect arch ($22).

12 E 16th Street (bet. Fifth & Sixth Aves) ☎ 989-8833 Ⓜ N•R•L•4•5•6 to 14th St-Union Sq; F to 14th St; L to 6th Ave ◑ 10am–7pm Mon–Fri; 9.30am–5pm Sat. 🚫 all ♿

The Service Station

The man in the street is taking better care of himself these days, and the Service Station is here to make sure it's a pleasurable experience. Kitted out like an old gas station, this is the original pampering place for men (although some women come too). They do tanning, massage ($65 per hour), manicures ($10), pedicures ($20) and hair ($35 for men; $45 for women).

137 Eighth Avenue (at 16th St) ☎ 243-7770 Ⓜ A•C•E to 14th St; L to 8th Ave ◑ 10am–10pm Mon–Sat; 12–8pm Sun. 🚫 AE/MC/V

hair care

Devachan

Having a haircut at Devachan – an airy Soho loft – is a spiritual experience… It all starts when they get you to lie down on a massage table, while they shampoo and give you a 10-min head massage ($60–$125 for cut; $65 and up for colour).

❶ If you have curly hair, try to see the owner Lorraine – she'll teach you how to 'cultivate your curls'.

558 Broadway (bet. Prince & Spring Sts) ☎ 274-8686 Ⓜ N•R to Prince St; 6 to Spring St ◑ 11am–7.30pm Tue–Fri; 10am–10pm Sat. 🚫 AE/MC/V

Jerry's Men's Hair Styling Salon

An old-school barbers, Jerry's provides shaves (with a steam towel), shoe shines, hair cuts ($20) and manicures. Walk in scruffy and leave like a gentleman.

635 Fifth Avenue (in the Rockefeller Center) ☎ 246-3151 Ⓜ B•D•F•Q to 47–50th Sts; Rockefeller Ctr; 6 to 51st St ◑ 8am–6pm Mon–Fri. 🚫 AE ♿

Mark Garrison Salon

This is as far away as you can get from the trad East Village hole-in-the-wall salon, where the specialty is usually crazy colour and funky cuts. One of the most chichi spots in town, this salon is beautiful, posh and a real indulgence. They'll give you that perfect cut (approx $100) and change your hair forever. For a true splurge, see Mark for $200.

820 Madison Ave (at 67th St) ☎ 570-2455 Ⓜ 6 to 68th St-Hunter College ◑ 9am–6pm Mon–Sat (to 8pm Tue & Thu). 🚫 MC/V

body art

Body Adorned

Looking to decorate your skin with some piercings or tattoos? Then head for the East Village. This neighbourhood is loaded with little haunts, but the ultra-hygienic Body Adorned is an especially friendly set-up. They have design books you can sift through for tattoo inspiration, and the professional artists (some of the most talented in town) will give you their advice before inflicting pain. Aside from tattoos (prices start at $75), they also have mendhei painters ($20 for a hand print), and a piercing service.

47 Second Avenue (bet. 2nd & 3rd Sts) ☎ 473-0007 Ⓜ F to 2nd Ave ◑ 1–8pm Sun–Thu (to 10pm Fri–Sat). 🚫 all ♿

body & soul

You might have been there or done that, but to get the feel of the city, open wide and really get your teeth into the Big Apple by joining the locals (plus those who long to be) at play...

↓ have a blast

Bowling

You can bowl your heart out all day long in the Big Apple, but for a different spin, why not 'rock 'n' bowl' at **Bowlmor Lanes** (Mon 10pm–4am) with Night Strike, NY's premier 'lights out' neon bowling party for the over-18's. Or, at **AMS Chelsea Bowl**, try 'extreme bowling'. When the lights go out, pins and balls go day-glo and you're surrounded by a laser light show. There's also a huge video games room.

Bowlmor Lanes
110 University Pl (at E 13th St) ☎ 255-8188 Ⓜ L•N•R•4•5•6 to 14th St–Union Sq ⎈ $4.95 per game Mon–Fri ($12 unlimited games Mon 10pm–4am); $6.45 Sat–Sun; Shoe rental $3. ◐ 10–1am daily (to 4am Mon & Fri–Sat; to 2am Thu). ⚐ ♻

AMS Chelsea Bowl
Pier 60 (bet. 20th St & Twelfth Ave) ☎ 835-2695 Ⓜ C•E to 23rd St ⎈ $7 per game; Shoe rental $4 ◐ 9am–midnight (to 4am Fri–Sat). ⚐ ♻

Chess ⚑

For activity of a more cerebral kind, bring or pair up with a chess partner at **Chess Forum**. You can even brush up on your moves beforehand with a private lesson or two. However, the quintessential NY chess experience is to challenge one of the local chess masters/hustlers who hang out in **Washington Square Park**. Should they suggest a wager, and you win the first game, it might be best to quit while you're ahead; there are a lot of scam artists out there...

Chess Forum
219 Thompson Street (bet. W 3rd & Bleecker Sts) ☎ 475-2369 Ⓜ A•B•C•D•E•F•Q

to W 4th St–Washington Sq ⎈ $1; private lessons $25 per hour ◐ 11–3.30am daily. ♻ ♻

Washington Square Park
Ⓜ A•B•C•D•E•F•Q to W 4th St–Washington Sq

Coney Island [→65]

The masses started coming to Coney Island in the early 1900s, and this Brooklyn outpost is still a great bet for an afternoon of amusement and some summer fun. Visit the 150ft-high Wonder Wheel (built in 1920) or the world-famous **Astroland**, home of the Cyclone (built in 1927), a 100-second, nine-hill roller-coaster ride that does its best to make you lose your cool – and your lunch. **Sideshows by the Seashore** is the last remaining 10-in-1 (10 acts, one admission price) sideshow in the US; expect bearded ladies, sword-swallowers and escape artists.

Astroland Amusement Park
1000 Surf Ave (at W 10th St) ☎ 1-718-372-0275 Ⓜ B•D•N•F to Stillwell Ave–Coney Island ⎈ $12.99 for unlimited major rides; single rides $1.75–$4 ◐ Memorial Day–Labor Day: 12pm–midnight daily. ♻

Sideshows by the Seashore
1208 Surf Ave (at W 12th St) ☎ 1-718-372-5159 Ⓜ B•D•F•N to Stillwell Ave–Coney Island ⎈ $3 ◐ May 1–Memorial Day: 1pm–midnight, Sat–Sun; Memorial Day–Labor Day: 2–10pm Fri; 1pm–midnight Sat–Sun; 2–8pm public holidays. ♻

Dance

For a full evening's entertainment, take advantage of the fact that swing is the hottest thing to hit the dance scene since Saturday Night Fever. At the **Supper Club**, zoot suits are prevalent and big bands

blast until the small hours. Before or after an optional dinner, you can practise your footwork in the lavish ballroom setting. Beginners, relax – you can pick up lessons. On your own-eo? No sweat, there's a hopping singles scene. And if you can't wait for the weekend, try the **Swing 46 Jazz & Supper Club**, where there are more live big band sounds to help you 'get hip, get hep, get right in step'.

Supper Club
240 W 47th Street (bet. Broadway & Eighth Ave) ☎ 921-1940 Ⓜ 1•9 to 50th St ⎈ $20 ($25 before 8pm) ◐ 5.30pm–4am Fri–Sat.

Swing 46 Jazz & Supper Club
349 W 46th Street (bet. Eighth & Ninth Aves) ☎ 262-9554 ⓦ www.swing46.com Ⓜ 1•9 to 50th St ⎈ $7 Sun–Wed, $12 Thu–Sat. Price includes free class at 11pm. ◐ 12pm–4am daily. ⚐ ♻

Games & Sports

A less frenetic game of pool or ping-pong might be more up your street. If so, **Fat Cat Billiards** is the real deal – a dingy hole-in-the-wall where you can kick back, shoot pool, slap a ping-pong ball around (with a net surround for minimum effort) and nurse a beer for hours. Or, with a more up-to-date take on games, **XS New York** is cyber heaven for those who digg state-of-the-art virtual reality games and simulated sports. You might not want to eat lunch before you climb into the simulated airplane/spaceship 'M4' or 'Indy 500 racecar' with surround sound and slam-bam realistic movement. Lazer Tag beckons in the basement. But if virtual thrills aren't your thing, try the awesome outdoor experience offered by **ParaSail NYC**. After a quick intro on the speedboat, you'll be strapped into a parachute harness and, before you know it, you're up and away, gliding 300 ft above the Hudson river. This exhilarating ride is the most unique way to spot the sights and take in Downtown's magnificent skyline. You can even fly with a friend to share the experience.

Fat Cat Billiards
75 Christopher Street (at Seventh Ave) ☎ 675-6056 Ⓜ 1•9 to Christopher St ⎈ $3.75 per hour per player. ◐ 2pm–2am daily. ⚐ ♻

ParaSail NYC

Liberty Harbor Marina, opposite the World Financial Center ☎ 490-9375 w www.parasailnyc.com Ⓜ C•E to World Trade Center 💲 $49 per person for a 10–15-min flight. ❶ May–Oct: 11am–nightfall daily. ♿

XS New York

1450 Broadway (bet. 41st & 42nd Sts) ☎ 398-5467 Ⓜ N•R• 1•2•3•7•9 to 42nd St-Times Sq 💲 video and virtual reality games $1.50–$5; Internet access $4.20 for 20 min. ❶ 12–10pm daily (to 2am Fri–Sat) (over 18's only after 8pm). ♿ ☃

Showtime

For a Chinese meal that's a little out of the ordinary, try **Lucky Chengs**, where their specialty is service with a song. There are nine cabaret shows a night (7.30, 8.30 and 10pm). If you're (un)lucky, your waitress may put whipped cream all over you and then lick it off, dance on your table and generally slither sexily around the room! If that's not your bag, there's **Kabuki Karaoke** downstairs. The service is fun, but the food… well, you don't come for the food. **Lips** will also give you a good lip sync show and better than average American cuisine. The ambience is laid-back downtown – banquettes, sofas and sexy red lights. Don't get too ga ga over your outrageously leggy waitress at either place, she's really a man in drag.

Lucky Chengs

24 First Ave (bet 1st & 2nd Sts) ☎ 473-0516 Ⓜ F to 2nd Ave 💲 appetizers $5–$11; entrées $12–$23 ❶ 6pm–2am (food served 'til midnight) daily. ♿

Lips

4 Bank Street (bet. Greenwich Ave & Waverly Pl) ☎ 675-7710 Ⓜ 1•2•3•9 to 14th St-Union Sq 💲 average meal: $30 (with appetizer and drink) ❶ 5.30pm–midnight Mon–Thu (to 1am Fri–Sat); 11.30am–4.30pm Sun brunch. ♿

Skate City

Ice-skating is big in NYC, and the city has several rinks. In Central Park [→84] is the secluded **Wollman Rink**, offering the great outdoors, music and, if you're looking and lucky, a little romance. It's especially busy at weekends during the Christmas season . The park is also prime rollerblading territory (especially in summer), but if you feel like taking to the streets with a crowd, join the huge number of bladers who gather on Wednesday evenings (summer months only) in Union Square for the weekly ritual.

Turn back the clock and head to the **Roxy**, a dance club where they turn the floor into a roller-rink on Wednesday nights. The DJ spins 70s and 80s disco tunes while some of the best skaters around trip the light fantastic. Even if you're not so hot on wheels, you'll appreciate others' talents – and it's a crazy flashback to headbands, glitter and bad hair. For 21's and over.

Union Square Mass Blade: meet by the parking lot on the east side of the square Ⓜ L•N•R•4•5•6 to Union Sq-14th St ❶ 8pm Wed.

The Roxy

515 W 18th Street (bet. Tenth & Eleventh Aves) ☎ 645-5156 Ⓜ A•C•E to 14th St 💲 $15 plus $5 for skate hire; $10 for blade hire. ❶ 8pm–2am daily. ▫

Wollman Rink

Park entrance at 59th St and Sixth Ave ☎ 396-1010 Ⓜ N•R to 5th Ave 💲 $7 (6–9.30pm Wed $3.50); $4 skate hire. ❶ Nov–Mar: 10am–3pm daily to 9.30pm Wed; to 5pm Thu; to 11pm Fri–Sat; to 9pm Sun). ❶ swing night (7–9pm Thu) with 30-min lesson. Adults only 💲 $15

Travel in Style

Who wouldn't willingly part with a few extra dollars to live the life of a celebrity For a few hours you can, by cruising Manhattan in the ultimate luxury, the stretch limo. Dress up, bring your friends – and pretend.

Smith Limousine Service

☎ 247-0711 💲 $70 per hour for 6 passengers (minimum 2 hours after 6pm); $85 per hour for 8 passengers plus tips, tolls and expenses.

Delancey Car Service

☎ 228-3301 💲 $50 per hour (minimum 2 hours) ❶ bring your own booze.

TV Heaven

Find yourself lamenting those missed episodes of *Baywatch* or wishing to revisit your childhood and favourite *Lost in Space* show? Run, don't walk, to the world's most comprehensive collection of TV shows and radio clips at the **Museum of Television and Radio**. Around 100,000 programmes are available for private viewing or listening on individual consoles, and you can see everything from a classic *I Love Lucy* to a wrap up of this year's Super Bowl commercials. There are also daily screenings and seminars in the museum's two screening rooms.

Museum of Television and Radio

25 W 52nd Street (bet. Fifth & Sixth Aves) ☎ 621-6800 Ⓜ E•F to 53rd St; N•R to 49th St; 1•9 50th St; B•D•F•Q to 47th-50th Sts at Rockefeller Center 💲 $6 ❶ 12–6pm Tue–Sun (to 8pm Thu; to 9pm Fri for screenings only). ♿ ▯

---

lottery

The New York State Lottery offers 10 different games to gamble with and you can grab a ticket in over 6500 locations citywide – look for the yellow and blue Lottery sign. Some games are more popular than others: if you need instant gratification, try the $1 and $2 scratch cards – the overall chances are 1 in 6, and you can win anything from $2 to $1 million. On Mon, Tue, Thu and Fri, a $1 TAKE 5 offers you a 1 in 9 chance of winning prizes worth up to $300,000. Choose five numbers

and watch ABC TV (Channel 7) at 11.21pm to see if your numbers come up. If you want the big bucks, play $1 LOTTO on Wed and Sat where the jackpot prize starts at $3 million. If no one wins, the winnings go up to $8, $12 and then $25 million. So what if the odds of winning the jackpot are only 1 in 12,913,583! You must be 18 or older to participate.

☎ 383-1300 for information on claiming prizes and checking numbers.

new york's top shopping zones

directory (downtown–uptown)

West Broadway (bet. Varick & Reade Sts) ⚑B6: Cutting-edge home furnishings and interesting up-and-coming designers.

Franklin Street (bet. Broadway & Church St) ⚑B6: More cutting-edge home furnishings and interesting up-and-coming designers.

Canal Street (bet. Bowery & West Broadway) ⚑B6–C6: Street vendors selling all manner of fruit and veg, knock-off designer watches and bags, cheap and gold jewellery, electronics, and the Pearl River Mart [→105].

Broadway (bet. Canal & Houston Sts) ⚑B6: Below Houston are superstores like Banana Republic and Sephora, plus lots of sportswear stores selling cut-price sneakers and trainers.

Houston to Grand Street (bet. Broadway & Bowery) ⚑B6–C6: The moment's hottest one-off boutiques, young designers, precious accessories stores, and some very cool home furnishings.

Houston to Canal Street (bet. Broadway & Sullivan St) ⚑B6: Peppered with major international designers from Anna Sui [→95] to Yohji Yamamoto [→97], upscale home furnishing stores, unique boutiques and commercial art galleries.

Ludlow and Orchard Streets (bet. Delancey & Houston Sts) ⚑C6: One-off boutiques selling cool clothing as well as vintage stores and record shops, plus traditional bargain vendors selling cut-price leather goods, bags and sportswear. There's a

▨ Lower East Side & Chinatown [→8–11]

▨ Tribeca [→12–14]

▨ Soho [→15–20]

▨ Nolita & Noho [→21–25]

▨ East Village [→26–31]

▨ West Village [→32–36]

▨ Chelsea District [→37–41]

▨ Gramercy Park & the Flatiron District [→42–45]

▨ Midtown & Hell's Kitchen [→46–51]

▨ Upper East Side [→52–55]

▨ Upper West Side [→56–58]

▨ Harlem & the Heights [→59–61]

▨ Brooklyn [→62–65]

Sunday market for bags, toys, general accessories like T-shirts and socks on Orchard Street.

Lafayette Street (bet. Spring & Houston Sts) ⚑C6: Cool clothing boutiques which cater to a young, downtown crowd. Vintage home furnishing stores selling Americana.

Broadway (bet. Houston & 12th Sts) ⚑B5: More sportswear and clothing boutiques, Tower Records and good bookstores like Shakespeare and Co, and Strand.

Christopher Street (bet. Sixth Ave & Bleecker St) ⚑B5: Erotic boutiques, gift stores and interesting one-offs.

Bleecker Street (bet. Hudson St & Sixth Ave) ⚑B5: Interesting one-off boutiques, some record stores, food shops.

Sixth Avenue (bet. 12th & W 4th Sts) ⚑B5: Historic stores like Balducci's [→108] and Bigelow's [→103], and chains like Urban Outfitters and Foot Locker.

E 7th Street (bet. Ave A & Second Ave) ⚑C5: Interesting one-offs, vintage furnishings, funky gift boutiques, cool clothing stores with a boho edge.

8th Street (bet. Broadway & Sixth Ave) ⚑B5: Shoes of all descriptions.

St Mark's Place (bet. Second & Third Aves) ⚑C5: Record stores, vendors selling cheap jewellery and sunglasses.

Chelsea (bet. 22nd & 24th Sts) ⚑A4: A burgeoning commercial gallery scene, plus radical chic from the Comme des Garçons boutique [→95] and Jeffrey's department store [→94].

E 9th Street (bet. Ave A & Second Ave) ⚑C5: More interesting one-offs, vintage furnishings, funky gift boutiques, and cool clothing stores with a boho edge.

Avenue A (bet. E 2nd & E 9th Sts) ⚑C5: One-off kooky gift boutiques and home accessories stores.

Broadway (bet. 12th & 14th Sts) ⚑B5: A cluster of antique stores.

Fifth Avenue (bet. 14th & 30th Sts) ⚑B4–B5: Interesting lesser known designer stores like Paul Smith [→97] and Intermix, big name chains such as Zara and Banana Republic, designer emporiums like Armani.

Broadway (bet. Union Sq & 23rd St) ⚑C4: One of a kind superstores like Paragon sports [→102] and ABC Carpet and Home [→104], with the emphasis firmly on home furnishings.

Sixth Avenue (bet. 17th & 26th Sts) ⚑B4: Megastores like Bed Bath and Beyond [→104], discount stores like Daffy's [→100].

W 18th and W 19th Streets (bet. Fifth & Sixth Aves) ⚑B4: Bookstores for new and used books, including Barnes & Noble [→106].

W 25th and W 26th Streets (around Sixth Ave) ⚑B4: Antique showrooms and the Annex Flea Market [→109].

W 28th Street (bet. Broadway & Seventh Ave) ⚑B4: Flower shops.

Sixth Avenue (bet. 30th & 36th Sts) ⚑B3 and **34th Street** (bet. Madison & Sixth Aves) ⚑B3: Around Herald Square are Macy's department store [→94], the Manhattan Mall, HMV, and sportswear chain stores like Footlocker and Modell's.

W 47th Street (bet. Fifth & Sixth Aves) ⚑B2: The jewellery stores of the Diamond District and the Gotham Book Mart.

Fifth Avenue (bet. 48th & 59th Sts) ⚑B2: Department stores like Saks Fifth Avenue [→94] and Bergdorf Goodman [→94], designer flagships like Gucci, Prada and Versace, the Gap flagship, historic one-of-a-kind stores like Tiffany's, and theme stores like the Disney Store [→102].

57th Street (bet. Madison & Seventh Aves) ⚑B2: Theme stores like Niketown [→102] and Warner Bros Studio Store [→102], commercial galleries, and Rizzoli book store.

Lexington Avenue (bet. 57th & 64th Sts) ⚑C1–C2: Bloomingdales [→94], the Diesel and Zara flagships, chain stores like Banana Republic, Express and Nine West shoes.

Madison Avenue (bet. 57th & 74th Sts) ⚑C1–C2: Every name designer in the known universe from Prada and Versace to Chlöe and Calvin Klein. Major designer 'event' flagships like the Ralph Lauren mansion [→96], cool department stores like Barneys New York [→94].

Columbus Avenue (bet. Broadway & 81st St) ⚑A1: Chains like Barnes & Noble and Gap. Interesting boutiques selling kids clothes and home furnishings.

125th Street (bet. Fifth & Eighth Aves) ⚑off map: Bargain stores, sportswear chains, ethnic stores, and the Studio Museum store.

getting your bearings

NYC, the epicentre of the shopping universe, has everything from couture to sneakers. If you can't find it here, you won't find it anywhere...

retail therapy

↓ department stores

Barney's New York

Working for one of NY's premier style bastion, Barney's brilliant buyers continue to seek out the very best in modern design. Fashion-forward clothing by such luminaries as McQueen and Margiela line the racks upstairs. On the ground floor the collection of accessories is breathtaking, and the two shoe departments hold some of the most interesting footwear around. The annual warehouse sale is as anticipated by New Yorkers as fireworks on the Fourth of July. $$$

660 Madison Ave (at 61st St) ☎ 826-8900 Ⓜ E•F•N•R to 5th Ave ◑ 10am–8pm Mon–Sat (to 7pm Sat); 12–6pm Sun. ▱ AE/MC/V

Bergdorf Goodman

For pure elegance, the one and only Bergdorf's is hard to top. Exclusives by designers such as Philip Treacy and Jo Malone attract fashionistas here like bees to a honey pot. But don't be intimidated by the big names, there are inspiring lines of casualwear and accessories too. The men's version is across the street. $$$

754 Fifth Ave (at 58th St) ☎ 753-7300 Ⓜ N•R to 5th Ave ◑ 10am–6pm Mon–Sat (to 8pm Thu; to 7pm Sat). ▱ AE/MC/V

Bloomingdale's

Bloomie's has seen better days, but it's making an effort to catch up fashion-wise by including some high-end urban-wear by the likes of Sean John, aka Puff Daddy. It is still also a key destination for New Yorkers looking for home furnishings. Make sure you check out the Barbie Boutique on the fifth floor, and the in-store chocolate factory on the sixth. $$–$$$

1000 Third Ave (at 59th St) ☎ 355-5900 Ⓜ N•R to Lexington Ave; 4•5•6 to 59th St ◑ 10am–8.30pm Mon–Sat (to 7pm Sat); 11am–7pm Sun. ▱ AE/MC/V

Jeffrey

Jeffrey Kalinsky, the ex shoe-buyer at Barneys, has built up a huge following, with this 18,000 sq-ft repository of designer clothes, shoes, accessories and home products. Jil Sander, Helmut Lang and Alexander McQueen are all on board.

The store also carries its very own private unisex label: KR. The prices may be high, but can you put a cost on style? $$–$$$

449 W 14th Street (at Ninth Ave) ☎ 206-1272 Ⓜ A•C•E•L to 14th St ◑ 10am–8pm Mon–Sat (to 9pm Thu; to 7pm Sat); 12.30–6pm Sun. ▱ AE/MC/V

Macy's

Famous for its sponsorship of the annual Thanksgiving Day parade [→147], Macy's also claims to be the world's largest department store. There's virtually nothing you can't buy here. With brand names ranging from Armani to Zenith, as well as cheaper, casual lines, Macy's covers all the bases. The Cellar, in the basement of course, carries home furnishings and there's also Eatzi's, an excellent deli. Don't miss Macy's notorious one-day sales. $$–$$$

151 W 34th St (bet. Seventh Ave & Broadway) ☎ 695-4400 Ⓜ B•D•F•N•Q•R to 34th St-Herald Sq ◑ 10am–8.30pm Mon–Sat; 11am–7pm Sun. ▱ AE/MC/V

Saks Fifth Avenue

Historic Saks should be visited as much for its famed Fifth Avenue setting as anything else. Best for top-of-the-line custom menswear and the exhaustive (and exhausting) bridal section, but the shoe and lingerie departments are loaded with treasures too. Also worth discovering is the surprisingly cutting-edge women's fashion on the fifth floor. $$–$$$

611 Fifth Ave (bet. 49th & 50th Sts) ☎ 753-4000 ◑ 10am–7pm Mon–Sat (to 8pm Thu; to 6pm Sat); 12–6pm Sun. Ⓜ B•D•F•Q to 47–50th Sts-Rockefeller Center; E•F to 53rd St ▱ all

Takashimaya

A very elegant Japanese department store, where every object has been carefully chosen. Whether you are looking for the perfect tea service, elegant home furnishings or an opulent piece of clothing, this is your store. The jungle-like garden shop on the ground floor is filled with fresh flowers by Christian Tortu, and the tea room in the basement is appropriately serene. $$–$$$

693 Fifth Ave (bet. 54th & 55th Sts) ☎ 350-0100 Ⓜ F to 53rd St ◑ 10am–7pm Mon–Sat. ▱ all

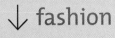
↓ fashion

for men & women

Anna Sui

Always young, fresh, fun and more than a little bit rock 'n' roll, Anna Sui's purple boutique in Soho is filled with clothes for the sartorially courageous, including a small men's collection popular with rock stars and male models. All of this NY designer's leather coats are perfection, her shoes are the funkiest, and the accessories legendary. Recently, Sui's own make-up line (including lots of sparkly nailpolish) has been added to the mix. $$

113 Greene St (bet. Prince & Spring Sts)
☎ 941-8406 Ⓜ N·R to Prince St ◐ 12–7pm daily (to 6pm Sun). 🚗 AE/MC/V

APC

The high-style basics from this French design company keep all those fashion-insider types well-dressed. Classically-cut clothes are made in interesting, contemporary fabrics. Even the T-shirts and underwear are luxe. $$

131 Mercer St (bet. Prince & Spring Sts)
☎ 966-0069 Ⓜ N·R to Prince St ◐ 11am–7pm Mon–Sat; 12–6pm Sun. 🚗 AE/MC/V

Calvin Klein

In Klein's spartan house of minimalist chic, designed by Brit architect John Pawson, you'll find the full complement of the designer's unfussy, clean-lined clothing. Also here is the cheaper CK line, a wide range of accessories (including a new handbag collection), plus the latest bed and bath range from one of America's favourite designers. $$–$$$

654 Madison Ave (at E 60th St) ☎ 292-9000 Ⓜ 4·5·6 to 59th St ◐ 10am–6pm Mon–Sat (to 8pm Thu); 12–6pm Sun. 🚗 AE

Comme des Garçons

The far west Chelsea shop of these fashion pioneers is as happening as many of the area's trendy art galleries. The beautifully-made clothes are always experimental and while all this fabulousness doesn't come cheap, Rei Kawakubo's brilliance makes every piece highly-collectible. $$$

520 W 22nd St (bet. Tenth & Eleventh Aves)
☎ 604-9200 Ⓜ C·E to 23rd St ◐ 11am–7pm Tue–Sat; 12–6pm Sun. 🚗 all

Costume National

In a store that looks like the inside of a very dark, monochrome space ship, Ennio Capasso's clothes are streamlined, sexy and artistic. While the fashion is pure genius, everybody really wants the shoes. Terminally trendy, the men's styles, especially, are unique and very flattering. $–$$$

108 Wooster St (bet. Prince & Spring Sts)
☎ 431-1530 Ⓜ N·R to Prince St; C·E to Spring St ◐ 11am–7pm Mon–Sat; 12–6pm Sun. 🚗 all

Diesel

The riotous Diesel flagship can sometimes seem as surreal as those ubiquitous adverts. Amidst the loud music and the 'art exhibits', you'll find urban, streetwise clothes that are casual with a cutting-edge twist. Even the underwear is trendy. Take a break from it all at the in-store café. $$

770 Lexington Ave (at 60th St)
☎ 308-0055 Ⓜ N·R to Lexington Ave-59th St ◐ 10am–8pm Mon–Sat; 12–6pm Sun. 🚗 all

DKNY

Donna Karan's flagship is just across the street from her all-American rival Calvin Klein. This is where she keeps her younger, DKNY line – the shapes borrow from classic sportwear silhouettes and the T-shirts make a great NY souvenir. $$

655 Madison Avenue (at 60th St)
☎ 223-3569 Ⓜ 4·5·6 to 59th St ◐ 10am–7pm Mon–Sat (to 9pm Thu); 12–6pm Sun. 🚗 all

DL. Cerney

Based mostly on vintage wear from the 40's, 50's and 60's, the collection here features casual, inexpensive, and well-cut clothing in good fabrics. Strong on hand-tailored shirts, an essential basic, as well as blazers, fitted pants, and lots of feminine shift dresses. $–$$

222 West Broadway (bet. White & Franklin Sts)
☎ 941-0530 Ⓜ 1·9 to Franklin St; A·C·E to Canal St ◐ 12–7pm Mon–Sat (from 11am Sat). 🚗 AE/MC/V

Dolce & Gabbana

The Italian design duo's fabulously sexy clothing will bring out the Sophia Loren (or Marcello Mastroanni) in you. Choose between the glamorous, high-end label, or the 'cheaper' D & G line which repeats themes from the uptown collection like lavish embroidery and flashy metallics: Each collection has its own store. $$–$$$

825 Madison Ave (bet. 68th & 69th Sts)
☎ 249-4100 Ⓜ 6 to 68th St-Hunter College ◐ 10am–6pm Mon–Sat (to 7pm Thu). 🚗 AE/MC/V
D&G: 434 W Broadway (bet. Prince & Spring Sts) ☎ 965-8000 Ⓜ B·D·F·Q to Boadway-Lafayette ◐ 11am–7pm Mon–Sat; 12–6pm Sun. 🚗 AE/MC/V

Emporio Armani

Armani is synonymous with Italian high-style. Minimalist chic from the master means simple shapes, decorated with lots of glitter and shine, and classic men's suits in rich fabrics. Uptown at Giorgio Armani, Italian ingenuity is applied to more expensive designs. $–$$$

110 Fifth Ave (at 16th St) ☎ 727-3240 Ⓜ L•N•R•4•5•6 to 14th St-Union Sq ◑ 11am–8pm Mon–Sat (to 7pm Sat); 12–6pm Sun. 🖃 all

Giorgio Armani: 760 Madison Ave (bet. 65th & 66th Sts) ☎ 988-9191 Ⓜ 6 to 68th St-Hunter College ◑ 10am–6pm Mon–Sat (to 7pm Thu). 🖃 AE/MC/V

Gucci

Tom Ford, who has radically changed the Gucci look, never fails to impress with his sensual, of-the-moment clothes for both sexes. The severely stylish also hanker after the amazing shoes and unbelievably tasteful home furnishings. $$$

10 W 57th St (bet. Fifth & Sixth Aves) ☎ 826-2600 Ⓜ E•F to 5th Ave ◑ 9.30am–6pm Mon–Sat (to 7.30pm Thu); 12–6pm Sun. 🖃 all

Helmut Lang

Lang is beloved of fashionable New Yorkers, who never say no to lots of expensive black designs in 'interesting' shapes. The spartan store houses his stark, poetic clothing including stunning men's suits and seemingly simple, yet high-constructed, frocks for women.$$$

80 Greene Street (bet. Broome & Spring Sts) ☎ 925-7214 Ⓜ 6 to Spring St; N•R to Prince St ◑ 11am–7pm Mon–Sat; 12–6pm Sun. 🖃 AE/MC/V

Hotel Venus

The Soho outlet for downtown style maven Patricia Field, this is the place for outlandish, clubby wear with a dash of class. Hotel Venus carries labels like Courrèges and Stephen Sprouse, plenty of fetish-inspired outerwear, stilettos, adorable accessories from Japan, and rhinestones for every occasion. $–$$

382 W Broadway (bet. Broome & Spring Sts) ☎ 966-4066 Ⓜ A•C to Prince St ◑ 12–8pm daily. 🖃 AE/MC/V

If Soho New York

With an intriguing mix of international fashion icons and brilliant newcomers, If Soho New York really gives any serious shopper a taste of the truly avant-garde. The entire Comme des Garçons collection is here, along with Martin Margiela and Dries Van Noten, plus designs from edgy local stars that change seasonally. $$$

94 Grand St (bet. Greene & Mercer Sts) ☎ 334-4964 Ⓜ N•R to Prince St; C•E to Spring St ◑ 11am–7pm daily (to 6.30pm Sun). 🖃 AE/MC/V

Polo Ralph Lauren

This historic, Upper East Side mansion provides the perfect environment for Ralph Lauren's classic look for men and women. Just as the setting appropriates the trappings of an English country castle, the clothing encorporates old world elegance with new world ease. The Polo Sport store (with its sporty creations) is just across the avenue. $$–$$$

867 Madison Ave (at 72nd St) ☎ 606-2100 Ⓜ 6 to 68th St-Hunter College ◑ 10am–6pm Mon–Sat. 🖃 AE/MC/V

Prada

No matter which lime green Prada store you happen into, plan on spending big bucks for some of the most modish clothes available anywhere. While her bags, shoes and shapes are endlessly imitated in the chain stores, Miuccia Prada's original and clean-lined designs for men and women are worth every penny. $$$

841 Madison Ave (at 70th St) ☎ 327-4200 Ⓜ 6 to 68th St-Hunter College ◑ 10am–6pm Mon–Sat (to 7pm Thu). 🖃 AE/MC/V 👜

Prada Sport

For those who worship at the altar of Prada, this latest addition to Miuccia's empire is a must. Filled with highly-designed sport clothes, utility wear and shoes. $$

116 Wooster St (bet. Prince & Spring Sts) ☎ 925-2221 Ⓜ N•R to Prince St; C•E to Spring St ◑ 11am–7pm Mon–Sat; 12–6pm Sun. 🖃 AE/MC/V

Shanghai Tang

Ultra-luxe clothes from China are the main attraction in this impressive, brightly-coloured art-deco store, which includes an in-store tailor who makes up garments in rich, expensive silks (5th flr). There are lots of mandarin-style jackets and gorgeous cashmere sweaters and a few, select home furnishings too. $–$$

714 Madison Ave (bet. 63rd & 64th Sts) ☎ 888-0111 Ⓜ N•R to 5th Ave ◑ 10.15am–7pm Mon–Sat; 12–6pm Sun. 🖃 AE/MC/V

Steven Alan

The eponymous owner is famous for his ability to sniff out new, young design talent before anybody else. His main women's store regularly showcases young designers who combine casual chic with a downtown aesthetic. Just west of Sixth Avenue is his first men's boutique, filled with smart utilitarian styles and accessories. $$

women: 60 Wooster St (bet. Broome & Spring Sts) ☎ 334-6354 Ⓜ N•R to Prince St; C•E to Spring St ◑ 1–8pm daily. 🖃 AE/MC/V men: 558 Broome St (bet. Sixth Ave & Varick St) ☎ 625-2541 Ⓜ 1•9 to Canal St ◑ 12–7pm Wed–Sat; 1–6pm Sun. 🖃 AE/MC/V

Untitled

Nestled among the inexpensive shoe shops on 8th Street, this two-storey abode carries a selection of clothes from hot, young designers from around the globe. Upstairs, the duds are mostly for dudes, and include desirable gear by Dirk Bikkemberg, Martin Margiela, Helmut Lang, maharishi Jean-Paul Gaultier and more. Downstairs, the women's clothes are equally illustrious and the accessories are divine. $$

26 W 8th St (bet. Fifth & Sixth Aves)
☎ 505-9725 Ⓜ A·B·C·D·E·F·Q to W 4th St-Washington Sq ◑ 11.30am–9pm Mon–Sat; 12–9pm Sun. ▤ AE/MC/V

Versace

Beloved by exhibitionist types (including lots of celebs), the entire Versace collection shines in a multi-level shop that is as lavish and vivid as the clothes it contains. Even if the colossal price tags are out of your league, stop in just for the wild Versace experience. $$$

815 Madison Ave (at 68th St) ☎ 744-6868
Ⓜ 6 to 68thSt-Hunter College ◑ 10am–6pm Mon–Sat (to 7pm Thu). ▤ AE/MC/V Flagship at 645 5th Ave (bet. 51st & 52nd Sts)
☎ 317-0224 for details.

Vivienne Westwood

British icon Vivienne Westwood has opened her first store stateside. The space (once a Soho art gallery) is filled with the entire range of Westwood's quirky English tailoring, including the hard-to-find Anglomania and her MAN collections. There are also loads of distinctive bags. $$$

71 Greene St (bet. Broome & Spring Sts)
☎ 334-5200 Ⓜ N·R to Prince St ◑ 11am–7pm Mon–Sat; 12–6pm Sun. ▤ AE/MC/V

Yohji Yamamoto

Yamamoto's all-white shrine of a store pushes forward the boundaries of fashion – so no wonder the sales help behave as if every item were a work of art. Consistently inventive and suprisingly wearable, Yamamoto's designs are like nothing else you'll see. $$$

103 Grand St (at Mercer St) ☎ 966-9066
Ⓜ J·M·N·R·Z·6 to Canal St ◑ 11am–7pm Mon–Sat; 12–6pm Sun. ▤ all

men's fashion

Nova USA

Nova offers occasionally severe, sporty clothes (like the perfect drawstring pants), meant for men, but worn by lots of women who appreciate the classic cut. $–$$

100 Stanton St (at Ludlow St) ☎ 228-6844
Ⓜ F to 2nd Ave ◑ 11am–8pm Mon–Sat; 12–7pm Sun. ▤ AE/MC/V

Paul Smith

Paul Smith's clothes are classically English but slightly wacky. His sweaters and shirts are highly-designed and made from luxe (ie expensive) materials, the ties often whimsical, and the suits amazing for both style and quality. There is a wonderful selection of toney accessories too. $$

108 Fifth Ave (at 16th St) ☎ 627-9770
Ⓜ L·N·R·4·5·6 to 14th St-Union Sq
◑ 11am–7pm Mon–Sat (to 8pm Thu); 12–6pm Sun. ▤ AE/MC/V

Sean

A recent addition to the menswear scene, Sean offers sporty clothes that are stylish without trying too hard. Ranging from corduroy shirts to tailored jackets, everything here is very wearable, with reasonable price tags. $$

132 Thompson St (bet. Houston & Prince Sts)
☎ 598-5980 Ⓜ Prince St ◑ 12–7pm daily (to 6pm Sun). ▤ all ▥

Yves Saint Laurent Rive Gauche

The elegant and spacious store is one of the few really stylish men-only outlets in Soho. With a new designer (Hedi Slimane) at the wheel, YSL Men is recycling the classics, but there's also a modern (and very dapper) aesthetic for guys who aren't afraid to make a fashion statement. $$$

88 Wooster St (bet. Broome & Spring Sts)
☎ 274-0522 Ⓜ N·R to Prince St; C·E to Spring St ◑ 11am–7pm Mon–Sat; 12–6pm Sun.
▤ AE/MC/V

women's fashion

Antique Boutique

This space-age store offers some of the best downtown fashion around. There are lots of up-and-coming local designers represented, plus many burgeoning European stars too. Things are grouped according to colour rather than designer, and err towards the avant-garde. $$

712 Broadway (bet. Astor Pl & 4th St)
☎ 460-8830 Ⓜ N·R to 8th St; 6 to Astor Pl
◑ 11am–10pm Mon–Sat; 12–8pm Sun. ▤ all

Betsey Johnson

Soho fashion pioneer (and survivor), Betsey Johnson, has decorated her flagship store in her signature and ultra-girly flower print, and it looks a bit like an upscale bordello. The clothes are directed at femmes of all shapes, sizes and ages: when you wear one of Betsey's frocks, you know you'll have lots of fun. $$

138 Wooster St (at Prince St) ☎ 995-5048
Ⓜ N·R to Prince St ◑ 11am–7pm Mon–Sat; 12–7pm Sun. ▤ AE/MC/V ▥

Calypso St Barths

This store is filled with a vibrant collection of truly pretty and feminine clothes from various designers. Along with the I-enjoy-being-a-girl outfits, there are brilliant little bags and accessories that can make getting dressed up a pleasure. Owner Christiane Celle's mini-empire also includes Jamin Puech [→101]. $$

280 Mott St (bet. Houston & Prince Sts) ☎ 965-0990 Ⓜ B•D•F•Q to Broadway-Lafayette St; 6 to Bleecker St ◑ 11am–7pm Mon–Sat; 12–6pm Sun. 🚍 all

Catherine

Well-known Parisian stylist, Malandrino has created a shop that looks like a very groovy, mid-60s living room. It's filled with colour-coordinated clothes that range from pretty beaded skirts to leathers, and lots of perfect tops to complete the outfit. The owner is also known for her high-style cowgirl hat in an array of pastel colours. $$

468 Broome St (bet. Greene & Mercer Sts) ☎ 925-6765 Ⓜ N•R to Prince St; C•E to Spring St ◑ 11am–7pm Mon–Sat; 12–6pm Sun. 🚍 AE/MC/V

Cynthia Rowley

Cute, sexy and all-girl is the theme at this wild and eclectic store. New York designer, Rowley does dresses the best: pretty fabrics,¹ots of beading and colour, plus cute accessories like charm bracelets and lipstick bags. Don't miss the fantastic collection of very femme shoes. $$

112 Wooster St (bet. Prince & Spring Sts), ☎ 334-1144 Ⓜ N•R to Prince St ◑ 11am–7pm Mon–Sat (to 8pm Thu–Fri); 12–6pm Sun. 🚍 all

Daryl K

Transplanted from Ireland, Daryl K has become an international style luminary with a huge, celebrity following (so much so her clothes are endlessly imitated by Seventh Avenue designers). In her futuristic cavern-of-a-store are sophisticated clothes under the Daryl K label, as well as funky and less-expensive pants and tops from her K-189 collection. $$

21 Bond St (at Lafayette St) ☎ 777-0713 Ⓜ 6 to Astor Pl; N•R to Prince St ◑ 12–7pm daily. 🚍 AE/MC/V

Fendi

The fabulous Fendi sisters continue to create super-stylish, offbeat clothes, using lots of fake fur and funky leather. But what everyone craves, season after season, are the 'baguette' bags, designed by Karl Lagerfeld, decorated with big 'F' buckles and even bigger price tags. $$$

720 Fifth Ave (at 56th St) ☎ 767-0100 Ⓜ E•F to 5th Ave ◑ 10am–6pm Mon–Sat (to 7pm Thu). 🚍 all

Issey Miyake Pleats Please

The store itself is as entertaining as the merch within – check out the windows which change from clear to opaque as you walk by. The clothes, which come in neutrals and bright patterns, are all totally pleated, and slide on the body like a second skin. It's a distinctive look, if you're feeling especially experimental. $$

128 Wooster St (at Prince St) ☎ 226-3600 Ⓜ N•R to Prince St; C•E to Spring St ◑ 11am–7pm Mon–Sat (to 6pm Sun). 🚍 AE/MC/V

Janet Russo

The homey shop of the former Madison Avenue fashion designer won't disappoint with its ultra-feminine floral print dresses, classic lines, and precious collectables from around the world, like Vietnamese dolls and pyjamas. This may well be where you'll find that perfect, pretty, little dress. $$

262 Mott St (bet. Houston & Prince Sts) ☎ 625-3297 Ⓜ B•D•F•Q to Broadway-Lafayette St, 6 to Bleecker St, N•R to Prince St ◑ 11am–7pm Mon–Sat; 12–6pm Sun. 🚍 AE/MC/V

Jeannette Lang

You don't have to be super skinny to fit into one of Lang's creations: there's no bias cut so anyone can enjoy her stretch silk looks, flowing lines and sexy touches. The German designer infuses a general sensuality to her creations and, for women who really want to stand out from the crowd, she also makes custom dresses. $$–$$$

171 Sullivan Street ☎ 254-5676 Ⓜ 1•9 to Houston St, A•C•E•D•F•B•Q to West 4th St ◑ 2–7pm Tue–Sun. 🚍 AE/MC/V

Kirna Zabete

Wonder where all the edgy fashion-forward women you see on the streets of Soho shop? Most likely it's at Kirna Zabete, the brainchild of two fashionista friends and always a safe bet for the coolest accessories and hottest looks of the season. Two levels of adornments and attitude include items from hard to find designers like Hussein Chalayan, Alain Tondowski, LuLu Guiness, and Martine Sitbon. $$–$$$

96 Greene St (bet. Prince & Spring Sts) ☎ 941-9656 Ⓜ B•D•F•Q to Broadway-Lafayette St, C to Spring St ◑ 11am–7pm Mon–Sat; 12–6pm Sun. 🚍 AE/MC/V

Marc Jacobs

Marc Jacobs has made a name for himself as the premier young American designer. Having been dubbed 'the new Calvin Klein,' Jacobs lives up to the moniker with refined, minimalist designs that are continuously fun, fresh, and really expensive. His cashmere sweaters are so popular, there's rumoured to be a long waiting list to get one. $$$

163 Mercer St (bet. Houston & Prince Sts) ☎ 343-1490 Ⓜ N•R to Prince St ◑ 11am–7pm Mon–Sat; 12–6pm Sun. 🚍 all

Miu Miu

This is the younger, sexier, slightly less expensive line from Prada. There are lots of little skirts, tops, dresses and coats that are modern yet flirtatious, with unique bags to match. Check out the super-trendy shoes too. $$

100 Prince St (bet. Greene & Mercer Sts) ☎ 334-5156 Ⓜ N•R to Prince St ◐ 11am–7pm Mon–Sat, 12pm–6pm Sun. 🖭 all

Morgane Le Fay

The world of Morgan Le Fay is totally original: meant to be layered, one piece on top of the other, the clothes are gypsy-meets-fairytale princess. This look is meant for the supremely-confident artsy type who likes to be noticed. $$$

151 Spring St (bet. W Broadway & Wooster St) ☎ 925-0144 Ⓜ N•R to Prince St; C•E to Spring St ◐ 11am–7pm daily. 🖭 AC/MC/V

Olive & Bette

In this cute neighbourhood shop (there's a sister store on the UES), the focus is on happening young designers like Daryl K and Vivienne Tam, along with genius jeans from Earl, those must-have T-shirts from 3 Dot and the most recent thing from Fiorucci. $–$$

252 Columbus Avenue (bet. 71st & 72nd St) ☎ 579-2178 Ⓜ B•C to 72nd St ◐ 11am–7pm Mon–Sun. 🖭 AE/MC/V

Scoop

One of downtown's favourite fashion outposts. Owner Stephanie Grenfield's taste in clothing runs from girly frocks to bold separates: young designers from New York and Europe are the lure, with lots of cute accessories to finish the look. Don't miss colourful T-shirts by Juicy USA – the best bargains in the store. $$

532 Broadway (bet. Prince & Spring Sts), ☎ 925-2886 Ⓜ C•E to Spring St ◐ 11am–8pm daily (7pm Sun). 🖭 all 👜

TG-170

Owner Terri Gillis was one of the original pioneers in the now happening LES fashion scene. This is one of the most distinctive and edgy collections in any store in New York, and many a designer has been launched here. The prices are impressively low for all this daring style. $–$$

170 Ludlow St (bet. Houston & Stanton Sts) ☎ 995-8660 Ⓜ F to 2nd Ave ◐ 1–8pm daily. 🖭 AE/MC/V

Tracey Feith

The interior here is all elegant dark wood and white walls – the perfect place to display Feith's colourful and seductive dresses, many of them inspired by vintage silhouettes and fabrics. There are darling shoes and bags, and plenty of room for Raj, the designer's less-expensive, hippie-gypsy clothes, that all downtown girls love. $$

209 Mulberry St (bet. Kenmare & Spring Sts) ☎ 334-3097 Ⓜ C•E to Spring St ◐ 11am–7pm daily. 🖭 AE/MC/V

Trufaux

PC animal prints and ultra-suede jackets, dresses and skirts at affordable prices. This is the place to shop for faux fur trim, giraffe print wrap dresses and washable and weatherproof leather-inspired looks that won't break your bank or your principles. $$

301 West Broadway (at Canal St) ☎ 334-4545 Ⓜ 1,9,A,C,E to Canal St ◐ 11am–7pm Mon–Sat; 12–6pm Sun. 🖭 AE/MC/V

chain stores

Once a suburban phenomenon, chain stores have become the first port of call for affordable copycat fashion. Indeed, it's not unusual to see catwalk trends translated to the chains before they reach the actual designer stores. The best places to look for the big names are Broadway (bet. 8th & Canal Sts), Herald Square, Fifth and Sixth Avenues, Lexington Avenue (bet. 57th & 61st Sts) Soho, South Street Seaport and the World Trade Center. Most carry both men's and women's apparel as well as footwear and accessories. All-American department store, *K-Mart*, is one of the best-priced with rock bottom bargains for the entire family. Also for all ages, the ubiquitous, unisex *Gap* features reasonably-priced understated basics like chinos and white T-shirts. The prime store is on Herald Square. *Old Navy* is in the same vein with even cheaper prices. Sweden's *H & M* has caused a big stir with their cheap, chic or streetwear styles, so be prepared to wait in long lines for the fitting rooms. *J Crew* and *Banana Republic* are good bets for timeless casualwear. But the more upbeat *XOXO* carries sexy clothing for female style vixens, while *Guess?* features the same sexy look at a higher price point. Other mid-priced stores include: *Express*, mainstream fashion for women, and its male counterpart, *Structure*. For streetwear, Urban Outfitters lives up to its name, offering the latest youth-oriented fashions. *Zara* injects a bit of European flair with its sleek separates, casualwear and shoes. *Club Monaco* and *French Connection* fit into the slightly more upscale and interesting, but still reasonably-priced, category. For something more rugged *Eddie Bauer* handles outdoorwear for men and women, while the more buttoned-down will appreciate the conservative *Brooks Bros* tailored suits. Its Wall Street style goes a long way with men, and the line of preppy womenswear is building momentum.

↓ vintage fashion

It's tough finding deals on vintage and antique clothing in New York where savvy store owners tend to know the value of a decent pair of used Levis. Although you might find some 'deadstock' (never-before worn vintage clothing), most stuff is pre-owned, so inspect all clothes well before purchasing as most places have a final sale only policy. The flea markets are a good place to start; after that, head to the East Village and the Lower East Side where you'll find the biggest concentration of stores. **Resurrection** is crammed with museum-quality antique and vintage pieces, which acts as a magnet to models and stylists. In addition to glorious vintage clothing, **Foley & Corinna** sells new bags made from antique fabrics as well as previously-loved models by Gucci and Fendi. Aficionados include Anna Sui and stylists from 'Sex and the City'. At **Timtoum**, the eclectic mix is more laid back and less expensive. Along the block, **Cherry** is a store devoted to collectible clothing and accessories (sometimes complete with original tags) from post-World War II forward. Elsewhere, **Stella Dallas**, in the West Village, has a girly collection of dresses, slips and nighties from the 30's and 40's at reasonable prices. In Noho, **Screaming Mimi's** and **Each and Them** are both purveyors of groovy yet chic threads, shoes, sunglasses

and bags from the 60's, 70's and 80's. Hit the lower level of Canal Jean Co on Broadway to find racks of vintage Levis, polyester shirts, jackets and accessories at OK prices. Consignment shops can also yield good buys. **Tokio 7** offers a broad spectrum of carefully-worn designer clothes with an avant-garde edge. But for the finest selection of pre-owned designer duds, go to **Ina**, which has stores for both men (Nolita) and women (Soho). True bargains are to be found at **Housing Works Thrift Shop** and Out of the Closet, where the clothing (especially men's suits), books, furniture and trinkets are exceptionally low in price. Both stores benefit AIDS charities.

Canal Jean Co
504 Broadway (bet. Spring & Broome Sts) ☎ 226-1130 Ⓜ 6 to Spring St; N•R to Prince St ◷ 10.30am–8pm daily. 🍽 all $

Cherry
185 Orchard St (bet. Houston & Stanton Aves) ☎ 358-7131 Ⓜ F to 2nd Ave ◷ mid-Apr–Nov: 12–9pm Sun–Wed; 12pm–midnight Thu–Sat (call for winter hours). 🍽 AE/V/MC $-$$

Each and Them
216 Lafayette St (bet. Spring & Broome Sts) ☎ 925-9699 Ⓜ 6 to Spring St ◷ 12–7pm daily. 🍽 all $-$$

Foley & Corinna
108 Stanton St (at Essex St) ☎ 529-2338 Ⓜ F to Delancey

St ◷ 12–7pm Mon–Sun (to 8pm Sun). 🍽 all $-$$

Housing Works Thrift Shop
143 W 17th St (bet. 6th & 7th Aves) ☎ 366-0820 Ⓜ 1•9 to 18th St ◷ 10am–6pm Mon–Sat; 12–5pm Sun. 🍽 AE/MC/V $

Ina
101 Thompson St (bet. Spring & Prince Sts) ☎ 941-4757 Ⓜ A•C•E to Spring St; N•R to Prince St ◷ 12–7pm daily 🍽 AE/MC/V $$ 💳

Out of the Closet
220 E 81st St (bet. 2nd & 3rd Aves) ☎ 472-3573 Ⓜ 4•5•6 to 86th St ◷ 10am–5pm Tue–Sat. 🍽 none $-$$

Resurrection
123 E 7th St (bet. 1st Ave & Ave A) ☎ 228-0063 Ⓜ F to 2nd Ave; L to 1st Ave; 6 to Astor Pl ◷ 1am–9pm daily (to 8pm Sun). 🍽 AE/MC/V $$ 💳

Screaming Mimi's
382 Lafayette St (at E 4th St) ☎ 677-6464 Ⓜ N•R to 8th St; 6 to Astor Pl ◷ 12–8pm daily (to 6pm Sun). 🍽 all $-$$

Stella Dallas
218 Thompson St (bet. Bleecker & W 3rd Sts) ☎ 674-0447 Ⓜ A•B•C•D•E•F•Q to W 4th St-Washington Sq ◷ 12–7pm daily. 🍽 AE/MC/V $-$$

Timtoum
179 Orchard St (bet. E Houston & Stanton Sts) ☎ 780-0456 Ⓜ F to 2nd Ave ◷ 1–8pm daily. 🍽 MC/V $-$$

Tokio 7
64 E 7th St (bet. 1st & 2nd Aves) ☎ 353-8443 Ⓜ 6 to Astor Pl ◷ 12–8.30pm daily. 🍽 AE/MC/V $$

---

discount stores

Century 21
Even uptown fashionistas aren't beneath shopping at this infamous clearing house. The store features 16 departments with most designer names at 25–75% off, but it's a real endurance test to pluck the diamonds from the trash. $-$$

22 Cortlandt St (bet. Broadway & Church St) ☎ 227-9092 Ⓜ N•R•1•9 to Cortlandt St ◷ 7.45am–8pm Mon–Fri (to 8.30pm Thu); 10am–7.30pm Sat. 🍽 all 💳

Daffy's
The masters of the outfit for under $100. Fight your way through the overcrowded racks for eveningwear, lingerie, and men's and women's clothes and shoes. $-$$

131 Broadway (at 34th St) ☎ 736-4477 Ⓜ B•D•F•N•Q•R to 34th St-Herald Sq ◷ 10am–9pm Mon–Sat (to 8pm Sat); 11am–7pm Sun. 🍽 all 💳

Loehmann's
Known for carrying tremendous high-end designer merchandise from DKNY, Versace, Dries van Noten and many more – all at eye-popping prices. $-$$

101 Seventh Ave (bet 16th & 17th Sts) ☎ 352-0856 Ⓜ 1•9 to 18th St ◷ 9am–9pm Mon–Sat; 11am–7pm Sun. 🍽 all 💳

Nice Price $$$
Each week several designers offer up delicious samples, old and new, at below-bargain prices. Marc Jacobs, Donna Karen, Urban Outfitters, and Kenar have all tested their wares here. $-$$

2nd floor, 261 W 36th St (bet. Seventh & Eighth Aves) ☎ 947-8748 Ⓜ A•C•E to 34th St-Penn Stn ◷ times vary, phone ahead 🍽 AE/MC/V

Find Outlet
New stock arrives every week in this store where last season's designer wares and accessories are sold at discount. Feminine designs by Paige Novick, Helmut Lang, and Jimmy Choo fill the neat, organized space. $-$$

229 Mott St (bet. Prince & Spring Sts) ☎ 226-5167 Ⓜ 6 to Spring St ◷ 12–7pm daily. 🍽 MC/V

shoe chains

*The ubiquitous **Nine West** always has plenty of well-priced styles which 'pay hommage' to the likes of Prada and Gucci. **9 & Co** is just as fashion-friendly, and in an even cheaper price bracket. **Kenneth Cole** is a favourite with smart, young New Yorkers of both sexes who flex their plastic for his cool, wearable styles (his bags and sharp separates are here too). Far more ostentacious are the platforms and fun sneakers on offer at **Steve Madden**, whose shoes are beloved of the dazed and confused set. **Sacco** is an excellent outpost for women's shoes and boots – although prices are a little higher than some of the other chains, sophistication is the payoff. For a more conservative look, **Joan & David** has a reliable selection with price tags to match. **Juno's** carries more edgy footwear, as well as a competitive selection of men's shoes. But for the ultimate bargain, **Payless** has footwear for men women for as little as $10. Just don't expect these shoes to outlive the month.*

↓ shoes

Europeans may be surprised to find the selection of footwear on offer in New York is not as great as the choice at home, but, hey, the sneakers are cheap (for good deals, trek up Broadway between Canal Street as far as 8th Street). If your credit is limitless, however, and you aren't afraid of vertigo, **Manolo Blahnik**'s heels are the kind no fashionista leaves the house without. In the same ultra-luxury category, Brit **Jimmy Choo** has just opened a snazzy, new boutique to house his collection of pretty heels and mules. But if you prefer to vamp it up, **Christian Louboutin**'s red-soled style statements will satiate even the most serious shopper. Fellow European **Stéphane Kélian**'s outlandish creations are in the same, high-end price bracket. Also on Madison is **Tod's** store. The brand's beloved (and expensive) leather 'driving loafer' is the kind worn by slumming movie stars.

Less pricey and infinitely more inventive are the 60s-style, mod designs on offer at **Sigerson Morrison**, one of the best little shoe stores in town and nearby, inside a tiny Spring Street boutique, are **Mark Schwartz**'s huge but super feminine skyscraper heels. **Jutta Neuman**'s hand-made sandals are a bit of a

bargain, considering the work that's gone into them. Career shoe shoppers, however, depend on the **Otto Tootsi Plohound** mini-chain for the best selection of high-fashion styles by various big names such as Free Lance.

For bargains, you'll have to head for 8th Street between Sixth Avenue and Broadway, where upwards of 20 one-off stores line the blocks (try **Petit Peton** for starters). And if your feet are worn out after looking for something to slip them into, you can get complimentary reflexology at the new **Rockport** 'concept' store in Soho where, thankfully, comfy footwear is the lure.

Christian Louboutin
941 Madison Ave (at 74th St) ☎ 396-1884 ⓶ 6 to 77th St ◑ 10am–6pm Mon–Sat. ▤ all $$$

Jimmy Choo
645 Fifth Ave (at 51st St) ☎ 593-0800 ⓶ E·F to 5th Ave ◑ 10am–6pm Mon–Sat. ▤ all $$$

Jutta Neumann
317 E 9th St (bet. 1st & 2nd Aves) ☎ 982-7048 ⓶ 6 to Astor Pl ◑ 12–8pm Tue–Sat. ▤ all $–$$

Manolo Blahnik
31 W 54th St (bet. Fifth & Sixth Aves) ☎ 582-3007 ⓶ E·F to 5th Ave ◑ 10.30am–6pm Mon–Fri (to 5pm Sat). ▤ AE/MC/V $$$

Mark Schwartz
45 Spring St (bet. Mulberry & Mott Sts) ☎ 343-9292 ⓶ 6 to Spring St ◑ 11am–7pm Tue–Sun. ▤ AE/MC/V $$$

Otto Tootsi Plohound
413 W Broadway (bet. Prince & Spring Sts) ☎ 925-8931 ⓶ N·R to Prince St; 6 to Spring St ◑ 10.45am–8.30pm Mon–Sat; 11.30am–7.30pm Sun. ▤ all $–$$ 📖

Petit Peton
27 W 8th St (bet. 5th & 6th Aves) ☎ 677-3730 ⓶ A·B·C·D·E·F·Q to W 4th St-Washington Sq ◑ 11am–9pm Mon–Sat; 12–8.30pm Sun. ▤ AE/MC/V $

Rockport
465 W Broadway (bet. Prince & W Houston Sts) ☎ 529-0209 ⓶ N·R to Prince St ◑ 11am–7pm Mon–Sat; 12–6pm Sun. ▤ AE/MC/V $–$$

Stéphane Kélian
717 Madison Ave (bet. 63rd & 64th Sts) ☎ 980-1919 ⓶ N·R to 5th Ave ◑ 10am–6pm Mon–Sat. ▤ all $$$

Sigerson Morrison
242 Mott Street (bet. Houston & Prince Sts) ☎ 219-3893 ⓶ B·D·F·Q to Broadway-Lafayette St ◑ 11am–7pm Mon–Fri; 12–6pm Sun. ▤ all $–$$

Tod's
650 Madison Ave (bet. 59th & 60th Sts) ☎ 644-5945 ⓶ N·R to 5th Ave ◑ 10am–6pm Mon–Sat (to 7pm Thu); 12–5pm Sun. ▤ all $$–$$$

↓ accessories

bags

Jamin Puech

Entirely precious bags by this Parisian designer in jewel-like colours are housed in a gorgeous, teeny boutique. $$$

252 Mott St (bet. Houston & Prince Sts) ☎ 334-9730 ⓶ B·D·F·Q to Broadway-Lafayette St ◑ 11am–7pm Mon–Sat; 12–7pm Sun. ▤ AE/MC/V

Kate Spade

Kate Spade's adorable bags are a New York status symbol, and range from everyday to evening glam. $$

454 Broome St (at Mercer St) ☎ 274-1991 ⓶ N·R to Prince St; C·E to Spring St ◑ 11am–7pm Mon–Sat; 12–6pm Sun. ▤ all

Manhattan Portage

The bag brand that's been so popular in Europe is finally making an impact at home. Stop by to find backpacks and DJ bags in the strongest canvas and lots of colours. $

333 E 9th St (bet. first & second Aves) ☎ 995-5490 ⓶ 6 to Astor Place ◑ 11am–7pm daily. ▤ all

eyewear

Robert Marc

A New York staple for excellent eyewear, this tiny chain has a good selection including hard-to-find makes like Prosh and Beausoleil. $$–$$$

1300 Madison Ave (at 92nd St) ☎ 722-1600 Ⓜ 6 to 96th St ◑ 9.30am–6pm Mon–Sat; 12–5.30 Sun. 🛒 all 🛍

Selima Optique

Selima's sexy, sleek line of eyewear is known for its cult-like following of everyone from the Dior-clad lady to edgy hipsters. There are loads of other designer frames too. $–$$

59 Wooster St (at Broome St) ☎ 343-9490 Ⓜ C•E to Spring St ◑ 11am–7pm Mon–Sat (8pm Thu); 12–7pm Sun. 🛒 all 🛍

hats

Amy Downs

Her hats are outrageous, and take a degree of courage to wear; some make you think the *Cat in the Hat* went couture. $–$$

103 Stanton St (at Ludlow St) ☎ 598-4189 Ⓜ F to 2nd Ave ◑ 1–6pm Wed–Sun. 🛒 all

Kelly Christie

Beautifully crafted, handmade hats, there's something for everyone. $–$$

235 Elizabeth St (bet. Houston & Prince Sts) ☎ 965-0686 Ⓜ N•R to Prince St ◑ 12–7pm daily (to 6pm Sun). 🛒 all

jewellery

Bond 07

Another store by the owner of Selima Optique. This one is filled with divine accessories (hats, glasses, shoes and trinkets), including lots of unique and beautiful jewellery. All irresistible. $$

7 Bond St (bet. Broadway & Lafayette St) ☎ 677-8487 Ⓜ 6 to Bleecker St; B•D•F•Q to Broadway-Lafayette St ◑ 11am–7pm Mon–Fri; 12–7pm Sun. 🛒 all

Fragments

Owner's Goldman and Moore keep this pretty Soho store filled with the inventive creations of 30 or so designers. Expect anything from Indian beadwork to rhinestone-studded bracelets, and even the occasional diamond. $$

107 Greene St (bet. Prince & Spring Sts) ☎ 334-9588 Ⓜ 6 to Spring St; N•R to Prince St ◑ 11am–7pm Mon–Sat; 12–6 Sun. 🛒 all

Me & Ro

Bohemian jewellery styles that subtly beautify the body are what's on offer at Me & Ro. Soon after designers Robin Renzi and Michelle Quan opened shop, a celebrity following appeared: Liz Taylor and Kate Moss are amongst those who love the religious-inspired artifacts, Indian style bell-drop earrings, and charm bracelets. $$

239 Elizabeth St (bet. Houston and Prince Sts) ☎ 917-237-9215 Ⓜ 6 to Bleecker St ◑ 11am–6pm Tue–Sat (to 6.30pm Fri–Sat); 12–6pm Sun. 🛒 AE/MC/V

sports gear

Foot Locker

43–45 W 34th St (bet. fifth & sixth Aves) ☎ 971-9449 Ⓜ B•D•F•N•Q•R to 34th St-Herald Sq ◑ 8am–9pm Mon–Sat (from 9am Sat); 11am–7pm Sun. 🛒 all 🛍 $

Modell's

901 Sixth Ave (at 33rd St in the Manhattan Mall) ☎ 594-1830 Ⓜ B•D•F•N•Q•R to 34th St-Herald Sq ◑ 10am–8pm Mon–Sat; 11am–6pm Sun. 🛒 all 🛍 $

Paragon

876 Broadway (at 18th St) ☎ 255-8036 Ⓜ L•N•R•4•5•6 to 14th St-Union Sq ◑ 10am–8pm Mon–Sat; 11am–6.30pm Sun. 🛒 all $–$$

Reebok Concept Store

160 Columbus Ave (bet. 66th & 67th Sts) ☎ 595-1480 Ⓜ 1•9 to 66th St ◑ 10am–8pm Mon–Sat; 11am–6pm Sun. 🛒 all $–$$$

---

theme stores

Disney Store

Strictly for kids and their adult companions, Disney is Mickey and more in an OTT setting. $–$$

711 Fifth Avenue (at 55th St) ☎ 702-0702 Ⓜ E• F to 5th Ave ◑ 10am–8pm Mon–Sat; 11–7pm Sun. 🛒 all 🛍

Niketown

At this temple to the 'swoosh', the experience of visiting is invigorating, even if the service is slow. $–$$

6 E 57th St (bet. 5th & Madison Aves) ☎ 891-6453 Ⓜ E•F•N•R to 5th Ave ◑ 10am–8pm Mon–Sat; 11am–7pm Sun. 🛒 AE/MC/V

Original Levi's Store

Four floors of this all-American brand, including non-denim clothing and accessories. Can't find a pair that fits? The store will custom-make some for you. $–$$

3 E 57th St (bet. 5th & Madison Aves) ☎ 838-2188 Ⓜ E•F•N•R to 5th Ave; B•Q to 57th St ◑ 10am–8pm Mon–Sat; 12–6pm Sun. 🛒 all

Sony Style

Shop for gadgets or simply test drive the Playstations in this technophile's paradise. $–$$$

550 Madison Ave (bet. 55th & 56th Sts) ☎ 833-8800

Ⓜ 4•5•6 to 51st St; E•F to 5th Ave ◑ 10am–6pm Tue–Sat (to 9pm Thu); 12–6pm Sun. 🛒 all

Warner Bros Studio Store

Products galore from the WB's cartoons, movies and TV shows plus interactive games on the top floor.

1 E 57th St (at 5th Ave) ☎ 754-0305 Ⓜ E•F•N•R to 5th Ave; B•Q to 57th St; 4•5•6 to 59th St ◑ 10am–8pm Mon–Sat; 12–8pm Sun. 🛒 all $–$$

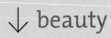
Aveda

This elegant space is easily the best smelling store in the world. If you're not going for Aveda's amazing hair care, aromatherapy, or bath and body collection, pop in for, at the very least, the soothing environment. The hair salon is upstairs, the spa is nearby on Spring Street. $$

456 W Broadway (bet. Houston & Prince Sts) ☎ 473-0280 Ⓜ C·E to Spring St; N·R to Prince St; 1·9 to Houston St ◑ *9am–9pm Mon–Fri; 10am–7pm Sun.* 🖃 AE/MC/V 📖

Bigelow Pharmacy

Founded in 1838, Bigelow's boasts a thoroughly modern variety of beauty products (hair accessories, essential oils, homeopathic remedies, and lots of good make-up). Spot the celebs at this quintessential West Village pharmacy. $$

414 Sixth Ave (bet. 8th & 9th Sts) ☎ 533-2700 Ⓜ A·B·C·D·E·F·Q to W 4th St-Washington Sq ◑ *7.30am–9pm Mon–Fri; 8.30am–7pm Sat; 8.30am–5pm Sun.* 🖃 AE/MC/V

Bliss Spa

While the who's who is making a bee-line to Bliss for spa treatments, the real treat at this chichi oasis is the boutique. All of the products are hand-picked by the spa's owner, skin-guru Marcia Kilgore. In addition to lines like Decleor and Yonka, Bliss sells everything you ever wanted beauty-wise, like upscale tooth-whitening paste and an at-home paraffin manicure kit. $$$

2nd flr, 568 Broadway (bet. Houston & Prince Sts) ☎ 219-8970 Ⓜ N·R to Prince St; B·D·F·Q to Broadway-Lafayette St; 6 to Spring St ◑ *9.30am–8.30pm Mon–Sat (to 6.30pm Sat).* 🖃 AE/MC/V

Creed

To see how well you really know your nose, stop by Creed where you can browse their scent library or join in a smelling seminars. To make you feel special, they also offer custom fragrance blending ($400–$1000) guaranteed to be yours and yours only for the next five years. $$–$$$

9 Bond St (at Broadway) ☎ 228-1940 Ⓜ 6 to Bleecker St ◑ *11.30am–730pm Mon–Sat; 12–6pm Sun.* 🖃 AE/V/MC

Face Stockholm

Face products have become a favourite amongst top make-up artists and the glitterati. You can choose from a bevy of all-natural beauty supplies – from make-up and utensils to bath gels and lotions. Check out the lip gloss – it's the best. $$

226 Columbus Ave (bet. 70th & 71st Sts) ☎ 769-1420 Ⓜ 1·9 to 72nd St ◑ *11am–7pm daily.* 🖃 AE/MC/V 📖

Kiehl's

Kiehl's is more than a beauty supply store – it's an American institution. This pharmacy-turned-beauty-brand's natural approach to products, and friendly, informative staff, make it a pleasure for you to financially submit (cost accumulates quite easily). They're best known for their lip balm and unisex appeal. $$

109 Third Ave (bet. 13th & 14th Sts) ☎ 677-3171 Ⓜ N·R·4·5·6 to 14th St-Union Sq; L to 3rd Ave. ◑ *10am-6.30pm Mon–Fri (to 7.30pm Thu); 10am–6pm Sat.* 🖃 AE/MC/V

M.A.C.

If you want the trendiest new colour for your lips, eyes, nails, or cheeks, then M.A.C. is the place to be. This make-up collection, which was created by a professional make-up artist, is known for its cutting-edge palette and sleek packaging. $$

113 Spring St (bet. Greene & Mercer Sts) ☎ 334-4641 Ⓜ N·R to Prince St ◑ *11am–7pm Mon–Sat; 12–6pm Sun.* 🖃 AE/MC/V 📖

Ricky's

This chain is a magnet for girlies who like their beauty products cheap and cheerful. The Soho branch has everything from fun-coloured wigs and nail polish to discounted high-end products. $

590 Broadway (bet. Prince & W Houston Sts) ☎ 226-5552 Ⓜ N·R to Prince St; 6 to Spring St ◑ *8am–9pm Mon–Fri; 9am–9pm Sat–Sun.* 🖃 AE/ MC/V 📖

Sephora

Product princesses will feel as if they've died and gone to heaven here. It's like a major department store, but just for cosmetics. Bath goods, make-up, perfume, skincare, and everything in between from big-name brands (Chanel, Lancôme, Dior) to more eclectic labels. $–$$$

555 Broadway (at Spring St) ☎ 625-1309 Ⓜ 6 to Spring St ◑ *10am–8pm Mon–Sat (to 9pm Thu–Fri); 12–7pm Sun.* 🖃 AE/MC/V 📖

Shu Uemura

The Armani of make-up, but from Japan. The store – and merchandise – has a Zen-like appeal in that less is more. Shu Uemura is not all about the moment's most fashionable colours, but minimalist beauty and quality. $$

121 Greene St (bet. Prince & W Houston Sts) ☎ 979-5500 Ⓜ N·R to Prince St; 6 to Spring St ◑ *11am–7pm Mon–Sat; 12–6pm Sun.* 🖃 AE/MC/V

↓ interiors

ABC Carpet & Home

One of the most popular and unique stores in NYC, it's got six floors crammed with the most luxurious items for bed, bath, table and kitchen – plus fine fabrics and trim, antiques and, of course, carpets. On the ground floor there's a great café and an exotic food shop. $–$$$

888 Broadway (at 19th St) ☎ 473-3000 Ⓜ L•N•R•4•5•6 to 14th St-Union Sq ◖ 10am–8pm Mon–Sat (to 7pm Sat); 11am–6.30pm Sun. ⊟ AE/MC/V

Ad-Hoc Software

Ad-Hoc Software's creative items always manage to fit the bill. Along with covetable bed and bath accessories (including some of the finest sheets and towels anywhere), there are lots of luxuries like French scented candles, gorgeous table linens, edgy dishware and cutlery, and even the latest in watch design. $–$$

136 Wooster Street (bet. Prince & Houston Sts) ☎ 925-2652 Ⓜ N•R to Prince St ◖ 11am–7pm Sat; 11.30am–6pm Sun. ⊟ AE/MC/V

Auto

Modern and must-have designs for the home, office and body. Off the beaten path, this immaculate shop-cum-showroom features items by young, free-thinking American designers like Elizabeth Powell, Fred Flare, and Kathleen Lewis. Auto's owners also represent the designers who've been snapped up by outlets like Barneys New York, Colette in Paris and DKNY. $–$$

805 Washington St (bet. Gansevoort & Horatio Sts) ☎ 229-2292 Ⓜ A•C•E to 14th St ◖ 2–7pm Wed–Sat (from 12pm Sat); 12–6pm Sun. ⊟ AE/MC/V

Bed Bath and Beyond

This gigantic superstore is the first place to check out when you're furnishing a new apartment. It carries a vast range of things for the home – some of it high-end and expensive, some of it a real bargain. For people used to shopping in crowded spaces with limited options, this place is a real treat, and the quality of the merchandise is pretty good. $–$$

620 Sixth Ave (at 19th St) ☎ 255-3550 Ⓜ 1•9 to 18th St; F to 23rd St ◖ 9.15am–9pm daily. ⊟ AE/MC/V

Fishs Eddy

Dishes are the name of the game at Fishs Eddy. The owners of this clever shop buy up sets of decorated dishes from country clubs, schools, hotels and other unlikely institutions, and sell them here. They also do their own retro designs – the one with the New York skyline is fab. $

889 Broadway (at 19th St) ☎ 420-9020 Ⓜ L•N•R•4•5•6 to 14th St-Union Sq; N•R to 23rd St ◖ 10am–9pm Mon–Sat; 11am–8pm Sun. ⊟ AE/MC/V

Gracious Home

Taking up almost both sides of one block, Gracious Home has all you need to line your nest. Everything here, from hardware to cleaning products, imported linens and towels, is sleek and highly-designed. $$

1217 & 1220 Third Ave (bet. 70th & 71st Sts) ☎ 517-6300 Ⓜ 6 to 68th St-Hunter College ◖ 8am–7pm Mon–Sat (from 9am Sat); 10am–6pm Sun. ⊟ AE/MC/V

Jonathan Adler

Designer of the moment, Adler is known for his whimsical home accessories blessed with bold, graphic designs. He has assembled a charming and aesthetically-pleasing selection of vases and tableware, along with other desirable objects culled from trips to flea markets – clearly his obsession. $$

465 Broome St (at Greene St) ☎ 941-8950 Ⓜ N•R to Prince St ◖ 11am–7pm Mon–Sat; 12–6pm Sun. ⊟ AE/MC/V

Las Venus

A staple for fashionable downtowners, Las Venus is all about 20th-century pop culture. It carries lots of graphic furniture and other colourful home furnishings (some of them quite kitsch) that any trendster would crave. $–$$

163 Ludlow St (bet. Stanton & E Houston Sts) ☎ 982-0608 Ⓜ F to 2nd Ave ◖ 12–9pm Mon–Thu (to 11pm Thu); 12pm–midnight Fri–Sat; 12–8pm Sun. ⊟ AE/MC/V

Moss

A showcase of the best designs past and present: if you like things for your home that are both functional and slick, Moss is nirvana. There are silver pieces from Alessi, fanciful glassware, jewel-toned Swedish crystal, and vases made from resin. The shop sometimes serves as a gallery for up-and-coming designers. $$

146 Greene St (at Houston St) ☎ 226-2190 Ⓜ N•R to Prince St ◖ 11am–7pm Tue–Fri; 12–7pm Sat; 12–6pm Sun. ⊟ AE/MC/V

Pottery Barn

As quintessentially American as Gap, this is a mass-market outlet for well-designed, countrified home furnishings at reasonable prices; it's hard to find anyone in New York who doesn't shop here. $–$$

600 Broadway (bet. Houston & Prince Sts) ☎ 219-2420 Ⓜ B•D•F•Q to Broadway-Lafayette St ◖ 10am–9pm Mon–Sat; 11am–7pm Sun. ⊟ AE/MC/V 👜

Shabby Chic

No false advertising here: the owners of this influential design store have made quite an impact with their laid-back take on contemporary elegance (think cosy, over-stuffed sofas and piles of downy pillows). The sheets made from T-shirt material have been much imitated. $$

93 Greene Street (bet. Spring & Prince Sts)
☎ 274-9842 Ⓜ C·E·6 to Spring St; N·R to Prince ◑ 10am–7pm Mon–Sat; 12–7pm Sun.
▤ AE/MC/V

TOTEM

One of the most modern home furnishing stores in the city, everything here is beautifully-designed; colourful, slick and functional. They carry loads of stylish plastic accessories, along with clean-lined furniture and distinctive rugs. $–$$

71 Franklin St (bet. Church St & Broadway)
☎ 925-5506 Ⓜ 1·9 to Franklin St ◑ 11am–7pm Mon–Sat; 12–5pm Sun. ▤ AE/MC/V

Williams-Sonoma

A big chain store from California, everything here is top-of-the-line: there are dishes from Italy, Calphon pans, plenty of glassware, food and gadgets that you can't do without. The real bargains here are the linens and napkins that look expensive but aren't. $–$$

110 Seventh Ave (bet. 16th & 17th Sts)
☎ 633-2203 Ⓜ 1·9 to 18th St; 1·2·3·9 to 14th St
◑ 10am–8pm Mon–Sat (7pm Sat); 12–6pm Sun.
▤ AE/MC/V

shops

Zona

Zona brings a bit of country life to the urban jungle. Filled with furniture and other items from around the world; the stock here is eclectic, deluxe and colourful. There are lots of little doodads that will brighten your pad, and don't cost much. The cult item here is the store's own hand-rolled candles that come in a rainbow of colours. $$

97 Greene St (bet. Prince & Spring Sts)
☎ 925-6750 Ⓜ C·E·6 to Spring St ◑ 11am–7pm Mon–Sat; 12–6pm Sun. ▤ AE/MC/V

↓ gift & museum stores

Cooper-Hewitt, National Museum of Design Store

The former music room of the Carnegie Mansion offers unexpected and unusual items that often tie in with the exhibitions: unique building toys, kitchen gadgets, stationery, and artsy books. Leave yourself a lot of time to browse. $$

2 E 91st Street (bet. Fifth & Madison Aves)
☎ 849-8355 Ⓜ 4·5·6 to 86th St
◑ 10am–5pm Tue–Sat (to 9pm Tue); 12–5pm Sun. ▤ all

Felissimo

New York's most unusual department store appeals to the rich hippy set. Brimful of amazing gift ideas, from wooden carvings to coloured candles, and beautifully stationery to indoor fountains, the products here are gathered from all over the world. Home furnishings, books and divine accessories are upstairs, as well as an elegant tearoom. $$

10 W 56th St (bet. Fifth & Sixth Aves)
☎ 247-5656 Ⓜ B·Q to 57th St ◑ 10am–6pm Mon–Sat (to 8pm Thu). ▤ all

Guggenheim Museum Store

Pricey merchandise for the art lover (and materialist) in you: Chinese paint and ink sets, geometric-shaped Japanese mobiles, decorated chopsticks as well as museum store staples like posters, prints, scarves, T-shirts and shoulder bags. $$

1071 Fifth Avenue (bet. 88th & 89th Sts)
☎ 423-3615 Ⓜ 4·5·6 to 86th St ◑ 9am–6pm daily (to 8pm Fri–Sat). ▤ AE/MC/V

Metropolitan Museum of Art Store

The mother of all museum shops, the Met's three spacious, colourful floors are an ode to art and commerce, and the book department can equal any art bookstore in the city. $$

Fifth Avenue (bet. 80th & 84th Sts)
☎ 650-2850 Ⓜ 4·5·6 to 86th St ◑ 9.30am–5.15pm Tue–Sun (to 9pm Fri–Sat). ▤ all

Museum of Modern Art Store

Most of the goods in the MoMA shop relate directly to the museum's permanent exhibits: its calendars, posters, monographs and books all make great gifts. Don't miss the MoMA design store across the street, which features rugs and kitchen accessories as well as contemporary remakes of furniture by designers like Charles Rennie Mackintosh. $$

11 W 53rd Street (bet. Fifth & Sixth Aves)
☎ 708-9700/767-1050 Ⓜ E·F to 5th Ave
◑ 10am–7pm daily (to 9pm Fri). ▤ AE/MC/V

Pearl River Mart

This Chinese emporium is packed with goodies: Chinese pyjamas and dresses, plain white T-shirts, great slippers, sandals, and loads and loads of oriental *tchotchkes*. Load up your baskets. $

277 Canal St (at Broadway) ☎ 431-4770
Ⓜ B·Q to Grand St; N·R to Canal St
◑ 10am–7.30pm daily. ▤ all

Troy

Troy's superb collection of strong design pieces by various New York and European names is offset by a sleek, all-white space. Hunt for the best in 90's design: unique lamps, small furniture and cool accessories like clocks and candles. Everything has a strong graphic edge. $$

138 Greene St (bet. Houston & Prince Sts) ☎ 941-4777 Ⓜ N•R to Prince St; C•E to Spring St; 6 to Bleecker St ◐ 11am–7pm Tue–Sat (to 6pm Sat); 12–6pm Sun. 🚊 AE/MC/V

Shi

Spare, sleek and modern is the style of this store, and everything in it from tiny lights on strings to perfectly-shaped ash trays. Very Zen. $$

233 Elizabeth St (bet. Houston & Prince Sts) ☎ 334-4330 Ⓜ 6 to Bleecker St ◐ 12–7pm Tue–Sat; 12–6pm Sun. 🚊 AE/MC/V

↓ books

In New York's ultra-competitive publishing world **Barnes & Noble** reigns supreme. With convenient locations in every pocket of New York (including Brooklyn), it carries selected hardcover new releases at 30% off. Author readings occur nightly and their cafés have a reputation as the pick-up bars of the 90's. In a similar vein, but with fewer locations, **Borders Books and Music** has a wide range of titles at reasonable prices. Of the smaller chains, the excellent **Rizzoli** is best for art and design books and **Shakespeare & Co** is strong on fiction, drama, film titles and British imports.

Other specialty bookstores fill the niches the chains haven't covered. **Tower Books** focuses on music titles, whereas the atmospheric **A Photographer's Place** offers secondhand photo books to stack up on the coffee table. East Village subversives adore their local **St Mark's Bookshop**, which puts the emphasis on politics, theory and the cutting-edge. The West Village literary set prefer New York's prettiest bookstore, **Three Lives and Company**, with its large fiction section. Judging by the number of mystery bookstores in town, New Yorkers have a voracious appetite for intrigue. **Murder Ink** is among the best of the bunch. Sci-fi, comic and graphic novel fans, meanwhile, will appreciate the massive range at **Forbidden Planet**. But if your idea of adventure is the rise and fall of a soufflé, then **Kitchen Arts**

& Letters is home sweet home. **A Different Light** ▶ is the largest gay and lesbian bookshop in NY. It's a genuinely fun place to hang out with a buzzing café where events are held regularly.

With a purported 8 miles of used books to choose from, **The Strand** has enough dusty tomes to keep the most avid bibliophile busy for days. Look out for new hardcovers at significant discounts too. For used books in a less intimidating environment, visit 80-year-old **Gotham Book Mart**, a NY literary landmark. Replete with used books on all subjects, its walls are lined with photos of folk who have read and met here over the years.

A Different Light

151 W 19th St (bet. Sixth & Seventh Aves) ☎ 989-4850 Ⓜ F•1•2• 3•9 to 14th St; L to 6th Ave ◐ 10am–midnight daily. 🚊 all $–$$

A Photographer's Place

133 Mercer St (bet. Prince & Spring Sts) ☎ 966-2356 Ⓜ C•E•6 to Spring St; N•R to Prince St ◐ 11am–8pm Mon–Sat; 12–6pm Sun. 🚊 all $–$$

Barnes & Noble

105 Fifth Ave (at 18th St) ☎ 807-0099 Ⓜ L•N•R•4•5•6 to 19th St-Union Sq ◐ 9.30am–7.45pm Mon–Sat (to 6.15pm Sat); 11am– 5.45pm Sun. 🚊 all $ 🛍

Borders Books and Music

5 World Trade Center (bet. Church & Vesey Sts) ☎ 839-8049 Ⓜ C•E to World Trade Center ◐ 7am–8.30pm Mon–Sat (from 10am Sat); 11am–8.30pm Sun. 🚊 all $–$$

Forbidden Planet

840 Broadway (at 12th St) ☎ 473-1576 Ⓜ L•N•R•4•5•6 to 14th St-Union Sq ◐ 10am–8.30pm daily. 🚊 all $–$$

Gotham Book Mart

41 W 47th St (bet. Fifth & Sixth Aves) ☎ 719-4448 Ⓜ B•D•F•Q to 47th–50th Sts-Rockefeller Ctr ◐ 9.30am–6.30pm Mon–Sat (6pm Sat). 🚊 AE/MC/V $

Kitchen Arts & Letters

1435 Lexington Ave (bet. 93rd & 94th Sts) ☎ 876-5550 Ⓜ 6 to 96th St ◐ 1–6pm Mon; 10am–6.30pm Tue–Fri; 11am–6pm Sat (closed Sat & Sun Jul–Aug). 🚊 MC/V $–$$

Murder Ink

2486 Broadway (bet. 92nd & 93rd Sts) ☎ 362-8905 Ⓜ 1•2• 3•9 to 96th St ◐ 10am–7.30pm Mon–Sat; 11am–6pm Sun. 🚊 AE/MC/V $–$$

Rizzoli

31 W 57th St (bet. Fifth & Sixth Aves) ☎ 759-2424 Ⓜ B•N•Q•R to 57th St ◐ 10.30am–9pm Mon–Sat; 12–7pm Sun. 🚊 all $–$$ 🛍

St Mark's Bookshop

31 Third Ave (bet. 8th & 9th Sts) ☎ 260-7853 Ⓜ 6 to Astor Pl ◐ 10am–midnight daily (from 11am Sun). 🚊 all $–$$

Shakespeare & Co

716 Broadway (at Washington Pl) ☎ 529-1330 Ⓜ 6 to Astor Pl ◐ 10am–11pm daily (to midnight Fri–Sat). 🚊 all $–$$

The Strand

828 Broadway (at 12th St) ☎ 473-1452 Ⓜ L•N•R•4•5•6 to 14th St-Union Sq ◐ 9.30am–9.30pm daily (from 11am Sun). 🚊 all $–$$

Three Lives & Company

154 W 10th St (at Waverly Pl) ☎ 741-2069 Ⓜ A•B•C•D•E•F•Q to W 4th St-Washington Sq ◐ 1pm–8pm daily (from 11am Thu–Sat; to 7pm Sun). 🚊 AE/MC/V $–$$

Tower Books

383 Lafayette St (at E 4th St) ☎ 228-5100 Ⓜ 6 to Astor Pl; B•D•F•Q to Broadway-Lafayette St ◐ 9am–midnight daily. 🚊 all $–$$

↓ electronics

For camera and electrical items go to any one of the numerous stores between 30th and 50th Streets, from Fifth to Park Avenues. They appreciate a good haggle but beware of inferior goods and fakes (which are plentiful). Comparative shopping is always your best bet, though some sales people are willing to lower on their prices to close the deal – especially if you're paying cash. **Nobody Beats the Wiz** and **Radio Shack** are the main chains. The Wiz specializes in television and sound equipment, and their bargains make up for the slow service. For years, consumers have thought of Radio Shack as a cheap imitation of the electronic big boys. But recently, their products have taken a giant step

forward in quality, and the slightly higher costs reflect it. A good one-off, **J & R Music & Computer World** has all the top-name computer and stereo equipment you could ever hope to use. There's also **B & H Photo-Video**, the home from home for many photographers looking for the best deal on professional quality lenses and bodies. For gadget freaks, the **Sharper Image** is your destination.

B & H Photo-Video
420 Ninth Ave (bet. 33rd & 34th Sts) ☎ 239-7500
Ⓜ A·C·E to 34th St-Penn Stn
🕐 9am–7pm Mon–Thu; 9am–1pm Fri; 10am–5pm Sun.
🍴 all $-$$

J & R Music & Computer World
23 Park Row (bet. Beekman & Ann Sts) ☎ 238-9100
Ⓜ J·M·Z·2·3·4·5 to Fulton St-Broadway Nassau;

N·R·4·5·6 to City Hall
🕐 9am–7pm Mon–Sat (to 7.30pm Thu); 10.30am–6.30pm Sun. 🍴 all $-$$

Nobody Beats the Wiz
555 Fifth Ave (at 46th St)
☎ 557-7770 Ⓜ B·D·F·Q to 47–50th Sts-Rockefeller Center; E·F to 5th Ave
🕐 9am–8.30pm Mon–Sat; 11am–7pm Sun. 🍴 all $-$$

Radio Shack
626 Broadway (bet. Houston & Bleecker Sts)
☎ 677-7069 Ⓜ B·D·F·Q to Broadway-Lafayette St
🕐 10am–8pm Mon–Sat; 11am–6pm Sun. 🍴 all $$

Sharper Image
4 W 57th St (bet. 5th & 6th Aves) ☎ 265-2550 Ⓜ B·D·F·Q to 47–50th Sts-Rockefeller Center; E·F to 5th Ave
🕐 10am–7pm Mon–Sat (to 6pm Sat); 12–5pm Sun. 🍴 all $$

↓ cds, records & tapes

NYC has every kind of record store from big-name chains to kooky specialty stores. **Tower Records** is a virtual music supermarket, its three floors of merchandise making a good starting point for any mainstream release. **HMV** is another giant with thousands of titles to browse as an in-store DJ entertains you. And the **Virgin Megastore** has the most comprehensive selection, which compensates for the slightly higher prices.

There's a string of music stores along St Mark's Place, which are good for price and selection. The best of these is **Kim's Video & Music**, with a great range and helpful staff. It's also a good spot for used CDs. **J & R Music & Computer World** is the best for bargains and carries all new releases at discount. There are separate departments for jazz and classical CDs.

DJs make their way to **Dancetracks** where all the latest dance music is car-

ried on vinyl. **8 Ball Records**, the record label's own store, is also excellent for house and other dance music. But for the newest in hip-hop, push your way past the DJs into **Fat Beats**, although DJs looking for bargains tend to frequent **Record Explosion**. For used CDs that also include fairly new pop hits, **Disco Rama** is hard to surpass.

If you want to go back in time, **Bleecker Bob's Golden Oldies** has vintage and collectible vinyl and the tour T-shirts to match. To pick up tour posters and recordings of your favourite live show, **Generation Records** is a gold mine. Jazz aficionados regularly make pilgrimages to the **Jazz Record Center** to get their fix, while those who love musicals head to **Footlight Records**. On Broadway, **Colony Records** also has an extensive collection of show tunes with the sheet music too. On a more classical note, **Academy Records** is especially good for used classical CDs. Hard-to-find titles are

tracked down by **Other Music**. The knowledge of their staff alone might make it the best record store in the city.

Academy Records
10 w 18th St (bet. 5th & 6th Aves) ☎ 242-3000 Ⓜ L·N·R· 4·5·6 to Union Sq 🕐 11am– 7pm daily. 🍴 AE/MC/V $

Bleecker Bob's Golden Oldies
118 W 3rd St (at MacDougal St) ☎ 475-9677 Ⓜ A·B·C· D·E·F·Q to W 4th St-Wash-inshgton Sq 🕐 12pm–1am daily (from 3am Fri–Sat).
🍴 all $-$$

Colony Records
1619 Broadway (at 49th St)
☎ 265-2050 Ⓜ N·R to 49th St; 1·9 to 50th St 🕐 9.30am– midnight daily. 🍴 all $-$$

Dancetracks
91 E 3rd St (at 1st Ave)
☎ 260-8729 Ⓜ F to 2nd Ave
🕐 12–9pm Mon–Sun (to 10pm Fri). 🍴 AE/MC/V $

Disco Rama
186 W 4th St (bet. 6th & 7th Aves) ☎ 206-8417 Ⓜ A·B·C· D·E·F·Q to W 4th St-Wash-inshgton Sq 🕐 10.30am– 10.30pm Mon–Sat (to 11.30pm Fri; from 12.30am Sat); 11.30am–8pm Sun. 🍴 all $

8 Ball Records
105 E 9th St (bet. 3rd & 4th Aves) ☎ 473-6343 Ⓜ 6 to Astor Pl; N·R to 8th St
🕐 12–9pm Mon–Sat; 1–7pm Sun. 🍴 AE/MC/V $

Fat Beats

406 Sixth Ave (bet. 8th & 9th Sts) ☎ 673-3883 Ⓜ A·B·C·D· E·F·Q to W 4th St-Washinshgton Sq ◑ 12–9pm daily (to 10pm Fri–Sat; 6pm Sun). 🖃 MC/V $–$$

Footlight Records

113 E 12th St (bet. 3rd & 4th Aves) ☎ 533-1572 Ⓜ L·N·R·4· 5·6 to 14th St-Union Sq ◑ 11am–7pm Mon–Fri; 10am–8pm Sat; 11am–5pm Sun. 🖃 AE/MC/V $–$$

Generation Records

210 Thompson St (bet. Bleecker & W 3rd Sts) ☎ 254-1100 Ⓜ A·B·C·D·E·F·Q to W 4th St-Washington Sq ◑ 11am–10pm Mon–Fri; 11–1am Sat; 12–10pm Sun. 🖃 AE/MC/V $–$$

HMV

57 W 34th St (at 6th Ave) ☎ 629-0900 Ⓜ B·D·F·N·R·Q to 34th St-Herald Sq ◑ 9am–10pm Mon–Sat; 11am–9pm Sun. 🖃 AE/MC/V $–$$ 🛍

Jazz Record Center

8th flr, 236 W 26th St (bet. 7th & 8th Aves) ☎ 675-4480 ◑ 10am–6pm Tue–Sat. 🖃 AE/MC/V $

J & R Music & Computer World

23 Park Row (bet. Beekman & Ann Sts) ☎ 238-9000 Ⓜ J·M·Z 2·3·4·5 to Fulton St-Broadway Nassau; N·R·4·5·6 to City Hall ◑ 9am–7pm Mon–Sat (to 7.30pm Thu); 10.30am–6.30pm Sun. 🖃 all $–$$

Kim's Video & Music

6 St Mark's Place (bet. 2nd & 3rd Aves) ☎ 598-9985, Ⓜ 6 to Astor Pl ◑ 9am–midnight daily. 🖃 AE/MC/V $

Other Music

15 E 4th St (bet. Broadway & Lafayette St) ☎ 477-8150 Ⓜ 6 to Bleecker St; B·D·F·Q to Broadway-Lafayette St ◑ 12–9pm daily (10pm Fri; 7pm Sun). 🖃 AE/MC/V $

Record Explosion

142 W 34th St (bet. 6th & 7th Aves) ☎ 714-0450 Ⓜ B·D·F·N·Q·R to 34th St-Herald Sq ◑ 9am–8.30pm Mon–Sat (to 9pm Sat); 10am–8pm Sun. 🖃 all $

Tower Records

692 Broadway (at E 4th St) ☎ 505-1500 Ⓜ 6 to Bleecker St ◑ 11am–11pm daily. 🖃 all $–$$

Virgin Megastore

1540 Broadway (bet. 45th & 46th Sts) ☎ 921-1020 Ⓜ A·C·E·N·R·1·2·3·7·9 42nd St-Times Sq ◑ 9–1am daily (from 2am Fri–Sat). 🖃 all $$ 🛍

↓ food stores

lower east side

Russ & Daughters

This cherished, spic-and-span Jewish deli has survived since World War I due to personalized service, and top quality smoked salmon (eight varieties), chopped liver, whitefish salad, sophisticated cheeses and dried fruits. So proud of their stock, they urge tastings on you (Eat!). $–$$

179 E Houston St (bet. Allen & Orchard Sts) ☎ 475-4880 Ⓜ F to 2nd Ave ◑ 9am–7pm Mon–Sat; 8am–6pm Sun. 🖃 MC/V

soho

Dean & Deluca

A huge white gallery with hundreds of mustards, vinegars, olive oils and herbs, plus gourmet cheeses, gorgeous breads, exotic flowers, professional kitchenware and cookbooks. Up front is a popular espresso bar. $$–$$$

560 Broadway (at Prince St) ☎ 226-6800 Ⓜ N·R to Prince St ◑ 10am–8pm daily (to 7pm Sun). 🖃 MC/V 🛍

Gourmet Garage

Groovy, food-conscious downtown types are always roaming the aisles here, filling their baskets with organic produce, European cheeses, house olive oil, salsa, tortilla chips and ice cream. Also a funky stop for bagels, sandwiches and soups to go. $–$$

453 Broome St (at Mercer St) ☎ 941-5850 Ⓜ N·R to Prince St ◑ 7am–9pm daily. 🖃 AE/MC/V 🛍

east village

Astor Wines & Spirits

Manhattan's biggest liquor store, with row upon row of bottles from around the world, including a trustworthy wine selection from New York State. The staff know their stuff and you can't beat the prices (check out the house brand liquors). Free wine tastings 3–6pm every Sat, and often 5–8pm Thu–Fri. $

12 Astor Pl (at Lafayette St) ☎ 674-7500 Ⓜ 6 to Astor Pl ◑ 9am–9pm Mon–Sat. 🖃 AE/MC/V

west village

Balducci's

Open since 1946, this virtual horn of plenty will astound you with its exquisite fruits and vegetables as well as lovely cheeses, pastries, chocolates, charcuterie and prepared foods. Most of it's costly, so sometimes it's just fun to look. $$–$$$

424 Sixth Ave (at 9th St) ☎ 673-2600 Ⓜ A·B·C·D·E· F·Q to W 4th St-Washington Sq ◑ 7am–8.30pm Mon–Sun. 🖃 MC/V

Murray's Cheese Shop

Manhattan's oldest cheese purveyor (opened 60 years ago) is beloved by foodies and locals alike – an old-world cornucopia of well-chosen international dairy produce, sold by a knowledgeable staff who have the gift of the gab. A fun Village stop for antipasti and sandwiches as well. $–$$

257 Bleecker St (bet. 6th & 7th Aves) ☎ 243-3289 Ⓜ 1·9 to Christopher St ◑ 8am–8pm Mon–Sat; 9am–9pm Sun. 🖃 AE/MC/V

chelsea

Garden of Eden

Both the Chelsea and East Village (314 Third Ave) locations display exotic, fascinating fruits you've never heard of: 'ugly fruit' from Jamaica, gold tamarilo from New Zealand, kiwana-horned melons, sweet feijoa, etc. This is a global, decently-priced farmers' market with dozens of types of marinated olives, fantastic prepared foods and cured meats. $$

162 W 23rd St (bet. 6th & 7th Aves) ☎ 675-6300 Ⓜ 1·9 to 23rd St ◑ 7am–10pm daily (9.30pm Sun). 🖃 AE/MC/V

upper east side

Best Cellars

Instead of classifying wines by grape or origin, here sections are labelled 'luscious', 'juicy', 'smooth', 'big', etc, so you can match them with mood or food. Better yet, every bottle is under $10 and has an evocative description to go with it. Free tastings daily from 5–8pm. $

1291 Lexington Ave (bet. 86th & 87th Sts) ☎ 426-4200 Ⓜ 4·5·6 to 86th St ◑ 10am–9pm Mon–Sat (10pm Fri–Sat). 🖃 AE/MC/V

Eli's Bread at The Vinegar Factory

Eli's is famous citywide for its cavernous warehouse of grocery items (the space formerly housed a vinegar factory). A salad bar holds dozens of choices and 10 fresh soups; the seafood counter, homemade potato chips and fresh squeezed juices also make it worth the trek. Upstairs is a café and exclusive housewares department. $$

431 E 91st St (bet. 1st & York Aves) ☎ 987-0885 🚇 4·5·6 to 86th St ⏰ 7am–9pm daily. 💳 AE/MC/V

upper west side

Zabar's

Beloved by New Yorkers and tourists alike, this landmark, labyrinthine store has a dizzying array of cheeses, coffee beans, bargain caviar, imported candies, baked goods and smoked salmon.

Upstairs are housewares at the cheapest prices in town. Nutty on the weekends. $

2245 Broadway (at 8oth St) ☎ 787-2000 🚇 1·9 to 79th St ⏰ 8am–7.30pm Mon–Sat (to 8pm Sat); 9am–6pm Sun. 💳 AE/MC/V

IDEAL 1st AVE @ 53rd cheese!

109

shops

↓ markets

Shopping al fresco is an alternative New York experience. Spring officially begins in the city when weekend street vendors put up their stands on streets like Astor Place, Columbus Avenue or along the sidewalks in the West Village to sell cheap clothes, handmade jewellery, and corndogs. A stall's merchandise tends to reflect the taste of the neighbourhood's residents. So it's downtown for hand-painted hash pipes, nose rings and kaftans and uptown for silk scarves, crystal necklaces and polished antiques.

Apart from street stalls, there are, luckily, several fixed markets which operate year round. On Sundays, **Orchard Street** is closed to traffic so local vendors can sell underwear, leather goods, and toys to the masses. Also on the weekend, the **Tower Market** is a small but crowded lot filled with knitted caps, T-shirts, and tapes. The **Spring Street Market** offers more of the same, with a particularly good selection of affordable knock-offs. Southeast of Central Park South's strip of hotels is **Columbus Circle Market** peddling art and antiques; it's a known hot spot for tourists, so prices tend to be higher. Uptown, the indoor and outdoor stalls at **PS 44** and **PS 183** sell upscale antiques, needlework, and various other arts and crafts. And way up in Harlem, the **Malcolm Shabazz Harlem Market**

is *the* place for colourful African imports.

Or have a rummage in one of the city's plentiful flea markets. The biggest and the best is Chelsea's **Annex Flea Market** which sells anything and everything. The next best place to check out is the **Soho Antique Fair Collectibles Market** on Broadway, which sells vintage clothing, old cameras, and crafts. **Columbus Flea** is, like Soho, on a much smaller scale than the Annex.

Farmers' markets sell fresh produce from New Jersey and Upstate New York. The open air one in **Union Square**, which sells fruit and vegetables, maple syrup, jams, flowers, and plants, is open year round. The indoor **Chelsea Market** houses about two dozen shops, specializing in delicious baked goods, seasonal produce, meat and fish.

Annex Flea Market
Sixth Ave (bet. 24th & 26th Sts) 🚇 F to 23rd St ⏰ 9am–5pm Sat–Sun.

Chelsea Market
75 Ninth Ave (bet. 15th & 16th Sts) ☎ 243-5678 🚇 A·C·E to 14th St; L to 8th Ave ⏰ 7am–7pm Mon–Sat; 10am–6pm Sun.

Columbus Circle Market
58th St & Eighth Ave 🚇 A·B·C·D·1·9 to 59th St-Columbus Circle ⏰ 11am–7pm daily.

Columbus Flea
77th St & Columbus Ave 🚇 B·C to 81st St-Museum of Natural History ⏰ 10am–5.30pm Sun.

Malcolm Shabazz Harlem Market
118 Lenox Ave (bet. 116th & 117th Sts) ☎ 987-8131 🚇 2·3 to 116th St ⏰ 10am–8.30pm daily

Orchard Street
Orchard St (bet. Delancey & Houston Sts) 🚇 F to Delancey St-Essex St ⏰ Sun.

PS 183
419 E 67th St (bet. 1st & York Aves) 🚇 6 to 68th St ⏰ 10am–6pm Sat.

PS 44
Columbus Ave (bet. 76th & 77th Sts) 🚇 1·9 to 79th St; B·C to 81st St ⏰ 10am–5.30pm Sun.

Soho Antique Fair Collectibles Market
Broadway & Grand St (nw corner) 🚇 J·M·N·R·Z·6 to Canal St ⏰ 9am–5pm Sat–Sun.

Spring Street Market
Spring & Wooster Sts 🚇 C·E to Spring St ⏰ 10am–7pm daily.

Tower Flea Market
Broadway (bet. W 4th & 3rd Sts) 🚇 B·D·F·Q to Broadway-Lafayette St ⏰ 10am–7pm Sat–Sun.

Union Square
(bet. 17th St & Broadway) 🚇 L·N·R·4·5·6 to 14th St-Union Sq ⏰ 8am–5pm Mon, Wed, & Fri–Sat.

new york's night-time hot spots

directory

Brighton Beach *♪off map*

Infamous Russian owned night-clubs and restaurants, popular with hen and stag nights, are sure to deliver too much vodka and kitsch floor shows

Chelsea *♪A5*

Lots of bustling restaurants and gay-slanted bars on Seventh and Eighth Avenues, plus some Off-Off Broadway theatres. Mega-clubs Twilo [→133] and Tunnel [→133] are located on the far west side.

Chinatown *♪B6*

Not great for bars or clubs, rather the streets here are thronged with those in search of excellent quality and reasonably-priced oriental food. The quintessential Chinatown.

East Village *♪B5*

One of New York's most active night-time hotspots, with abundant and varied restaurants, cool bars, live music venues, clubs and alternative theatre spaces.

Fort Greene *♪C6*

Nightlife tends to be dominated by the Brooklyn Academy of Music (BAM) [→140], which also has its own cinema. Nearby restaurants and cafés keep going into the early hours. Spoken word aficionados should investigate.

Harlem *♪A1–A2*

Once strictly no-go by day, let alone by night, Harlem is now quite a night-time destination, but it's still not advisable to loiter on quieter streets. Down by Columbia University, the scene is dominated by students.

Lower East Side *♪B5*

Ludlow and Orchard Streets are the focus for a happening bar and club scene; a mix of well-established and brand new – with something for everyone. There are also some interesting alternative performance spaces and lots of small live music venues.

Meatpacking District *♪A5*

A real happening hotspot. Several excellent restaurants, bars, and clubs are situated here.

Midtown *♪A4*

Away from the Theater District [→Theater District], there are lots of cinemas, and a good choice of restaurants and swank hotel bars.

Noho *♪B5*

Exceedingly hip restaurants, bars, and lounges are crammed into this tiny area. Also the location of the well-respected Joseph Papp Public Theater [→137].

Nolita *♪B5*

Neighbouring Nolita has an even greater concentration of bars and eateries including some of the moment's most fashionable destinations in NYC.

Soho *♪A5–A5*

Super-stylish restaurants and bars, loungey bar-clubs with velvet ropes and strict door policies. Club music venue Shine [→133] is located here, plus New York's leading arthouse cinema The Angelika [→139]. Very *Sex in the City*.

Theater District *♪A4*

The jewel in Midtown's crown. The location of around 30 Broadway theatres, plus lots of Off-Broadway ones too – as well as restaurants catering to the early evening theatre crowd. Times Square might be a shadow of its former seedy self, but the bright neon lights still cannot fail to impress. There are a few old-time dive bars around Hell's Kitchen, and lots of restaurants, especially those along Ninth Avenue.

Tribeca *♪A6*

Quite a well-behaved and local nightlife scene, centered around lots of restaurants and a few bars and lounges. Great music venues such as the Knitting Factory [→143], as well as the movie house, the Screening Room [→139].

Upper West Side *♪A3*

The Lincoln Center is the hub of nightlife in the lower reaches of the UWS, with its various concert and performance halls, great for opera, dance, classical and the occasional world music and jazz. Also many restaurants and bars in the 70's along Columbus Avenue.

Washington Heights *♪A1*

To the north of Harlem is Washington Heights with a happening bar scene, including lots of live music, especially jazz and Latin. Again, not an area to stroll around after dark.

West Village *♪A5*

Cosy Off-Off Broadway theatres, lots of smoky jazz clubs and laid back music cafes. A great number of excellent restaurants of all shapes and sizes, plus diverse lounges and bars, many for gay men and women, and their friends.

getting your bearings

restaurants, bars & clubs La Cote Basque

what's where

bars & restaurants chart

↓ brooklyn heights

Grimaldi's | $$ [→120] 🐧°

Junior's | $$ [→119] 🐧°

Peter Luger Steakhouse | $$$ [→121] 🐧° 🍴

Pour House [→132] 🍴

Stinger Club [→129] 🍴

↓ chelsea/meatpacking district

Baktun [→133] ●

Cafeteria | $$ [→118] 🐧°

Ciel Rouge [→129] 🍴

Empire Diner | $–$$ [→119] 🐧°

Florent | $–$$ [→114] 🍴 🐧°

Fressen | $$–$$$ [→118–119] 🐧° 🍴

Hell [→128] 🍴

Joe Jr's | $ [→119] 🐧°

Limelight [→133] ●

O Padeiro | $–$$ [→127] 🐧° 🍴

Pastis | $$ [→119] 🐧° 🍴

Tunnel [→133] ●

Twilo [→133–134] ●

↓ east village

Alphabet Lounge [→128] 🍴

Angelica Kitchen | $–$$ [→123] 🐧°

Angel's Share [→132] 🍴 🐧°

Baraza [→128] 🍴

The Cock [→132] 🍴

Decibel [→131] 🍴 🐧°

Dick's [→132] 🍴

First | $–$$$ [→126] 🐧° 🍴

Il Bagatto | $ [→119] 🐧° 🍴

KGB [→131] 🍴

Lakeside Lounge [→129] 🍴

Lei Bar [→131] 🍴

Old Devil Moon | $–$$ [→121] 🐧° 🍴

Pisces | $–$$ [→127] 🐧° 🍴

Prune | $$ [→127] 🐧° 🍴

Second Avenue Deli | $–$$ [→115] 🐧°

7A | $ [→124] 🐧°

Spa [→133] ●

Takahachi | $$–$$$ [→123] 🐧°

Wonder Bar [→132] 🍴

↓ gramercy park/flatiron district/union square/madison square

Chicama | $$–$$$ [→122] 🐧° 🍴

Eleven Madison Park | $$–$$$ [→118] 🐧° 🍴

Gramercy Tavern | $$–$$$ [→115] 🐧° 🍴

Mesa Grill | $$–$$$ [→122 & 124] 🐧° 🍴

Park Avenue Country Club [→130] 🍴

Patria | $$$ [→123] 🐧° 🍴

Tabla | $$$ [→123] 🐧° 🍴

Union Pacific | $$$ [→125] 🐧°

Union Square Café | $$$ [→116] 🐧° 🍴

Verbena | $$$ [→125] 🐧° 🍴

Veritas | $$$ [→127] 🐧° 🍴

Zen Palate | $–$$ [→123] 🐧°

↓ harlem/morningside heights/washington heights

Coogan's [→130] 🍴

Copeland's | $–$$$ [→114] 🐧° 🍴

Sylvia's | $–$$ [→124] 🐧°

Tom's Restaurant | $ [→119] 🐧°

↓ lower east side/chinatown

Baby Jupiter [→128] 🍴 🐧°

Fun [→133] ●

Good World Bar & Grill [→131] 🍴 🐧°

Joe's Shanghai | $–$$$ [→122] 🐧°

Katz's Deli | $ [→115] 🐧°

Kush [→131] 🍴

Max Fish [→131] 🍴

Meow Mix [→129] 🍴

Orchard Bar [→128] 🍴

71 Clinton Fresh Food | $$–$$$ [→126] 🐧° 🍴

Tonic [→129] 🍴 🐧°

Winnie's [→129] 🍴 🐧°

↓ midtown/hell's kitchen

Aquavit | $$$ [→116] 🐧° 🍴

Blue Bar [→132] 🍴

Chase [→132] 🍴

Cho Dang Gol | $–$$ [→122] 🐧°

Ess-a-Bagel | $ [→115] 🐧°

Island Burgers & Shakes | $ [→120] 🐧°

Jimmy's Corner [→130] 🍴 🐧°

La Bonne Soupe | $–$$ [→124] 🐧° 🍴

Le Bernardin | $$$ [→117] 🐧° 🍴

Lespinasse | $$$ [→117]

Michael Jordan's The Steakhouse | $$$ [→121]

Oyster Bar | $–$$$ [→115]

Regents [→132]

Rudy's [→132]

The Russian Samovar [→131]

Siberia [→132]

Swine on Nine [→131]

Top of the Tower [→130]

Trattoria dell'Arte | $$–$$$ [→115]

'21' Club | $$$ [→116]

↓ nolita/noho

Acquario | $–$$ [→126]

Balthazar | $$–$$$ [→118]

B-Bar and Grill [→118]

Bond St | $$–$$$ [→118]

Botanica [→128]

Il Buco | $–$$$ [→119]

Joe's Pub [→129]

Le Jardin Bistrot | $$–$$$ [→124]

Lombardi's | $$ [→121]

Mare Chiaro [→131]

Rialto | $$$ [→120]

Sweet & Vicious [→128]

↓ queens/jackson heights

Pearson's Texas Barbecue | $$ [→121]

↓ soho

Bar 89 [→129]

Blue Ribbon | $–$$$ [→126]

Grand Bar [→130]

Jerry's | $$ [→114]

Mercer Kitchen | $–$$$ [→119]

Pepe Rosso | $ [→121]

Quilty's | $$$ [→125]

Raoul's [→130]

357 [→130]

Void [→131]

↓ tribeca/lower manhattan

American Park | $$–$$$ [→124]

Bayard's | $$$ [→116]

Bouley Bakery | $$$ [→116]

Bubble Lounge [→130]

Capsouto Frères | $$–$$$ [→124]

The Greatest Bar on Earth [→130]

Lush [→130]

Nancy Whiskey Pub [→131]

Nobu | $$$ [→117]

The Odeon | $$–$$$ [→115 & 124]

Rosemarie's | $$–$$$ [→125]

Screening Room | $$–$$$ [→125]

Shine [→133]

Spartina | $$–$$$ [→125]

Vinyl [→134]

↓ upper east side/central park

Café Boulud | $$$ [→116]

Comfort Diner | $–$$ [→120]

Daniel | $$$ [→117]

Elaine's [→129]

Feinstein's at the Regency [→129]

Harry Cipriani | $$$$ [→130]

Jackson Hole | $ [→120]

Park View at the Boathouse | $$–$$$ [→124]

Payard Patisserie & Bistro | $$–$$$ [→127]

↓ upper west side

Artie's New York Delicatessen | $$ [→115]

Barney Greengrass | $$–$$$ [→115]

Big Nick's Burger | $ [→120]

Café des Artistes | $$$ [→114]

Calle Ocho | $$–$$$ [→122]

Jean Georges | $$$ [→117]

Pampa | $–$$ [→121]

↓ west village

Babbo | $$–$$$ [→118]

Bar d'O [→128–129]

Bar Pitti | $–$$ [→126]

Chumley's [→129]

Corner Bistro | $ [→120]

Gotham Bar and Grill | $$$ [→117]

Grange Hall | $$–$$$ [→126]

Halo [→128]

'ino | $ [→120]

Japonica | $$–$$$ [→122]

Joe Jr's | $ [→126]

Lupa | $$ [→127]

Nell's [→133]

Pó | $$ [→127]

Surya | $–$$$ [→123]

Tea & Sympathy | $–$$ [→121]

Waterloo | $$$ [→120]

Key	
$	main courses up to $10
$$	main courses up to $20
$$$	main courses above $20
🍴	restaurant/café
🍺	bar/pub
⚫	club

bars & restaurants chart

New York has always been a major chowtown but never so much as today – even the most dedicated foodie has trouble keeping up. You'd need a King Kong appetite and a Rockefeller-sized fortune to try it all, so sample what you can of the amazing variety of eateries – high-priced and low – in neighbourhoods all over the city.

eat up

↓ timeless classics

Café des Artistes 1 W 67th Street (bet. Columbus & Central Park W) | UWS

Intimate and extravagantly filled with flowers and sensual murals, Café des Artistes is not for the claustrophobic. Patrons are well-heeled and it's perfect for cozy dates and smart family dinners. The French fare is consistent and classic, with salmon served four ways (smoked, poached, dill-marinated and tartare) a highlight. Hungarian owner George Lang has also sneaked in some of his native dishes (like chicken paprika, and goulash soup). Service is cutely formal, and it's tough getting a reservation. The polished bar.is romantic for drinks.

☎ 877-3500 Ⓜ B·C to 72nd St; 1·9 to 66th St ◑ 12–2.30pm (from 11am Sat; from 10am Sun) & 5.30pm–midnight daily. ♂ 110 ♿ 🖥 ⤵ 🎵 🍽 all $$$

Copeland's 547 W 145th Street (bet. Amsterdam Ave & Broadway) | Harlem

If you're curious about Harlem, Copeland's is an excellent introduction. There's a veneer of formality and decor that recalls a 70s-style country club. The wine list is economical and the homey Southern cooking accomplished: fried chicken, collard greens, spicy Louisiana gumbo, and delectable candied yams. Sunday brunch features gospel, and every night it's live, glorious jazz (no cover charge).

☎ 234-2357 Ⓜ 1·9 to 145th St ◑ 4.30–11pm Tue–Sat (to midnight Fri–Sat); 12–11pm Sun. ♂ 85 ♿ 🖥 ⤵ 🎵 Tue–Sun Ⓢ (buffet Tue–Thu) 🍽 AE/MC/V $–$$$

Florent 69 Gansevoort Street (bet. Greenwich & Washington Sts) | Meatpacking District

Fêted institutions should often be avoided, but this drag queens' French diner on a cobblestone street is so much fun. You'll go away hoarse and deaf (especially late on weekends) and will eat amply, if not memorably. Best bets are roast chicken with mustard sauce and mash, boudin noir and fries, mussels, smoked trout, French toast, or steak frites. It's an ideal pitstop on your way home after an exhausting evening. Best to be decisive about what you want because some of the waiters are verging on cruel.

☎ 989-5779 Ⓜ A·C·E·L to 14th St ◑ 9–5am Mon–Thu; open 24 hrs Fri–Sun. ♂ 70 ♿ 🖥 ⤵ bar only 🖥 Ⓥ 🍽 none $–$$

Jerry's 101 Prince Street (bet. Greene & Mercer Sts) | Soho

Nearly the only soulful restaurant in the Soho 'mall', Jerry's red booths, mosaic-tiled floor, zinc bar and zebra-striped walls have held up well over time, as has much of the American comfort food with slight pretensions – well, mostly. Portions of roast chicken; seasonal vegetable plate; cajun shrimp salad; devilishly good chocolate brick cake – aren't exactly diner-sized, but the French toast, made with baguette, is the best in town. Watch out for the brunch crush and occasionally deranged service.

☎ 966-9464 Ⓜ N·R to Prince St ◑ 9am–11pm Mon–Sat (to 11.30pm Fri–Sat); 10.30am–5pm Sun. ♂ 70 ♿ 🖥 🖥 Ⓥ 🍽 all $$

Gramercy Tavern 42 E 20th Street (bet. Broadway & Park Ave S) | Gramercy

If your pocket's not up to it, you can sidestep the gastronomic prix fixe dinner at this extremely popular and lively temple to New American cuisine by sauntering into the tavern area (no reservations needed) where lower-priced à la carte items are featured. The wine selection is excellent, and they'll open just about anything for you to try by the glass. Everything – either in the tavern or in the dining room – is well prepared, such as fondue of sea urchin and crabmeat with curry essence, and roasted monkfish with pancetta and truffle vinaigrette. Lunch is happening, too, with a more reasonable set menu.

☎ 477-0777 Ⓜ N·R to 23rd St ◑ Dining room: 12–2pm Mon–Fri; 5.30–11pm Sat–Sun; Tavern: 12–11pm daily (to midnight Fri–Sat). 👤 140 (dining room); 52 (tavern) 🚻 ☐ 🍽 🅱 $ ☐ all $$–$$$

The Odeon 145 W Broadway (bet. Duane & Thomas Sts) | Tribeca

If Downtown had to eliminate all but one restaurant, the vote would definitely be to keep Odeon, the ideal place for all occasions (date, birthday, hunger), all hours (still busy at midnight Mondays), all moods (it can cure misery), and all types (though predominantly arty and cool). In the early 80s art boom, it was the place to be seen (Warhol et al), then it died a little, now it's here to stay. Food is American bistro (burgers, seared tuna, beet and fennel salad, steak frites); service is brisk. Enjoy.

☎ 233-0507 Ⓜ A·1·2·3·9 to Chambers St ◑ 11.45–1am Mon–Wed; 11.30–3am Thu–Sat; 11.30–1am Sun. 👤 120 🚻 limited ☐ 🍸 bar only 🍽 🅾 Ⓥ ☐ all $$–$$$

Oyster Bar Lower Level | Grand Central Station | Midtown

Somehow, visiting the Oyster Bar is a little like going to Coney Island: corny yet peculiarly charming. Essentially, it's expensive, ultra-fresh fish and seafood in an old-fashioned setting with gruff yet winsome servers who've been at it for decades. The vaulted space is vast and sitting at the counter for chowder, fresh oysters (tons of different types) and a glass of beer is an after-work treat. House specials include bouillabaisse, Maryland crab cakes and Arctic char. The big, dark bar at the back feels like a wood-lined steamship cabin.

☎ 490-6650 Ⓜ 4·5·6·7 to Grand Central-42nd St ◑ 11.30am–9.30pm Mon–Sat (from 5.30pm Sat). 👤 480 🚻 🍽 ☐ all $–$$$

Trattoria dell'Arte 900 Seventh Avenue (at 57th St) | Midtown

The price of the cracker-thin, fresh clam pizza makes you wonder if the little molluscs were flown in first class from the ocean, but you know what? It's worth it. So is the creative antipasti, and there is a special fish dish every day. An illustrious set regularly gathers at this attractive, bustling Italian establishment, with Tina Brown, Steve Martin and actor William Baldwin being spotted in a single lunch sitting. If no stars are around, feast your eyes on the strange art bedecking the walls.

☎ 245-9800 Ⓜ N·R to 57th St ◑ 11.30am–2.45pm & 5–11.45pm daily (to 10.45pm Sun). 👤 300 🚻 ☐ 🍽 ☐ all $$–$$$

↓ eat-in delis

Artie's New York Delicatessen 2290 Broadway (bet. 82nd & 83rd Sts) | UWS
New kid on the block doles out great old-time deli favourites.
☎ 579-5959 Ⓜ 1·9 to 86th St ◑ 9am–11pm daily (to midnight Fri–Sat). 👤 100 🚻 🍽 🅾 Ⓥ ☐ AE/MC/V $$

Barney Greengrass 541 Amsterdam Avenue (bet. 86th & 87th Sts) | UWS
Topnotch Jewish specialties, velvety lox and knishes big as baseballs.
☎ 724-4707 Ⓜ 1·9·B·C to 86th St ◑ 8.45am–4pm Tue–Sun (to 5pm Sat–Sun). 👤 80 🚻 🍽 Ⓥ ☐ none $$–$$$

Ess-a-Bagel 831 Third Avenue (bet. 50th & 51st Sts)| Midtown
Charmless atmosphere but bagels like no other, plus everything else under the sun.
☎ 980-1010 Ⓜ 6 to 51st St ◑ 6.30am–10pm Mon–Fri; 8am–5pm Sat–Sun. 👤 100 🚻 🍽 Ⓥ ☐ none $–$$

Katz's Deli 205 E Houston Street (at Ludlow St)| LES
A funky cafeteria with incredible pastrami and chopped liver, around forever for good reason.
☎ 254-2246 Ⓜ F to 2nd Ave ◑ 8am–10pm daily (to 11pm Wed–Thu; to 3am Fri–Sat). 👤 100 🚻 🍽 Ⓥ ☐ AE/MC/V $–$$

Second Avenue Deli 156 Second Avenue (at 10th St) | East Village
Always a line but worth it for huge portions of quality meats and homemade pickles.
☎ 677-0606 Ⓜ 6 to Astor Pl ◑ 7am–midnight daily (to 3am Fri–Sat). 👤 110 🚻 🍽 Ⓥ ☐ AE/MC/V $–$$

'21' Club 21 W 52nd Street (bet. Fifth & Sixth Aves) | Midtown

What?! You might harrumph at paying $27 for a hamburger (potatoes and green beans included!), or $33 for chicken hash (Joe DiMaggio's favourite). But this Prohibition-era speakeasy is such a charming landmark it's hard to be curmudgeonly. Newish chef Erik Blauberg, a culinary historian, has taken standards to a new level of excellence. Flaming baked Alaska and caramelized banana flan lit with Malibu rum produce exciting pyrotechnics. Hang out at the bar and feel the tippling spirits of old regulars Ernest Hemingway and Humphrey Bogart.

☎ 582-7200 Ⓜ E•F to 5th Ave ◑ 12–2.30pm Mon–Fri & 5.30–10.15pm Mon–Sat (to 11pm Fri–Sat). 🍴 140 ♿ 🖥 ⏤ ▭ all $$$

Union Square Café 21 E 16th Street (bet. Fifth Ave & Union Sq W) | Union Square

You can see clear to America's heartland through chef Michael Romano's vibrant cooking, matched by a brilliant wine list. The ambience is streamlined and comfortable. Serving such innovative delights as risotto with foie gras, savoy cabbage and sage, and lobster 'shepherd's pie', it is not surprising that this is many New Yorkers' favourite restaurant. If you can't get a table, swing by and request a seat at the bar, order some wine, a hamburger and hot garlic chips, and you'll feel like the smartest cookie in town.

☎ 243-4020 Ⓜ L•N•R•4•5•6 to 14th St-Union Sq ◑ 12–2.30pm & 6–10.30pm Mon–Sat (to 11.30pm Fri–Sat); 5.30–10pm Sun. 🍴 125 ♿ 🖥 ▤ ▭ all $$$

↓ big bucks

Aquavit 13 W 54th Street (bet. Fifth & Sixth Aves) | Midtown

Named after an icy eau de vie, Aquavit aptly offers a broad selection of fluid flavours infused with lemon, dill or anise. They go best with herring (four types of saltwater fillets are available), and other unusual Swedish specialties, like crispy smoked salmon with fingerling dumplings and dill-sevruga broth. Chef Marcus Samuelsson experiments with global influences, both in the intimate (and less expensive) upstairs café and in the formal downstairs atrium, which dramatically shoots up six storeys towards the skylights. A sculpted waterfall whispers in the background.

☎ 307-7311 Ⓜ E•F to 5th Ave ◑ 12–2.15pm Mon–Fri; 5.30–10.30pm Mon–Sat; 12–4pm Sun. 🍴 75 🖥 ⏤ ▤ Ⓥ Ⓢ ▭ all $$$

Bayard's India House | 1 Hanover Square | Lower Manhattan

Maritime history and gentlemen's club elegance evoke an aura of privilege. Even though you might think Bayard's is just for Wall Street tycoons, you're wrong. Everyone who walks through the hallowed India House doors is treated like royalty by one of the best-trained, most personable staffs in the city. Sensational contemporary French cuisine is by chef Luc Dendievel; sautéed Hudson Valley foie gras, poached Maine lobster, and loin of venison in red wine are all divine, as is the wine list.

☎ 514-9454 Ⓜ 2•3 to Wall St ◑ 3.30–10pm Mon–Fri; 5.30–11pm Sat. 🍴 85 🖥 ⏤ ▤ ▭ all $$$

Bouley Bakery 120 W Broadway (at Duane St) | Tribeca

Some describe the space at Bouley as 'intimate' – others go for 'cramped'. But regardless, everyone agrees on the food: it's succulent and flavourful, an unadulterated party for your tastebuds. Chef David Bouley has long been revered for his creations, and despite the name 'Bakery' this is a fully-fledged NY culinary hotspot. Think filo-dusted shrimp with Maine crab meat and baby squid, Maple Leaf Farm duck with glazed turnips. While the service is often quite surly, tables are booked way ahead, and even though the prices get steep, no one seems to mind or complain. It's delish!

☎ 964-2525 Ⓜ 1•9 to Chambers St ◑ 11.30am–3pm & 5.30–11.30pm daily. 🍴 80 ♿ Ⓢ lunch only ▭ AE/MC/V $$$

Café Boulud 20 E 76th Street (bet. Fifth & Madison Aves) | UES

Since chef/owner Daniel Boulud is busy over at his four-star restaurant Daniel, he has appointed rising star Andrew Carmellini to man the stove at the smaller, more relaxed Café Boulud. His take on traditional French (chicken fricassee), seasonal specialties (smoked salmon latkes with caviar), vegetarian creations (cassoulet of root vegetables with garlic crust), and featured world cuisines (anything from Basque to Louisiana cooking) is subtle and deeply resonant. The warm, cosmopolitan room is plushly upholstered and usually filled with powerbrokers (but ties aren't required).

☎ 772-2600 Ⓜ 6 to 77th St ◑ 12–2.30pm & 5.45–11pm Tue–Sat; 5.45–11pm Sun–Mon. 🍴 90 ♿ 🖥 ▤ 🎨 Ⓥ Ⓢ ▭ all $$$

Daniel 60 E 65th Street (bet. Madison & Park Aves) | UES

Daniel Boulud is a god-like chef, and this pink parlour vindicates his reputation. He does serious, sit-up-straight French cuisine: incredible dishes include a chestnut-celery root soup with a braised apple slice and a tranche of foie gras immersed within; a *boeuf aux carottes* – perfect, peasanty braised beef and carrots; or roasted Arctic char with béarnaise and baby vegetables. Desserts are equally sublime – an espresso cup of foamy chocolate with a thick chocolaty bottom; a fruit soup with apple beignets... To die for.

☎ 288-0033 Ⓜ 6 to 68th St ◑ 12–2pm & 5.45– 11pm Mon–Sat. 🧍 130 ▯ ⏤ bar only 📋 Ⓢ 🍽 all $$$

Gotham Bar and Grill 12 E 12th Street (bet. Fifth Ave & University Pl) | West Village

Alfred Portale's edible sculptures have been amazing New Yorkers since 85. His kitchen has been a training ground for several of the city's top chefs, educated in his visionary architecture of flavours and beauty. The soaring room is lit by billowy parachutes, a great invitation to carefully savour sweetwater shrimp salad with papaya and curry vinaigrette, and seared yellowfin tuna with *pappardelle* and *caponata*. The polished, friendly service also sets the standard, and the crowd is sophisticated too.

☎ 620-4020 Ⓜ L•N•R•4•5•6 to 14th St-Union Sq ◑ 12–2.15pm Mon–Fri; 5.30–10pm daily (to 11pm Fri–Sat; 9.45pm Sun). 🧍 153 ♿ ▯ 📋 🍽 all $$$

Jean Georges Trump International Hotel | 1 Central Park W (bet. 60th & 61st Sts) | UWS

Eating at this four-star mega blockbuster is not going to be easy. Tables are booked 30 days in advance with every foodie in town eager to explore Jean-Georges Vongerichten's eclectic palette, which might include black sea bass with Sicilian pistachio crust, and loin of lamb dusted with black trumpet mushrooms and leek purée. The dining room's floor-to-ceiling windows and neutral canvas of colours is a soothing backdrop for the smart, refined clientele, who discuss their dishes in low, thrilled tones. The kitchen also turns out grilled meats, salads and cold soups for the Mistral Terrace (summer only) which overlooks Central Park.

☎ 299-3900 Ⓜ A•B•C•D•1•9 to 59th St-Columbus Circle ◑ 12–2.30pm & 5.30–11pm Mon–Fri; 5.30–11pm Sat. 🧍 70 ♿ ▯ ⏤ 📋 🦋 Ⓢ 🍽 all $$$

Le Bernardin 155 W 51st Street (bet. Sixth & Seventh Aves) | Midtown

Chef Eric Ripert is so skilled he might spoil you for seafood prepared by anyone else. Based in corporate, moneyed Midtown, Le Bernardin has started to attract a cool, younger clientele flush with newfound-but-not-obnoxious wealth. The quiet, wood-lined dining room is Frank Lloyd Wright-inspired, embellished with gorgeous floral arrangements. It's flying first class all the way. Sit in the kitchen (six available seats) to observe the French master more closely, but only the very brave would try to duplicate dishes like roasted lobster tail with finely diced foie gras or skate in goosefat with caramelized confit of artichokes and fennel.

☎ 489-1515 Ⓜ N•R to 49th St; 1•9 to 50th St ◑ 12–2.30pm Mon–Fri; 5.30–10.30pm Mon–Sat (to 6pm Mon; to 11pm Fri–Sat). 🧍 120 ♿ ▯ ⏤ 📋 Ⓢ 🍽 AE/MC/V $$$

Lespinasse St Regis Hotel | 2 E 55th Street (bet. Fifth & Madison Aves) | Midtown

The grandest of Gotham City's French restaurants is named after Mademoiselle Lespinasse who, during Louis XV's reign, entertained philosophers, nobles and diplomats in her Paris salon. The restaurant's exquisite atmosphere may evoke a past era, but you'll hear big money deals discussed more than ideas. Chef Christian Delouvrier is highly trained in classic French techniques, using only the best ingredients in dishes like hare stew in red wine, and confit of baby pig in rich cassoulet. Before or after dinner, take time to luxuriate in the glowing King Cole Bar.

☎ 339-6719 ◑ 7–10.30am, 12–2pm & 5.30–10pm Tue–Sat. 🧍 88 ♿ ▯ 📋 🍽 AE/MC/V $$$

Nobu 105 Hudson Street (at Franklin St) | Tribeca

Nobu's nouvelle-Japanese morsels are remarkable in flavour, freshness and sheer artistry. With no holds barred, dinner for two in this dramatic blond-wood setting easily costs $200 with items like abalone and sea urchins on the menu, but eating here for half that amount is possible if you stick to regular sushi items with salmon, squid, mackerel or white fish. (The more intriguing-sounding sakes and seafood specialties can really add up.) Film and music big-shots, and a galaxy of pretty faces fill the soaring, dramatic stage where the sushi bar stools look like oversized chopsticks, wall sconces resemble crossed samurai swords, and lights are embedded within towering birch tree sculptures.

☎ 219-0500 Ⓜ 1•9 to Franklin St ◑ 11.45am–2.15pm & 5.45–10.15pm Mon–Fri; 5.45–10.15pm Sat–Sun. 🧍 140 ♿ ▯ 📋 🍽 all $$$

↓ talk of the town

restaurants & cafés

Babbo 110 Waverly Place (bet. MacDougal St & Sixth Ave) | West Village

Everything good you hear about Mario Batali's gorgeous place in the old Coach House is true. Two spacious lemon-yellow rooms (upstairs is fancier), and meticulous service are merely the backdrop to the most original Italian food around. Read and salivate: goat's cheese tortellini with dried orange and wild fennel pollen; chestnut gnocchi with wild boar – and that's just the *primi*. Entrées are equally imaginative and desserts such as poached kumquats with gorgonzola are delectable.

☎ 777-0303 Ⓜ A·B·C·D·E·F·Q to W 4th St-Washington Sq ◑ 5–11.30pm Mon–Sun (to 11pm Sun). 🧍 100 ♿ limited 📱 📋 ⑤ 📇 all $$–$$$

B-Bar & Grill 40 E 4th Street (bet. Bowery & 4th St) | Noho

Here, in the sexy, aviary-themed dining room, in the huge bar and out on the enclosed patio, interesting faces and fashions are sure to be seen. Even though it's been around a few years, B-Bar (formerly the Bowery Bar) still hosts tons of private music biz parties, and there's always a line of stretch limos purring outside. American favourites, like crab cakes and roast chicken with mash, are dead certs.

☎ 475-2220 Ⓜ 6 to Astor Pl ◑ Restaurant: 11.30am–midnight daily (from 10.30am Sat–Sun), Bar: 10.30am–4am daily). 🧍 180 ♿ 📱 ⤹ 📋 📇 Ⓥ 📇 all $–$$$

Balthazar 80 Spring Street (bet. Broadway & Crosby St) | Nolita

When this spot-on facsimile of the perfect Parisian bistro opened in 1997, it was a too-hot-to-handle celebrity-model nightmare, but now it's assumed its rightful place as the young sibling of New York's most lovable restaurant, Odeon [→115]. Order very good renditions of French faves – plateau de fruits de mer; the Balthazar salad of greens, green beans, sheep's cheese and truffle oil; steak-frites; rabbit *pappardelle* – all accompanied by fine sourdough bread baked at the next-door boulangerie. This is a guaranteed fun meal out.

☎ 965-1414 Ⓜ N·R to Prince St; 6 to Spring St ◑ 7.30–2am Sat–Thu (to 3am Sat–Sun). 🧍 150 ♿ 📱 ⤹ bar only 📋 📇 all $$–$$$

Bond St 6 Bond Street (bet. Broadway & Lafayette Sts) | Noho

This is the three-storey Japanese restaurant that out-Nobus Nobu. The lower ground floor is a loud bar where you pick your sake by personality, eg 'cool, subtle and refined' or 'warm, rich and complex'; above, there are two floors of packed, dimly-lit, minimalist dining rooms. Drop your entire budget on *osetra* caviar sushi, select spotted sardine, needle fish and basil-smoked salmon *nigiri*, or get fab, fun rolls like sesame-crusted shrimp with orange curry dressing. Absolutely not your everyday sushi joint.

☎ 777-2500 Ⓜ B·D·F·Q to Broadway-Lafayette St; 6 to Bleecker St ◑ 6pm–midnight daily (to 11pm Sun). 🧍 135 📱 ⤹ bar only 📋 ⑤ 📇 all $$–$$$

Cafeteria 119 Seventh Avenue (at 17th St) | Chelsea

Don't be fooled by the name – this is the furthest thing from a typical cafeteria. In fact, it's one of the city's sleeker hot spots, so try not to gawp when Kate Moss, Calvin Klein or Evan Dando sit at the cushy booth right next to you and order from a menu packed with cholesterol-rich comfort food like old-fashioned macaroni cheese, fries, milk shakes, and jaw-breakingly huge sandwiches. Downstairs, there's a funky lounge where late-night crawling lizards may languish.

☎ 414-1717 Ⓜ L·1·2·3·9 to 14th St ◑ 24 hours daily. 🧍 80 ♿ limited 📇 all $$

Eleven Madison Park 11 Madison Park (at 14th St) | Gramercy Park

Danny Meyer, restaurateur supreme (Union Square Café, Gramercy Tavern, Tabla) scores another success with this swanky eaterie located in a former bank. It's his most corporate place, from the lobby-like soaring marble-floored room to the Yankee-French food and the suits at the tables. Menus read like a butcher's display: foie gras several ways (with pomegranate essence, toasted walnuts and sage), braised pork shoulder, dry-aged sirloin strip, loin of lamb, saddle of venison, roast chicken (with potato speck tart); accompaniments are invariably hearty. Not for vegetarians, anorexics or dates.

☎ 889-0905 Ⓜ N·R to 23 St ◑ 5.30–10.30pm Mon–Sat (to 11pm Sat; to 9.30pm Sun). 🧍 168 ♿ 📱 📋 📇 all $$–$$$

Fressen 421 W 13th Street (bet. 9th Ave & Washington St) | Meatpacking District

More nightclub than restaurant when it first opened, in the summer of 1999, Fressen has mellowed a tad, making it easier to enjoy the organically-focused American cuisine. The seasonal menu changes daily, but you'll always find pristine fish, crispy Amish chicken and tender grilled meats, along with fresh-off-the-farm vegetables.

The concrete industrial space is warmed by oxblood lacquered walls, and the dimly-lit dining room is split up by handsome mahogany screens. Overzealous, slickly groomed boulevardiers sully it at weekends; to avoid them stick to weeknights.

☎ 645-7775 Ⓜ A·C·E to 14th St; L to 8th Ave ◐ 6pm–midnight daily. 👤 250 🖨 🍷 ⬛ ⊿ ▤ Ⓡ 2 weeks in advance 🖃 AE/MC/V $$–$$$

Il Bagatto 192 E 2nd Street (bet. Aves A & B) | East Village

If you never had the stereotypical Italian mamma (you know... killer cook, killer instinct) but always felt the need, head to this charming restaurant, where there are two rules: no cheese on seafood pasta, and be on time. While the service is often offhand and the seating cramped, the homemade gnocchi and lasagne will leave you begging for more. Everything is stuffed full of the best, hand-picked ingredients and made with love, so it's no wonder that the jewel box of a space is always packed with a hip crowd of downtown gurus, models and celebs. Warning: smoking's allowed here, and everyone does – with gusto.

☎ 228-0977 Ⓜ F to Second Ave ◐ 6.30–11.30pm Mon–Sat (to midnight Sat); 6–10.30pm Sun. 👤 34 🖨 🍷 ⊿ ▤ none $

Il Buco 47 Bond Street (bet. Bowery & Lafayette St) | Noho

On any night of the week, well-coiffed young debs and their Newport-type dates mob this dark, romantic restaurant filled with vintage toys and bookshelves of wine bottles. Long-haired, carefully dishevelled downtown artists also gather around the big wooden tables. A rustic Spanish/Italian theme is carried through from the country decor to such luscious tapas plates as polenta with goose ragu and duck prosciutto with port wine. Pasta specials are heavenly, like penne with artichoke, pancetta and cream. The wine list is wide-ranging and discriminating.

☎ 533-1932 Ⓜ 6 to Bleecker St ◐ 6pm–midnight Mon–Sat; 5–11pm Sun. 👤 80 🍷 🖨 ⊿ ▤ ▤ AE $–$$$

restaurants & cafés

Mercer Kitchen 147 Mercer Street (at Prince St) | Soho

Raw tuna pizza, black sea bass carpaccio, slow-cooked rabbit, garlic-spiked duck – you can't go wrong with anything you order in this ultra-cool, roomy subterranean restaurant in the fashionable Mercer Hotel [→152]. The food (prepared by one of New York's most acclaimed chefs, Jean Georges Vongerichten) is superb, though the crowd, decked out in the latest creations by Gucci, Prada and Helmut do their best to out-shine the menu. Whether you're a fashionista or Madonna, so long as you look the part, the staff will treat you like a star. Book way ahead.

☎ 966-5454 Ⓜ N·R to Prince St ◐ 8–10.45am, 12–2.45pm & 6pm–midnight daily. 👤 150 🍷 🖨 ⊿ bar only 🖃 all $–$$$

Pastis 9 Ninth Avenue (at Little W 12th St) | Meatpacking District

Über-restaurateur Keith (Balthazar) McNally set out to make his latest enterprise, Pastis, an everyday sort of bistro. Intents aside, he created a monster. The casual, faux-aged setting is an impeccable re-creation of a Provençal village café, so appealing that some nights it feels like all of Manhattan is trying to squeeze inside. Go early or very late (at midnight), as a two-hour wait during prime hours is standard, due to a no reservations policy. Dishes such as hearty pastas, roasted chicken with garlic confit, and supple braised beef are reliable and modestly priced.

☎ 929-4844 Ⓜ A·C·E to 14th St; L to 8th Ave ◐ 9–3am daily (to 4am Fri–Sat). 👤 150 🍷 🖨 ⊿ ▤ Ⓡ only for tables booked 6–7pm 🖃 AE/MC/V $$

↓ diners

Empire Diner 210 10th Avenue (at 22nd St) | Chelsea
Comfort food sassily served 24 hours a day, often accompanied by live piano music.
☎ 243-2736 Ⓜ C·E to 23rd St ◐ 24 hours daily (closed 4–8.30am Tue). 👤 100 ⊿ ▤ ▤ all $–$$

Joe Jr's 482 Sixth Avenue (at 12th St) | Chelsea
Cinematic diner dollhouse with lots of heart but no vitamin content.
☎ 924-5220 Ⓜ F to 14th st; L to 6th Ave ◐ 6–1am daily. 👤 90 ⊿ ▤ ▤ none $

Junior's 386 Flatbush Avenue (at De Kalb Ave) | Brooklyn
The blintzes and world-famous cheesecakes are showstoppers. Go on, live a little.
☎ 1-718-852-5257 Ⓜ D·M·N·Q·R to De Kalb Ave ◐ 6.30–12.30am daily (to 2am Sat). 👤 100 🖨 🖃 ▤ all $$

Tom's Restaurant 2880 Broadway (at 112th St) | Harlem
Immortalized by Seinfeld, with satisfying greasy-spoon specialties for student budgets.
☎ 864-6137 Ⓜ 1·9 to 110th St-Cathedral Pkwy ◐ 6–1.30am daily. 👤 85 ⊿ ▤ ▤ none $

Waterloo 145 Charles Street (at Washington St) | West Village

If you aren't in a good mood when you arrive here, you will be when you leave – the party-on atmosphere is up there with the best. The industrial, flatteringly-lit dining room is filled with arty types, and the tight seating promotes merrymaking. Sharing a black kettle of mussels and frites over a delicious Belgian beer is a bonding experience, and you'll also want to dig into each other's full-flavoured Belgian-accented chocolatey-rich desserts. One of the best of Manhattan's crop of Belgian eateries.

☎ 352-1119 Ⓜ 1·9 to Christopher St ◑ 6pm–1am Mon–Sun (to 2am Fri–Sat). 🍴 75 ♿ 🚻
⊿ bar only 🖃 AE/MC/V **$$$**

↓ bargain gourmet

Comfort Diner 142 E 86th Street (at Lexington Ave) | UES

New York is filled with greasy spoon diners with acceptable grub, but at the Comfort Diner (two locations), it's butter, not bacon grease, that will shoot up your cholesterol level. Owned by a nostalgic soul named Ira Freehof, the place is polished to a sheen. The idea is kitschy, but also authentic, with crunchy grilled cheese sandwiches, macaroni and cheese, and thick chocolate malteds. Soups and lighter sandwiches cater to healthier tastes. No alcohol served.

☎ 369-8628 Ⓜ 4·5·6 to 86th St ◑ 7.30am–11pm daily (from 9am Sat–Sun). 🍴 140 ♿ 🖼
🖃 all **$–$$**

Grimaldi's 19 Old Fulton Street (bet. Front & Water Sts) | Brooklyn Heights

Beneath the Brooklyn Bridge lies a paean to pizza lovers and Frank Sinatra (walls are littered with autographed photos of him as well as other bygone celebrities). Even the 'small' pizza is obscenely huge, the crust slightly charred, the fresh mozzarella bubbling from the brick oven. Conventional toppings are generous, the only gourmet touches being fresh basil leaves and a twist of fresh ground pepper. It may look tacky, and crass pop plays more than Ol' Blue Eyes, but it's hard to find a better pie.

☎ 1-718-858-4300 Ⓜ A·C to High St; 2·3 to Clark St ◑ 11.30am–10.45pm Mon & Wed–Fri (to midnight Fri); 2pm–midnight Sat; 2–11pm Sun. 🍴 70 ♿ 🖼 Ⓥ 🖃 none **$$**

'Ino 21 Bedford Street (bet. Sixth Ave & Downing St) | West Village

Tucked down a little West Village side street, this is exactly the kind of cheery nook you'd love to find on a roadside in Italy. The staff are warm and don't rush you, allowing time to sit and read, think, or chatter all afternoon and night. What's more, the light snacking food is delicious: marinated olives, bruschetta with a number of toppings and flavourful panini with quality ingredients. Smooth music and interesting wines served by the glass, half carafe and bottle help wash cares away.

☎ 989-5769 Ⓜ A·B·C·D·E·F·Q to W 4th St-Washington Sq ◑ 8–2am daily (from 11am Sat–Sun).
🍴 21 ♿ ⊿ 🖼 Ⓥ 🖃 none **$**

burgers

Big Nick's Burger 2175 Broadway (at 77th St) | UWS
24-hour Upper West Side dump that inspires affection; loosen your belt buckle.
☎ 362-9238 Ⓜ 1·9 to 79th St ◑ 24 hours daily. 🍴 110 ⊿ 🖼 🖃 all **$**

Corner Bistro 331 W 4th Street (at Jane St) | West Village
Cheap, juicy burgers in a dark saloon that do the trick after a night of drinking.
☎ 242-9502 Ⓜ A·C·E to 14th St; L to 8th Ave ◑ 11.30–4am daily (from 12pm Sun). 🍴 100 🚻
⊿ 🖼 Ⓡ 1–2 weeks 🖃 none **$**

Island Burgers & Shakes 766 Ninth Avenue (bet. 51st & 52nd Sts) | Midtown
Move over McDonald's. You can have it any way you like it here. But no fries.
☎ 307-7934 Ⓜ C·E to 50th St ◑ 12–01.30pm daily (to 11.30pm Fri–Sat). 🍴 100 ⊿ 🖼
🖃 none **$**

Jackson Hole 1270 Madison Avenue (at 91st St) | UES
Get lots of napkins for these messy burgers, especially good for kids.
☎ 427-2820 Ⓜ 4·5·6 to 86th St ◑ 6.30am–11pm Mon–Sat (from 8pm Sun); 8am–10pm Sun.
🍴 90 ⊿ 🖼 AE **$**

Rialto 265 Elizabeth Street (bet. Houston & Prince Sts) | Nolita
Groovy bistro with lots of inventive choices but nothing beats their thick, quality burgers and crispy fries.
☎ 334-7900 Ⓜ N to Spring St ◑ 5–12.30pm Mon–Sat (dinner); 11am–4.30pm Sat–Sun (brunch).
🍴 100 🚻 ⊿ 🖼 Ⓡ 1–2 weeks 🖃 all **$$$**

steaks, grills & bbq

Michael Jordan's The Steakhouse Grand Central | 23 Vanderbilt Ave | Midtown

Eat enough of his steak and lamb chops and you too might grow tall and strong – just like Mike.

☎ 655-2300 Ⓜ 4•5•6•7 to Grand Central-42nd St 🌓 12–3pm & 5–11pm Mon–Sat; 1–10pm Sun. 🍴 120 ♿ 🖺 ⤷ 🖾 𝄢 Ⓡ 3 days 🍽 all $$–$$$

Pearson's Texas Barbecue 71–04 35th Avenue (bet. Vernon blvd & East River) | Queens

Ensconced in a new home, Pearson's still serves up the best bbq in town. Get those fingers dirty and chow down.

☎ 1-718-779-7715 Ⓜ N to Broadway 🌓 12–9pm Tue–Sat (to 10pm Sat); 2–8pm Sun. 🍴 100 🖵 ⤷ 🖾 🍽 none $$

Peter Luger Steakhouse 178 Broadway (at Driggs Ave) | Brooklyn Heights

Don't ask for a menu: this century-old institution is strictly for carnivores who love the legendary dry-aged steaks. Go so hungry you could eat a cow – the portions are large.

☎ 1-718-387-7400 Ⓜ Z•M•J to Marcy Ave 🌓 12–9.45pm daily. 🍴 140 ♿ 🖵 ⤷ 🖾 𝄢 Ⓡ 8–10 weeks 🍽 none $$–$$$

Lombardi's 32 Spring Street (bet. Mott & Mulberry Sts) | Nolita

This little place is satisfyingly cinematic, with its brick walls and chequered cloths, but the point is the 1905 coal oven and the pizza that emerges from it, which is – honest – the best in Manhattan. The crust is the crispest, the mozzarella the freshest, the toppings (pancetta, sweet Italian sausage, anchovies, roasted peppers, fresh basil, etc) the finest. They also do a fresh clam pie without tomato or cheese, and a white pizza (no tomato), with mozzarella, romano, ricotta and garlic, with a salad on the side. That's all you need.

☎ 941-7994 Ⓜ 6 to Spring St 🌓 11.30am–11pm daily (to midnight Fri–Sat). 🍴 60 ♿ ⤷ 🖾 Ⓥ 🍽 none $$

Old Devil Moon 511 E 12th Street (bet. Aves A & B) | East Village

This is where your 'white trash diner' meets the edgy East Village. In a funky-looking flea market of mismatched chairs, booths, kitsch and fairy lights, gigantic portions of meatloaf with mash, stews, salads and – the best dish – country ham are served by unbelievably sweet waitpersons. The pies (peanut butter cream and the like) are so loved, that you can place orders for whole pies, to go.

☎ 475-4357 Ⓜ F to 2nd Ave 🌓 5–11pm Mon–Fri; 10am–midnight Sat–Sun. 🍴 60 ♿ 🖵 ⤷ 🖾 𝄢 Ⓥ 🍽 all $–$$

Pampa 768 Amsterdam Avenue (bet. 97th & 98th Sts) | UWS

If you're looking for a festive place to meet friends, you can't beat Pampa, even though they don't take reservations. It's a cool, lively spot and cheap enough for everyone. Argentine steaks, fries coated in garlic and parsley, juicy roasted chicken, flaky empanadas, and South American wines that start at $15 – all justify the trip Uptown. Waiters are so cute and sweet you'll want to take them home.

☎ 865-2929 Ⓜ 1•2•3•9 to 96th St 🌓 4pm–midnight Mon–Thu (to 11pm Mon); 12pm–midnight Fri–Sun (to 11pm Sun). 🍴 85 ♿ ⤷ 🖾 🍽 none $–$$

Pepe Rosso 110 St Mark's Place (bet. Ave A & First Ave) | Soho

Stop by Pepe Rosso's tiny Sullivan Street shop in Soho for a delicious hunk of focaccia to snack on while strolling around. With just a few cramped tables, it's not very comfortable to linger. However, their larger outpost in the East Village is a destination on its own. Dirt cheap pastas (spaghetti with pesto for $5.95!), salads and grilled vegetables are robustly flavoured. The dark, funky setting is utterly without pretension and wine is poured in fat, stemless glasses. Service is haphazard but when the food's this cheap and good, who cares?

☎ 677-6563 Ⓜ N•R to 8th St; 6 to Astor Pl 🌓 12pm–midnight daily. 🍴 55 ♿ ⤷ bar only 🖵 🖾 Ⓥ 🍽 none $

Tea & Sympathy ⤷ 108 Greenwich Avenue (bet. 12th & 13th Sts) | West Village

Anglos and Anglophiles alike can't get enough of Tea & Sympathy which is why it's often packed tight. Authentic English breakfasts, typical pub items (shepherd's pie, bangers and mash) and tea from mismatched pots are low-priced and satisfying. It looks like your favourite auntie's living room, the one who still cries over Diana (Royals) memorabilia is everywhere).

☎ 807-8329 Ⓜ A•C•E• 1•2•3•9 to 14th St 🌓 11.15am–10.30pm Mon–Fri; 10.30am–10.30pm Sat–Sun (to 10pm Sun). 🍴 23 ⤷ 🖾 Ⓥ 🍽 none $–$$

restaurants & cafés

↓ ethnic spice

Calle Ocho 446 Columbus Avenue (bet. 81st & 82nd Sts) | UWS

Past a warren of secret loungey nooks is a cavernous, dazzling dining room lit by huge burlap lampshades that resemble hoop skirts. One wall is dominated by a dramatic, faux-aged Cuban mural, and more Cuban imagery is evoked when wonderful rolls and muffins arrive in a lined cigar box. Alex Garcia's stimulating Pan-Latino cooking radiates fragrance and spice (octopus and calamari with palm hearts, chick peas and olives, or side dishes like *malanga* mash and green plantains), while fun rum drinks like *mojitos* and *caipirinhas* prime the palate.

☎ 873-5025 Ⓜ 1·9 to 79th St ◑ *6–11pm Mon–Fri (to midnight Fri); 5pm–midnight Sat–Sun (to 10pm Sun).* 🍴 180 ♿ ▯ ⚊ bar only 📖 🖿 all **$$–$$$**

Chicama 35 E 18th Street (bet. Broadway & Park Ave South) | Union Square

The exclusive emporium ABC Carpet & Home now houses a festive Nuevo Latino restaurant that is festooned with Peruvian rugs and constructed from a Brazilian country inn that was imported beam by beam. The sprawling, evocative space notwithstanding, the real draw here is ex-Patria chef Douglas Rodriguez, who stimulates palates with crispy fried oysters, citrusy ceviches, and spicy Peruvian hen stew with blue potatoes. The wine list is heavy on earthy South American choices, but it's the frothy Latino-inspired cocktails that really get the party going.

☎ 505-2233 Ⓜ L·N·R·4·5·6 to 14th St ◑ *12–3pm & 6pm–midnight Mon–Sat (to 1am Fri & Sat); 5.30–10pm Sun.* 🍴 100 ♿ ▯ ⚊ 📖 Ⓡ 2 weeks in advance 🖿 all **$$–$$$**

Cho Dang Gol 55 W 35th Street (bet. Fifth & Sixth Aves) | Midtown

This may be the only Korean restaurant that makes its own tofu, which sounds a missable experience, until, that is, you try the *Doo-Boo-Doo-Roo-Chi-Gi* (*kimchi* fermented cabbage with tofu and pork) or the *Mo-Doo-Boo Nak-Ji-Bok-Um* (octopus with tofu, vegetables and noodles), after your *Pa-Jun* – a delicious, thin, chewy pancake – and the Panjan of assorted fiery vegetable and fish side dishes. No place in Koreatown is friendlier. The lovely people seem to like helping neophytes with the mysteries of the menu.

☎ 695-8222 Ⓜ B·D·F·N·Q·R to 34th St-Herald Sq ◑ *11.40am–10.30pm daily.* 🍴 90 ♿ 📖 Ⓥ 🖿 all **$–$$**

Japonica 100 University Place (at 12th St) | West Village

There has been a long-time debate in NY sushi-eating circles over which place serves the best. Now it's official – well at least among the sushi-eating set. Whether you're a die-hard *Yama*-ite, a *Tomoe*-addict or a dedicated *Iso* fan, Japonica has the best. The beautifully-presented sashimi and sushi is swimmingly fresh (albeit pricey), their cooked delights are delicious, and there's always a colourful selection of specials. It's short on atmosphere and long on queues (so book ahead), but it's about a taste of Japan, not the trend factor.

☎ 243-7752 Ⓜ L·N·R·4·5·6 to 14th St-Union Sq ◑ *12–10.30pm Mon–Fri (to 11pm Fri); 1–11pm Sat–Sun (to 10.30pm Sun).* 🍴 90 ♿ 🖿 AE/DC **$$–$$$**

Joe's Shanghai 9 Pell Street (bet. Bowery & Mott St) | LES

The best joint in Chinatown. Sure, the insane queues, borderline rude service and communal tables may be frustrating, but there is nothing like their soup dumplings (scoop 'em up in a spoon, bite the top off, drink the soup inside, and then eat the crab meat and pork filling) and fried ricecakes. Get the real Shanghai experience, overorder, over-eat and share with friends...

☎ 233-8888 Ⓜ N·R·6 to Canal St; B·D·Q to Grand St ◑ *11am–11pm daily.* 🍴 110 ♿ Ⓥ 🖿 none **$–$$$**

Mesa Grill 102 Fifth Avenue (bet. 15th & 16th Sts) | Gramercy Park

Everything is oversized in the design of this airy, two-level space, from the huge pillars to the blown-up pop art, to fans as big as propellers on a B-52. The Southwestern flavours are tremendous, too. There's nothing cowardly about sweet potato and Scotch bonnet pepper ravioli, Yucatan-spiced venison or red snapper with roasted *poblano* sauce. Brunch is a standout, with Bloody Marys to knock your socks off. Cut down on the cost by visiting the long bar and sampling potent margaritas and spicy appetizers.

☎ 807-7400 Ⓜ L·N·R·4·5·6 to 14th St-Union Sq ◑ *12–2.30pm & 5.30–10.30pm Mon–Fri; 11.30am–3pm Sat–Sun.* 🍴 130 ♿ ▯ ⚊ bar only 📖 Ⓥ 🖿 all **$$–$$$**

restaurants & cafés

Patria 250 Park Avenue South (at 20th St) | Gramercy Park

Patria is the patriarch of the Nuevo Latino trend, and electrifying for lunch or dinner. Even though many other restaurants have copied its use of South American and Latin American ingredients, nobody can match chef Douglas Rodriguez's exceptional brilliance. The spacious, creatively-designed dining room sports mosaic touches reminiscent of Gaudi. The three-course set menu features dishes like incredible crispy oysters, 'fire and ice' tuna ceviche, and plantain-coated *mahi mahi*.

☎ 777-6211 Ⓜ 6 to 23rd St 🕐 12–2.30pm & 6–11pm Mon–Fri; 5.30pm–midnight Fri–Sun (to 10.30pm Sun). 🙆 120 ♿ 🖵 🗐 Ⓢ ⊟ all $$$

Surya 302 Bleecker Street (bet. Grove St & Seventh Ave S) | West Village

A former beauty queen from India is the hostess, setting the tone for a stylish room full of beautiful people. Exotic spices from Southern India blaze in dishes like *dosai* crêpes filled with sea bass, and grilled halibut with ginger and coconut cream. Unique vegetarian choices abound, making use of lentils in cakes, pancakes and soups; and spice-lifted aubergines, okra and potatoes in dishes served with mint rice or *paratha*. It's as modern as Indian restaurants get, also featuring spectacular, photogenic cocktails. The main dining room can be deafening, so when weather cooperates, opt for the serene courtyard.

☎ 807-7770 Ⓜ 1·9 to Christopher St-Sheridan Sq 🕐 11am–3pm Sat–Sun; 6.30–11.30pm Sun–Thu; 6pm–midnight Fri–Sat. 🙆 63 🖵 ⇴ lounge & bar only 🗐 🌐 Ⓥ ⊟ all $–$$$

Tabla 11 Madison Avenue (at 25th St) | Gramercy Park

Want a typical Indian dinner? This is not the place. Chef Floyd Cardoz may be a Bombay native but he's more influenced by his training in haute cuisine at Lespinasse. Tabla's food is actually American with a profusion of Indian spices, the flavours intense and controversial, provoking feelings of love and hatred. See which way you turn with dishes like tandoori rabbit, or lobster with pink lentils and five-spice sauce. The fricassee of shellfish comes with turmeric mash and curry leaves. The beautiful, two-level space has dynamic views of Madison Square Park; downstairs is the more casual Bread Bar (lentil soup and lamb tandoori are delicious); upstairs there's a $48 set menu.

☎ 889-0667 Ⓜ N·R·6 to 23rd St 🕐 12–2.30pm & 5.30–10.30pm Mon–Thu (to 11pm Fri); 5.30–11pm Sat. 🙆 75 Bread Bar; 116 main dining room ♿ 🖵 🗐 Ⓢ ⊟ all $$$

Takahachi 85 Avenue A (bet 5th & 6th Sts) | East Village

Unless you come before 7pm, you'll have to join the long line of East Village locals who know that the sushi here is worth the wait. Takahachi scores on its perfect, delicate *shumai* (steamed dumplings), its insistence on fresh crab instead of the stringy reconstituted stuff, and, in fact, the consistent super-freshness of everything. As an extra plus, it's also not too expensive and the portions are generous. The space is ugly standard-issue – pine tables and bright white light, but it's the food that people come back for.

☎ 505-6524 Ⓜ F to 2nd Ave 🕐 5am–midnight daily. 🙆 79 🗐 Ⓥ ⊟ all $$–$$$

↓ veg out

Angelica Kitchen 300 E 12th Street (bet. 1st & 2nd Aves) | East Village

During the day Angelica Kitchen is a place to unwind over well-prepared dragon bowls of rice, beans, tofu and sea vegetables. Instead of salt and pepper on the tables, it's soy sauce and a shaker of sesame seeds. They also have good marinated tofu sandwiches and rich walnut-lentil paté. It's a homey, bright place with bronze Aztec-designed walls, an open kitchen and plain wood tabletops. At night it's more hectic so you won't absorb the same Zen-ness. Note: no alcohol served.

☎ 228-2909 Ⓜ L·N·R·4·5·6 to 14th St-Union Sq 🕐 11.30am–10.30pm daily. 🙆 65 ♿ 🗐 Ⓥ ⊟ none $–$$

Zen Palate 34 Union Square E (at 16th St) | Union Square

Luckily there is a Zen Palate Downtown, Midtown and Uptown so you never have to go too far to enjoy its meditative, unusual Asian compositions in a poetic atmosphere. The Union Square location is perhaps the most popular, with a busy downstairs area (and cheaper prices), and a tranquil, airy upstairs room (with fancier veggie offerings) affording views of the park. Patrons are chic but not horribly so. Real thought and creativity goes into dishes you feel you could eat into infinity. Note: no alcohol served.

☎ 614-9291 Ⓜ L·N·R·4·5·6 to 14th St-Union Sq 🕐 11am–11pm Mon–Sat; 12–10.30pm Sun. 🙆 200 ♿ 🗐 Ⓥ ⊟ all $–$$

restaurants & cafés

↓ brunch

Mesa Grill 102 Fifth Avenue (bet. 15th & 16th Sts) | Gramercy Park
Creative twists on Southwestern brunch, blazing with flavour – along with sensational drinks.
☎ 807-7400 Ⓜ L•N•R•4•5•6 to 14th St-Union Sq ◖ 12–2.30pm; 5.30–10.30pm Mon–Fri; 11.30am–3pm; 5.30–10.30pm Sat–Sun. ♦ 110 ♿ ☐ ☐ ☑ Ⓡ Ⓢ ☐ all $$–$$$

The Odeon 145 W Broadway (bet. Duane & Thomas Sts) | Tribeca
Forever cool in every way, a delectable bread basket and big tables for brunching parties.
☎ 233-0507 Ⓜ 1•2•3•9 to Chambers St ◖ 11.45–1am Mon–Wed; 11.30–3am Thu–Sun (to 1am Sun). ♦ 120 ♿ limited ☐ ☐ bar only ☐ ✍ ☐ all $$–$$$

7A 109 Avenue A (at 7th St) | East Village
Cheap, hangover heaven. Bring sunglasses for sidewalk tables and reading material for the wait.
☎ 673-6583 Ⓜ 6 at Astor Pl ◖ 24 hours daily. ♦ 70 ♿ ☐ ☐ ✍ ☑ ☐ all $

Sylvia's 328 Lenox Avenue (bet. 126th & 127th Sts) | Harlem
Skip church and get your gospel here, along with church lady fashions.
☎ 996-0660 Ⓜ 2•3 at 125th St ◖ 7.30am–10.30pm Mon–Sat (from 8am Fri–Sat); 11am–8pm Sun. ♦ 90 ♿ ☐ ☐ ✍ ☐ Ⓡ Ⓢ ☐ all $–$$

↓ romantic rendezvous

American Park Battery Park (opposite 175 State Street) | Lower Manhattan

Smack dab on the harbour and near the Staten Island ferry, American Park's towering windows afford an incomparable view of passing boats and the Statue of Liberty. But this is no tourist trap. The seafood tastes of the sea it just came from, and is swimming with global influences. How about grilled *mahi mahi* with Vietnamese rice noodles, Japanese eggplant and shiitake mushrooms in spicy lemongrass coconut broth? It works. A table on the outdoor patio at sunset is a lovely experience and service is friendly and proficient.

☎ 809-5508 Ⓜ 1•9 to South Ferry; 4•5 to Bowling Green ◖ Restaurant:12–3pm & 5–10pm Mon–Fri; 5–10pm Sat; Patio: 12–10pm daily. ♦ 130 ♿ ☐ ✍ bar & patio only ☐ ✍ ☐ AE/MC/V $$–$$$

Capsouto Frères 451 Washington Street (at Watts St) | Tribeca

The out-of-the-way address may exasperate your cab driver, but it really does exist, and it's well worth seeking out. Three brothers with lots of savvy opened this gracious Tribeca loft-space nearly 20 years ago, and new chef Eric Heinrich have recently reinvigorated the French cuisine. The temple to magnificent soufflés, *saucisson chaud* and fork-tender duckling now boasts creative specials like *tian* of venison with parsnip purée. Brunch is fab, the crowd distinguished but dressed down. And, oh, the wine list!

☎ 966-4900 Ⓜ 1•9 to Canal St ◖ Restaurant: 6–10pm Mon; 12–3.30pm & 6–10pm Tue–Sun (to 11pm Fri–Sat). ♦ 90 ♿ ☐ ✍ bar only ☐ ☐ all $$–$$$

La Bonne Soupe 48 W 55th Street (bet. Fifth & Sixth Aves) | Midtown

Utterly retro from the red-and-white check cloths to the fondues, this adorable bistro anachronism makes a fantastic Midtown bolt-hole. Ignore the terrifying menu prose ('this omelette masterpiece, almost austere in its simplicity', 'transformed by the art of France into a sophisticated delight'), because the food is just fine. Onion soup; Emmenthal fondue; great brandade and quiche; and little tables in two straight lines are the essence of cozy.

☎ 586-7650 Ⓜ E•F to 5th Ave ◖ 11.30am–11pm daily. ♦ 70 ♿ limited ☐ ✍ bar only ☐ Ⓢ ☐ AE $–$$

Le Jardin Bistrot 25 Cleveland Place (bet. Spring & Lafayette) | Nolita

One hesitates to recommend this perfect bistro for fear of its being overwhelmed by success, but Breton chef-patron, Gérard Maurice, can surely handle it. The bucolic garden is full of grape vines, herb and tomato plants and Gérard's extensive collection of frog *tchotchkes*. Satisfy your yearnings for bouillabaisse, cassoulet, steak (or tuna) tartare, steak, moules-frites and coq au vin; there is not a bad dish on the menu, though desserts (tarte tatin, chocolate marquise, creme caramel) tend not to be as successful.

☎ 343-9599 Ⓜ 6 to Spring St ◖ 12–3pm & 6–11.30pm Mon–Sat; 6–11pm Sun. ♦ 80 ♿ ☐ ✍ ☐ AE/MC/V $$–$$$

Park View at the Boathouse Central Park (bet. East Park Drive & 74th St) | UES

A shuttle bus leaves from Fifth Avenue and 72nd Street every ten minutes to ferry customers to this rustic chalet in the middle of Central Park. Open all year round, the cozy interior glows from the slate fireplace in winter and there's a bar where you can warm up on hot toddies. In good weather the outdoor tables are romantically lakeside.

The American menu with global touches is strong on seafood, such as Indian-spiced salmon tartare with mango, and spinach and potato crusted monkfish with Barolo sauce.

☎ 517-2233 Ⓜ 6 to 68th St-Hunter College ◑ 11.30am–4pm & 5pm–midnight Mon–Sat (to 1am Fri–Sat); 11am–4pm Sun. ♠ 200 ♿ ▯ ⌣ 🗐 ⊘ ▤ all $$–$$$

Quilty's 177 Prince Street (bet. Sullivan & Thompson Sts) | Soho

Chef Katy Sparks knows how to wow and woo diners with her spectacularly innovative cuisine. It is American food taken to a higher form of evolution, with Asian and French influences that accent each other in an eloquent way. For instance, you've never tasted anything quite like her tuna medallions with sesame-wilted Savoy cabbage, papaya coulis and macadamia couscous. The far-reaching wine list is nearly as amazing. Moneyed corporate types impress clients here with the cool Soho vibe, so go later for more quiet romance.

☎ 254-1260 Ⓜ N·R to Prince St ◑ 6–11pm Mon; 12–3pm (from 11.30am Sat–Sun) & 6–11pm Tue–Sun. ♠ 60 ♿ ▯ ⌣ 🗐 ⊘ ▤ all $$$

Rosemarie's 145 Duane Street (bet. Church St & W Broadway) | Tribeca

Considering this excellent northern Italian in Tribeca doesn't put a foot wrong, it's remarkably underpopulated. The room is calm and grown up, the service is caring, and the small menu is good-to-spectacular. Go for wild mushrooms with polenta, pancetta and sage, or white bean crostini; a half order of pasta (orecchiette with Manila clams or rigatoni with lamb bolognese); then seared skate with brown butter over red cabbage, or a veal chop with porcini sauce – and your stomach will be happy. Buzz factor is low.

☎ 285-2610 Ⓜ 1·9 to Franklin St ◑ 12–2.30pm Mon–Fri; 5.30–9.30pm Mon–Sat. ♠ 84 ♿ ▯ ⌣ bar only 🗐 Ⓢ ▤ AE/MC/V $$–$$$

Screening Room 54 Varick Street (bet. Canal & Laight Sts) | Tribeca

All under one roof, at The Screening Room you can enjoy cinematic cocktails at the bar (the 'Clockwork Orange', the 'Lolita'), tuck into rapturous dishes like pan-fried artichokes and cedar-planked salmon, and then move into the 40s-style theatre showing independent and foreign films. The attractive dining room is downtown casual, and the best deal is the $30 prix fixe, which includes three courses plus the screening. Brunch is also fun when they regularly show old cult favourites like Breakfast at Tiffany's and Valley of the Dolls.

☎ 334-2100 Ⓜ A·C·E··9 to Canal St ◑ 12–3pm Mon–Thu; 5.30–11pm Thu–Sat (to midnight Fri–Sat); 11.30am–3.30pm Sun. ♠ 150 ♿ ▯ ⌣ 🗐 ⊘ ▤ all $$–$$$

Spartina 355 Greenwich Street (at Harrison St) | Tribeca

Tribeca residents probably wish they could keep Spartina to themselves, but that's too bad. The warmth of the stylish room enfolds you, and the Mediterranean dishes further seduce. The place specializes in fish and seafood, such as roasted trout stuffed with brandade and wrapped in smoked bacon, but chef-co-owner Stephen Kalt also excels at slow-cooked short ribs and mash. Then there are the divine, crispy grilled pizzas, and over 80 types of wine. What more could you need?

☎ 274-9310 Ⓜ 1·9 to Franklin St ◑ 11.20am–3pm Mon–Fri; 5.30–11pm daily (to midnight Thu–Sat). ♠ 100 ♿ ▯ ⌣ bar only 🗐 ⊘ ▤ all $$–$$$

Union Pacific 111 E 22nd Street (bet. Lexington & Park Ave S) | Gramercy Park

At this smart restaurant, expect some of the most succulent and creatively prepared seafood your tongue could hope to tangle with. Sashimi-quality Taylor Bay scallops with sea urchin; wild sturgeon with morels; and for the non-fish-eaters, there's always steak and chicken, prepared with the chef's innovative touch. And the richly-decorated space is just as smart as the menu – a plush lounge filled with chic velvet sofas and over-stuffed chairs in the basement level – it's the perfect place to impress.

☎ 995-8500 Ⓜ 6 to 23rd St ◑ 12–2pm Mon–Fri; 5.30–10.30pm Mon–Sat (to 11pm Sat). ♠ 109 ♿ limited Ⓢ ▤ AE/MC/V $$$

Verbena 53 Irving Place (bet. 17th & 18th Sts) | Gramercy Park

If Edith Wharton were alive today, she would probably dine at Verbena; she lived near here and the place manages to be civilized and daring at the same time. The townhouse setting is lovely and spare, with two fireplaces, and botanical touches throughout. The courtyard garden is bordererd by herbs and vegetables, which chef-owner Diane Forley employs in American dishes like butternut squash ravioli with roasted oranges and sage, and red snapper with braised cabbage and salsify.

☎ 260-5757 Ⓜ L·N·R·4·5·6 to 14th St-Union Sq ◑ 5.30–10.30pm daily (to 11pm Fri–Sat); 11.30am–2.30pm & 5.30–9.30pm Sun. ♠ 55 dining room; 75 garden ♿ ▯ 🗐 ⊘ Ⓥ ▤ all $$$

restaurants & cafés

restaurants & cafés

71 Clinton Fresh Food 71 Clinton Street (at Rivington St) | Lower East Side

A tatty Lower East Side block is luring uptown, moneyed patrons who brave the unsavoury journey to partake of Wylie Dufresne's far tastier, inspired American cooking. Yet this is no place for stiffs; it's small and boisterous and attracts hip locals, too. The precocious young chef was tutored for years by the fabled Jean-Georges Vongerichten, and it shows in his diverse, market-driven menu. Shrimp-stuffed squid is dashed with blood orange emulsion, and rye bread and *edamame*-crusted sea bass is anchored by chive mashed potatoes. Think yummy but not fussy.

☎ 614-6960 Ⓜ F to Delancey St ◗ 6–10.30pm Mon–Sat (to 11.30pm Fri & Sat). ♠ 34 ♿ ▯ ◢ ▤ Ⓡ 1 month in advance ▭ AE/MC/V $$–$$$

Acquario 5 Bleecker Street (at Bowery) | Noho

Apparently, everybody in this small, cozy brick-lined restaurant, sister to the popular Il Buco [→119] is from Europe, smokes and abuses cellphones, but don't let that discourage you. A Sicilian/ Portuguese/Spanish menu offers no division between appetizers and mains, encouraging mix-and-match and sharing – *boquerones* with green pepper couscous and salsa verde; grilled octopus; baked Asiago cheese with prosciutto and fresh figs; clam linguine; grilled *gambas* with fennel and *mache* salad.

☎ 260-4666 Ⓜ B·D·F·Q to Broadway-Lafayette St; 6 Bleecker St ◗ 12–3pm Mon & Wed–Sun; 6–11.30pm daily (to midnight Sat–Sun). ♠ 40 ♿ ◢ ▤ ▭ none $–$$

Bar Pitti 268 Sixth Avenue (bet. Bleeker & Houston Sts) | West Village

A simple Tuscan restaurant that's best in summer, when tables line up on the wide sidewalk, and the marble floors and white walls inside are super cool. The *fettunta* (bread salad) is the best dish on the menu, but the blackboard specials are all usually good, from spinach with garlic and lemon to marinated quail or homemade pasta. Bar Pitti feels genuinely European, as opposed to Eurotrashy (that's what Da Silvano, the expensive schmoozy joint next door, is for).

☎ 982-3300 Ⓜ A·B·C·D·E·F·Q to W 4th St-Washington Sq ◗ 12pm–midnight daily. ♠ 77 ♿ limited ▯ ▤ ⌨ Ⓥ ▭ none $–$$

Blue Ribbon 67 Sullivan Street (bet. Prince & Spring Sts) | Soho

The waiting-in-line situation is absurd (even at 3am), but the people-watching (superchic and supermodels) is almost an essential part of the experience. While it tends to get sceney, it's never obnoxious – because everyone is there for one thing... fabulous, eclectic, innovative food, like the flavour-bursting fondue, roasted duck club sandwich and whole steamed flounder. Calorie counters, beware: it's impossible to stick to your diet here... and with a menu this diverse and tempting, you wouldn't want to.

☎ 274-0404 Ⓜ C·E to Spring St ◗ 4pm–4am Tue–Sun. ♠ 55 ♿ ▯ ▭ AE/MC/V $–$$$

First 87 First Avenue (bet. 5th & 6th Sts) | East Village

First has an undeniable groove, even though you'd never notice it passing by. The commodious booths are ideal for groups, and dim lighting enhances everybody's appearance. The new American cuisine is generously portioned, so beware the addictive warm bread with infused olive oil. Martinis are served in their own cute pitchers on ice, keeping them cold for refills. Pizza with condiments on the side (like fresh pesto) is wonderful, as is the vegetable extravaganza and grilled lamb steak.

☎ 674-3823 Ⓜ 6 to Astor Pl; F to 2nd Ave ◗ 6pm–2am Mon–Sat (to 3am Fri–Sat); 11am–1am Sun. ♠ 90 ♿ ▯ ▤ Ⓥ ▭ AE/MC/V $–$$$

Grange Hall 50 Commerce Street (at Barrow St) | West Village

So homey, you'll feel like you're dining in your friend's ultra-cool art deco apartment. And the fact that it's nestled on one of NYC's most beautiful streets makes this restaurant even more of a draw. The service is sweet and the portions are waist-strainingly huge, so go hungry and prepare to scarf down some old-fashioned comfort food like creamy garlic mashed potatoes, herb-breaded organic chicken, and a big slab of aged shell-steak with pickles. It always brings in a crowd, especially for brunch.

☎ 924-5246 Ⓜ 1·9 to Christopher St–Sheridan Sq ◗ 12–3pm & 5.30–11pm Mon–Wed & Fri–Sun (from 11am Sat & 10.30am Sun; to 11.30pm Tue–Wed & midnight Fri–Sat). ♠ 90 ▯ ▭ AE $$–$$$

Lupa 170 Thompson Street (bet. Bleecker & Houston St) | West Village

Secluded on a West Village street, this Roman-style trattoria is delightfully lacking in pretension, with terracotta floors, and wooden tables set with candles. Mario Batali and Joseph Bastianich, of Po, Babbo and Esca fame, are the formidable team behind it, ensuring value at a fair price. The menu is replete with straightforward pastas (silky fettuce alfredo) and expertly prepared seafood (crusty salt cod with fennel and mint), along with paper-thin antipasti meats shaved to order. Courses can be matched with rustic Italian wines served by the *quartino*.

☎ 982-5089 M 1•9 to Houston St; N•R to Prince St ◑ 12–3pm & 5.30–11.30pm Tue–Sun. 🍴 80 ♿
☐ ⚊ 📖 🍸 ℝ up to 1 month in advance 💳 AE/MC/V $$

O Padeiro 641 Sixth Avenue (bet. 19th & 20th Sts) | Chelsea

If you're in need of some hardcore carbohydrate action, then this adorable Portuguese bakery/tapas bar will be right up your alley. Their baked goods, and eclectic wine selections are outrageously good and their small-sized entrées (like salt cod layered with potato, chopped eggs and olives) demand indulgence. Every so often, a Portuguese singer adds a little more authentic flavour to the tile-embellished ambience.

☎ 414-9661 M 1•9 to 23rd St ◑ 7am–10pm Mon–Sat (to 11pm Fri–Sat); 10am–7pm Sun. 🍴 40
♿ ☐ 📖 💳 AE/MC/V $$

Payard Patisserie & Bistro 1032 Lexington Avenue (bet. 73rd & 74th Sts) | UES

Children (and the child in you) will be filled with wonder at the tiers of tea cakes, tarts, éclairs, fancy pastries and handmade chocolates in the Parisian-style patisserie. A few small tables provide room for immediate gratification. Ladies who 'tea' will be entranced by the $14.50 afternoon delights of brioche, scones and madeleines. Those desirous of classic, but equally calorific, French fare can tuck into bouillabaisse and cassoulet in the bi-level bistro.

☎ 717-5252 M 6 to 77th St ◑ Patisserie: 7am–11pm Mon–Sat; Bistro: 12–2.30pm (to 3pm Fri–Sat) & 6–10.30pm Mon–Sat (to 11pm Fri–Sat). 🍴 100 ☐ 📖 💳 all $$–$$$

Pisces 95 Avenue A (at 6th St) | East Village

What's so great about Pisces is that you can get really fresh seafood prepared in eclectic ways and still walk out with money in your pocket. At weekends it's a challenge to snag a table even though they open the second deck upstairs for the overflow. In summer, the wraparound windows are flung open, making it feel like you're out at sea on Avenue A. Brunch is also a big attraction, with several egg dishes for under $8, which includes a Mimosa (champagne and OJ) and coffee.

☎ 260-6660 M F to 2nd Ave; 6 to Astor Pl ◑ 5.30–11.30pm Sun–Fri (to 1am Fri); 11.30–1am Sat–Sun. 🍴 140 ♿ ☐ ⚊ 📖 💳 all $–$$

Pó 31 Cornelia Street (bet. Bleeker & W 4th Sts) | West Village

'Molto' Mario Batali is famous for his colourful TV cookery programme, popular cookbooks and a clutch of fine Italian restaurants. Pó is the original, and still packed after a number of years. The small, unfussy space feels like a well-oiled machine, with every detail seen to in a professional, unpretentious manner. Garlicky white bean bruschetta comes gratis, and pastas are big in size and flavour. The six-course tasting menu is a real deal: and goes on and on, and on...

☎ 645-2189 M 1•9 to Christopher St ◑ 5.30–11pm Tue; 11.30am–2.15pm & 5.30–11pm Wed–Sun (to 11.30pm Fri–Sat; to 10pm Sun). 🍴 34 ☐ 📖 Ⓥ Ⓢ 💳 AE $$

Prune 54 E 1st Street (bet. 1st & 2nd Ave) | East Village

So sweet and charming, this tiny spot is dear to many, though cramped seating might gall anti-social types. The creative, very personal menu is often revised by chef owner Gabrielle Hamilton: grilled artichokes with fried fava beans; pasta kerchiefs with asparagus, ham and poached egg; and roasted slab bacon with okra and pickled radish are all boldly flavoured. Desserts are equally singular, such as strawberry-rhubarb cobbler with brown sugar ice cream, and chocolate cashew tart with sour cherry compote. Sunday night 'firehouse suppers' are family affairs, with everyone getting the same thing.

☎ 677-6221 M F to 2nd Ave ◑ 6–11pm Tue–Sat (to midnight Fri & Sat); 5–10pm Sun. 🍴 25 ☐ ⚊
📖 ℝ 1 week in advance Ⓢ 💳 AE/MC/V $$

Veritas 43 E 20th Street (bet. Broadway & Park Ave S) | Flatiron District

This muted, shimmering room gets rave reviews for one of the most astonishing wine lists in the city. What's more, bottles are not overpriced – certainly not for the quality and rare vintages. Owners Gino Diaferia and Scott Bryan are sharp guys, already having the extremely good Indigo and Siena restaurants under their belts. Veritas is their real showplace, with subtle yet exhilarating contemporary American inventions like warm truffled oysters with Riesling, roasted squab with foie gras emulsion, and pepper-crusted venison with sour cherry-Armagnac sauce.

☎ 353-3700 M N•R to 23rd St ◑ 12–2.30pm & 6–11pm Mon–Sat; 5–10pm Sun. 🍴 65 ♿ ☐ ⚊ 📖
💳 all $$$

restaurants & cafés

New York's bars are as varied as the city's denizens. Get louche in plush lounges, hang with the barflies at a local dive, or sip superb cocktails alongside the chic and sleek set. Everything's open 'til late, so you can take your time.

drink up

club mode

Alphabet Lounge

The best the Village has to offer: plush banquettes, monster-sized martinis, a rotating roster of DJs and an address so far east that no drunken frat boys can find it. Best of all: no bouncers or velvet ropes – just lotsa groove.

104 Avenue C (at 7th Street), East Village ☎ 780-0202 Ⓜ L to 1st Ave; 6 to Astor Pl ◑ 8pm–4.30am daily. ⏤ 🗐 ✎ vary ◯ vary

Baby Jupiter

A bar, club, performance space and restaurant all squeezed into one, Baby Jupiter is always packed. Their popular club nights change frequently, so call ahead to confirm scheduling. Perfect for cheap dates and indecisive groups.

170 Orchard St (at Stanton St), LES ☎ 982-2229 Ⓜ F to 2nd Ave ◑ 11–3/4am daily. ♿ 🍴 ⏤ ✎ ◯

Baraza ✓

Can't afford that tropical vacation? Take a trip to Baraza, an Alphabet City bar where DJs spin salsa and samba, bartenders serve *mojitos* and *caipirinhas* and the average duration of relationships formed on the premises is ten days.

133 Ave C (at 8th St), East Village ☎ 539-0811 Ⓜ L to 1st Ave ◑ 7.30pm–4am daily. ♿ ⏤ 🗐 🎦 ◯ Mon & Thu

Botanica

Sick of the megaclubs? Come to Botanica for jungle, dub and drum 'n' bass spun by top DJs in a cozy basement lounge. Cheap drinks and a monthly surf music party too.

47 E Houston St (bet. Mott & Mulberry Sts), Noho ☎ 343-7251 Ⓜ B·D·F·Q to Broadway-Lafayette St ◑ 5pm–4am daily (from 6pm Sat–Sun). ⏤ 🗐 ◯ Mon–Fri & Sun

Halo

Wanna hang out with Puffy, Leo, and the rest of the fabulous ones at this white-hot, basement-level lounge? Get in line... behind the velvet rope. Flash your smile (and your Prada) at the doorman, then order some $100 champagne and revel in your own fabulousness.

49 Grove Street (bet. Seventh Ave & Bleecker St), West Village ☎ 243-8885 Ⓜ 1·9 to Christopher St ◑ 6pm–4am Mon–Sat. ♿ 🎦 before 1am ⏤ 🗐 ◯ nightly

Hell

This is a gay bar that goes out of its way to welcome a mixed crowd. DJs spinning 70s and early 80s disco get the crowd moving on the dance floor, and Hell's potent house martinis (some more appealing than others) keep lazy loungers blissful.

55 Gansevoort St (bet. Greenwich & Washington Sts), Chelsea ☎ 727-1666 Ⓜ A·C·E to 14th St; L to 8th Ave ◑ 5pm–4am Fri; 7pm– 4am Sat–Thu. ♿ ⏤ 🗐 ◯ Tue–Thu

Orchard Bar

DJs spin all forms of electronica nightly in an atmosphere more reminiscent of a terrarium than a bar. From the foliage-filled glass tanks to the apples suspended in jars, an unnatural green glow pervades everything in the room – including visitors, who take excessive advantage of the bar's cheapish drinks.

200 Orchard St (bet. Houston & Stanton Sts), LES ☎ 673-5350 Ⓜ F to 2nd Ave ◑ 7pm–3am daily (to 4am Tue–Sat). ♿ ⏤ 🗐 ◯

Sweet & Vicious

The best time to enjoy this sleek, sexy lounge is on a Sunday night, when the weekend crowds have dissipated, DJs spin break beats and you can linger over your raki. Come summer, the garden is an urban oasis.

5 Spring St (at Elizabeth St), Noho ☎ 334-7915 Ⓜ 6 to Spring St ◑ 5pm–3am daily. ⏤ 🗐 🎦 ◯ Wed & Sun

lively sounds

Bar d'O

New York's premiere venue for drag entertainment just keeps getting better. Intimate and glamorous, Bar d'O continues to attract a devoted following thanks to weekly performances by downtown legends Raven O and Joey Arias – a brilliant, Billie Holiday-esque chanteuse.

29 Bedford St (at Downing St), West Village ☎ 627-1580 🅜 1·9 to Houston St ◗ 7pm–3am daily. ◖ ☄ Sat, Sun & Tue ◉ Mon & Wed–Sat

Ciel Rouge

More like Weimar Berlin than modern-day Chelsea, Ciel Rouge serves up sexy torch singers and exceptional cocktails in its plush, decadent lounge. When no one's performing, the CD player is partial to opera arias and Marlene Dietrich. Gorgeous garden, too.

176 Seventh Ave (at 20th St), Chelsea ☎ 929-5542 🅜 1·9 to 23rd St ◗ 7pm–2am daily (to 3.30am Fri–Sat). ◖ 🍴 📖 ✎ ☄ Tue, Wed & Thu

Feinstein's at the Regency

Life is a cabaret, old chum – especially in this oh-so-swank Park Avenue club, where songbirds like Rosemary Clooney serenade stars, society mavens and anyone else who can afford the cover charge. It's pricey, but the lavish setting and attentive staff will make you feel like royalty.

540 Park Avenue (at 61st St), UES ☎ 759-4100 🅜 4·5·6 to 59th St; N·R to Lexington Ave ◗ 8–2am daily (to 1am Sun). ◖ 🍴 ☄ bar only 📖 · shows: 8.30pm Tue–Thu; 8.30 & 11.30pm Fri–Sat 💲 $35 and up; cover charge: $60

Joe's Pub

Built into the Public Theater, Joe's Pub has remained one of New York's hottest nightspots since its arrival stirred up the Noho scene. It is both an elegantly modern lounge and an intimate performance space [→141] with inebriated models performing unintentionally between sets.

425 Lafayette St (bet. Astor Pl & W 4th St), Noho ☎ 539-8770 🅜 6 to Astor Pl ◗ 5pm–4am daily. 🍴 ☄ 📖 ☄ vary ◉ vary (NB entrance fee for shows)

Lakeside Lounge

Catch some of New York's best indie bands at Lakeside Lounge, before they hit the charts. A few big names play here as well, and, on nights when no one performs, you'll find plenty of out-of-work musicians slumped over their beers.

162–164 Ave B (at 10th St), East Village ☎ 529-8463 🅜 L to 1st Ave ◗ 4pm–4am daily. ◖ ☄ 📖 ☄ vary

Meow Mix

Unlike its older, quieter counterparts in the West Village, Meow Mix – the only lesbian bar in the Lower East Side – offers live music seven nights a week and enough hard-rocking girls to keep the party going all night.

269 E Houston St (at Suffolk St), LES ☎ 254-0688 🅜 F to 2nd Ave ◗ 3pm–4am daily. ◖ ☄ 📖 ◖ ◉ ◖·

Stinger Club

Looking for a great martini, a game of pool, or a half dozen abstract-impressionist sculptors? You'll find 'em all in this trendy Williamsburg haunt, a red-lit, occasionally raucous tavern, renowned for its fabulous jukebox and even more fabulous clientele. It's all in the name of art, baby.

241 Grand Street (bet. Driggs & Roebling Sts), Brooklyn ☎ 1-718-218-6662 🅜 J·M·Z to Marcy Ave ◗ 5pm–4am daily (from 3pm Sun). ☄ 📖 ☄ weekends ◉ Wed

Tonic

Ever had a drink in a giant wine barrel? This former Kosher wine shop now houses a performance space, an alternative press, and a basement bar featuring oversized casks that have been converted into miniature private rooms, complete with seating. Movies shown on Mondays.

107 Norfolk St (at Delancey St), LES ☎ 358-7504 🅜 F·J·M·Z to Delancey St-Essex St ◗ 11–1am daily. ◖◻ ☄ ☄ Wed–Sun

Winnie's

Tucked away on a side street in Chinatown, Winnie's caters to both Asian and non-Asian karaoke fans. A makeshift stage inspires seasoned songsters to ham it up, while copious quantities of Tsing Tao beer encourage novices to screech at the bar. A fun, boisterous crowd.

104 Bayard St (bet. Mulberry & Baxter Sts), Chinatown ☎ 732-2384 🅜 J·M·N·R·Z·6 to Canal St ◗ 12pm–4am daily. ◖◻ ☄ 📖 ☄ karaoke nightly ◖·

the status quo

Chumley's

A former speakeasy with two secret entrances, Chumley's was once a literary hang-out for the likes of John Reed, Eugene O'Neill, John Dos Passos, TS Eliot and many others. Today, in this last remaining vestige of New York's prohibition era, there's a friendly neighbourhood crowd; a choice of over 25 beers on tap; and a varied steak and pasta menu.

86 Bedford St (bet. Bleecker St & Seventh Ave), West Village ☎ 675-4449 🅜 1·9 to Christopher St ◗ 4pm–midnight daily (to 1am Sat–Sun). ◖ ◖◻ ☄

Elaine's

This Upper East Side establishment has managed to maintain a loyal local clientele and attract enough swells to keep the gossip columnists busy. And yes, Billy Joel did write a song about it. Dress up for this chic Italian with fresco-like wall paintings and literary parties galore.

1703 Second Ave (at 88th St), UES ☎ 534-8103 🅜 4·5·6 to 86th St ◗ 6pm–4am daily. ◖◻ ☄ 📖

Raoul's

There may be no better end to the week than a glass of wine and a steak at Raoul's. Reservations are a must in the dining room, but you may prefer to eat at the bar where after-work drinkers gather to soak up the pub-like atmosphere – although this gets crowded too.

180 Prince St (bet. Sullivan & Thompson Sts), Soho ☎ 966-3518 Ⓜ N•R to Prince St ◐ 12pm–2am daily. ✆ ◢ 📋

live it up

Bar 89

Bar 89 was built for bull-market imbibing. If 40-ft ceilings and bottomless martinis aren't enough to make you feel like a master of the universe, steal one of the trophy girlfriends sitting at the banquettes.

89 Mercer St (at Spring St), Soho ☎ 274-0989 Ⓜ N•R to Prince St ◐ 1pm–2am daily. ⅙ ✆ ◢ 📋

Bubble Lounge

Exceptional champagnes, tempting appetizers and enough platinum cards to buy a small Central American nation can all be found at the Bubble Lounge. Wear this season's Gucci to fit in.

228 W Broadway (at White St), Tribeca ☎ 431-3433 Ⓜ 1•9 to Franklin St ◐ 5pm–4am Mon–Sat. ⅙ ✆ ◢ 📋 ✎ Mon &Tue

Grand Bar

Barely removed from the bustle of Soho, the Grand Bar is ideal for both stylish midday drinks and comfortable nightcaps à deux: just don't expect too much privacy at weekends when footsore shoppers and cultured-out gallery-goers take over.

Soho Grand Hotel, 310 W Broadway (at Canal St), Soho ☎ 965-3000 Ⓜ A•C•E to Canal St ◐ 12pm–2am daily. ⅙ ✆ ◢ 📋

The Greatest Bar on Earth

The view from here is spectacular. Bring your friends, order a round of classic cocktails and stick someone else with the tab. After 10pm, the Wall Street crowd goes home and the kids come out for swing music and Sidecars. Be sure to visit on Wednesdays, when Lucien the Loungecore DJ spins kooky soundtracks and other lounge music staples.

107th Floor, 1 World Trade Center, Lower Manhattan ☎ 524-7011 Ⓜ N•R•1•9 to Cortlandt St; 2•3 to Park Pl; A•C•E to Chambers St ◐ 12pm –midnight Mon–Tue (to 1am Wed–Sat); 11am –10pm Sun. ⅙ ✆ ◢ 📋 ✎ Mon–Sat ◉ Mon–Sun

Harry Cipriani

Nostalgic for Italy? Visit Harry Cipriani, where bartenders pour the same Bellinis made famous at Harry's Bar in Venice. If power lunches frighten you, request your midday meal at the bar. (The downtown outpost of Harry's is worth a visit for its rooftop garden.)

781 Fifth Ave (at 59th St), UES ☎ 753-5566 Ⓜ N•R to 5th Ave ◐ 12–10.30pm daily. ✆ ◢ 📋 +B

Lush

When you crave luxury, head to Lush, a favorite of dotcom moguls and Tribeca film execs. The velvet banquettes are sumptuous; the specialty cocktails are spectacular; and everyone looks good beneath the amber lights. If you don't like crowds, find yourself a private nook – and someone to share it with.

110 Duane Street (bet. Church St & Broadway), Tribeca ☎ 212-766-1275 Ⓜ A•C to Chambers St ◐ 5pm–2am Tue–Thu; 5pm–4am Fri–Sat (from 9pm Sat). ◷ 5.30–7pm Tue–Fri ✆ 📋 ✎ Tue jazz singer ◉ nightly

357

A resolutely swanky champagne lounge serving both bubbly and booze by the bottle or glass. The crowd is equal parts downtown hipster and well-heeled Soho-ite. Regular club nights – call ahead for DJ information.

357 W Broadway (at Broome St), Soho ☎ 965-1491 Ⓜ N•R to Prince St ◐ 9pm– 4am daily. ⅙ ✆ ◢ 📋 ◉ daily

Top of the Tower

Top of the Tower is the epitome of old New York elegance. The views from this art deco hotel bar – located on the 26th floor – are stunning. Ancient waiters (not aspiring actors) are on hand to serve classic cocktails and a piano player performs nightly.

Beekman Tower Hotel, 3 Mitchell Place (bet. E 49th St & First Ave), Midtown ☎ 355-7300 Ⓜ E•6 to 51st St ◐ 5pm–1am daily. ⅙ ✆ 📋 ✆ ✎ nightly

sports bars

Coogan's

4015 Broadway (bet. 168th & 169th Sts), Washington Heights ☎ 928-1234 Ⓜ A•B•C•1•9 to 168th St-Washington Heights ◐ 11am–4am daily. ◢ 📋 ◷

ESPN Zone

1472 Broadway (bet. 42nd St & Broadway), Midtown ☎ 921-3776 Ⓜ N•R•S•1•9•2•3•7 to 42nd St-Times Sq ◐ 11.30am–midnight Mon–Fri (to 1am Fri); 11–1am Sat–Sun (to midnight Sun). ⅙ ✆ ◢ 📋 ◷ Two 16ft video walls

Jimmy's Corner

140 W 44th St (bet. Sixth & Seventh Aves), Midtown ☎ 764-2366 Ⓜ N•R•S•1•9•2•3•7 to 42nd St-Times Sq ◐ 11–4am daily. ✆ snacks ◢ 📋 ◷

Park Avenue Country Club

381 Park Ave (at 27th St), Gramercy Park ☎ 685-3636 Ⓜ 6 to 28th St ◐ 11.30am– 2am Mon–Sat; 11.30am–10pm Sun. ◢ 📋 ◷

themes & schemes

Decibel

Sample the sake at Decibel and you'll never settle for a flavourless flask of rice wine again. An impressive selection of premium sakes, mixed sake cocktails and Japanese munchies (hot peas, shrimp crackers) are offered at the bar, while full meals are served at the tables.

240 E 9th St (at 2nd St), East Village ☎ 979-2733 ⓜ 6 to Astor Pl ◐ 8pm–3am daily (to 1am Sun). ▤ AE/MC/V ⌇ ⌣ 🗏

Good World Bar & Grill

New York's only Swedish-themed bar serves up more than 60 beers, tasty bar snacks like cured herring and meatballs and a crowd of hotties so hip they can actually find this way out-of-the way hotspot. No, you don't have to try the herring.

3 Orchard Street (at Canal St), LES ☎ 925-9975 ⓜ F to East Broadway ◐ 4pm–4am Mon–Sat (from 11am Fri–Sat). ❡ snacks ⌣ 🗏 Thu–Sat

KGB

Don't be fooled by the commie-chic decor. Commercially successful authors read here regularly, as do a number of the literary world's brightest young stars. A haven for aspiring literati and their devotees.

85 E 4th St (bet. Bowery & Second Ave), East Village ☎ 505-3360 ⓜ 6 to Astor Pl ◐ 7.30pm–4am daily. ⌣ 🗏

Kush

Flop on a pillow-strewn couch, smoke a hookah and make believe you're in Marrakech. Kush brings the Middle East to the Lower East Side every Tuesday night with belly dancers, henna hand-painting and tarot card readings. Other nights feature live jazz or DJs but the vibe's still mellow.

183 Orchard St (bet. Houston & Stanton Sts), LES ☎ 677-7328 ⓜ F to 2nd Ave ◐ 6pm–3am Mon–Sat; 7pm–3/4am Sun. ⌘ ⌣ 🗏 ⌇ Tue & Sun ◉ Mon–Sat

Lei Bar

Nestled in the basement of Niagara, this tiny East Village bar-within-a-bar boasts a DJ spinning surf-movie soundtracks and a bamboo-lined bar serving kitschy frozen drinks – all garnished with fruit kebabs and paper umbrellas.

112 Avenue A (at 7th St), East Village ☎ 420-9517 ⓜ 6 to Astor Pl ◐ 4pm–4am daily. ⌣ 🗏 ◉

The Russian Samovar

Idle Russian beauties line the bar; a piano tinkles in the background; dozens of infused vodkas beckon to be sampled: the Cold War may be over, but intrigue lingers on at this gaudy and elegant Theater District bar and restaurant. Bar snacks include boiled potatoes and black bread!

56 W 52nd St (bet. Broadway & Eighth Ave), Midtown ☎ 757-0168 ⓜ 1·9 to 50th St ◐ 12pm–midnight daily (to 3am Thu–Sat). ⌘ ❡ ⌣ 🗏 ⌇ nightly

Swine on Nine

Swine on Nine may be the most garishly entertaining paeon to pigs man has ever known. Pig murals, drawings and figurines line the walls, and a giant besuited boar greets visitors at the door. A dive at heart, Swine offers dirt-cheap drinks, free chicken soup and a complimentary pink porcelain piggy bank for ladies.

693 Ninth Ave (bet. 47th & 48th Sts), Midtown ☎ 397-8356 ⓜ C·E to 50th St ◐ 8–4am daily (from 12pm Sun). ⌘ ⌣ 🗏

Void

Dark, cavernous and striving for an air of deviance, Void has to be one of New York's best cyber bars, with film screenings (think *Blade Runner* and *Badlands*) every Wednesday, and DJs spinning electronica every Tuesday and Thursday, while punters surf the Web.

16 Mercer St (at Howard St), Soho ☎ 941-6492 ⓜ N·R to Canal St ◐ 8pm–3am Tue–Sat. ⌣ 🗏 ◉ Tue & Thu.

great dives

Mare Chiaro

This is the quintessential Italian dive bar. Once a popular stop for visiting celebrities, and then a favourite haunt of downtown literati, Mare Chiaro is now seeing increased traffic from Nolita's fashionable new residents. Avoid weekends, when cigar-chomping bridge-and-tunnel types pour in from nearby restaurants.

176 Mulberry St (bet. Broome & Grand Sts), Nolita ☎ 226-9345 ⓜ 6 to Spring St ◐ 12pm–1am daily (to 3am Fri–Sat). ⌣ 🗏 ◐

Max Fish

The best dive bar in the Lower East Side is packed every evening with indie-rockers, students, artists and locals. Long since discovered by the outside world, Max Fish has managed to retain its edge without scaring off new visitors; the pool table, however, remains viciously competitive.

178 Ludlow St (bet. Houston & Stanton Sts), LES ☎ 529-3959 ⓜ F to 2nd Ave ◐ 5.30pm–4am daily. ⌘ ⌣ 🗏

Nancy Whiskey Pub

A dive bar in Tribeca, Nancy Whiskey Pub is the real thing with a motley clientele, high-stakes shuffleboard tournaments, and a bartender who steals sips of your beer when you aren't looking.

1 Lispenard St (at 6th St), Tribeca ☎ 226-9943 ⓜ A·C·E to Canal St ◐ 8.30am–3am daily. ⌘ ⌘ ⌣ 🗏 ◐

Pour House

Unlike many of its sleek, Williamsburg neighbours, Pour House is not a place to 'see and be scene'. It is, however, a laid-back, lively local bar where neighbours young and old toss back brews, play pin-ball, and wonder why the bar down the street charges $6 for a beer.

790 Metropolitan Avenue (at Humboldt St), Brooklyn ☎ 1-718-599-0697 Ⓜ L to Graham Ave ◑ 4pm–4am daily (from 12pm Sat–Sun). ◔ to 7pm Sat–Sun ⬜📱

Rudy's

The $3.00 pitchers and free hotdogs are legendary, but the real reason everyone loves this dingy dive is the eclectic crowd. Models, mobsters, and local drunks share rickety tables, overflowing shots, and quarters for the juke. If you don't leave with a story – and a hangover – you're doing something wrong.

627 Ninth Avenue (bet. 44th & 45th Sts), Midtown ☎ 212-974-9169 Ⓜ A•C•E to 42nd St ◑ 8–4am daily (from 12pm Sun). ⚲ hot dogs ⬜📱📖

Siberia

Located in a subway station (and Russian only in decor) this joint is a welcome break from the overgrown theme palaces taking over Times Square above ground. The bar is tiny, the proprietor is gregarious and patrons are encouraged to cut loose, often with complimentary shots of chilled vodka. Not many dive bars can shut off your shy side like Siberia. Great jukebox, too.

1627 Broadway (at 50th St), Midtown ☎ 333-4141 Ⓜ 1•9 to 50th St ◑ 3pm–4am daily (from 8pm Sun). ⬜📖◔

gay thirst

Chase

An urbane, upscale gay bar where buff boys in DKNY mix, mingle, and share some of the city's best margaritas. During peak hours, it gets stuffy in the front room – but we hear it's even hotter in the back lounge. Ladies are more than welcome to join in the fun.

255 W 55th Street (bet. Eighth Ave & Broadway), Midtown ☎ 333-3400 Ⓜ A•B•C•D; 1•9 to 59th St-Columbus Circle ◑ 4pm–4am daily. ♿⬜📖

The Cock

Drag thespians Sherry Vine and Jackie Beat are moonlighting as party hosts at the East Village's hottest gay bar. Homo heart-throb Mario Diaz and a gaggle of go-go dancers are on hand, while DJs spin classic rock 'n' roll, and more, nightly.

188 Ave A (bet. 11th & 12th Sts), East Village ☎ 777-6254 Ⓜ L to 1st Ave ◑ 10pm–4am daily. ♿⬜📖◔

Dick's

Famed for its cheap booze and superb jukebox, Dick's is one of Manhattan's best-loved gay dives. $2 shots and a few Morrissey singles should lower your inhibition. Cruising strongly encouraged.

192 Second Ave (at 12th St), East Village ☎ 475-2071 Ⓜ L to 1st Ave ◑ 2pm–4am daily. ♿⬜📖

Regents

A quiet focal point for the older gay male community, Regents is a swell midtown townhouse with a restaurant, lounge and piano bar. Casually but neatly dressed gentlemen gather round the piano to sing show tunes and standards, taking a break to stroll out onto the ter-race or sit with friends. A heart-warming gem, refreshingly free of young hustlers.

317 E 53rd St (at Second Ave), Midtown ☎ 593-3091 Ⓜ F to 53rd St ◑ 12pm–1am daily. 🍽 all ⚲ ⬜📖⚲🔨

Wonder Bar

One of the rare gay nightspots that wel-comes straight friends without putting a damper on cruising. Excellent DJs keep the crowd happy, but some of the boys still pine for the old porn videos and cur-tained back room. Hey, it's Giuliani time.

505 E 6th St (at Ave A), East Village ☎ 777-9105 Ⓜ 6 to Astor Pl ◑ 8pm–4am daily. 🍽 none ♿⬜📖◐

quiet retreats

Angel's Share

Don't come in a group: well-concealed Angel's Share enforces a strict four-person limit per group, making it most suitable for first-time dates and social recluses. The biggest draw here is the Japanese bartenders, known for mixing marvellous cocktails with expert precision.

8 Stuyvesant St (bet. Second & Third Aves), East Village ☎ 777-5415 Ⓜ 6 to Astor Pl ◑ 7pm–3am daily. ⚲ ⬜📖

Blue Bar

The rarefied, literary atmosphere of the historic Algonquin Hotel [→156] provides the setting for this friendly, low-key mid-town bar. Non-guests are warmly wel-comed and the loquacious bartenders will brew you a warming Irish coffee on cold winter days.

59 W 44th St (bet. Fifth & Sixth Aves), Midtown ☎ 840-6800 Ⓜ B•D•F•Q to 42nd St (Bryant Park) ◑ 12pm–1am daily. ♿

bars

night fever

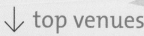

Despite Mayor Giuliani's 'Quality of Life' laws putting a stranglehold on NY nightlife, club promoters still cook up the new, the retro and the extravagant and dish it out at venues all over the city. The club beat goes on, even if at some of the city's lounges, dancing isn't strictly allowed...

↓ top venues

Baktun

Music comes first at this sleek, cozy and truly unique lounge, with staple nights providing different types of dance or electronic music. Creative party promotions, video projections, modest bar prices and friendly staff make it a diamond in the rough.

418 W 14th St (bet. 9th & 10th Aves), Chelsea ☎ 206-1590 **w** www.baktun.com Ⓜ A•C•E to 14th St; L to 8th Ave ⚏ $5–$10 ◐ 10pm–4am Wed–Sun. 🚊 AE/MC/V ⬚ ⚕ casual ⟳ Bang The Party deep house night (first Fri of the month).

Fun

Party people have a great time at Fun, a vast space under the Manhattan Bridge, where the music comes in hip-hop, funk, reggae and house colours. Suited doormen meet and greet at the entrance, but there are no guest lists nor cover charges! The drinks are pricey but that's all you'll have to pay for. You'll need a sense of humour to pay a visit, though: the sinks in the bathrooms have surveillance monitors (so guys can spy on girls, and vice versa).

130 Madison St (at Pike St), LES ☎ 964-0303 Ⓜ F to East Broadway ⚏ $10–$15 ◐ 8pm–4am daily. 🚊 all ⚕ casual-smart ⟳ Never a cover. DJ Bax or special events on Saturdays. ⚐ Hard to find/out of the way.

Limelight

The controversy surrounding owner Peter Gatien's involvement with drug rings and murder has made his club a must-see for the curious. By day, Limelight presents art shows and theatre; by night, it's home to themed parties. Hard house is usually featured on the main floor, while hip-hop and pop are elsewhere. The huge, thumping fiestas allow you to appreciate how they can charge top whack admission.

660 6th Ave (bet. 20th & 21st Sts), Chelsea ☎ 807-7780 Ⓜ F•N•R to 23rd St ⚏ $15–$20 ◐ 10pm–5am daily. 🚊 MC/V ⚕ dress up

Nell's

Having hit on the recipe for success way back, Nell's has changed little over the years. Upstairs, a lush bar has a DJ playing between live R&B sets, while downstairs pulsates to a classic dance mix. It's renowned for a picky door policy so come well-dressed (and men come with a woman). Particularly popular is Voices (Tue) where amateur songbirds and the occasional celeb-birdie perch on the open mic.

246 W 14th St (bet. 7th & 8th Aves), West Village ☎ 675-1567 Ⓜ A•C•E to 14th St; L to 8th Ave ⚏ $10–$15 ◐ 10pm–4am daily (to 1am Mon). 🚊 MC/V ⬚ ⚕ dress up

Shine

A rock 'n' roll venue transformed into a party paradise, Shine radiates good clean fun. There are cushy couches and a mini-stage hosting everything from dance and drag to burlesque and comedy. Promoters bring all sorts of special events and parties. ⟳ Home Cookin' hip-hop party (Wed).

285 West Broadway (at Canal St), Tribeca ☎ 941-0900 Ⓜ A•C•E•1•9 to Canal St ⚏ $5–$15 ◐ 10pm–4am daily. 🚊 MC/V ⬚ ⚕ smart casual.

Spa

After being The Grand, System, and Key Club, the Spa incarnation at this address is the most glamourous. Its white decor is accented with 'spa' touches, such as sauna-like bathrooms, and a tanning bed above the dancefloor. But the sound system has been neglected. Great if you don't mind paying top dollar for a cocktail in a plastic cup for a chance to see and be seen.

76 E 13th St (bet. Broadway and Fourth Ave), East Village ☎ 388-1060 Ⓜ N•R•L•4•5•6 to 14th St-Union Sq ⚏ $20 (Tue–Thu); $25 (Fri–Sat) ◐ 10pm–4am Tue–Sat. 🚊 all ⬚ ⚕ to impress ⟳ Lovely decor. Thursday night Ultra party with DJ Jackie Christie. ⚐ Expensive bar

Tunnel

Thousands of people from all walks of life converge at this megaclub. Every area – even the bathroom – has its own bar and sound system; so weave in and out through hard house, 80s pop, hip-hop, and deep house. Admission's expensive, but there's more than enough bang for the buck with smash hit nights and special events. Dress up; and men, come with a woman.

220 12th Ave (at 27th St), Chelsea ☎ 695-4682 Ⓜ C•E to 23rd St ⚏ $15–$25 ◐ 10pm–6am Thu–Sun. 🚊 MC/V ⬚ ⚕ smart casual. ⟳ Saturday night 'Kurfew' hard house.

Twilo

The huge dancefloor dominates this magnet for an energetic gay crowd. Large psychedelic globes hang from the ceiling and movies are screened on the walls, giving this club a rich, yet frivolous atmosphere. ⟳ Ultimate Twilo (Fri) and Twilo & Junior Vasquez Presents (Sat).

530 W 27th St (bet.10th & 11th Aves), Chelsea
☎ 268-1600 w www.twiloclub.com 🚇 C•E to
23rd St; 1•9 to 28th St 🔢 $15–$25 🌓 10pm–8am
Fri, 10pm–noon Sat. 🚻 MC/V 🔲 🎩 casual.

Vinyl

This hallowed patch of land is the birth-place of legendary clubs of old: Area, Quick, and Shelter. Now known as Vinyl, it's dance heaven, still carving out a giant reputation. Usually closed in the week, weekends see queues wrapping around the corner. No alcohol is served.

6 Hubert St (at Hudson St), Tribeca ☎ 343-1379
🚇 A•C•E to Canal St; 1•9 to Franklin St
🔢 $10–$15 🌓 vary. 🚻 none 🔲 🎩 very casual.
♫ Body & Soul deep and underground house music tea party (Sun all day long).

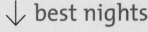

↓ best nights

monday

Giant Step @ Shine

Giant Step returns with their musically innovative event and it now features Chicago house producer Ron Trent as resident. The funky, Afro-infused, danceable tunes allow early-week scenesters and record industry shmoozers to party hearty.

285 West Broadway (at Canal St), Soho
☎ 941-0900 🚇 A•C•E•1•9 to Canal St 🔢 $10
🌓 10pm–2am. 🚻 all 🔲 🎩 Casual-smart
♫ Great music. ♫ It's only four hours long.

Sleaze Factor @ Sapphire

Partiologist Adam Goldstone mingles and mixes on the wheels of steel at this unexpected gem, where dancing is guaranteed. Guest DJs of the highest underground caliber pop by for stints of hard house, hip-hop, funk, trip-hop at this shabby-chic club.

249 Eldridge Street (bet. Houston & Stanton Sts), LES ☎ 777-5153 🚇 F to 2nd Ave 🔢 $5
🌓 7pm–4am. 🚻 none 🔲 🎩 casual
♫ Fun-loving crowd; affordable night out.
♫ Crowd can be somewhat random.

tuesday

Easy Star Reggae Tuesdays @ Black Star Lounge

As NYC has a dearth of good reggae parties, the guys from Easy Star Records fill the void with this weekly do. DJ King Crown spins real roots-reggae for a cool eowntown crowd. The night starts early; there's no cover charge; and the vibe is laid back.

92 Second Ave (bet. 5th & 6th Sts), East Village ☎ 254-4747 🚇 F to 2nd Ave 🔢 free
🌓 8pm–4am. 🚻 all 🔲 🎩 casual ♫ Casual atmosphere with great music. ♫ Can be too mellow.

The Murray & Penny Show @ The Slipper Room

Lil' lady of nightlife Penelope Tuesdae gets together with drag king Murray Hill to inject some burlesque, music, and comedy into New York (showtimes 11pm & 12.30am). Dress to impress and party with an interesting crowd of locals and drag luminaries.

167 Orchard St (bet. Houston & Stanton Sts), LES ☎ 253-7246 🚇 F to 2nd Ave 🔢 free 🌓 *from* 11.30pm. 🚻 all 🔲 🎩 casual ♫ Quirky crowd.

Velveteen @ Serena

Velveteen provides a little glamour for your rump shakin'. Party promoter Audrey Bernstein joins up with talented resident DJ/promoter Johnny 'Don Flan' Sender and playgirl Oberon Sinclair to create a haven for hipsters and their wannabe friends.

Chelsea Hotel, 222 W 23rd St (bet. 7th & 8th Aves), Chelsea ☎ 255-4646 🚇 C•E to 23rd St 🔢 free 🌓 10.30pm–4am. 🚻 all 🔲 🎩 smart-casual ♫ Hip, young and fashionable crowd.
♫ Hip, young and fashionable crowd.

wednesday

Dance Ritual @ Vinyl

Deep house lovers let rip on the dancefloor as internationally renown DJ/producer 'Little Louie' Vega lets loose on the booming system. Liquor-lovers will be disappointed by the beer-and-wine-only license.

6 Hubert St (at Hudson St), Tribeca ☎ 343-1379 🚇 A•C•E to Canal St; 1•9 to Franklin St 🔢 $12 ($7 until 10pm) 🌓 9pm– 3am. 🚻 none 🔲 🎩 dance-casual ♫ Lots of space.

Latin Tribe @ Gemini Lounge

This small, sexy venue lends itself well to the sexy vibe of Latin Tribe. DJ/promoter Babaloo makes a musical offering every week, with Latin jazz, salsa, meringue, and cha-cha. Wallflowers also fit right in at a bar of Cuba Libre sippers.

221 Second Ave (bet. 13th & 14th Sts), East Village ☎ 254-5260 Ⓜ L to 3rd Ave ⓢ $5 ❶ *from 9pm.* 🍴 all ⬜ ⓓ casual-smart ⚭ Friendly mixed crowd. ⚫ Not as high-energy as trad Latin clubs.

thursday

Say it Loud @ Opaline

After sundown, basement restaurant Opaline turns into a party hot spot every Thursday. Cool DJ Marv spins a smooth selection of hip-hop, soul classics, and R&B for a crowd of up-for-it young professionals.

85 Ave A (bet. 5th & 6th Sts), East Village ☎ 475-5050 Ⓜ F to 2nd Ave ⓢ $5 women (free until 11am); $7 men ❶ *from 10pm.* 🍴 all ⬜ ⓓ Fun mix of music & people

Subliminal Sessions @ Centro Fly

Subliminal Records proprietor DJ Eric 'More' Morillo brings this house party to Centro-Fly, whose psychedelic decor, high-tech sound system, and funky restaurant please the most fickle nightclub aficionado. Huge DJs such as Armand Van Helden sometimes make guest appearances.

45 W 21st St (bet. 5th & 6th Aves), Chelsea ☎ 627-7770 Ⓜ F•N•R to 23rd St ⓢ $10 ❶ *10pm–6am.* 🍴 all ⬜ ⓓ casual-smart ⚭ World-famous DJs every week. ⚫ Selective door policy

Trannie Chaser @ NowBar

NY's only transexual promoter Glorya Wholsome has made a perfect place for Trannies and their Chasers to meet and cavort. Men of all shapes and sizes woo the 'ladies' downstairs, while in the upstairs 'lap dance' lounge, they go that bit further.

22 Seventh Ave S (at Leroy St), West Village ☎ 293-0323 Ⓜ 1•9 to Houston St ⓢ $15 ($10 for women, TV's and TS's) ❶ *10pm–4am.* 🍴 MC/V ⬜ ⓓ casual

friday

Twilo @ Twilo

Anyone who enjoys a big club experience will love Twilo. Fab DJs like Sasha, Digweed, and Carl Cox tweak the state-of-the-art sound system for a sea of hard-house revelers. High-tech visuals and occasional art installations enhance the fun.

503 W 27th St (bet. 10th & 11th Aves), Chelsea ☎ 268-1600 ⓦ www.twiloclub.com Ⓜ C•E•1•9 to 23rd St ⓢ $25 ❶ *11pm–7am.* 🍴 all ⬜ ⓓ casual-smart ⚭ Great sound system. ⚫ High admission price.

Squeezebox @ Don Hills

A night of fun and frolics at this long-established punk (as in Sex Pistols) party. Experience Downtown's decadence with a room full of limber go-go dancers and daring drunks. Come early to catch live sets.

511 Greenwich St (at Spring St), West Village ☎ 334-1390 Ⓜ C•E to Spring St ⓢ $10 ❶ *9pm–4am.* 🍴 AE/MC/V ⬜ ⓓ funky casual.

saturday

Foxy @ The Cock

A quirky night, where between dancing and drinking, patrons are invited to strut their stuff on stage – and win $100. Judged by the crowd, contestants do dastardly deeds ranging from acrobatics to anal probing.

188 Ave A (at 12th St), East Village ☎ 777-6254 Ⓜ L to 1st Ave ⓢ $5 ❶ *11pm–4am.* 🍴 none ⬜ ⓓ casual.

Direct Drive @ Baktun

Direct Drive provides a much-needed night of drum 'n' bass with an unbelievable roster of DJs: Seoul, Seen, and Reid Speed are among the residents, and guests drop in on occasion. Enjoy it hard and fast in this high tech, yet warm and intimate, atmosphere.

418 W 14th St (bet. 9th Ave & Washington), Meat Packing District ☎ 206-1590 Ⓜ A•C•E to 14th St; L to 8th Ave ⓢ $12 (women free before midnight) ❶ *from 8pm.* 🍴 all ⬜ ⓓ casual ⚭ Friendly vibe; great music. ⚫ Young crowd.

Shelter @ Vinyl

Shelter attracts older souls as well as younger house disciples. The original DJ Timmy Regisford keeps the underground crowd dancing, twirling, and flipping to the classics non-stop until 9am.

6 Hubert St (at Hudson St), Tribeca ☎ 343-1379 ⓦ www.clubshelter.com Ⓜ A•C•E to Canal St; 1•9 to Franklin St ⓢ $12 ($10 with membership) ❶ *from 11pm.* 🍴 none ⬜ ⓓ dance-casual ⚭ Wonderful dancers & music. ⚫ Doesn't get going until late.

sunday

Shout @ 13

Anglophiles gather in sleek, comfy surroundings to listen to all-night Brit-pop. 13's low-key atmosphere makes it a good place to wind down your weekend, especially in summer when the roof-deck is open.

35 E 13th St (at University Pl), East Village ☎ 979-6677 Ⓜ L•N•R•4•5•6 to 14th St-Union Sq ⓢ free ❶ *10pm–4am.* 🍴 MC/V ⬜ ⓓ smart casual.

Body & Soul @ Vinyl

Probably the best-known dance party in NYC, attracting house heads from the world over. Doors open at 3pm, and it's packed by 6pm. Residents François K, Joe Claussell, and Danny Krivit take dancers on a journey in house, world beat, soul et al.

6 Hubert St (at Hudson St), Tribeca ☎ 343-1379 ⓦ www.bodyandsoul-nyc.com Ⓜ A•C•E to Canal St; 1•9 to Franklin St ⓢ $14 ($10 with membership) ❶ *3–10pm.* 🍴 none ⬜ ⓓ dance-casual ⚭ Wonderfully mixed crowd of dancers. ⚫ Usually gets crowded.

New York, the USA's undisputed cultural capital, throws up an infinite number of top-notch amusements on any given night. The only problem is how to choose between them...

that's entertainment
↓ get in on the act

Recently, Disneyfication has become the byword of the Theater District (bounded by 41st and 53rd Streets, and Sixth and Eighth Avenues): the Disney Store lights up the 'new' Times Square and Disney musicals dominate the stages. Disney's latest venture, Tim Rice's and Elton John's *Aida* at the **Palace Theater**, was panned by the critics, but *Beauty and the Beast* and *The Lion King* are both still going strong (at the **Lunt-Fontanne** and **New Amsterdam** theatres respectively). The latter was partly created by bril-liant puppet theatre director Julie Taymor. Her latest, non-musical venture, *The Green Bird* at the **Cort Theater**, a retelling of an 18th-century Italian fairy tale, is more offbeat – and an easier ticket.

In the world of musicals, *Cats* finally closed in June 2000 after nearly 18 years – the longest run in Broadway history. Alas, there wasn't much on the hori-zon to replace it or other enduring blockbusters such as *Phantom* (**Majestic Theater**) or *Les Miz* (**The Imperial**). And none of the younger US composers came close to touching the genuine success of the last truly new American musi-cal hit, Jonathan Larson's long-running *Rent* at the **Nederlander Theater**, a modern *La Bohème* set in funky East Village. In fact, the most successful American musical produc-tions of late have been revivals: *Annie Get Your Gun* at the **Marquis Theater**; the excellent *Kiss Me, Kate* at the **Martin Beck Theater**; or the longer-running *Chicago* at the **Shubert**. Movie buffs should check out Brit import *Cabaret* at **Studio 54** – the first stateside the-atre success of Oscar-win-ning director Sam Mendes.

This year's spoken offer-ings centre around revivals as well: currently a new production of Eugene O'Neill's *A Moon for the Misbegotten* with Gabriel Byrne at the **Walter Kerr Theater** has been critically feted. Another British West End import, Michael Frayn's *Copenhagen* at the **Royale Theater**, is the sole claimant to the contempo-rary drama crown.

Until the 60s, theatre in NY meant Broadway block-busters, but today Off-Broadway is just as vital. These are the theatres that mounted the first produc-tions of the works of play-wrights like Tennessee Williams and David Mamet, and recently more than a few hits (like *Rent* for example) have origi-nated here. Off-Broadway theatres tend to be more experimental and less commercial, and top writ-ers and directors are lured here by the prospect of a greater artistic freedom than they get on Broadway. Technically, they're venues with 100–499 seats but aren't

tickets & reviews

There are two central ticket agencies responsible for credit card phone orders for all the Broadway theaters: **Ticketmaster** ☎ 307-7171 and **Telecharge** ☎ 239-6200. Each makes a small surcharge for telephone reserva-tions; tickets can then be picked up at the box office (show your credit card as proof of identity). Tickets can also be purchased directly over the internet from the Ticketmaster website **w** www.ticketmaster.com. You can also buy tickets directly from the theatre box offices. There are often special discounts for those with disabili-ties: call Telecharge wheelchair hotline ☎ 239-6280.

On the day of the performance, you can get half-price tickets to both Broadway and Off-Broadway shows at the TKTS booths in Times Square (at 47th St) and at the World Trade Center (often less busy). Lines are long, but move quickly. Tickets for these booths cannot be pur-chased by phone or credit card (cash only).

☼ Broadway theatres are dark on Monday, and many shows are closed Sunday night as well. The main Broadway theatres usually have Wednesday, Saturday and Sunday matinees. Performances generally start at 8pm (matinees 2pm Wed & Sat; 3pm Sun).

♠ Phone the venues direct to get the low-down on seating. Many Broadway theatres now carry infra-red hearing enhancement (headsets available on request).

⊠ Expect to pay $75 plus for the big Broadway shows; tickets for Off-Broadway shows are usually between $25 and $40, and Off-Off Broadway tickets are roughly $15 to $25.

❶ The *New York Times* prints theatre listings every day but the Friday and Sunday papers tend to have the most theatre coverage – critics on the New York Times and the *New Yorker* are especially well respected. There are also listings in the weekly magazines [→145]. *New York City Onstage* ☎ 768-1818 gives recorded information on shows and *Playbill's* website, **w** www.playbill.com, has the low-down on what's on, plus seating plans for the main theatres.

necessarily outside the Theater District: Theater Row, the stretch of 42nd Street west of Ninth Avenue, sports a whole row of Off-Broadway theatres. One Off-Broadway hit of growing grassroots fame is *The Vagina Monologues* at the **Westside Theater**, a show that began as a one-woman monologue and has evolved into a showcase for threesomes of notable women, all discussing the subject of the title openly, sensitively and, often, as humorously as is possible. Granddaddy of the Off-Broadway, non-profit scene is Noho's **Public Theater**, which legendary New York director Joseph Papp founded in 1954. The Public presents productions in every stage of development, including a First Stages series which tests brand-new dramas and musicals in front of small audiences. Emulating the Public, the **Manhattan**

Theater Club also presents readings of new work and fully-fledged stagings in its two small theatres at **City Center**, and has built up a healthy reputation of its own over the last 30 years. The **Atlantic Theater Company**, created out of workshops taught by William H Macy and David Mamet, also stages challenging scripts. And the **Mitzi E Newhouse Theater**'s polished productions of unknown plays almost come with a warranty.

As Off-Broadway became an increasingly established entity in its own right, the development of an even more alternative Off-Off-Broadway scene was inevitable. Anything goes on Off-Off Broadway, where even the definition of a 'theatre' is subject to interpretation. The theatres can be located anywhere from East Village to Brooklyn and they usually have less than 100 seats. Off-Off

Broadway shows tend to be hit or miss, but venues and companies that frequently show excellent productions are the **Jean Cocteau Repertory**, the **Adobe**, the **Irish Rep**, **PS 122**, the **Performing Garage and Second Stage**.

festivals

Shakespeare in the Park is the quintessential New York summertime theatre event [→147]. The **Lincoln Center Festival** (July) ☎ 875-5127 includes theatre in its broad and varied programme. During the regular season, the *Encores!* at **City Center** series presents three revivals of classic-but-forgotten American musicals, in concert version. Leading Broadway stars take time out from their regular shows to appear in the events, and the quality is consistently high. You have to be on the ball to get tickets.

theatre | cabaret

↓ in the spotlight

When people hear the word 'cabaret' they often shudder and think 'show-tunes'. True, you'll often find numbers from the best (and sometimes the worst) in American musical theatre, but in New York – perhaps the world capital of cabaret – the scene is constantly re-inventing itself and becoming a showcase for new, exciting music, in addition to the classic tunes of yesteryear.

For high glamour, try **Café Carlyle**, where singer-pianist and enduring favourite Bobby Short is usually in residence, and cabaret legends Barry Manilow, Barbara Cook and the outrageous Eartha Kitt frequently perform. Another quintessential, all-singing cabaret experience is the elegant **Feinstein's at the Regency**, which puts on a perfect mix of all-time favourites (Rosemary Clooney to mention but one) and newcomers. Though the

$60 cover charge might put some people off, the high-class entertainment is guaranteed to keep punters happy. **FireBird Café**, a tiny piano-bar, also boasts some first-class talent: you can catch the dapper Steve Ross chanelling Cole Porter, or actress-singer

tickets & reviews

There's no central booking agent, so contact venues directly to book tickets.

🕐 Most cabaret performances are Tuesday–Saturday, with a few smaller shows on Sundays and Mondays.

❶ Except for the big extravaganzas, almost all theatres are dark on Mondays, so you might find a singer from a Broadway musical doing a one-night-only event at a cabaret venue.

🎤 Shows with very big names often sell out quickly, so reservations are highly recommended. Reservations are often not required for smaller shows, but it's a good idea to call ahead for seats.

💲 Most cabaret venues have a cover charge and a one-to two-drink minimum. Restaurants offering entertainment sometimes require guests to dine at earlier shows, so it's best to ask when making a reservation. Cover charges range from $10–$15 to $50 at more high-end spaces. Most smaller clubs take only cash, but the larger venues take credit cards.

❶ Cabaret listings change weekly, and the best resources are weekly publications like *Time Out New York*, *In Theater* and *Back Stage*. The *New York Times*, the *New York Daily News* and the *New York Post* often review performances, but you sometimes have to hunt to find cabaret coverage in between other entertainment news. The internet is often a good alternative and you can sometimes book tickets on-line [→145].

→directory 146

and Marlene Dietrich sound-alike, Sian Phillips. Nestled in the Algonquin Hotel (of Dorothy Parker fame) [→150], **The Oak Room** is an intimate club where some of the biggest names in cabaret play. Slip into a velvet banquette to hear timeless tunes interpreted by luminaries like Andrea Marcovicci and Maureen McGovern.

If you enjoy talent spotting, try **Don't Tell Mama**, where many a musical theatre career has been launched. The show is as much in the two show rooms as in the piano bar, where singing waiters set the scene. One of the friendliest spaces in town is **Eighty Eights**, which features an eclectic range of performers, from well-known cabaret singers to comics. Just as friendly and informal is **Judy's Chelsea**, hosting a variety of new and traditional talent in fabulously modern surroundings. Also does a great Sunday jazz brunch.

In the heart of Noho, **Joe's Pub** – a plush club in the Public Theater – manages to be hip and elegant at the same time. There's a great trend of theatre stars making their cabaret debuts here. Don't let the cruisy atmosphere at **Wilson's** put you off: it's often home to Judy Barnett, whose velvety powerhouse of a voice and inventive jazz arrangements will have you cheering. **Torch**, an LES supper club [→10], is where every Monday, you'll find Nicole Renaud, an enchanting Parisian songbird. Her cristalline voice, clever play list and bizzarely beautiful costumes make for a decidedly different evening. Best of all, there's no cover charge.

↓ stand-up new york

If you're looking for comedy of the 'politically correct, fun-for-the-whole-family' variety in New York City, plop yourself in front of a TV set. But if it's irreverent, aggressive, take-no-prisoners entertainment that you're after, New York's top comedy clubs are sure to deliver. The majority of the acts you'll see in New York are stand-ups, but improv comedy is also starting to make big waves.

The city has a long tradition of nurturing breakaway talents like Jerry Seinfeld and Eddie Murphy. Recent, well-known comics who call the city home include Chris Rock (an edgy urban comedian), Janeane Garafolo (who you might recognize from the Larry Sanders Show), Colin Quinn (a down-to-earth Brooklynite) and Ray Romano (of Everybody Loves Raymond fame). Don't be surprised if any of these comedians makes an impromptu appearance, especially during the summer television-taping hiatus. Comedians like to frequent local clubs to test out new material before going on TV shows like The Late Show with David Letterman.

Starting Downtown, New York's alternative comedy scene centres round **Luna Lounge**, whose stark atmosphere epitomizes LES style: some of the city's hippest comedians come here regularly to test the water. Showcasing sassy comics who scoff at the notion of hitting the stage with polished material, the club typifies the belief that it is better to be daring than safely funny. The **Comedy Cellar** offers great comics in a cozy setting and is home to many comedy legends: Robin Williams is known to drop by unannounced.

In Chelsea, the elegant **Gotham Comedy Club** has consistently strong lineups, and is one to check out if you're looking for comedy that pushes down barriers without pushing up your credit limit. Further uptown you'll find New York's premier venue, **Caroline's on Broadway**. This club will cost you, but it's rich, 18-year tradition of hosting America's major comic talents (such as Jerry Seinfeld and Richard Belzer) will assure you of top acts. The UES is home to **Dangerfield's**, founded by comedy legend Rodney Dangerfield. The upscale club harks back to the days of the notorious Catskills comedy circuit, where Mel Brooks got started in the 50s. Lineups are a little uneven, but fairly strong. **Comic Strip Live** may not boast the best decor, but the lineups are good. Well-knowns like Chris Rock and Adam Sandler have done sets on occasion.

tickets & reviews

Make reservations by calling the club directly. Be sure to book a day or two in advance, especially for weekend shows or those with big-name headliners. All clubs mentioned take most major credit cards apart from Dangerfield's.

⏲ As far as seasons go, comedy in New York never takes a vacation – clubs run shows year round. Typical weekday shows (Sun–Thu) run continuously from 9pm–midnight. Weekend shows (Fri & Sat) are more structured, with shows at 8pm, 10pm and 12.30am. The later the show, the racier the material gets.

👤 Reservations don't guarantee a seat: seating is first come, first served, so get there at least half an hour before show time otherwise you stand a good chance of paying $20 to watch the back of another punter's head.

💲 Cover charges range from $5– $25 and almost all clubs have a two-drink minimum, with prices ranging from $3 (non-alcoholic drinks) to $8 (mixed drinks).

❶ Check listings in the weekly mags [→145] but your best bet is to call the club direct: most venues have recorded listings detailing the week's lineups.

↓ reel time

New York is, indisputably, the axis around which the international film world revolves, and on any given day the capital bursts with film-going options: if a recently released film isn't showing here, it very likely isn't worth the projector time.

New releases break in the Big Apple every week, usually before they open anywhere else. The city harbours approximately 185 screens, most of them occupied by the 60 or more films on current release. If big, Dolby-powered Hollywood blockbusters are up your street, there are enough screens in Manhattan, especially round the neon-lit Times Square, to meet your needs at practically any time of the day or night. In most listings magazines [→142] cinemas are conveniently listed by area so you can easily find a screen close by. **The Sony Lincoln Square** is New York's mega-cinema with 12 screens, and a 3D IMAX. But **Clearview's Ziegfeld** (once home to the Follies) is the ultimate movie-going experience, with its huge screen, great sound and ultra-comfy seats. It's the venue for many a glitzy premiere. For those on a budget, the **CO Encore Worldwide** shows films which have recently completed their general release, at half the price.

Manhattan is awash with alternative movie venues. A good 40 screens, evenly distributed between Up- and Downtown, run imported, revived and avant-garde fare, sometimes with schedules that change every day. New York's indie showplace is the **Angelika Film Center**, which routinely screens the moment's finest low-budget films, and programmes the coolest midnight revivals. The beautifully restored **Paris Theatre** also shows regular revivals, especially of French films. The city's surviving repertory outlets are legendary – and deservedly so. **Film Forum**, on the edge of Soho, runs alternative film (documentaries, animations, underground and unorthodox indies) on one screen, and the city's most audience-friendly revival programming on another. **Quad** also includes documentaries in its programme as well as a healthy smattering of foreign films. And the **Anthology Film Archives** shows new experimental films and vintage art-film classics that no one else will touch; when Theo Angelopoulos's prize-winning *Ulysses' Gaze* came to town, this is where it was shown. Even more off-beat movies are screened at the intimate **Cine-Noir Film Society** but only one night a week. For something more highbrow try the **Walter Reade Theater**, located in the Lincoln Center complex, with a comprehensive international series. More arcane, thanks to its curatorial agenda, is the **Museum of Modern Art**; it is always engaged in some series of rare screenings (such as a survey of Cuban films), which are free with museum admission. The **NYU Cantor Film Center** has an interesting programme of studenty cult revival movies and tickets won't break the bank. Look out, as well, for foreign screenings at the **Asia Society**, the **Japan Society** (always good for some Kurosawa or Japan-imation), **Goethe House** (for something German), the **French Institute** (for er... French films) and the **King Juan Carlos I Center** (for occasional screenings of Spanish movies).

During the summer, there are free *Cinema Paradiso-esque* outdoor screenings of golden oldies at **Bryant Park** [→85] every Monday ☎ 391-4248. **Two Boots**, a pizza parlour in the East Village, also has free screenings of classics movies in the downstairs basement, and the gay bookstore, **A Different Light**, shows a free gay-oriented film once a week.

For a night out with a difference, try **Void**, a cyber-age nightclub showing alternative classics, and the **Screening Room** for dinner and a movie; it mainly plays alternatives and classics, and is a great spot for late-night weekend screenings.

cinema

tickets & reviews

It's best to buy or book tickets in advance, and you can do this for most cinemas (but not some of the independents) via the credit-card reservation at ☎ 777-FILM (3456) – they charge a booking fee of $2 per ticket). The service is very easy to operate. It also gives preview information.

☉ New films generally open on Fridays. Screening times vary, but usually start around 10am and run 'til around midnight (there are many more midnight shows at the weekends). In general, movies have only a few trailers and maybe an ad preceding them, so don't assume there's masses of time to spare after the official programme start time.

♿ Automated booking services means the early bird gets the best seats.

⑤ Ticket prices are currently about $9, and slightly less for the smaller, artier theatres.

❶ Film reviews and information about shows can be found in listings mags [→145]. Generally the quickest and hippest place to look for what's happening cinematically is the *Village Voice*, and *Time Out New York*. On the net, **w** www.nytoday.com/movies will help you find a film nearby. The *New York Times* and *New York Observer* run regular film reviews.

→directory 146

festivals

The city hosts more than 30 film festivals during the year. The two biggest are the Lincoln Center's **New York Film Festival** [→147]; and MoMA's **New Directors/New Films Festival** (March) ☎ 708-9480, which shows films from film-makers who are about to 'make it'. The **New York Underground Film Festival** is also in spring [→148]. This is followed by the **Women's Film Festival** in April ☎ 465-3435 at the NY Cantor Center and in July, the **New Festival** (lesbian & gay) ☎ 254-7228.

movie landmarks

New York has constantly been featured on celluloid, and everywhere you go there are famous locations. The most touted by the location scouts is Katz's diner (on Houston Street on the corner with Ludlow), the setting for the fake orgasm scene in **When Harry Met Sally**. Also Downtown, the cab rank where Travis Bickle works in **Taxi Driver** is the real taxi hangout at the bottom of Sixth Avenue (just above Canal Street). And the scene where Madonna buys the sparkly boots in **Desperately Seeking Susan** was filmed in a store called Love Saves the Day on Second Avenue (bet. 6th & 7th Sts). Moving Uptown, the Daily Planet of **Superman** fame is based in the building inhabited by the Daily News (22 E 42nd Street). But the scariest movie ever made, **Rosemary's Baby**, took place in the Dakota Building [→69] – that creepy old apartment probably still echoes with Mia Farrow's screams.

cinema | classical music & opera

↓ new world symphonies

From grand opera at the Met to experimental performances at the avant-garde Kitchen, New York offers a breathtaking range of musical events. Lincoln Center alone boasts four major auditoria – the Metropolitan Opera House, the New York State Theater, Alice Tully Hall and Avery Fisher Hall – which stage performances year round.

The **Metropolitan Opera House**, or Met (Oct–Apr), is arguably the best place in the world to see traditional productions of the standard repertory, but European-style stage direction, with its focus on re-interpreting opera for a contemporary audience, is still in its infancy. Met audiences dote on Franco Zeffirelli, who fills the stage with props, spectacle and casts of thousands in *Turandot* or *La Traviata*; but when Robert Wilson, whose distinctive, minimalist theatrical language is taken for granted in Europe, staged *Lohengrin* here, he was booed: the production was just too innovative for New York.

By contrast, New York City Opera, based next door in the **New York State Theater**, is more ambitious in the stage direction department. Here, singers who are younger and less well known than their Met counterparts, appear in innovative versions of both classics and recent American operas.

When there's no opera at the Met, there are other options. Year after year, the tiny **Amato Opera Theater** cranks out idiosyncratic productions on a shoestring, and the city's music schools, including **Mannes** (Sep–Jun) and the legendary **Juilliard**, stage full student performances. There's also the Opera Orchestra of New York, which gives three different operas a year in concert version at **Carnegie Hall**. Founder-conductor Eve Queler specializes in discovering new singers, and a lot of major stars have made their New York debut under her baton.

A symbol of New York's musical conservatism is the great New York Philharmonic. While former principal conductor Leonard Bernstein – one of America's best known artistes – is still lionized, the Philharmonic today has returned to the orchestral tradition's 19th-century European roots, offering the standard symphonic repertoire. The Philharmonic's home, **Avery Fisher Hall**, is one of Lincoln Center's ugliest buildings – the Beast, as it were, to the Beauty of Carnegie Hall, which has preserved its famous acoustic for more than a century. It also boasts a recital annexe, the **Weill Recital Hall**. Brooklyn's leading arts venue is the **Brooklyn Academy of Music** (BAM), the oldest academy in the US, where the wide and eclectic classical range extends from the Brooklyn Philharmonic to European opera productions.

For chamber music, the leader is, yet again, the Lincoln Center, where **Alice Tully** is the hall of preference. There's also **Merkin Concert Hall**, a couple of blocks north, another venue for chamber and lieder recitals. Across town, at the **92nd Street Y**, violinist Jaime Laredo runs the acclaimed chamber music series 'Chamber Music at the Y' and composer Ned Rorem has been presenting and performing here for the last 50 years.

Of course music isn't restricted to the concert hall stage. One insider tip is the acclaimed series of classical chamber concerts (sometimes with related lectures) at the **Metropolitan Museum of Art** [→73]. In the same vein, the **Frick Collection** [→76] has presented recitals by such international soloists as James Levine. For cutting-edge performances and avant-garde music, the diminutive downtown **Kitchen** is where it's at. And on a barge docked on the Brooklyn side of the East River, you can enjoy the Manhattan skyline while listening to chamber music presented by the popular series **BargeMusic**. For church concerts, check out **Trinity Church**, one of the oldest in New York, **St Ignatius Loyola** or, of course, the Cathedral of **St John the Divine** (see local listings for schedules).

festivals

Granddaddy of New York festivals is the **Mostly Mozart Festival** at Lincoln Center ☎ 546-2656 which has offered summertime classical concerts for over two decades. **The Lincoln Center Festival** ☎ 875-5127 in July brings in funky events from around the world, effectively serving as a summertime pendant to **BAM's Next Wave Festival** every autumn ☎ 1-718-636-4111. The epitome of summer in New York are the appearances of the Metropolitan Opera and New York Philharmonic in various city parks: picnickers enjoy performances like *Aida* under the stars ☎ 362-6000.

tickets & reviews

Tickets for the Lincoln Center venues can only be booked through the agencies, with a surcharge of $4.80 to $5.50 per ticket. Call **Centercharge** ☎ 721-6500 for Alice Tully Hall and Avery Fisher Hall; **CarnegieCharge** ☎ 247-7800 for Carnegie Hall; and ☎ 362-6000 for the Metropolitan Opera. Tickets for other main venues, like the BAM, can be booked through **Ticketmaster** ☎ 307-7171 (surcharges vary by venue). Performances at smaller venues are less likely to be booked out; for tickets call the venues direct.

👕 Dress codes are a thing of the past: even at the Met, anything and everything goes, from jeans to tuxedos.

🕐 The Metropolitan Opera only plays from October toApril. Evening performances generally begin at 8pm (occasionally, at 7 or 7.30pm). There are no Sunday performances at the Met. As a rule classical music performances generally begin at 8pm, but Sunday performances and recitals are sometimes earlier.

🔭 Binoculars are useful accessories in Lincoln Center's huge auditoria. Sitting at the top of the Met isn't necessarily a liability – the acoustics are great here.

💲 Tickets vary from $10 to $180 for events featuring the top performers. At the Met, standing-room tickets for the week go on sale the preceding Saturday morning; people line up before dawn to procure the $12 spots. At music schools, performances are often free.

❶ Listings of the week's cultural events appear in all the weekly mags [→145]. Classical music performances and opera are reviewed in most of the daily papers, usually two to three days after the event. The *New York Times* is the most respected but the critics on the *New York Post* and *Newsday* are usually spot on.

dance | classical music & opera

↓ perpetual motion

The New York dance scene is alive and kicking. At its heart is the New York City Ballet, created by the brilliant choreographer George Balanchine. Today, long after his death, the choreographer's spare and elegant non-story ballets (Balanchine eschewed the word 'abstract') remain benchmarks of American dance. Current director, and former soloist, Peter Martins has kept up the company's Balanchine and Jerome Robbins (of *West Side Story* fame) classics, while adding his own new works. The New York City Ballet (NYCB) shares the **New York State Theater**

with the New York City Opera; their seasons run from November to February, and April to June.

New York's other leading classical ballet company, the American Ballet Theater (ABT), based at the **Metropolitan Opera House** (Apr–Jun), presents a broad range of ballets, traditional and modern. Many are homegrown but big-name international companies like the Kirov and the Royal Ballet are also included in the programme. You are more than likely to see a star or two here.

What Balanchine was to ballet, Martha Graham was to modern dance; and her company continues to perform works from her repertoire. One Graham protégé was Merce Cunningham, a Graham soloist before founding his own avant-garde company, which he still heads today. He has collaborated on productions with Andy Warhol and, more recently, Comme des Garçons. Another seminal, New York-based choreographer is the idiosyncratic and gifted Twyla Tharp (of *The Fugue* and *Push Comes to Shove* fame). She has her own touring outfit but tends to

→directory 146

work with established companies like the NYCB. Another key figure is the inventive Paul Taylor, who, in 1957, established the renowned Paul Taylor Dance Company, which holds its New York season at **City Center**. Just as popular is the Alvin Ailey American Dance Theater, a troupe of mainly black dancers which, thanks to director Judith Jamison, maintains a strong international presence. Sadly, performances from the Dance Theater of Harlem are rare these days. It is now a New York institution but was started in a garage in 1958 by NYCB dancer Arthur Mitchell, who wanted to give the kids of Harlem the opportunities he'd had.

These companies perform mainly at **City Center**, the **Brooklyn Academy of Music** (BAM), acknowledged as the New York centre of modern dance, and the smaller **Joyce Theater** in Chelsea. This former art deco-style cinema was converted into a dance venue by Cora Cahan and Eliot Feld, a fomer NYCB dancer. The Feld Ballet, recently reincarnated as the more experimental Ballet Tech, is based here. The Joyce also presents the short seasons of a

wide spectrum of companies both local and international, famous and less established.

Not far away, the Dance Theater Workshop, in the **Bessie Schonberg Theater**, provides young choreographers with a place to test their mettle. The other place to see truly cutting-edge choreographers is **PS 122** in the East Village. For all these venues, check the listings mags to find out what's on when [→145].

tickets & reviews

Some of the larger companies sell through ticket agencies such as **Ticketmaster** ☎ 307-7171. The **TKTS booth** (at Times Square and the World Trade Center) sometimes has dance tickets for City Center or Joyce performances. Tickets can only be purchased on the day, and they don't accept credit cards. Smaller venues have their own box office and booking system. Most companies' seasons last only a week or two. In smaller venues, there's often no assigned seating: first come, first served.

🕐 Most companies' seasons last only a week or two so you have to be on the ball to get tickets. Show times vary depending on the company and the length of the run. There are often weekend matinees.

👁 It's advisable to bring binoculars for better viewing at the Met and the New York State Theater.

💲 Ticket prices vary from $10 for the smaller venues up to $200 for popular companies at the big venues.

❶ The listings mags [→145] are the best bet to find out what's going on. The main papers all review dance, but sporadically. *The Times* is the best bet but it's the luck of the draw as to which day reviews will run.

festivals

Known as a forum for many things new and interesting in the performing arts, the **BAM's Next Wave Festival** ☎ 636-4100 each autumn, includes dance on its programme. At the Joyce, the **Altogether Different Dance Festival** (January) ☎ 242-0800, now in its 14th year, features choreographers working in novel directions. The **Lincoln Center Festival** ☎ 875-5127 (July) also features dance, and includes companies ranging from Merce Cunningham to the Stuttgart Ballet.

↓ urban verse

Poetry in NYC is becoming as omnipresent as yellow cabs; spoken word events and slams take place all over the city in all sorts of venues, from bookstores to cafés. Not since the 50s Beat generation has poetry been so big. The popularity of verse was confirmed by its appearance on the big screen in *Slam* (director Marc Levin's winner at the 1998 Sundance Festival), which has inspired yet another generation to recycle their innermost thoughts in public.

When big names like Maya Angelou or John Ashbery want to reach the people live, they read in the eru-

dite atmosphere of the **92nd Street Y, Barnes & Noble** bookstores [→106] or the **New York Public Library**. On a cozier note, **Poets House** describes itself as a 'home to all the poetic traditions'. It boasts a 35,000 volume library and literary centre. One of their signature series, *Passwords* presents poets reading and discussing the work of other poets.

Spoken word – poetry written for performance – is still riding high on the poetry and rap hybrid that originated in the city. It is a particularly NY phenomenon and the cross-fertilization was encouraged at

clubs like Fez, where rappers read alongside scene stalwarts such as 99, Todd Colby, and Tracie Morris. Morris, together with the legendary scene godmother, Jayne Cortez, comes from a long-standing tradition of combining poetry with politics and activism.

As ever, though, Downtown is where it's at, the premier spoken word venue is the **Nuyorican Poets Café.** Founded by veterans Miguel Algarin, Bob Holman and Lois Elaine Griffith, it presents plays and verse, and it was here that poetry slams (spoken word competitions), triggered the appearance of spoken word on MTV. A bohemian, beatnik sanctuary of verse is the **Poetry Project at St Mark's**. This is where Allen Ginsberg and Patti Smith have performed more recently. Its New Year's Eve marathon poetry all-nighters are a tradition. A few blocks further east, the ultra-fringe A Gathering of Tribes base their monthly rovings at the **Tribes Gallery** presided over by the poetry guru Steve Cannon, who first encouraged Gil Scott-Heron and Ishmael Reed.

Way Uptown, every Friday night in Harlem, the **National Black Theatre** hosts the Hottest Poetry Slam, the live aspect of the

Hottest Poets Radio Satellite Network (WEVD, 1050 AM). In the comparatively plush theatre setting, poets battle for a $500 prize. And the borough of Brooklyn boasts an ever-increasing number

of cafés hosting poetry events, such as the **Brooklyn Moon Café** and the **Demu Café**, where hipsters can eat and enjoy music and open-mic sessions.

↓ the beat goes on

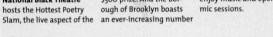

Even if Mayor Giuliani did bring the nightlife tempo down along with the murder rate, New York is still the city that never sleeps, with a wealth of musical performances happening every night. American and international music, from avant-garde to rock, jazz or blues, abounds in surroundings grand and down-home.

If it's international pop stars you're after, then the world-famous **Madison Square Garden** is a must, hosting big acts like the Rolling Stones. Stepping down in size, there are other seated venues like the beautiful **Beacon Theater**, which presents a mix of rock and reggae, ranging from Natalie Merchant to Bob Dylan. Be warned that many other venues are standing room only, like the enormous **Roseland**, a regular spot for big name acts, and the atmospheric **Irving Plaza**; despite its size, it still manages to be a cozy venue for rock, reggae and African artists. And there are always class acts at the **Hammerstein Ballroom**, the elegant **Webster Hall** and the **Bowery Ballroom** where up-and-comers who are denting the charts hone their craft.

New York has a huge array of smaller, more cutting-edge venues too. In the mid-70s, the local rock scene that dared to call itself punk exploded out of **CBGB**. They launched Blondie and Talking Heads and have now given way to the likes of the Chainsaw Kittens. In the middle of St Mark's Place is **Coney Island High**, a popular rock venue for local bands and bigger names. On the traditional rock front, **The Bottom Line** is a West Village institution dating back to the early 70s and is a regular record company showcase. But the LES and East Village is musically where it's at if you want to see the next generation of indie rock and folk stars in the making. Bars and clubs are teeming with aspiring artists and you can spend nights on end here hopping from gig to gig. Another music biz showcase is **Mercury Lounge**, the anchor of the buzzing Ludlow/Orchard Street scene. Really getting down and dirty, **Brownies** is a dark bar that showcases budding rock stars for eager record company scouts. There's also ever-changing live action in small clubs like the lesbian bar **Meow Mix**, the **Luna**

Lounge, **Max Fish**, **Tonic**, the **Living Room** and **Arlene Grocery**. This tiny but trendy club in a former grocery store, where all performances are free includes events like the monthly Rock & Roll and Heavy Metal Karaoke night with a live band.

Musically speaking, the bastion of the avant-garde is the busy **Knitting Factory**. A small empire, it promotes art rock; John Cale, Yoko Ono and Lou Reed, among others, work out their new material here. In the heart of the Meatpacking District, the **Cooler** is named for its former purpose. It's a subterranean meat locker, called 'spooky-cool' by in-the-know locals. It isn't unusual to see experimental performances here by Thurston Moore and Beck.

NYC is a dream made real for jazz fans – bands like the Vanguard Jazz Orchestra and Mingus Big Band all play here once a week. Big jazz names can be seen at deliciously close quarters in clubs like **Sweet Basil**, the **Village Vanguard**, **Smalls Underground** and **Fez**. All of which vie for attention with the **Blue Note**, the renowned home of jazz. They've all gigged

→directory 146

here, from Sonny Rollins to Dave Brubeck.

Self-appointed guardians of big-band jazz, **Jazz at Lincoln Center**, fronted by trumpeter Wynton Marsalis, has a programme of musical events aimed at keeping alive the work of artists like Duke Ellington. The premier jazz club **Birdland** is in itself a nod to jazz tradition, taking its name from Charlie 'Bird' Parker. Parker himself played here along with other great jazzers. Across the road from Lincoln Center, the lurid, surreally decorated **Iridium** attracts vocalists of the calibre of Dee Dee Bridgewater. It's also worth taking the A train up to Harlem to explore the renaissance of jazz that's happening in intimate spots like **St Nick's Pub** and **Perk's**. Meanwhile the **Supper Club**, a lovely ballroom in Midtown, holds big swing nights with the likes of the Charlie Watts Big Band providing the music. There are surprisingly few blues places in the Big Apple, but **Chicago BLUES** presents both local blues players and icons. For under $20, you can enjoy musicians such as Johnnie Johnson or Son Seals.

New York has a significant Latin and world music scene. The regular watering-hole of New York's Latin and world music aficionados is the venerable **SOB**'s (Sounds of Brazil), with a stage that's usually overflowing with large Latin, African or Caribbean bands. The city's most elegant venue of world music is the **Town Hall**, a formal, classical space often booked out by the World Music Institute. For the pop-ier sides of world music, see what's happening at **Symphony Space**. If you're in search of salsa, dance your pants off at big halls like **Latin Quarter** and the **Copacabana**. Or way up in the Bronx is the lively pan-Latin hangout, **Jimmy's Bronx Café**, run by the redoubtable Jimmy himself, with live salsa and merengue on Saturday

nights. For more intimate Latino jazzy jams, it is always wise to see if any music's going down at the **Nuyorican Poets Café**.

Rootsy and hip-hop artists, from singer-songwriter Amanda McBroom to funk and R&B singer Tamar-Kali, can occasionally be found at **Joe's Pub**. Alternatively, the shabby country house chic of **Nell's** (founded by English expat Nell Carter) succeeds in remaining endlessly in fashion. Open-mic sessions here attract visiting VIPs like Stevie Wonder. London-born Nigerian singer, Wunmi, ex Soul II Soul, plays here too. The legendary **Apollo Theatre** is still going, and is home to the famous Wednesday 'Amateur Night', as well as a steady stream of soul and hip-hop stars. And Harlem's churches, like the **Abyssinian Baptist Church**, are the real deal for a Sunday gospel experience.

Considering New York City gave birth to rap, there's a serious dearth of venues booking rap acts. But rap artists like the Roots have begun using a stretch at **Wetlands** (ordinarily a Grateful Dead-type hangout) to warm up for major tours.

tickets & reviews

You can get tickets from venues in advance, but the main purveyor is the monolithic **Ticketmaster** ☎ 307-7171, which can also be accessed on the internet at w www.ticketmaster.com. As everywhere, good shows get sold out quickly. The desperate can join the tradition of being ripped off by ticket scalpers outside major events.

☾ There are gigs every night of the week but many more on Friday and Saturday nights. Most start between 8/9pm. Big names will often have a support band, which will start earlier.

♠ Larger venues tend to be seated and smaller ones seating room only.

☷ Tickets for the big names are around $40–$50 mark but otherwise reckon on paying between $8–$20.

❶The weekly mags have comprehensive listings [→145]. Web-sites offer invaluable info, too [→145]. Up-to-date scoop can also be gleaned from Funkmaster Flex's radio show on 96 Kiss FM every night of the week. Hip happenings can be discovered by making enquiries at places like Earwax Records, 204 Bedford Ave (bet. N 5th & 6th Sts) ☎ 1-718-218-9608. Or trail the underground scene on the internet at sites like w www.supa.com

festivals

Music festivals are a pressure valve for New York in the summertime and are usually free. **Summerstage** is the musical highlight of summer [→147]. The **Guinness Fleadh** ☎ 307-7171 is a Celtic fun-fest weekend held in June on Randall's Island and one of the most romantic events is the **Midsummer Swing Series** at the Lincoln Center ☎ 875-5766 (Jun–Jul). Dance lessons are held an hour before the start of the show, and the outdoor dance floor within the main plaza is inevitably packed. There are also free summer concerts in the **World Trade Center** ☎ 435-4170 by artists like Ryuichi Sakamoto and DJ Spooky, and **Celebrate Brooklyn** ☎ 1-718-855-7882 is a free weekend concert series held between Jul–Aug in Prospect Park [→85], with African music, soul, and silent movies with the score performed by a full live orchestra. Jazz buffs should enjoy the **Bell Atlantic** (☎ 219-3055) and **JVC Jazz Festivals** (☎ 501-1390) held one after the other in summer. Many of the former's performances are free and both festivals include R&B and world music.

↓ get switched on

listings magazines & the free press

Time Out New York has made a comfortable niche for itself in the market of weekly listings mags, which include the more conservative *New Yorker* and yuppie-ish *New York Magazine*. Supposedly providing the skinny on the scene is *Paper* (monthly), though it's a little old hat nowadays.

the papers

Picking up your preferred local paper from one of the city's many street-side newsstands is a morning ritual in NYC. Perhaps with the exception of *The Washington Post*, the *New York Times* is the most well respected paper in America; it prides itself on its world news analysis and, despite its stuffy tone and appearance, is a comprehensive read. The Sunday version weighs in like a set of encyclopedias. As far as tabloids go, the *Daily News* and the *New York Post* can't touch the down-and-dirty tactics of the British rat-pack but, with Rupert Murdoch at the helm of the *Post*, it can't be long in coming. As for the top financial paper, the *Wall Street Journal*: no WSJ...no comment.

An excellent way to check out the press without spending a cent is to try a café that has newspapers and magazines: the Pink Pony on Ludlow Street and the News Café on University Place at Union Square are just a couple. Also Barnes & Noble stores all have cafés where you can read for free after you've paid to sup. For foreign press go to Hudson News (753 Broadway at 8th St), Tower Books (383 Lafayette Street at 4th St) or branches of Universal News.

Free listings magazines and newspapers can be found all over the place, from the laundromat to the bank foyer, or in boxes on the sidewalk, and combine listings with local and national interest features. *The Village Voice*, a long-standing liberal mouthpiece, has declined recently, partly due to competition from the equally liberal listings mag, the *New York Press*. A rash of free specialty publications such as *NYC*, *NYPress*, *HX*, *Next*, *Flyer*, with up-to-date club gossip, and *Literal Latte*, a café-society rag, have become omnipresent in public spaces.

radio

New York is equally well endowed with 24-hour radio stations, featuring all manner of music and talk shows. FM stations are your best bet but AM stations can also entertain, if not inform. Hot 97 (WBLS, 97.1 FM) provides the essential hip-hop accompaniment to a New York day, while K-Rock (WXRK, 92.3 FM) is shock-jock Howard Stern's personal soapbox every morning. WBGO (88.3 FM) is a round-the-clock jazz station, and the station of choice for rock 'n' roll classics is WNEW (102.7 FM). What you'll hear in most cabs is WKTU (103.5 FM) – pumped-up versions of mainstream house anthems. College radio stations showcase big name DJs at weekends to get you in the party spirit. Non-music alternatives are WNYC (820 AM), a member station of National Public Radio or WBAI (99.5 FM), both of which have public-forum type news discussions and good coverage of politics

television

Americans are a nation of TV junkies and New Yorkers, no matter how cosmopolitan they seem, are no exception. There are 70-odd channels to be had

if you have cable and around a dozen if you don't, but for the visitor the novelty soon wears off. Exceptions to the rule are channels 13, 21 and 31, which are given over to public broadcasting and have higher quality programming. To get your fix of the big-name shows, channel 11 screens re-runs of Friends, Seinfeld and Cheers every night, and NBC shows the phenomenally successful ER. Channel 21 also shows BBC world news every night at 11.30pm. The main television news slot is 10pm on terrestrial channels, but there are plenty of all-news-all-the-time cable channels: MSNBC (15), CNN (10), Fox News (46) and, for good local info, New York News One (1). MTV deserves a mention if only because of its popularity. Don't forget to have a quick flick past the public access channels for freak-show-style laughs.

websites

www.newyork.citysearch.com has up-to-the-minute info on events; *www.clubnyc.com* is nightlife oriented; *www.sidewalk.com* is Miscrosoft's comprehensive listings and information network, covering everything from restaurant reviews to club listings. If these don't help you out, *www.nynetwork.com* has a listing of all New York websites. But if your hotel doesn't have internet access, try the terminals at the New York Public Library [→71] for free access, or one of the city's cyber cafés:

Cyber café
273 Lafayette Street
(at Prince St) ☎ 334-5140

Internet café
82 E 3rd Street (bet. First & Second Aves) ☎ 614-0747

Void [→132]
16 Mercer St (at Howard St)
☎ 941-6492

media

→directory 146

Abyssinian Baptist Church
☎ 862-7474

A Different Light
☎ 989-4850

Adobe
☎ 352-0441

Alice Tully Hall
Lincoln Center
☎ 875-5050

Amato Opera Theater
☎ 228-8200

Angelika Film Center
☎ 995-2000

Anthology Film Archives
☎ 505-5110

Apollo Theatre
☎ 513-5300

Arlene Grocery
☎ 358-1633

Asia Society
☎ 288-6400

Atlantic Theater Co
☎ 645-8015

Avery Fisher Hall
Lincoln Center
☎ 875-5030

BargeMusic
☎ 1-718-624-4061

Beacon Theater
☎ 496-7070

Bessie Schonberg Theater
☎ 924-0077

Birdland
☎ 581-3080

Blue Note
☎ 475-8592

The Bottom Line
☎ 228-6300

Bowery Ballroom
☎ 533-2111

Brooklyn Academy of Music (BAM)
☎ 1-718-636-4100

Brooklyn Moon Café
☎ 1-718-243-0424

Brownies
☎ 420-8392

Café Carlyle
☎ 744-1600

Carnegie Hall
☎ 247-7800

Caroline's on Broadway
☎ 367-9000

CBGB
☎ 982-4052

Chicago BLUES
☎ 924-9755

Cine-Noir Film Society
☎ 253-1922

City Center
☎ 581-1212

Clearview's Ziegfeld
☎ 777-FILM 602

CO Encore Worldwide
☎ 246 1583

Comedy Cellar
☎ 254-3480

Comic Strip Live
☎ 861-9386

Coney Island High
☎ 674-7959

Cooler
☎ 229-0785

Copacabana
☎ 582-2672

Cort Theater
☎ 239-6200

Dangerfield's
☎ 593-1650

Demu Café
☎ 1-718-875-8484

Don't Tell Mama
☎ 757-0788

Eighty Eights
☎ 627-4351

Feinstein's at the Regency
☎ 339-4095

Fez
☎ 533-2680

FireBird Café
☎ 586-0244

Film Forum
☎ 727-8110

French Institute
☎ 355-6100

Frick Collection
☎ 288-0700

Goethe House
☎ 439-8700

Gotham Comedy Club
☎ 367-9000

Hammerstein Ballroom
☎ 564-4882

The Imperial
☎ 239-6200

Iridium
☎ 582-2121

Irish Rep
☎ 727-2737

Irving Plaza
☎ 777-6800

Japan Society
☎ 832-1155

Jean Cocteau Repertory
☎ 677-0060

Jimmy's Bronx Café
☎ 1-718-329-2000

Joe's Pub
☎ 539-8777

Joyce Theater
☎ 242-0800

Judy's Chelsea
☎ 929-5410

Juilliard Theater
☎ 769-7406

King Juan Carlos I Center
☎ 689-4232

Kitchen
☎ 255-5793

Knitting Factory
☎ 219-3055

Latin Quarter
☎ 864-7600

Living Room
☎ 533-7235

Luna Lounge
☎ 260 2323

Lunt-Fontanne Theatre
☎ 307-4100

Madison Square Garden
☎ 465-6741

Majestic Theater
☎ 239-6200

Manhattan Theater Club
☎ 399-3000

Mannes College of Music
☎ 580-0210

Marquis Theater
☎ 307-4100

Martin Beck Theater
☎ 239-6200

Max Fish
☎ 529-3959

Meow Mix
☎ 254-0688

Mercury Lounge
☎ 260-4700

Merkin Concert Hall
☎ 501-3330

Metropolitan Museum of Art
☎ 570-3949

Metropolitan Opera House
☎ 362-6000

Mitzi E Newhouse Theater
☎ 239-6200

Museum of Modern Art
☎ 708-9480

National Black Theatre
☎ 722-3800

Nederlander Theatre
☎ 921-8000

Nell's
☎ 675-1567

New Amsterdam Theater
☎ 307-4100

New York Public Library
☎ 930-0830

New York State Theater
☎ 870-5570

92nd Street Y
☎ 996-1100

Nuyorican Poets Café
☎ 505-8183

NYU Cantor Film Center
☎ 998-4100

The Oak Room
☎ 840-6800

Palace Theater
☎ 307-4747

Paris Theatre
☎ 688-3800

Performing Garage
☎ 966-3651

Perk's
☎ 666-8500

Poetry Project at St Mark's
☎ 674-0910

Poets House
☎ 431-7920

PS 122
☎ 228-4249

Public Theater
☎ 260-2400

Quad
☎ 255-8800

Roseland
☎ 247-0200

Royale Theatre
☎ 239-6200

St Ignatius Loyola
☎ 288-3588

St John the Divine
☎ 316-7540

St Nick's Pub
☎ 283-9728

Shubert Theater
☎ 239-6200

Screening Room
☎ 334-2100

Second Stage
☎ 246-4422

Smalls Underground
☎ 929-7565

SOB's
☎ 243-4940

Sony Lincoln Square
☎ 336-5000

Studio 54
☎ 239-6200

Supper Club
☎ 921-1940

Sweet Basil
☎ 242-1785

Symphony Space
☎ 864-5400

Tonic
☎ 358-7504

Torch
☎ 228-5151

Town Hall
☎ 997-6661

Tribes Gallery
☎ 674-3778

Trinity Church
☎ 602-0872

Two Boots
☎ 254-1441

Village Vanguard
☎ 255-4037

Void
☎ 941-6492

Walter Kerr Theater
☎ 239-6200

Walter Reade Theater
Lincoln Center
☎ 875-5600

Webster Hall
☎ 353-1600

Weill Recital Hall
Carnegie Hall
☎ 247-7800

Westside Theater
☎ 239-6200

Wetlands
☎ 966-4225

Wilson's
☎ 769-0100

new york agenda

A year's worth of events and happenings in and around the big apple...

summer

Bell Atlantic & JVC Jazz Festivals

Both Bell Atlantic and JVC celebrate summertime by sponsoring great music acts in venues all over town. The impressive lineups are not only about jazz but also feature R&B and world music. The Bell Atlantic festival, organised by the Knitting Factory [→143], usually offers more free concerts. See listings mags for details [→145].

◑ *June*
Various locations ☎ 484-1222 (Visitor Information Center) ⊠ free–$65

Puerto Rican Day Parade

The parade honours the 2 million plus Puerto Rican residents of New York, but all over town cars beep their horns and sport the flags and banners of their owners' native island.

◑ *June*
Fifth Avenue, from 44th to 79th Sts ☎ 1-718-665-4009 Ⓜ B·D·F·Q to 47th-50th Sts-Rockefeller Center; any stops on 4·5·6 from Grand Central - 42nd St to 77th St ⊠ free

Restaurant Week

For five days, a selection of New York's best restaurants offer special three-course prix-fixe lunches. Restaurant Day opens the feast, when participating restaurants serve tasting plates for $3–$5.

◑ *mid-June*
various locations ☎ 484-1222 (NYC Visitor Information Center) ⊠ $20 (three-course lunch)

Gay and Lesbian Pride Day

Body-beautiful, bare-chested men (and women) take to the streets to celebrate Gay Pride and show off their pecs.

◑ *end June*
Fifth Avenue, from 80th Street to Greenwich Village; street party along Christopher Street to West Side Piers ☎ 620-7310 Ⓜ 6 to 77th St (start); 1·9 to Christopher St (finish) ⊠ free

New York Philharmonic & Metropolitan Opera in the Park

Humid summer evenings are best spent in the park with the strains of classical music wafting over one's picnic – see listings mags for details [→145].

◑ *June–August*
Rumsey Field, mid-park ☎ 875-5709 Ⓜ 6 to 68th St-Hunter College or 77th St; 1·2·3·9 to 72nd St ⊠ free

Central Park Summerstage

Weekend afternoon concerts feature big name music acts such as Roy Ayres and James Brown. Spoken word and dance recitals on week nights – see listings mags for details [→145].

◑ *June–August*
Rumsey Field, mid-park St-Hunter College or 77th St; 1·2·3·9 to 72nd St ⊠ free

Mermaid Day Parade

King Neptune chomping on a hot dog while dozens of mermaids and other fairy-tale creatures cavort on the boardwalk at Coney Island make for a real off-beat experience.

◑ *end June*
From Steeplechase Park to Boardwalk (at 8th St), Coney Island ☎ 1-718-372-5159 Ⓜ B·D·F·N to Stillwell Ave-Coney Island ⊠ free

Shakespeare in the Park

Every season the Delacorte Theater in Central Park shows two plays: one by Shakespeare and one American classic.

◑ *late June–late August*
Delacorte Theater, mid-park ☎ 539-8500 Ⓜ 6 to 68th St-Hunter College or 77th St; 1·2·3·9 to 72nd St ⊠ free

Washington Square Music Festival

Continuing a long-running Greenwich Village tradition of a civilized night out, this festival provides chamber music for an appreciative audience.

◑ *July–August*
West Village ☎ 431-1088 Ⓜ A·B·C·D·E·F·Q to W 4th St-Washington Sq ⊠ free

Macy's Fourth of July Fireworks

14,000 aerial shells and special effects explode over the East River. The hour-long extravaganza ends with a rousing rendition of 'The Star Spangled Banner'.

◑ *Independence Day*
East River; for the best view get down to FDR Drive (bet. 14th & 51st Sts) ☎ 494-4495 Ⓜ L to 1st Ave; or 4·5·6·7 to Grand Central-42nd St; 6 to 51st St ⊠ free

Harlem Week

The highlight of this uptown extravaganza is the street festival on Fifth Avenue between 125th and 135th Streets with live jazz, gospel and R&B.

◑ *early–mid-August*
Throughout Harlem ☎ 862-8477 Ⓜ 2·3 to 125th St or 135th St ⊠ free

autumn

US Open Tennis Tournament

Pete Sampras, Stefi Graf and Monica Seles have all strutted their stuff here, at one of the most demanding tennis tournaments on the world circuit.

◑ *end August–early September*
USTA Tennis Center, Flushing, Queens ☎ 1-718-760-6200 Ⓜ 7 to Willets Point-Shea Stadium ⊠ approx $30–$65

Feast of San Gennaro

Spicy Italian sausages, fairground games and pumping house music. Crowds flock from the outer boroughs for this raucous 10-day street party.

◑ *mid-September*
Mulberry Street, from Houston to Canal Streets, Nolita ☎ 764-6330 Ⓜ B·D·F·Q to Broadway-Lafayette St; 6 to Bleecker St; N·R to Prince St; J·M·Z·6 to Canal St ⊠ free

Wigstock

As the name implies, it's all about hair – and stilettos and frocks, with a salubrious stage show hosted by the reigning drag queen. See listings mags [→145] or call the Lesbian & Gay Center for details.

◑ *Labor Day weekend*
Pier 54, West Side Highway, West Village Ⓜ 1·9 to Christopher St ⊠ free

West Indian-American Day Carnival

Not on the scale of London's Notting Hill but excellent beef patties, jerk chicken and many sound systems make for a carnival spirit nonetheless.

◑ *Labor Day*
Eastern Parkway, Brooklyn ☎ 1-718-467-1797 Ⓜ 2·3 to Grand Army Plaza ⊠ free

New York Film Festival

A wide range of new films from established directors debut before a critical audience. Tickets sell out fast in this film-crazed community.

◑ *end September–mid October*
Alice Tully Hall, Lincoln Center, Columbus Avenue (bet. 62nd & 66th Sts), UWS ☎ 875-5610 Ⓜ 1·9 to 66th St-Lincoln Center ⊠ approx $15 per screening

Hispanic Day Parade

Thousands of flag-waving New Yorkers line Fifth Avenue to salute a parade of floats and dancers representing the Hispanic nations.

◑ *early October*
Fifth Avenue, from 44th to

72nd Street ☎ 864-0715
Ⓜ B•D•F•Q to 47th-50th Sts-Rockefeller Center; any stops on 4•5•6 from 42nd St-Grand Central to 77th St 🚯 free

Columbus Day Parade

The official celebration of Columbus's so-called 'discovery' of America with an Italian-oriented show of floats and military marching bands.

◑ *early October*
Fifth Avenue, from 44th to 72nd Streets ☎ 249-9923
Ⓜ B•D•F•Q to 47th-50th Sts-Rockefeller Center; any stops on 4•5•6 from Grand Central-42nd St to 77th St 🚯 free

Rangers Ice Hockey Season

NYC is big on local sports – the Rangers are home grown heroes and have a huge following.

◑ *October–April*
Madison Square Garden (bet. W 33rd St & Seventh Ave), Midtown ☎465-6741 Ⓜ A•C•E•1•2•3•9 to 34th St-Penn Station 🚯 varies

Greenwich Village Halloween Parade

An orgy of freaks, ghouls and outlandish costumes. Gay New Yorkers guarantee a totally uninhibited, high-spirited affair.

◑ *31 October*
Sixth Avenue, from Spring to 21st Streets ☎ 1-914-758-5519
Ⓜ C•E to Spring St; A•B•C•D•E•F•Q to W 4th St-Washington Sq; 1•9 to 18th St 🚯 free

winter

New York City Marathon

Cheering on the stragglers can be combined with a beautiful day in the park – or, if it's your thing, sign up! Best views are usually from within Central Park.

◑ *end October/early November*
Verazzano Bridge on Staten Island (start); Tavern on the Green, W 67th Street (finish) ☎ 860-4455 (for details of route) 🚯 free

'Knicks' Basketball Season

New Yorkers are a loyal bunch and despite the Knicks' patchy track record, diehard fans like Spike Lee and Woody Allen, who are at every home game, keep on cheering and hoping.

◑ *November–April*
Madison Square Garden (bet. W 33rd St & Seventh Ave), Midtown ☎ 465-6741 Ⓜ A•C•E•1•2•3•9 to 34th St-Penn Station 🚯 varies (tickets are hard to get hold of)

Macy's Thanksgiving Day Parade

Balloons of suitably skyscraper proportions are inflated in Central Park the day before and paraded on Thanksgiving Day – this pre-turkey spectacular is unmissable.

◑ *Thanksgiving Day*
From Central Park W (at 77th St), down Broadway and finishing at Herald Square ☎ 494-4495 Ⓜ 1•2•3•9 to 72nd St (start); B•D•F•N•Q•R to 34th St-Herald Sq (finish) 🚯 free

Lighting the Rockefeller Center Christmas Tree

Traditional and kitschy with twinkling lights, Christmas carollers and throngs of shopping-bag-toting tourists.

◑ *early December*
47th to 50th Street (at Sixth Ave), Midtown ☎ 632-3975
Ⓜ B•D•F•Q to 47th-50th Sts-Rockefeller Center 🚯 free

'Dropping the Ball'

You thought the subway at rush hour was crowded? A generally well-mannered crowd counts down to the New Year.

◑ *New Year's Eve*
Times Square, Midtown ☎ 922-9393 Ⓜ N•R•1•2•3•7•9 to 42nd St-Times Sq 🚯 free

Midnight Footrace in Central Park

A festive race around the park, and plenty of champagne when you make it to the finishing line. Good healthy fun.

◑ *New Year's Eve*
Tavern on the Green, Central Park ☎ 860-4455 Ⓜ 1•2•3•9 to 72nd St 🚯 free

Tax Free Week!

No tax on all retail items twice a year – takes the sting out of shopping.

◑ *mid-January & September*
☎ 788-3000 (mayor's office)

Martin Luther King Jr Day

A solemn tribute to Dr King, the parade also serves as a memorial to all black soldiers who have fought for America.

◑ *late January*
Fifth Avenue (bet. 60th and 68th Streets), UES ☎ 374-5176
Ⓜ 4•5•6 to 59th St (start); 6 to 68th St-Hunter College (finish) 🚯 free

Chinese New Year

Strict enforcement of the firecracker ban has dampened this manic celebration, but dragons still dance around Chinatown.

◑ *February*
Chinatown Ⓜ J•M•N•R•Z•6 to Canal St ☎ 373-1800 🚯 free

spring

St Patrick's Day Parade

The city's Irish contingent turns out to parade (and drink) in celebration of their cultural heritage: a rowdy day-out.

◑ *17 March*
Fifth Avenue, from 44th to 86th Streets, then east to Third Ave ☎ 1-718-357-7532

Ⓜ 7 to 5th Ave; any stop on Sixth Ave, from 51st to 86th Streets 🚯 free

New York Underground Film Festival

A young, downtown audience critiques over 120 new movies. Brit films also showcased since 1999.

◑ *March*
Anthology Film Archives, Second Avenue (at 3rd St), LES ☎ 925-3440 w www.nyuff.com
Ⓜ F to 2nd Ave 🚯 $7.50

Easter Sunday Parade

Pet dogs dressed up as Easter bunnies, kiddies in bonnets – and eggs galore.

◑ *Easter Sunday*
Fifth Avenue (bet. 49th & 57th Sts), Midtown ☎ 484-1222
Ⓜ B•D•F•Q to 47th-50th Sts-Rockefeller Center; E•F to 5th Ave 🚯 free

Yankees & Mets Baseball Season

Tickets are easy to come by, unlike basketball games. The Yankees are team winners and have a huge home following.

◑ *April–October*
Mets: Shea Stadium, 126th St (at Roosevelt Ave), Queens ☎ 1-718-507-8499
Ⓜ 7 to Willets Point-Shea Stadium 🚯 $9–$23
Yankees: Yankee Stadium, 161st St & River Ave, Bronx ☎ 1-718-293-6000 Ⓜ C•D•4 to 161st St-Yankee Stadium 🚯 $12–$23

Spring Festival

Stalls selling home-baked goods rub shoulders with carnival games and bouncy castles. Sound systems get everyone dancing in the streets.

◑ *April*
Broadway (bet. 110th & 118th Streets), Morningside Heights ☎ 764-6330 Ⓜ 1•9 to Cathedral Pkwy (110th St) 🚯 free

Bike New York: The Great Five Boro Bike Tour

The largest mass bike ride passes through Manhattan, the Bronx, Queens, Brooklyn and Staten Island, covering 42 miles in a single day.

◑ *early May*
Starts Battery Park; finishes Staten Island ☎ 932-2453 (for details of route) 🚯 free

Memorial Day Parade

Old soldiers are remembered by their comrades in arms. The city is eerily quiet when the minute of silence is observed.

◑ *end May*
Fifth Avenue, from 44th to 72nd Street ☎ 374-5176
Ⓜ B•D•F•Q to 47th-50th Sts-Rockefeller Center; any stops on 4•5•6 from Grand Central-42nd St to 77th St 🚯 free

New York has some of the trendiest, coolest hotels in the world, from the super smooth Time to the thoroughly modern, touch-of-a-button Peninsula. But there is also plenty of trad chintzy and more elegant old-world comfort too. Bedrooms tend to be larger than in European city hotels; they also tend to cost more. Find your niche in the following selections – from no-expense-spared to budget – in all areas of the big apple.

sleep easy
what's where

↓ brooklyn
Bed & Breakfast On The Park | $195 [→157]

↓ chelsea
Chelsea | $185 [→151]
Chelsea International Hostel | $60 [→154]
Leo House | $78 [→156]

↓ gramercy park
Carlton Arms | $73 [→154]
Hotel 17 | $109 [→156]
Inn at Irving Place | $295 [→157]

↓ lower east side (LES)
Off Soho Suites | $179 [→154]

↓ midtown east
Avalon | $275 [→150]
Box Tree | $230 [→155]
Fitzpatrick | $325 [→155]
Four Seasons | $615 [→152]
Gershwin | $129 [→156]
Gramercy Park Hotel | $170 [→156]
Kitano New York | $315 [→155]
Morgans | $320 [→152–153]
New York Palace | $465 [→152]
Omni Berkshire Place | $389 [→155]
Peninsula | $535 [→152]
Plaza | $425 [→151]
St Regis | $580 [→152]
Shelburne Murray Hill | $306 [→154]
Waldorf Astoria | $250 [→151]
W New York| $279 [→153]

↓ midtown west
Algonquin | $329 [→151]
Broadway Inn | $135 [→157]

midtown west (continued)
Casablanca | $265 [→155]
Edison Hotel | $140 [→154–155]
Hudson | $95 [→156]
Mansfield | $255 [→150]
Paramount | $290 [→153]
Southgate Tower Suite Hotel | $200 [→154]
Royalton | $385 [→153]
Time | $285 [→153]

↓ soho
Mercer Hotel | $400 [→152]
Soho Grand | $419 [→153]

↓ tribeca
Tribeca Grand Hotel | $399 [→153]

↓ upper east side (UES)
Carlyle | $450 [→151]
Hotel Élysée | $325 [→150]
Hotel Wales | $265 [→150]
Franklin | $269 [→150]
Lowell | $445 [→155]
Pierre | $480 [→152]
Plaza Athénée | $475 [→151]

↓ upper west side (UWS)
Country Inn The City | $150 [→157]
Hotel Beacon | $170 [→154]
Hostelling International New York | $75 [→156]
Malibu | $99 [→156]
Pickwick Arms Hotel | $130 [→157]

↓ west village
Abingdon | $165 [→157]
Larchmont Hotel | $100 [→156]
Washington Square Hotel | $129 [→157]

prices – lowest quoted, excluding taxes, for double room in peak season 2000 (unless otherwise stated)

↓ chic boutiques

Avalon 16 E 32nd Street (bet. Fifth & Madison Aves) | Midtown | 10016

One of New York's newest, privately owned, one-off hotels. Bordering lower Madison Avenue, a white-hot area of new restaurants and shops, the hotel manages to feel both grand and cozy. The lobby is definitely grand, with Veronese marble and opulent centre rotunda with black marble columns. At night, snuggle up with the hotel's unique, full-size body pillows. Green-and-cream bedrooms feature luxurious details like Frette bathrobes, Irish cotton towels and marble bathrooms.

☎ 299-7000 **F** 299-7001 **w** www.theavalonny.com **M** 6 to 33rd St ✦ 100 ⌨ 🗐 ↔ 🖉 🕸 🖵 ♿ ☐ AE (singles from $225; doubles from $275)

Hotel Élysée 60 E 54th Street (bet. Park & Madison Aves) | UES | 10022

An impressive list of famous people have called this place home when it housed longer-term residents. Both Joe DiMaggio and Marlon Brando have lived here, Tallulah Bankhead had public tantrums, Tennessee Williams wrote and died here, and Vladimir Horowitz left his piano behind. The public spaces are large with cheerful bright furnishings. Quirky oil paintings are everywhere, and the large bedrooms contain some lovely antiques. The Monkey Bar has a packed bar scene, with a sexy red dining room next door.

☎ 753-1066 **F** 980-9278 **e** elysee99@aol.com **M** E•F to Lexington Ave-3rd Ave ✦ 99 ⌨ 🗐 🖉 🕸 ☐ **P** ♿ ☐ all (singles & doubles from $325)

Hotel Wales 1295 Madison Avenue (at 92nd St) | UES | 10128

Staying a block away from Museum Mile makes sense if art grazing is the plan. Conveniently located in the schmoozy Carnegie neighbourhood, this grand old dame of Madison Avenue has had a facelift, designed to recreate the civilized New York of a bygone era. Its collection of children's book illustrations graces the public spaces, a touch of whimsy in the classically European rooms. The large tea room, where guests take breakfast, afternoon tea and light desserts, has a plush library feel. Sarabeth's restaurant downstairs provides the hotel's room service.

☎ 876-6000 **F** 860-7000 **e** hotelwales@mindspring.com **M** 6 to 96th St ✦ 87 ⌨ 🗐 ↔ 🖉 🕸 ♿ ☐ all (singles & doubles from $265)

Franklin 164 E 87th Street (bet. Lexington & Third Aves) | UES | 10128

This hotel is diminutive in size, from the cherrywood lobby to the elegant breakfast room and café-style lounge. Compact, chic rooms in soft neutral colours are offset by black-and-white photos of contemporary NYC, and filmy fabric headboards extend overhead in a modern canopy effect. The CD and video library is for all.

☎ 369-1000 **F** 369-8000 **M** 4•5•6 to 86th St ✦ 47 ⌨ 🗐 ☐ all (singles from $245; doubles from $269)

Mansfield 12 W 44th Street (bet. Fifth & Sixth Aves) | Midtown | 10036

The clean, modern entranceway leads on to a lobby of polished marble floors, dark woodwork and hip 30s furniture. Original features of the building have been restored, like the elaborate wrought-iron spiral stairwell. Rooms (on the small size) have modern sleigh beds with mesh headboards, and contemporary black and white prints. Laze around in comfy chairs in the lounge where you can sip free espressos 24 hours a day.

☎ 944-6050 **F** 764-4477 **w** www.mansfieldhotel.com **M** B•D•F•Q to 42nd St ✦ 124 ⌨ 🗐 🖉 **P** ☐ all (singles & doubles from $255)

hotels

Plaza Athénée 37 E 64th Street (bet. Park & Madison Aves) | UES | 10021

Once upon a time Lady Di's choice of hotel when in town, this jewel has the look of a French château. Hand-painted wallpaper and dark green leather chairs lend style to the marble-floored lobby. Smart French decor in the rooms includes original antique oil paintings, grey silk moiré-covered walls and elegant blue and green fabrics for bedcovers and curtains. Lovers of luxury will adore the rose-coloured marble bathrooms, flowers and Italian Frette bathrobes. Some rooms have terraces.

☎ 734-9100 **F** 772-0958 **W** www.plaza-athenee.com **M** N·R to Lexington Ave ◆ 153 ㉔ ↔ ✎ ☎
▯ **P** ♿ ▭ all (singles from $440; doubles from $475)

↓ dead famous

Algonquin 59 W 44th Street (bet. Fifth & Sixth Aves) | Midtown | 10036

The personality of this literary landmark oozes from the fabulously restored public spaces. This was where Dorothy Parker headed up the Round Table, and the *New Yorker* cartoon wallpaper in the hall is a nod to the local magazine whose staff famously used the Algonquin as their watering hole [→138]. The rooms are a decent size, in soft colours, and carry wonderful examples of old black-and-white photos of 50s New York.

☎ 840-6800 **F** 944-1419 **W** www.camberleyhotels. com **M** 7 to 5th Ave ◆ 165 ▭ ▤ ↔ ✎ ☎ ▯
♿ ▭ all (singles from $329; doubles from $329)

Chelsea 222 W 23rd Street (bet. Seventh & Eighth Aves) | Chelsea | 10011

Check out the pinnacle of kitsch in the Chelsea's Room 822, where Madonna and Drew Barrymore have both staged photoshoots. Artists and creatives of all kinds love this place – crushed velvet chaises longues are tucked into light-filled bay windows, and rooms may sport leopard print curtains, hot pink 70s-style couches with lime green pillows and ornate fireplaces. No two rooms are alike. The lobby is famous for its paintings by artists who've lived here, like Julian Schnabel.

☎ 243-3700 **F** 675-5531 **W** www.chelseahotel.com **M** 1·9 to 23rd St ◆ 250 ▤ ㉔ ☎ ▯ **P** ▭ all
(singles from $165; doubles from $185)

Plaza Fifth Avenue (at 59th St) | Midtown | 10019

Arguably NYC's most famous hotel: site of Truman Capote's legendary Black and White Ball, and once home to Scott and Zelda (who frolicked in the hotel's fountain), and Marlene Dietrich (who was better behaved). A New York sight in itself, the Plaza was built in 1907 in the style of a French château. Bedrooms feel sparsely furnished only because of their generous size. Decorative fireplaces, crystal chandeliers and elaborate ceilings embellish every grand and conservatively elegant room.

☎ 759-3000 **F** 759-3167 **W** www.fairmont.com **M** N·R to 5th Ave ◆808 ▤ ㉔ ↔ ✎ ☎ ▯ **P** ♿
▭ all (singles from $335; doubles from $425)

Waldorf Astoria 301 Park Avenue (bet. 49th & 50th Sts) | Midtown | 10022

Every President since Hoover has stayed here when in town. Sure, the presidential four-bedroom suite with dining room is roomy, but you'd be away from the fun if you missed out on people-watching in the enormous lobby (Cole Porter's piano is here). Public rooms exemplify tasteful American excess and even the standard bedrooms are large with classic decor. With nearly 1400 of them, plus restaurants and shops, this hotel resembles a mini-city.

☎ 355-3000 **F** 872-0204 **W** www.hilton.com **M** 6 to 51st St ◆ 1385 ▤ ㉔ ↔ ✎ ☎ ▯ **P** ♿
▭ all (singles from $210; doubles from $250)

↓ last word in luxury

Carlyle 35 E 76th Street (bet. Madison & Park Aves) | UES | 10021

With 65 permanent residents, the Carlyle feels like a club but is glad to consider new 'members'. World-famous rooms like Bemelmans Bar, with murals by the eponymous children's book illustrator and author, and Café Carlyle [→137] where Bobby Short has tinkled the ivories for patrons for 30 years, are all part of New York history. Many of the large rooms have baby grand pianos, are decorated in restrained yellows and greens, and dotted with elegant antiques.

☎ 744-1600 **F** 717-4682 **M** 6 to 77th St ◆ 180 ▤ ㉔ ↔ ✎ ☎ ▯ **P** ♿ ▭ all
(singles & doubles from $450)

hotels

Prices exclude all taxes

Four Seasons 57 E 57th Street (bet. Madison & Park Aves) | Midtown | 10022

'Monumental' best describes the theatrical entrance and lobby of this IM Pei-designed building. The Four Seasons boasts the largest (and most expensive) rooms in town. Decor is updated art deco in muted colours with plenty of warm wood. Luxuriate in the sheer space, with walk-in dressing rooms, and opulent marble bathrooms with deep baths, which fill in 60 seconds. The view of the Chrysler building from the jacuzzi on the 51st floor is drop-dead amazing.

☎ 758-5700 **F** 758-5711 **w** www.fourseasons.com **M** N•R to 5th Ave 🔱 370 📃 🎓 ↔ 🖋 🕸 ❑ **P** 🔥 🖃 all (singles from $565; doubles from $615)

New York Palace 455 Madison Avenue (bet. 50th & 51st Sts) | Midtown | 10022

The historical exterior of this 1882 landmark building is intact, making the hip reception area a surprising contrast. A team of French designers revamped the place to include high-back modern couches in the lobby with a Moroccan carpet and quirky gold lamps. Bedrooms come in a choice of two styles; Empire furnishings or updated art deco, inspired by the buildings of the nearby Rockefeller Center.

☎ 888-7000 **F** 303-6000 **w** www.newyorkpalace.com **M** 6 to 51st St 🔱 897 📃 🎓 ↔ 🖋 🕸 ❑ **P** 🔥 🖃 all (singles $425; doubles $465) (weekend rates are 50% less all year)

Peninsula 700 Fifth Avenue (at 55th St) | Midtown | 10019

Located in a turn-of-the-century beaux-arts building, the Peninsula has reopened after renovations. It is now totally high-tech with stereos in the bathrooms (automatically muted if your hands-free phone rings...), built-in TVs, control of humidity and warmth and, of course, mood lighting. Technology aside, wallow in comfy velvet chairs, or dine at gold-leaf tables. Matisse prints and oversized fireplaces all contribute to a surprisingly unfussy, modern look.

☎ 956-2888 **F** 903-3949 **w** www.peninsula.com **M** E•F to 5th Ave 🔱 241 📃 🎓 ≋ ↔ 🖋 🕸 🕸 ❑ **P** 🔥 🖃 all (singles & doubles from $535)

Pierre 2 E 61st Street (at Fifth Ave) | UES | 10021-5402

A hotel within an apartment building for the elite, the Pierre makes you feel that you too are living an upper crust existence. It's a social hub for the NY elite; you can rub elbows with distinguished residents at afternoon tea (the 'in' thing) in the muralled Rotunda Room. Rooms are individual; some French in style with navy toile bedcovers, matching curtains, and botanical prints. Amazing views of Central Park help to keep the elegant, largely European clientele coming back time after time.

☎ 838-8000 **F** 826-0319 **w** www.fourseasons.com **M** N•R to 5th Ave 🔱 202 📃 🎓 ↔ 🖋 🕸 ❑ **P** 🔥 🖃 all (singles from $430; doubles from $480)

St Regis 2 E 55th Street (bet. Fifth & Park Aves) | Midtown | 10022

The St Regis, doyenne of Fifth Avenue hotels, harks back to a glamour-filled era. Cherubs draped in roses recline on the ceiling, while baroque gold and Louis XVI furniture fills a lobby which invites you into a gentle 'old money' existence. Feel like a pearl in an oyster shell as you recline in bedrooms decked out in shades of green and grey. Pampering the Gucci and Prada shopping-laden clientele seems to be the life-mission of the solicitous staff.

☎ 753-4500 **F** 787-3447 **w** www.luxurycollection.com **M** E•F to 5th Ave 🔱 314 📃 🎓 ↔ 🖋 🕸 ❑ **P** 🔥 🖃 all (singles & doubles from $580)

↓ designer label

Mercer Hotel 147 Mercer Street (at Prince St) | Soho | 10012

For the madly hip who have to stay Downtown, the hotel of the moment is the Mercer. Smack dab in the heart of Soho, it's the place to be seen for a drink or lunch [→119] and music and entertainment industry-types hang out with flip-phones clamped to their ears. Deep, comfy chairs and couches in the lobby are seductively inviting. Rooms are minimal, clean, spare: shades of white on white with fun marble bathrooms, whose walls fold out to expose the big tubs to the room.

☎ 966-6060 **F** 965-3838 **w** www.themercer.com **M** N•R to Prince St 🔱 75 📃 🎓 🖋 🕸 ❑ 🔥 🖃 all (singles from $375; doubles from $400)

Morgans 237 Madison Avenue (at 37th St) | Midtown | 10016

Ian Schrager's first NY hotel continues to be the place of choice for the fashion industry. Refurbishment has lightened up the rooms: cream, buff and soft greys with contrasting textures of soft corduroy, silks, maple wood and an ultra-suede window seat to warm up the space. Wide, low-slung beds make the smallish bedrooms appear larger. The lobby is Eastern in feel with a carpet of Escher cubes and brown leather armchairs.

☎ 686-0300 **F** 779-8352 **M** 6 to 33rd St 🛎 113 🖙 🔲 📠 🕙 🚭 🗗 ♿ 🍽 all
(singles from $295; doubles from $320)

Paramount 235 W 46th Street (bet. Eighth Ave & Broadway) | Midtown | 10036

Billed as Schrager's 'cheap chic' hotel, there is still plenty of style and attitude in the Paramount. Though small, any feeling of claustrophobia is ruled out by ingenious room layouts and decor: large Vermeer prints as headboards, white bedlinen, white leather furniture and you gotta love the hip black and white tiled bathrooms with cool stainless steel sinks. The foyer's intimate seating arrangements encourage lobby socializing. Shades are warmed-up green and orange.

☎ 764-5500 **F** 354-5237 **M** N•R to 49th St 🛎 600 📠 ↔ 🚭 🗗 ♿ 🍽 all (singles from $200; doubles from $290)

Royalton 44 W 44th Street (bet. Fifth & Sixth Aves) | Midtown | 10036

Ian Schrager's Midtown hotel is a cool-yet-fun Philippe Starck tribute to modernism. A long lobby of poured concrete is softened with cartoonish wing chairs and eccentric tables. Practical things like elevators and lobby desks are tucked out of sight. The large, minimal-decor rooms with real fireplaces reflect the tastes of the cool, trendy clientele – largely media and fashion folk. Splash in the large round tubs after a day's tough shopping and you'll feel like royalty.

☎ 869-4400 **F** 768-5191 **M** B•D•F•Q to 42nd St 🛎 169 🖙 📠 🕙 🚭 🗗 ♿ 🍽 all (singles from $365; doubles from $385)

Soho Grand 310 W Broadway (bet. Grand & Canal Sts) | Soho | 10013

Located in chic Soho, this hotel pays homage to the loft-style industrial buildings of the area, and the art community on its doorstep. A dramatic cast iron stairwell leads to the upper lobby area. The modern decor, complete with drafting table desks and mock sculptures as nightstands, reflects an artistic theme, and there's an added bonus for pet owners: Soho Grand is owned by the family who run Hartz (pet products) and there are cat and dog menus, and even a pick-up dog washing service.

☎ 965-3000 **F** 965-3200 **w** www.sohogrand.com **M** A•C•E to Canal St 🛎 369 📠 🕙 ↔ 🚭 🗗 ♿ 🍽 all (singles from $399; doubles from $419)

Time 224 W 49th Street (at Broadway) | Midtown | 10019

Restaurant designer Adam Tihany's first venture into hotels was much anticipated. In the lobby designed around a sculpture by Richard Serra – known for massive minimalist pieces which challenge your sense of space – you start to get an idea of Tihany's mission. The stylish rooms have soft furnishings in a choice of primary colours like red and blue, and you can choose one to suit when you book.

☎ 320-2925 **F** 320-2926 **M** N•R to 49th St 🛎 192 📠 ↔ 🚭 🗗 ♿ 🍽 all (singles from $265; doubles from $285)

Tribeca Grand Hotel 2 Avenue of the Americas (at White St) | Tribeca | 10013

This über-hip sibling of the Soho Grand is an equally alluring downtown destination. The triangular building has an understated brick exterior, but inside the decor takes a decidedly plush, modern turn, with impressive range of in-room amenities and guest services. Follow the cleft-stone ramp into Church Lounge, a bar-cum-dining-cum-living room with low, curved loveseats and slipper chairs. The breath-taking eight-story atrium supplies the necessary Tribeca magic, as does the Grand Screen, a projection room that serves film fare seat-side.

☎ 519-6600 **F** 519-6700 **w** www.tribecagrand.com **M** 1•9 to Franklin Street 🛎 209 📠 🕙 ↔ 🚭 🍽 (rooftop terrace with the Grand Suite) 🚭 🗗 🍽 all (singles from $399; suites from $649)

W New York 541 Lexington Avenue (at 49th St) | Midtown | 10022

You can't shake the feeling that you're worshipping at the temple of a kinder, gentler chic at the new W Hotel. Maybe it's the huge Mondrian-style stained glass windows dominating the lobby area. These David Rockwell-designed masterpieces cast a warm glow with their earthy colours. Guest rooms are small but beautifully designed and packed with fun luxury touches like feather top mattresses and the finest quality sheets embroidered with soothing phrases like 'Sleep With Angels'.

☎ 755-1200 **F** 319-8344 **w** www.starwoodlodging.com **M** 6 to 51st St 🛎 717 📠 🕙 ↔ 🚭 🗗 ♿ 🍽 all (singles & doubles from $339)

Prices exclude all taxes

↓ home from home

Hotel Beacon 2130 Broadway (at 75th St) | UWS | 10023

This lovely, privately-owned hotel is a bargain considering the high quality of the accommodation. Make the most of large, light-filled rooms with classical decor, city and Hudson River views, and pristine bathrooms. Cook in your own fully-equipped kitchen, picking up ingredients at local stores, or grab a takeout from one of the area's ethnic restaurants. Convenient for the Met, so you may catch a glimpse of sweeping dresses and black ties zipping out for some culture. ◆

☎ 787-1100 F 724-0839 w www.beaconhotel.com M 1•2•3•9 to 72nd St ◆ 220 ▤ ◌ᵒ ◨ ♿ ⊟ all
(singles from $175; doubles from $205)

Off Soho Suites 11 Rivington Street (at Bowery) | Lower East Side | 10002

Location, location, location should be the mantra of guests of Soho Suites. You'll be minutes only from Soho, Little Italy and Chinatown with all those ethnic food shops and restaurants. Rooms are basic motel fare with faintly Eastern decor. If you're travelling with friends and gotta stay downtown, this spot is a good money-saving option – rooms have double beds as well as a separate living room with sofabed.

☎ 979-9808 F 979-9801 w www.offsoho.com M J•M to Bowery ◆ 35 ▤ ↔ ◌ᵒ ♿ ⊟ AE/MC/V
(singles from $97.50; doubles from $179)

Shelburne Murray Hill 303 Lexington Avenue (at 37th St) | Midtown | 10016-3104

Located in the 19th-century brownstone area of Murray Hill, the Shelburne has a genteel lobby belying all its wonderful practicality. Pretty, generously proportioned rooms have fully equipped kitchens, and washers and dryers in the basement, and you can relax and check out the views from the roof terrace.

☎ 689-5200 F 779-7068 M 6 to 33rd St ◆ 258 ▤ ↔ ✏ ◌ ◌ᵒ ▢ ◨ ♿ ⊟ all
(singles from $269; doubles from $306)

Southgate Tower Suite Hotel 371 Seventh Avenue (at 31st St) | Midtown | 10001-3984

This place is ideal if you're in town for a Madison Square Garden event. Rooms are beautifully furnished, considering the reasonable price, classical in style with chintz spreads and matching curtains. Suites with two double beds and sofabeds are a boon to families. All the rooms have well-equipped kitchenettes and even better, someone who comes in each day to wash your dishes.

☎ 563-1800 F 643-8028 w www.mesuite.com M 1•2•3•9 to 34th Street-Penn Station ◆ 522
▤ ↔ ✏ ◌ᵒ ▢ ◨ ♿ ⊟ all (singles & doubles from $200)

↓ budget beds

Carlton Arms 160 E 25th Street (at Third Ave) | Gramercy Park | 10010

This hotel is perfect for art students. There are cartoons in the stairwells, and fourth floor corridors have 3D models. Every room has its own theme (with murals and collages) and you may find owner John hands you several sets of keys so you can pick your favourite. Bathrooms (if you get one in your room) are bare bones, but you pay for what you get, and this place is fun.

☎ 679-0680 M 6 to 23rd St ◆ 54 ⊟ MC/V (singles from $57; doubles from $73)

Chelsea International Hostel 251 W 20th Street (bet. Seventh & Eighth Aves) | Chelsea | 10011

Centrally located in Chelsea, this hotel is opposite a police precinct, which may put the city-timid at ease. Rooms are very small and simple with bunk beds, lockers and a sink, but the public rooms (TV, billiards and two kitchens) are full of a young, beautiful and budget-challenged clientele. Making friends is easy here, and the garden set-up with picnic tables and barbecue grills sets the scene for impromptu summer parties.

☎ 647-0010 F 727-7289 w www.chelseahostel.com M 1•9 to 18th St ◆ 255 ✏ ⊟ AE/MC/V
(singles from $25; doubles from $60)

Edison Hotel 228 W 47th Street (bet. Broadway & Eighth Ave) | Midtown | 10036

This large, 900-room, pre-war building, just one block away from Times Square, is a tribute to the art deco era. The busy, gargantuan lobby has lovely high ceilings and elaborate mouldings in pale peach, turquoise and pink with murals of the Radio City Rockettes and the Cotton Club. The bedrooms, although lacking authentic 20s details, are attractive and newly furnished. Guests are a varied bunch, though generally on the younger side, and all are out to have fun.

☎ 840-5000 **F** 596-6850 **e** edisonnyc@aol.com **M** N•R to 49th St ✦ 900 🖥 💻 📶 🚪 **P** ♿ 🖨 ▭ all (singles from $125 doubles from $140)

↓ themes & variations

Box Tree   250 E 49th Street (bet. Second & Third Aves) | Midtown | 10019

Tucked into two fabulous side-by-side townhouses, the Box Tree is for romantics. Design references range from a Versailles-style private dining room to another with a table for 12 and a fireplace big enough to roast a wild boar. The main dining room is reminiscent of a Swiss chalet: the lobby, with chairs around a fireplace, could have come straight from *Wuthering Heights*. Individual bedrooms like the Fabergé Room have hand-painted murals, French canopied beds and real fires.

☎ 758-8320 **F** 308-3899 **M** 6 to 51st St ✦13 💻 🖥 📶 🚪 ▭ all (singles & doubles from $230)

Casablanca   147 W 43rd Street (bet. Sixth Ave & Broadway) | Midtown | 10036

This Moroccan theme hotel in Times Square provides a touch of the theatrical. The original wrought-iron staircase transports you up to Rick's Café, furnished with a beautiful Moroccan tiled fireplace, Moorish arches, wicker chairs, ceiling fans, and of course, a piano. Potted palms and antique weavings add to the exotic mood. Decent-sized rooms have carved headboards and prints of Moroccan villages. Here's looking at you as you curl up to watch the famous film – every room has a copy.

☎ 869-1212 **F** 391-7585 **e** casahotel@aol.com **M** N•R•1•2•3•7•9 to Times Sq-42nd St ✦ 48 💻 🖥 ✐ 📷 **P** ♿ 🖨 ▭ all (singles from $265 doubles from $295)

Fitzpatrick   687 Lexington Avenue (bet. 56th & 57th Sts) | Midtown | 10022

If peacock blue walls and the Celtic-patterned emerald green carpet of the lobby aren't clues enough, then the enormous photo of the President of Ireland, Mary MacAleese, should do it. The Fitzpatrick is a corner of Ireland set slap bang in the middle of New York. Bedrooms are of a fair size with dark furnishings and crystal chandeliers. The towels are thick and the soaps are Irish. There is also a good selection of Irish mags as well as all the practicals such as hairdryers and coffee machines.

☎ 355-0100 **F** 355-1371 **w** www.fitzpatrickhotels.com **M** 4•5•6 to 59th St ✦ 96 🖥 ✐ 📷 🚪 **P** ♿ ▭ all (singles & doubles from $335)

Kitano New York   66 Park Avenue (at 38th St) | Midtown | 10016

The Kitano attracts a largely Asian clientele and caters for them with a wonderful kaiseki restaurant, as well as providing clean, minimal rooms painted in soothingly muted tones. Authentic Japanese bedroom suites offer deep soaking tubs, roll-out futon beds and a tea ceremony room. The lobby is streamlined mahogany and marble, with a large Botero bronze: owner Mr Kitano is an avid art collector and his large collection of works appears in the halls and rooms.

☎ 885-7000 **F** 885-7100 **e** reservations@kitano.com **M** 4•5•6•7 to Grand Central-42nd St ✦ 149 🖥 ✐ 📷 🚪 ♿ 🖨 ▭ all (singles & doubles from $410)

Lowell   28 E 63rd Street (bet. Park & Madison Aves) | UES | 10021

This hotel confirms that good things come in small packages. Immaculately groomed women sit in the bijou lobby on dainty love seats. Neo-Classical fixtures, trompe-l'oeil marble walls, real marble floors and exquisite Empire-style furniture surround them. Luxurious bedrooms are impeccably furnished with tapestry bedcovers and real fires. For a themed stay, try the Garden Suite, where breakfast can be taken on the terrace.

☎ 838-1400 **F** 319-4230 **e** lowellhtl@aol.com **M** N•R to Lexington Ave ✦ 65 🖥 🕓 ↔ 📷 🚪 **P** ▭ all (singles from $345; doubles from $445)

Omni Berkshire Place   21 E 52nd Street (bet. Fifth & Madison Aves) | Midtown | 10022

Behind the walls of this 1926 landmark hotel, you'll find a modern oasis of stream-lined serenity. A $70 million renovation created an enormous lobby with honey-toned wood and peach-coloured marble floors. Large, modern rooms have Giacometti-style lamps and silk fabrics galore. Prints hang above velvet couches; the touch of a button controls lights, TV, and music. In a literary mood? Ask for the Author's Suite, where novelists have stayed and left signed copies of their books.

☎ 753-5800 **F** 754-5018 **w** www.omnihotels.com **M** E•F to 5th Ave ✦ 396 🖥 ↔ ✐ 📷 🚪 **P** ♿ ▭ all (singles from $199; doubles from $389)

Gershwin 7 E 27th Street (bet. Fifth & Madison Aves) | Midtown | 10016

The Gershwin looks like a Chinese theatre run amok. Step in and the wackiness is confirmed by murals everywhere and hip Euro-type travellers buzzing by. An art collector is a co-owner and you can see his booty everywhere, including a real Lichtenstein in the lobby. Private rooms have TVs and voicemail, dorms are cheaper and much more basic.

☎ 545-8000 **F** 684-5546 **w** www.gershwinhotel.com **M** N·R to 28th St ◆ 106 ▭ AE/MC/V (economy $89; standard $129)

Gramercy Park Hotel 2 Lexington Avenue (at 21st St) | Midtown | 10010

International and unpretentious is the order of the day. The halls and rooms have a boarding-house feel to them, and the doors still require old-fashioned keys. All rooms are spacious with minty green walls and dark wood furniture. Some suites have fridges, others kitchenettes; in-room phones have voicemail. Guests also have access to Gramercy, a rare private park.

☎ 475-4320 **F** 505-0535 **M** 6 to 23rd St ◆ 509 ▤ ✇ ▯ ▭ all (singles from $165; doubles from $180)

Hostelling International New York 891 Amsterdam Avenue (bet. 103rd & 104th Sts) | UWS | 10025

This Victorian Gothic building is just a couple of blocks from Central Park. The rooms are pristinely clean, large and light-filled. You have your own room key, and keep your gear in lockers. The best deal comes in the form of large family rooms with private bathrooms and bunk beds for two kids for an unbeatable $100. Public areas include a library with web-linked computers, a café, kitchen facilities and a garden.

☎ 932-2300 **F** 932-2574 **w** www.hinewyork.org **M** 1·9 to 103rd St ◆ 624 ✇ ✇ ✇ ♿ ▭ MC/V/JCB (singles from $22; family rooms from $75)

Hotel 17 225 E 17th Street (bet. Second & Third Aves) | Gramercy Park | 10003

You know how to whistle, don't you? With its eccentric decor and a staff comprised of models, this 100-year-old landmark has just completed a renovation, maintaining the noir-ish glamour that draws fashionistas and savvy travelers alike. The rooms are eclectic and deco, with fake wood wallpaper and the occasional decorative wooden fireplace. The shared loo, though shining clean, is an ironic twist, considering stars such as Madonna and Sharon Stone have been photographed here.

☎ 475-2845 **F** 677-8178 **w** www.hotel17.citysearch.com **M** L·N·R·4·5·6 to 14th St–Union Sq ◆ 160 ▤ ✇ ▭ none (singles from $86; doubles from $109)

Hudson 356 W 58th Street (bet. Eighth and Ninth Aves) | Midtown | 10019

Ian Schrager's latest masterpiece is due to open in October and at publication remained shrouded in secrecy. At 24 stories high and a stone's throw from Central Park, insiders dish that this a hotel like nothing you've ever seen before. With Philippe Starck aiding once again in the design and the restaurant expertise of Jeffrey Chodorow (of Asia de Cuba fame), guests will surely be thinking that they've fallen on their feet.

☎ 554-6000 **F** 554-6054 **w** www.hudsonhotel.com **M** A·B·C·D·1·9 to Columbus Circle ◆ 825 ▤ 24 ↔ ✇ ✇ ✇ ▯ ♿ ▭ all (rooms from $95)

Larchmont Hotel 27 W 11th Street (bet. Fifth & Sixth Aves) | West Village | 10011

Behind the bright red door on this quiet street, you'll find a pleasant, cozy brownstone hotel. Rooms are large, with pretty rattan furnishings, and floral bedcovers. No en-suite bathrooms, but the shared baths and showers are sparkling clean and all the rooms have their own sinks. Balducci's [→108], the famous gourmet food grocery store, is just around the corner.

☎ 989-9333 **F** 989-9496 **w** www.larchmonthotel.citysearch.com **M** L to 6th Ave ◆ 55 ▭ ▤ ♿ ▭ all (singles from $85; doubles from $100)

Leo House 332 W 23rd Street (bet. Eighth & Ninth Aves) | Chelsea | 10011

An unusual not-for-profit hotel, run by a Catholic organization, though everyone, whatever their belief, is welcome. Bedrooms are clean and basic. The dining room overlooking a garden offers an all-you-can-eat breakfast for a bargain $5. Non-standard facilities include a chapel and a priest on 24-hour call.

☎ 929-1010 **F** 366-6801 **M** C·E to 23rd St ◆ 58 ✇ ▭ MC/V (singles from $72; doubles from $78)

Malibu 2688 Broadway (at 103rd St) | UWS | 10025

A particular favourite with Europeans, this hotel is a great choice for the budget-conscious. The clean, modern, good-sized rooms – most with their own bathrooms, and all with cable TV and compact disc player – are in minimal black and white.

☎ 222-2954 **F** 678-6842 **M** 1·9 to 103rd St ♠ 150 ⊟ 🖥 **24** 🖶 MC/V
(singles & doubles from $99)

Pickwick Arms Hotel 230 E 51st Street (bet. Second & Third Aves) | UWS | 10022

This is one of the best-priced hotels in town. A modern lobby with a beautiful fire-place welcomes you, as do the friendly staff. Rooms are on the small side, but they're pretty and very clean. There's a wine bar, Le Bateau Ivre, on the ground floor and the large roof garden is open to everyone staying.

☎ 355-0300 **F** 755-5029 **M** 6 to 51st St ♠ 350 🖥 🖋 🖥 🖶 all (singles from $70; doubles from $130)

Washington Square Hotel 103 Waverly Place (at MacDougal St) | West Village | 10011

Smack bang in West Village is this family-owned hotel, which pays tribute to the lovely Washington Square park outside with a lobby of beautiful antique wrought-iron garden furniture. Rooms are comfortable and decked out in pastel colours. For the full effect of staying here, ask for a room with a park view.

☎ 777-9515 **F** 979-8373 **M** A·B·C·E·F·Q to W 4th St-Washington Sq ♠ 170 ⊟ 🖥 ↔ 🖋 🖥 🖶 AE/MC/V (singles from $121; doubles from $142)

↓ city b & b's

Abingdon 13 Eighth Avenue (at 12th St) | West Village | 10014

A rare city find in the West Village, the Abingdon is a New England-style charmer. Each bedroom has its own distinct personality, displaying bits and pieces gathered by the owner on his global wanderings. The Ambassador room could be renamed 'Out of Africa' with its rattan mats, African masks on paprika-red walls and an enormous four-poster bed. Definitely for those who appreciate a quiet stay.

☎ 243-5384 **F** 807-7473 **w** www.abingdonguesthouse.com **M** A·C·E to 14th St ♠ 396 🖥 ↔ 🖋 🖋 🖥 ♿ 🖶 all (singles from $155; doubles from $165)

Bed & Breakfast On The Park 113 Prospect Park West (bet. 7th & 8th Sts), Park Slope | Brooklyn | 11215

Staying in this fabulous period brownstone is worth the 20-minute subway ride from Manhattan. Owner Liana Paolella was in the antiques business and 'kept the good stuff for herself'. The best of her furniture is exquisitely arranged in every room. The Brooklyn Museum of Art and the Botanical Garden [→85] are minutes away.

☎ 718-499-6115 **F** 718-499-1385 **w** www.bbnyc.com **M** F to 7th Ave ♠ 7 ⊟ 🖥 🖋 🖶 AE/MC/V (singles & doubles from $135 shared bathroom; $195 separate bathroom)

Broadway Inn 264 W 46th Street (bet. Eighth & Ninth Aves) | Midtown | 10036

The lobby is full of antique charm with an open fire and book-lined shelves, where you can read the papers over your continental breakfast. Bedrooms are modern and snug and triple-glazed windows provide a soundless night's sleep in one of the liveliest blocks on the planet. Larger 'suite' rooms are ideal for families or groups, but be warned, there's no elevator up from the lobby. The staff are friendly and happy to help.

☎ 997-9200 **F** 768-2807 **w** www.broadwayinn.com **M** A·C·E to 42nd St-Port Authority ♠ 41 ⊟ 🖥 ↔ **P** 🖶 all (singles from $95; doubles from $135)

Country Inn The City 270 W 77th Street (bet. Bwy & West End Ave) | UWS | 10024

Reserve early to stay in one of four of the homiest rooms in town. Owners Larry and Fergus describe these large apartments as being non-chaperoned, meaning; you check in, get your own front door key, and you're on your own. You make your own breakfast with ingredients found in your kitchenette. Rooms have antique four-poster or sleigh beds, with decorative fireplaces, oil paintings and fresh roses. Room 6 even has its own terrace with wisteria-covered arbour. Minimum stay three nights.

☎ 874-3981 **F** 501-9647 **w** www.countryinnthecity.com **M** 1·9 to 79th St ♠ 4 ⊟ 🖥 🖶 none (singles & doubles from $150)

The Inn at Irving Place 56 Irving Place (bet. 17th & 18th Sts) | Gramercy Park | 10003

These adjoining 1830 townhouses ooze the charm of a bygone era. Both have been immaculately restored with an astonishing array of antique pianos, chandeliers, hand-painted beds and elaborate ceiling roses. The staff are model-beautiful if a little temperamental. Plop down post-shopping and wallow in pillow-piled couches as you take afternoon tea by the fire.

☎ 533-4600 **F** 533-4611 **w** www.irvingplace.com **M** L·N·R·4·5·6 to 14th St-Union Sq ♠ 12 ⊟ 🖥 🖶 all (singles & doubles from $295)

↓ arrivals

Two international airports serve New York: JFK is the larger, although Newark is actually busier. La Guardia, the closest to Manhattan, is used for domestic flights only.

John F Kennedy [JFK]

JFK, in the borough of Queens, covers an area equal to the lower half of Manhattan: annually, around 31 million people pass through this chaotic 'perpetual construction site', with 353,000 flights in and out out of the nine terminals.

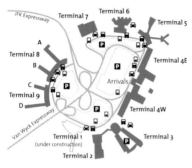

☎ useful numbers:

Enquiries: 1-718-244-4444
Lost and found:
1-718-244-4225/4226
Ground Transportation:
w www.jfk-airport.com
1-800-247-7433
☞ **Ramada Plaza**
1-718-995-9000
☞ **Holiday Inn**
1-718-659 0200
General enquiries on transport to/from NYC's airports and parking:
1-800-247-7433 (Port Authority)
w www.panynj.gov

transport options

Ⓜ Public Transportation

60–75 min to/from Howard Beach on Rockaway A train.

⏱ 24 hours daily, every 10–15 min at peak times 7.30–9.30am, 4.30–7pm, every 15–30 min offpeak.

🎫 $1.50

Connects with free bus service (yellow, white and blue bus) to all terminals, every 15 min, approx 30-min ride.

↻ The cheapest option and not dependent on traffic.

⚠ 1| Avoid late at night.
2| The journey can feel arduous with heavy bags.

❶ 1| Make sure you get trains going to Rockaways and not Ozone Park-Lefferts Blvd.
2| Howard Beach is not the last stop on the line.
3| Allow enough time a) for both parts of the journey and b) delays on the subway.

☎ 1-718-330-1234

🚌 Shuttle Buses

New York Airport Service

60–75 min to/from Grand Central Station, Port Authority and Penn Station.

⏱ 6.05am–1pm every 30 min, and 1–11.40pm every 15 min, daily.

🎫 $13

↻ Set schedule and well-marked bus stops.

↻ Travel times are dependent on traffic.

☎ 1-718-875-8200

❶ Formerly Carey Airport Express.

Gray Line Airport Shuttle

60–75 min to any Midtown hotel.

⏱ 5am–11pm, daily.

🎫 $19

↻ Door-to-door service.

↻ Up to a 20-min wait for the shuttle bus.

☎ 315-3006/757-6840 allow an hour if booking to go to the airport, or order service from Ground Transportation.

Super Shuttle

60–75 min to/from Midtown.

⏱ 24 hours, daily.

🎫 $19 for the first person; $9 for each additional person in your party to east/west

Manhattan (up to 110th St).

↻ Service through the night.

⚠ 1| Allow a 30-min wait at the airport.
2| Buses accomodate up to seven people – drivers wait until enough people want to go to the same part of town before departing.

☎ 258-3826 or order service from Ground Transportation.

🚕 Taxis, limos & cars

Taxis

45–65 min journey

⏱ 24 hours, daily.

🎫 $33 flat rate, plus tolls ($3.50) and tip.

↻ Most convenient.

↻ Relatively expensive.

❶ 1| At the airport, only accept a cab from an official taxi dispatcher.
2| If you decide to share a cab to split the cost, note that after the first stop the meter starts running.

Limos & Cars

45–65 min to/from Manhattan.

⏱ 24 hours, daily.

$30–$35 for cars (minicabs). $70–$80 for limos. Plus tolls ($3.50) and tip.

♻ Travel in style.

♻♻ Most expensive option.

❶ 1| If you call a Manhattan company, ensure they already have a car at the airport.

2| It is illegal for cars to make pick-ups without being formally dispatched.
3| Make sure you know which terminal you are at when you give the pick-up details.
☎ Some companies have direct phones located at terminal exits, or call:

Town Cars Anywhere: 1-800-532-3730
Carmel: 1-800-924-9954
Classic Limousine: 1-800-666-4949
Tel Aviv: 1-800-222-9888

Newark [EWR]

Passenger traffic figures at Newark – New York's second largest international airport, based in New Jersey – now exceed JFK's, with over 32 million people using the 56 airlines flying from its three terminals each year.

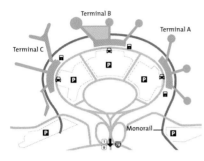

Terminal B
Terminal A
Terminal C
Monorail

transport

☎ useful numbers

Enquiries: 1-973-961-6000
Lost and found: 1-973-961-6633
Ground transportation:
w www.panynj.gov
1-800-247-7433
☞ **Days Inn:** 1-973-242-0900

transport options

▣ Public Transportation

Airlink Bus & PATH/New Jersey Transit Trains [→161]

1| Airlink Bus: 15–30 min to/from Penn Station.

⏱ 6.15–1.45am daily, every 20 min.

▣ $4, exact fare only.

☎ 1-800-626-7433

2| Connecting with either:
a) PATH train, 15–25 min ride, via Christopher St; 9th St & Sixth Ave; 14th St & Sixth Ave; 23rd St & Sixth Ave and 33rd St & Sixth Ave.

⏱ 24 hours daily, every 15 min.

▣ $1

☎ 1-800-234-7284

Or b) NJT train, 20 min to/from 34th St (bet. Seventh & Eighth Aves).

⏱ 24 hours daily, every 15–20 min.

▣ $2.50

☎ 1-800-626-7433

♻ Cheapest way to get to the city.

♻♻ Unreliable scheduling and connection times.

❶ 1| Have small bills and change for your fares.
2| Connections with the subway involve quite a walk.
3| Trains run 24 hours, but the bus link does not.

▣ Shuttle Buses

Olympia Trails Bus Company

30–40 min to/from Grand Central Station or Penn Station to Newark.

⏱ 5am–11pm daily, every 20–30 min.

▣ $11/$20 return

♻ Very convenient and there are always places available.

♻♻ Allow a 20-min wait at the airport.

❶ For an additional $5 fare, there is a hotel connection bus (8am–9pm) to/from Grand Central Station.

☎ 964-6233 or order minibus from Ground Transportation.

Gray Line Airport Shuttle

30–60 min to/from any Midtown hotel.

⏱ 6am–11pm, daily.

▣ $14 ($19 return)

♻♻ Allow a 20-min wait at the airport.

☎ 315-3006/757-6840 or order minibus from Ground Transportation.

Super Shuttle

60–90 min to/from Midtown.

⏱ 24 hours daily.

▣ $19 for the first person; $9 for each additional person in your party to east/west

Manhattan (up to 110th St).

♻ Door-to-door drop off throughout the night.

♻♻ 1| Up to a 30-min wait at the airport.
2| Buses take up to seven people and drivers wait until enough people want to go to the same part of town before departing.

☎ 258-3826 or order from Ground Transportation.

▣ Taxis, limos and cars

50–60 min to/from Midtown.

⏱ 24 hours daily.

▣ $40 and up, plus tolls ($5.70) and tip.

☎ Some cab companies have direct phones near the terminal exits, or call:
Route 22: 1-800-680-3334
Airport Express: 1-877-546-6332
Carmel: 1-800-924-9954
Tel Aviv: 1-800-222-9888

♻ The luxury way to travel.

♻♻ Most expensive option.

❶ 1| Be sure you know which terminal you are at when you give the pick up details.
2| If you take a car from the rank, check the price of your exact destination before you set out.

La Guardia [LGA]

La Guardia sees 22 million people and 355,000 planes come and go each year. Twenty-three airlines, serving destinations all over the US, fly from this convenient Queens base with four terminals.

transport

☎ useful numbers:

General enquiries:
1-718-533-3400
Emergencies:
1-718-533 3900
Lost and found:
1-718-533-3988
w www.panynj.gov
☞ **Marriott:**
1-718-565-8900

transport options

Ⓜ Public Transportation

Subway/Bus

1| To/from 74th St-Roosevelt Ave on E•F•G•R•7 trains. (approx 30-min ride to/from Midtown) ⏱ 24 hours daily, every 10–15 min. 💲 $1.50

Connecting with 33 bus – a 10-min ride to/from the central terminal building. 💲 $1.50 (or free subway transfer).

2| Around 30 min to/from Astoria Blvd on N train; 125th St on A•B•C•D•2•3•4•5•6 trains; 116th St-Columbia University on 1•9 trains ⏱ 24 hours daily, every 10–15 min. 💲 $1.50

Connecting with M60 bus, a 20–60-min ride to/from La Guardia with bus stops outside each terminal. 💲 $1.50 approx 5–1am daily, every 15–30 min.

❶ Ask the driver for a transfer so you can hook up with another bus route.

☎ 1-718-330-1234

🚌 Shuttle Bus

New York Airport Service

approx 50 min to/from Grand Central Station or the Port Authority bus terminal. ⏱ 5.10am–10 pm daily, every 15–30 min. 💲 $10

👍 **1|** Grand Central Station is convenient for Midtown hotels. **2|** Set schedule.

👎 **1|** Travel times are dependent on traffic. **2|** Port Authority has lots of escalators and stairs to reach street and subway levels.

☎ 1-718-875-8200

New York Airport Express Connection

Bus (approx 30-min ride) to/from Jamaica station (Queens). ⏱ 7am–10pm daily, hourly from outside each terminal. 💲 $5

Connect with LIRR [→161] to Penn Station, approx a 20-min ride. ⏱ 24 hours daily, every 10–15 min. 💲 $5.50 (7.30–9.30am & 4.30–7pm), $3.75 (off-peak).

👍 The cheapest option.

👍 **1|** Making connections with luggage is difficult. **2|** The LIRR is often busy.

☎ 1-718-217-5477

🚕 Taxis, limos and cars

30–45 min to/from Midtown. ⏱ 24 hours daily. 💲 approx $26 and up, plus tolls and tip. Surcharge of $1.50 per trip between 8pm–6am

☎ Contact Ground transportation, or call:
Carmel: 1-800-924-9954
Tel Aviv: 1-800-222-9888

👍 The luxury way to travel.

👎 Most expensive option.

🚢 Ferry

Delta Water Shuttle

30–45 min to/from E 62nd St pier, E 34th St pier, or Pier 11 (Wall Street). ⏱ every hour, 6.30am–5.30pm to La Guardia; 7.45am–6.45pm to Manhattan. 💲 $15 ($25 round trip).

👍 fun, quick and easy.

👎 essentially only runs during office hours.

☎ 1-800-533-3779

↓ general info

▤ metrocards

These come in a variety of denominations. The pay-per-ride card allows you to put money on your card in whatever increment you choose ($3–$80). For refills of more than $15, there is a bonus ride – that's 11 for the price of 10. You can get cards valid for seven days ($17) or 30 days ($63). The Fun Card offers unlimited rides on buses and subways for a whole day ($4).

With all MetroCards™, you can make a free transfer within two hours subway-to-bus, bus-to-subway and bus-to-bus (the ticket machines

will display 'Xfer' for transfer). As well as in stations, $3, $6 and $15 MetroCards™ are sold in delis and supermarkets. For up-to-date information on where to buy MetroCards™ call ☎ 638-7622.

❶ Fun Cards are sold at Grand Central Station at the transit museum store; Times Square Visitors' Centre; some pharmacies and cheque agencies.

🧒 kids

Children under 44 inches high ride free on subways and buses.

♿ disabled travellers

Access for the disabled in New York is good; buses are the best option, as they are all fully equipped for wheelchairs and the drivers are good-hearted folk. For bus and subway travel enquiries ☎ 1-718-596-8585. Accessible Travel is a free guide with a Braille subway map, available from the MTA New York City Transit. ☎ 1-718-330-1234
For private car hire, Upward Mobility Limousines have roll-in wheelchair-accessible cars. ☎ 1-718-645-7774

❶ the disabled travel at half-fare on public transportation.

↓ going underground

The subway is as chaotic as the city and people it serves – on average it carries 3.8 million customers a day.

subway map [→back cover]

Maps are available free upon request from all stations. They are the definitive user's guide – the one drawback is that they are huge.

↓ using the subway

• There are 25 routes, all colour-coded and identified by a number or letter. Local trains stop at all stations; express trains stop only at stations marked with a black-ringed white circle.

• Transfers are possible when two or more lines serve one station. On maps, two stations connected with a line shows a transfer point.

☎ useful numbers:

Information: 1-718-330-1234
Transit police: 1-718-254-1990
Lost and found: 1-718-712-4500

❶ subway essentials

⏲ 24 hours daily, every 2–5 min (6.30–9.30am & 3.30–8pm Mon–Fri), every 10–15 min at other times. Reduced service after midnight – check official subway map as some stations close.

💳 $1.50 flat fare. You must buy a MetroCard™ or a token to pass through the turnstiles.

👍 1| Cheap and handy.
2| Much cleaner and less intimidating than anything you may be expecting.

👎 1| Not ideal for crosstown journeys.
2| If you are not used to the subway system, it is easy to miss your stop, get on the wrong train or go in the wrong direction – some trains go for miles between stops.

3| The idiosyncratic service can be a nuisance if you don't know which lines and stations to avoid.

❶ Some stations have different entrances for downtown or uptown platforms – usually on opposite sides of the street. Check on a map before going through the turnstile.

do
1| Double-check to see if you are on the local/express or uptown/downtown platform.
2| Stand in the designated area, or wait near the manned ticket booth after peak hours or at empty stations.
3| Be aware of your belongings.
4| Ask fellow passengers if you're unsure as not all subway cars have line route maps inside.

don't
1| Smoke anywhere on the subway.
2| Jump the turnstiles: police will give you an on-the-spot fine or even arrest you.

MUNY (Music Under New York)

Performing arts are making subway travel more attractive thanks to MUNY – a creative arts programme funded by the Metropolitan Transportation Authority. Call for details of performances (Cajun, bluegrass, African, South American and jazz) scheduled in subway and commuter rail stations.

☎ 362-3830

suburban trains

Ⅲ Long Island Rail Road (LIRR)
The LIRR network stretches from the eastern tip of Montauk, Long Island to Penn Station (at 33rd St & Seventh Ave) nearly 120 miles away. Tickets purchased on trains when ticket offices are open cost more, so buy before you board. Most stations now have ticket-vending machines. Travelling offpeak saves you about 30%; rush-hour times are 6–10am and 4–7pm. These trains are good for getting to the beaches [→85].

☎ 1-718-217-5477

Ⅲ New Jersey Transit
NJ Transit operates trains and buses throughout New Jersey. Commuter trains have two terminals: Hoboken, in northern NJ where passengers can transfer to the PATH trains, ferries or buses to

continue to NYC; and Newark Penn Station, which has services to NY Penn Station. There is a $3 penalty for purchasing a ticket on the train when the station's ticket office is open.

☎ 1-973-762-5100

Ⅲ PATH
PATH (Port Authority Trans-Hudson) rapid trains run between New Jersey and NYC. Newark, Harrison and Hoboken Stations 24 hours a day, seven days a week.

☎ 1-800-234-7284

Ⅲ Metro-North Railroad
Serves lower New York State and SW Connecticut out of Grand Central Station (Lexington Ave at 42nd St).

☎ 532-4900

long-distance travel

Ⅲ Amtrak
All long-distance rail services operate out of Penn Station.
☎ 1-800-872-7245

🚌 Long distance bus travel

These services operate out of Port Authority Bus Terminal, 40th–42nd Sts (bet. Eighth & Ninth Aves).

☎ 564-8484

↓ on the buses

NYC's buses carry 1.5 million people daily – and it feels like it. Because of their plodding progress, buses carry a certain kind of New Yorker – late-night workers, families and kids going to and from school. They tend to be neighbourhood-oriented, with many passengers and drivers on first-name terms.

bus map

Free from all subway stations, the bus map is easy to read and doubles as a tourist guide, with major sights clearly marked.

↓ using the buses

• Bus stops are located every two or three blocks, marked by route signs and yellow-painted curbs. Abbreviated route maps (occasionally) appear at the bus stops, showing the buses that run along that avenue or street. The printed times are highly unreliable.

• The driver will stop if he sees you, but to make sure, hold out your arm and wave. After 11pm drivers will pick up and drop off between official stops.

• To indicate that you want to get off at the next stop, press any part of the 'strip' that runs in between and above the windows.

• The back doors take a bit of getting used to. Push on the yellow strip and the doors will slowly open – follow up with a firm shove. You can also get off at the front.

• There are two types of buses: regular, making all stops, and Limited (an LED sign with the word 'Limited' is displayed in the front window). Limited buses stop only at major cross streets and transfer points.

❶ bus essentials

⏰ 24 hours daily, but run less frequently after midnight.

💳 $1.50 flat fare.
Paying by MetroCard™: insert card as you get on. This entitles you to a free ride when connecting with the subway or another bus within two hours. Paying by coins: drop into slot in front of the driver. Exact fare only, but you can also use subway tokens.

🗨 1| Buses run along all avenues and on major cross-streets; generally they are the best public transport option for cross-town travel.
2| Free sightseeing tour of the city.

❶ Even when paying for your ride with coins or a token, you can ask for a transfer ticket, which allows you to catch another bus for free (within two hours); ie after a cross-town bus ride, you can also hop on an uptown or downtown bus and vice versa.

🗨 Don't go anywhere near a bus if you're in a hurry.

do
1| Have your exact fare, token or MetroCard™ ready.
2| Shout if the driver forgets to open the back doors.

don't
Smoke on buses.

☎ **useful numbers:**

Travel info (6am–9pm daily):
1-718-330-1234
Customer service:
1-718-330-3322
Lost and found:
1-718-625-6200

↓ catch a cab

The yellow cab is synonymous with Manhattan. Careering madly through traffic, cabs seem able to move in even the thickest of jams; nevertheless in gridlocks the predominant colour is always yellow.

cab spiel

In case you forget to 'belt up, take all of your belongings and get a receipt', an automated celebrity voiceover will remind you. Everyone from Dr Ruth, the sex columnist, to Pavarotti has given their two-cents worth.

↓ using yellow cabs

• You can stop a cab if the middle panel only on the cab is lit. During rush hours, the competition is fierce.

• It is a good idea to have at least a vague notion of how to get where you want to go. 'Politely' suggest your favoured route and keep an eye open for unnecessarily long detours.

• As a rule, yellow cabs only take four people.

☎ **useful numbers:**

Lost property: 302-8294
Taxi Limousine Commission: 676-1000 (for complaints)

❶ cab essentials

Taxis are metered: the fare starts at $2 and rises 30¢ per 1/5 mile, or 30¢ per 90 seconds in slow traffic or when stationary.

Having successfully hailed a cab, get in quickly. The driver is likely to start moving before you've even told him where you want to go.

Tip 15–20% – or else!

Most drivers don't like to change anything bigger than a $20 note.

Pay the driver while still seated in the back of the cab.

🗨 There are lots and lots!

🗨 1| Although plentiful at all other times, in bad weather conditions – forgeddaboutit.
2| Get in before you ask to go to Brooklyn or the Bronx, as legally they cannot then refuse you, but most drivers have threadbare knowledge of the outer boroughs.

do
Use them – taking a cab is not considered a luxury in NY.

don't
1| Argue with the driver: in yellow cabs the customer is never right.
2| Smoke – the driver could lose his licence.

car services

Generally referred to as 'cars', not 'minicabs', and suitable for longer journeys. For instance, if you need to go to/from Brooklyn, the company should supply a driver who is familiar with the neighbourhood.

❶ 1| When they say they'll be there in '5 minutes', they mean it!
2| You must look out for them – drivers never ring the bell.
3| Check the price of the ride before you set off or, better still, with the controller when you order the car.

👍 1| Convenient if you are not near a busy main street, or if it is late or raining.
2| You can specify what kind of car (eg 'station wagon' for more than four of you).

👎 Poor language skills, bad driving and no sense of direction ... only the worst-case scenario.

do
Only call when you are ready to leave.

don't
Get in a gypsy cab (unlicensed, unmarked cars) – they will rip you off.

☎ useful numbers:

Downtown Delancey Car Service: 228-3301
Brooklyn Evelyn Car Service: 1-718-230-7800/8244
Random Carmel: 1-800-924-9954/666-6666
Tel Aviv: 1-800-222-9888/777-7777

↓ freewheeling

Since New York's public transport system is both relatively efficient and inexpensive, the only reason to rent a car is to get out of town. Driving and parking in the city gives new meaning to the word nightmare, and only the most foolhardy would want to share the road with New York's army of yellow cab maniacs.

↓ rules of the road in NYC

• Drive on the right.

• You cannot make a right turn on a red light.

• Seatbelts are compulsory in front and rear seats.

• School buses are sacred and the fines for passing one which has stopped are huge.

• Do not park within 50 ft of a fire hydrant.

• Speed limit is 30 mph.

• Vandalism and car theft are rife.

At the wheel

Nowhere do the rules of supply and demand apply more than in New York's car rental business – prices rocket on a holiday weekend. If you call one of the major rental agencies, be prepared: know from what location you want to rent, how long for and the exact dates – all of these factors affect cost and availability (average $50–60 per day). You must have a major credit card, a passport and a valid driver's licence (foreign licences are accepted). Large companies have a minimum age of 25, but for an extra $10–30 per day, they'll bend the rules.

❶ 1| Always get the most comprehensive insurance.
2| It's cheaper to rent from outside the city. Ask the big companies for their regional office locations.

☎ Car hire:

A-1 Value: 348-5151
Avis: 1-800-831-2847

Budget: 1-800-527-0700
Enterprise: 1-800-325-8007
Hertz: 1-800-654-3131
Rent-a-Wreck: 1-718-784-3302
They will pick you up at the station (based in Long Island City)

gas

Gas stations in Manhattan are few and far between. These two are reliable and open 24 hours:
Uptown: Atlas Garage 303 W 96th St (bet. West End Drive & Riverside Drive).
Downtown: Amoco 610 Broadway (at Houston Street).

Parking meters and lots

Meters: depending on the neighbourhood and the time of day, it will cost you anything from 25¢ (for 20 min) to 25¢ (for 1 hr). If you are towed, call the helpline (Mon–Fri) and expect a fine of around $150. ☎ 1-718-422-7800

Lots: private parking lots are more expensive but at least you are guaranteed to find your car in one piece.

do
Note signs on opposite side of street, indicating which days the street cleaners come.

don't
Park anywhere a sign says 'no stopping' or 'no standing'; in a bus stop; or by a fire hydrant.

Bicycles

Most cycle routes are in city parks, but if you've got the guts, cycling is an excellent way to see the city. Though not illegal, it would be unwise to ride without a helmet or lights.

Cyclists must follow the same road rules as car drivers and fines for running red lights or riding without a bell (!) in Midtown are commonplace.

Bike rental: A security deposit of $150 held on a credit card is usually required:

☎ Bike hire:

Bikes in the Park, Loeb Boathouse, Central Park (summer only)
🚲 $8–$10 per hr (5 or 10 speed bikes) ☎ 861-4137
Bicycles Plus, Second Ave (West 87th & 88th Sts). 🚲 $7.50 per hr/$25 per day ☎ 722-2201
Metro Bike .
🚲 $7 per hr; $45 per day.
14th St (bet. First & Second Aves) ☎ 228-4344
1311 Lexington Ave (at 88th Street) ☎ 427-4450
Sixth Avenue (at 15th Street) ☎ 255-5100
417 Canal Street ☎ 334-8000

Roller Blades

So, you really want to get around in a hurry, while looking cool. Try blading it [→91]. Only for the very proficient.

☎ Roller Blade hire:

Blades East & West
🛼 $16 per day Mon–Fri; $27 per day Sat–Sun
❶ hire includes free protective gear.
160 E 86th St (bet. Lexington & Third Aves) ☎ 996-1644
105 W 72nd St (bet. Columbus Ave & Broadway) ☎ 787-3911
Second Ave (at 74th St) ☎ 249-3178

↓ a–z essentials

admission charges

Charges for museums and sights vary; it's always worth checking if there are any concessions. The larger museums have one evening a week when admission is cheaper.

banks

New York's major banks are the Bank of New York, Chase Manhattan, Citibank and Fleet. Opening hours are usually 9am–3pm on weekdays (and often 4pm Thu & Fri), with limited service at most branches on Saturday (10am–2pm).
Fleet (318 Grand St bet. Allen & Orchard Sts & 50 Bayard St at Bowery), and **Chase Manhattan** (180 Canal St at Mott St) are open on Sundays (10am–2pm) for foreign currency exchange only. Bank rates are slightly less competitive than bureaux de change [→bureaux de change; credit & debit cards]. To transfer money from abroad call:
American Express Moneygram
☎ 1-800-543-4080
Western Union ☎ 1-800-325-6000

bars

Most bars open from around 5pm–4am, but bartenders will close earlier when the tips aren't up to much [→tipping]. Carry picture ID (eg passport) to prove you are of drinking age (ie over 21 years) – they can 'card' anyone! If you're told not to dance in a bar, don't laugh – they're serious. Dancing licences are hard to come by and unauthorized boogying incurs fines for the bar owner. NB: it is illegal to drink a can or bottle of anything alcoholic in the street – even if it is in a brown paper bag.

bureaux de change

Rates can be slightly more competitive than the banks'.
AmEx charges $3 commission.
200 Vesey Street (at West St) ☎ 640-5998
◑ 8.30am–5.30pm Mon–Fri; 12–8pm Sat–Sun.
Avis charges $4.50 minimum or 1% commission, whichever is higher.
1451 Broadway (bet. 41st & 42nd Sts) ☎ 944-7600 ◑ 10am–8pm Mon–Fri; 12–8pm Sat–Sun.
Chequepoint USA charges 9¢ on every $1.
22 59th Street (bet. Fifth & Sixth Aves)
☎ 750-2400 ◑ 8am–8pm daily.
Thomas Cook charges $5 minimum or 1% commission, whichever is higher.
1590 Broadway (at 48th St) ☎ 265-6049
◑ 9am–7pm Mon–Sat; 9am–5pm Sun.

children

Activities: there are lots of magazines with kid-orientated listings; see also kids' sections of New York Magazine; Time Out; Village Voice; the Friday edition of the New York Times and NY Family Calendar and Resource Book. Or try the
Big Apple Parents' Paper ☎ 533-2277
Parent Guide ☎ 213-8840
Babysitting: two agencies to try are:
The **Babysitters' Guild** ☎ 682-0227
Frances Stewart Agency ☎ 439-9222
Hotels: most allow young children to stay in their parents' room at no extra charge. Age limits vary.
Restaurants & bars: It's not illegal for kids to go into bars but on the whole they're not places for family outings (many bars are shut during the day anyway). On the whole cheap and cheerful restaurants and cafés welcome kids but upscale places tend to be more formal and less well equipped.

consulates

Australia: 150 E 42nd Street ☎ 351-6500;
Canada: 1251 Sixth Avenue ☎ 596-1600;
Ireland: 345 Park Avenue ☎ 319-2555; **New Zealand:** suite 1904, 780 Third Avenue ☎ 832-4038; **UK:** 845 Third Avenue ☎ 745-0200

conversion chart

Clothing	Women's				Men's			
US	6	10	14	16	36	40	44	46
British	8	12	16	18	36	40	44	46
European	36	40	44	46	46	50	54	56
Shoes	Women's				Men's			
US	5	6	7	8	7	8	9	10
British	4	5	6	7	6	7	8	9
European	37	38	39	40	40	42	43	44

courier services

For services within Manhattan:
Breakaway ☎ 219-8500; **CD&L** (for a pick-up or delivery) ☎ 337-1460 (for prices and administration) ☎ 337-1450.
National and international services:
DHL ☎ 1-800-225-5345; **FedEx** ☎ 1-800-247-4747; **UPS** ☎ 1-800-742-5877

credit & debit cards

Automated Teller Machines (ATMs) are on almost every street corner in Manhattan, in delis, supermarkets, and even some bars. Internationally recognized debit cards can be used to withdraw cash at any ATM displaying the appropriate card sign; normal bank charges apply. Or you can use your credit card if you have a PIN number. Cash advances are also available with your credit or debit card with appropriate picture ID (eg passport). Again, normal bank charges apply.
To report lost cards:
American Express ☎ 1-800-528-4800
Diners Club ☎ 1-800-234-6377
MasterCard ☎ 1-800-826-2181
Visa ☎ 1-800-336-8472

currency

The dollar is made up of 100¢. Coins are 1¢ (pennies); 5¢ (nickels); 10¢ (dimes) and 25¢ (quarters) – the most useful change for buses, vending machines and public telephones. Occasionally you might come across a JFK half-dollar (50¢) or $1 coins, which are annoyingly oversized and often rejected in stores. Dollar bills are uniformly green and of one size; they come in denominations of $1; $5; $10; $20; $50 and $100. Commemorative issues include extremely rare $2 bills.

customs

All passengers arriving in the US are given a customs declaration form to fill out on the airplane. Don't bring in anything from 'unfriendly' countries (Cuban cigars are a no-no) and, while we are on the subject, drugs are not only illegal but you risk being denied entry to the US ever again.

dates

Abbreviated dates are usually given as month/day/year in the USA.

practical information

dentists

Although there is no free dental care in the US, the dental schools offer the most cost-effective treatments.

The New York University Dental Center charges a fee of $85 to cover the cost of pain relief and emergency treatment. *345 E 24th Street (at First Ave)* ☎ *998-9800* ◗ *8am–9pm Mon–Thu; 9am–7.30pm Fri.*

Columbia University School of Dental Surgery has a walk-in clinic for emergencies only; the $65 fee covers pain relief and emergency treatment. *Vanderbilt Clinic (7th floor), 622 W 168th Street (at Broadway)* ☎ *305-6726* ◗ *8.30am–2pm Mon–Fri.*

Private Practise offers a 24-hour call-out service *3 E 74th Street (at Fifth Ave)* ☎ *737-1212*

disabled visitors

Access For All is a guide to disabled access to NYC's cultural institutions. To obtain a copy, send $5 to Hospital Audiences Inc, 3rd fl, 548 Broadway (for all general enquiries call ☎ 1-888-424-4685).

I Love New York Travel Guide, available from tourist information points and some hotels, also includes accessibility ratings.

For information on transport [→160].

duty free

When entering the US, the allowance on duty-free goods is: one litre of alcohol, 50 cigars and 200 cigarettes. The duty (per extra litre) on wine is $1.07 and a pricey $13.50 on spirits (for 40% proof; the higher the alcohol content the more you pay!). There is a limit of $100 allowed for gifts and souvenirs. Money over $10,000 must be declared. For more information call the US Duty Office at JFK ☎ 1-718-553-5470

electricity

Electrical supply is 110 volts AC with mainly two-pronged plugs, although the newest sockets and appliances are now made for three prongs. British appliances need an adaptor.

email & internet

Public libraries offer free internet access with time restrictions and inevitably long waits. For information call ☎ 930–0800. There are a few internet cafés; prices are around $10 per hour [→142].

emergencies

For emergency police, ambulance and fire services, dial ☎ **911**.

In a medical emergency, get yourself to one of the 24-hour emergency rooms at one of these hospitals:
Bellevue Hospital, *First Ave (at E 27th St)* ☎ *562-4141*; **Mount Sinai Hospital**, *100 Madison Ave (bet. 99th & 100th Sts)* ☎ *241-7171*; **New York Presbyterian Hospital**, *510 E 70th St (at York Ave)* ☎ *746-5050*; **St Vincent's Hospital**, *Seventh Ave (bet. 11th & 12th Sts)* ☎ *604-7997*
More often than not (depending on the cost of treatment), you must pay the bill, then reclaim the expense from your insurance provider.

help & advice lines

AIDS Hotline ☎ *447-8200*
Lesbian & Gay
Community Center ☎ *620-7310*
Missing Persons Bureau ☎ *374-6922*
Travelers' Aid/Victim Services ☎ *577-7777*

hotels

Book early, especially in December when hotels are usually full to capacity. Apart from the room price (and NY hotels don't come cheap!), you'll have to pay a sales tax (13.25%) and an occupancy tax ($2 per night). NB: some hotels take a fraction of the room cost for a late cancellation (the amount varies from hotel to hotel).

You could consider choosing a small b&b [→155], or an unhosted apartment (if you're staying more than seven days – you won't have to pay sales tax). For information call the **Bed & Breakfast Network** ☎ *645-8134* or **A Hospitality Co** ☎ *965-1102* **w** *www.acompanies.com*

Most hotels offer discount rates, especially for weekend stays in non-peak season. Or, there are agencies who buy blocks of rooms and offer as much as 50% off regular rates.
Central Reservations Service, *11420 North Kendall Drive, Miami, Florida, FL 33176* ☎ *1-305-274-6832*; **Accommodations Express**, *801 Asbury Avenue 6th floor, Ocean City, New Jersey, NJ 08226* ☎ *1-609-391-2100*; **Quikbook** *381 Park Avenue South, New York, NY 10016* ☎ *779-7666* **w** *www.quikbook.com*

For general information on room availability call the **Visitors' Bureau** ☎ *484-1200*

immigration

US immigration control has become increasingly strict. If you are entering as a student or to work, make sure you have the appropriate visa and that your papers are in order. For enquiries while in the country, contact the **Immigration and Naturalization Service (INS)** *26 Federal Plaza* ☎ *264-5650; 1-800-375-5283* ◗ *7.30am–3pm Mon–Fri.* No vaccinations are needed.

insurance

It is foolhardy to travel in the US without medical insurance. Without it, you will just about be treated in an emergency, but you will spend the rest of your working days paying off the debt. It is wise to have your personal effects covered as well. Keep all receipts (including medical bills) to substantiate a claim.

left luggage

The only place to leave luggage in the city ($2 per item per day) is at Grand Central Station. ☎ *340-2555* ◗ *7am–11pm Mon–Fri; 10am–11pm Sat–Sun.*

lost property

Report the loss to the police and get an incident report to present to your insurance agency. The Police Property Clerk's office is where all lost articles may eventually end up. Call them only after all else fails (and not before one week). ☎ *374-5084*

measurements

As a rule, imperial measures are used.

imperial : metric	metric : imperial
1 inch = 2.5 cm	1 mm = 0.04 inch
1 foot = 30 cm	1 cm = 0.4 inch
1 mile = 1.6 km	1 m = 3.3 ft
1 ounce = 28 g	1 km = 0.6 mile
1 pound = 454 g	1 g = 0.04 oz
1 pint = 0.6 l	1 l = 0.6 (US) gallon
1 (US) gallon = 3.8 l	

medical care

There is no national healthcare service. Look under 'physicians and surgeons' or 'clinics' in the Yellow Pages. Ask at your hotel or contact your consulate for more advice.
[→emergencies & insurance]

medicines

Most delis carry your vital pharmaceutical needs, and many are open all night. The official line on filling foreign prescriptions is that it can't be done, but try any drugstore (many are open 24 hours – some even deliver), or go to a doctor's office or an emergency room [→emergencies]. The chain drugstore Duane Reade (others include Rite Aid, McKays and CVS) has three stores that are open 24 hours:
224 W 57th Street (at Broadway) ☎ 541-9708
2465 Broadway (at 91st Street) ☎ 799-3172
485 Lexington Avenue (at 47th St) ☎ 682-5338

office & business

Most upscale hotels operate 24-hour business centres, though usually only for guests only. Computer terminals, photocopiers, fax machines and printing facilities are available at Kinko's 20 branches around the city (including Brooklyn) – 19 are open 24 hours. For general enquiries ☎ 1-800-2546567
Mail Boxes etc ☎ 642-5000 will accept deliveries like dry-cleaning and parcels on your behalf, and have cheap mailboxes to rent. For stationery try Staples ☎ 929-6323. Mobile phones can be hired from: AT & T Wireless ☎ 333-3150 (charge $7.99 per day and 69¢ per min); Robert's ☎ 734-6344 (charge $5 per day and $1.45 per min).

opticians

A walk-in eye examination will probably set you back around $50. With a prescription, the chainstore Lenscrafters, open daily (including most evenings), can make glasses up in less than an hour and have contact lenses available over the counter. For locations call ☎ 967-4166 or see 'opticians' in the Yellow Pages.

photography

Camera Repair does just that at 37th W 47th St (bet. Fifth & Sixth Aves) ☎ 382–0550
CLIK for a one-hour service.
23rd St (bet. Fifth & Sixth Aves) ☎ 645-1971
Spectra, pricier than the average one-hour place, produces professional quality prints.
293 E 10th Street (at Avenue A) ☎ 529-3636

police

For emergencies only, call ☎ 911. To find your nearest police precinct, dial ☎ 374-5000.
Crime Victims Hotline ☎ 577-7777 will give you advice on making a report.
For any troubles on public transport call the Transit Police on ☎ 1-718-330-3330.
Don't antagonize the NYPD's officers in blue; jay walking, for example, incurs tickets and fines.

postal services

Post office lines at peak hours (early mornings and lunchtime) can stretch out the door; allow extra time to avoid stressing out. For any enquiries or to find your nearest branch call ☎ 1-800-725-2161. Stamps can also be bought from most delis (although they sell domestic 33¢ stamps only). For postcards outside the US, use one 55¢ stamp. The international letter rate starts at 60¢. Letters can be posted in rail and bus terminals, post offices and the rather scarce blue mail boxes (pull the handle to use).

To receive mail it should be addressed to you c/o General Delivery, General Post Office, 421 Eighth Avenue, New York, NY 10001.

public holidays

While banks, offices and museums close on national holidays, most convenience stores remain open for business year round.
Columbus Day: 9th Oct 2000; **Veterans' Day:** 10th Nov 2000; **Thanksgiving:** 23nd Nov 2000; **Christmas Day:** 25th Dec 2000; **New Year's Day:** 1st Jan 2001; **Martin Luther King Day:** 15th Jan 2001; **Presidents' Day:** 19th Feb 2001; **Memorial Day:** 28th May 2001; **Independence Day:** 4th Jul 2001; **Labor Day:** 3rd Sep 2001

religion

Avodah Jewish Services Corp ☎ 545-7759;
Bah'ai Center ☎ 330-9309; Baptist
☎ 283-6517; Buddhist ☎ 406-5109;
Catholic ☎ 1-516-333-6470; Evangelical
☎ 867-2066; Jehovah's Witnesses
☎ 862-0945; Mormon ☎ 928-0714;
Muslim ☎ 481-5244; Quakers ☎ 682-2745

restaurants & cafés

Hours: Double-check closing times – restaurants with slow service tend to close the kitchen up to an hour earlier than stated. Best to call before you jump in a cab.
Payment: The majority of restaurants accept credit cards and dollar travellers' cheques with picture ID (eg passport).
Reservations: Always book ahead: the same day is fine for neighbourhood restaurants but for upscale eateries, call as far ahead as you can.
❶ You can eat at the bar if you want to check out a great place but can't spend a lot (or just aren't that hungry).
❶ Pricey restaurants have slightly cheaper menus at lunchtime (set hours), and neighbourhood restaurants often offer special lunch deals (usually served all day).
❶ Be wary of 'upselling'; that is waiters subtly suggesting you choose pricier drinks and dishes.
❶ If you don't like something, send it back – but complain nicely: it pays to be friendly to NY waiters. Portions are often massive – no-one will mind if you ask for a doggie bag [→tipping].

safety

NY is now the safest big city in the US. However, precautions should be taken: it is inadvisable for women to walk alone late at night (carrying whistles, CS gas or pepper spray can give extra confidence and is legal); and certain areas are dodgier than others. Out of hours, wait for subway trains in the designated area on the platform, where there's video surveillance, or by the ticket booth.

sales tax

NY sales tax is 8.25% and it is added at the cash register on top of the price of goods or services purchased [→hotels & shopping].

shopping

Export: tourists do not get a refund on sales tax when leaving the country.
Opening times: in Manhattan, shops generally stay open late until around 7pm. Downtown shops often open until midnight. Nearly all stores are open on Sundays.
Payment: even small shops take the major credit cards. Dollar travellers' cheques with picture ID are widely accepted too.
Returns: keep the receipt and you will be able to return your purchase, although most

stores only offer exchange or store credit. Your rights as a shopper include having the right to know the store's refund policy before you buy: if there is none displayed, then you are entitled to a full refund if you return the item within 20 days. If you feel you have been ripped off, call **Consumer Affairs** ☎ *487–4444*. **Sales:** twice a year (usually mid-January & mid-September) during 'no tax week' the state forgoes the sales tax on items and shopping mayhem ensues (NB sales tax on clothing and footwear under $110 has now been eliminated). There are also summer and winter sales in May–Jun & Jan–Feb respectively.

smoking

Strictly speaking, it is illegal to smoke in hotel lobbies, banks, public restrooms, taxis, playgrounds, sports stadiums, and in restaurants with seating for over 36 people. It is permitted in bars, and restaurants with bars, if the bar is at least two yards from the nearest table.

students

STA Travel (*10 Downing Street* ☎ *1-800-777-0112*) and **Council Travel** (*205 E 42nd Street* ☎ *1-800-226-8624*) offer discounted travel. They also issue the International Student Identity Card (ISIC), which entitles full-time students to travel discounts and reduced entrance fees. In the US, the card costs $20: it could be worth getting one before you leave home (eg in the UK it's only £6).

telephoning

Calling collect (reverse charge): dial *0* then ☎ *1-800-265-5328* or *1-800-225-5288*. The surcharge on Bell Atlantic payphones is $1.58.
Directory enquiries: call ☎ *411* (addresses are given too). These calls are free from payphones.
International calls: for direct calls overseas dial *011* plus the country code: **Australia:** *61*; **Ireland:** *353*; **New Zealand:** *64*; **UK:** *44*. For operator assistance dial *01* plus city code.
Local codes: Manhattan mostly uses *212*. Omit the code when dialling from within Manhattan. In this guide, all telephone numbers without a code are *212* Manhattan numbers. New Manhattan numbers currently being introduced will have *646* and *917* codes, which must be dialled if you're calling from a *212* number. For Brooklyn, Bronx and Staten Island the code is *718*; for Queens it's *917*. When dialling another borough put '1' in front of the area code – the same goes for dialling a number outside the city, and toll-free *800* numbers.
Operator: ☎ *0*. From here you can also ask for international operator or enquiries.
Payphones: street phone booths are plentiful – stick to the Bell Atlantic ones as the rates are steadier. Payphones take 25¢, 10¢ and 5¢ coins. Local calls cost 25¢ for the first three minutes. The cheapest way to call long distance at a public phone is to buy a prepaid 'charge card', or phone card in varying denominations (dial number on card for instructions), widely available from delis and news stands.
Phone directories: the *White Pages* lists private phone numbers and businesses, the *Yellow Pages* details every consumer-oriented business and service.
Phone sounds: steady 'brrrrrr' = go ahead and dial; long low-pitched tone with short gaps = ringing tone; repeated short beeps = busy tone; single high-pitched tone = unobtainable.
Private phone rates: local calls cost 10.6¢ no matter how long you talk, with discounts for certain times of the day and all weekend.

Toll-free numbers: all numbers preceded by *1-800* are free (standard rate applies when calling a *1-800* number from overseas).

time

The US has four different time zones – Eastern (including New York) is five hours behind GMT. Clocks go forward by one hour in spring and back one hour in the fall. Speaking clock: ☎ *976-0001*.

tipping

Tipping is a vital part of America's service-industry culture.
Bars: leave 'good' tips (around a dollar a drink) for your first two or three rounds, and the bartender will often buy you a round back known as a 'buy-back'.
Restaurants: a minimum of 15% is the bottom line – anything less is considered an insult. And at the finer establishments, it's more like 18–20%. For easy maths, double the sales tax at the bottom of the check.
Taxis: cab drivers expect a 15% tip and are not shy about voicing their dissatisfaction if you offer them any less.

tourist information

New York Convention and Visitors' Bureau (NYCVB) *810 Seventh Ave (bet. 52nd & 53rd Sts)* ☎ *484-1200* ◑ *8.30am–6pm Mon–Fri; 9am–5pm Sat–Sun.* (London office: *33–34 Carnaby St, London W1* ☎ *0171–437 8300* ◑ *10am–4pm Mon–Fri)*
New York by Phone call ☎ *484-1222* for the NYCVB's voice-activated information service.
Times Square Visitor Information Center *1560 Broadway (bet. 46th & 47th Sts)* ☎ *869-1890* ◑ *8am–8pm daily.*
on the internet: **w** www.nycvisit.com, **w** www.newyork.citysearch.com, **w** www.sidewalk.com and **w** www.nyctourist.com give comprehensive listings of where to go, eat, stay and shop.

travellers' cheques (US 'checks')

These are still the safest way to carry your money, with instant refunds if lost or stolen. American Express and Visa are the most widely recognized, with Thomas Cook not far behind. Buy your cheques in US dollars – it's easier than dealing with fluctuating exchange rates, and they are more versatile [→shopping & restaurants]. If you lose your cheques call:
American Express ☎ *1-800-221-7282*; **Master Card** ☎ *1-800-223-9920*; **Thomas Cook** ☎ *1-800-287-7362*; **Visa** ☎ *1-800-227-6811*

visas & entry requirements

For visitors from Australia, New Zealand, the UK, Ireland and most European countries, a passport valid for at least six months after entry is all that is needed. A 'visa waiver' allows a short-stay visit of up to 90 days: the visa waiver form, to be filled out on the incoming plane, must have the address of where you will be staying on your first night in the country. All other nationals must check visa requirements at their local US embassy.

weather

Spring and fall are ideal times to visit. In the winter, the cold can be ferocious, and in summer, it's often too hot.

practical information

A
À Détacher 21
A Different Light 38, **106**
films 139
A Photographer's Place 106
A-1 Value 163
ABC Carpet & Home 43, **104**
ABC Parlour 44
Abingdon 157
Abyssinian Baptist Church 144
Academy CDs & Records 43, **107**
accessory shops **102**
Ace Gallery 81
Acquario 23, **126**
Ad-Hoc Software 17, **104**
admission charges 164
Adobe Theater 137
Africa 60
African Paradise 60
Air Market 27
airports 158–160
Algonquin hotel 151
Alice Tully Hall 140
Alison on Dominick Street 18
Allan & Suzi 55
Alley's End 39
Alpana Bawa 16
Alphabet City 7
Alphabet Lounge 30, **128**
Alphaville 33
alternative therapies 89
Altogether Different Dance Festival 142
Alvin Ailey American Dance Theater 141–142
Amalgamated Hardware 33
Amalgamated Home 33
Amato Opera Theater 140
American Ballet Theater (ABT) 141
American Craft Museum 67, **78**
American Express Moneygram 164
American Fine Arts 81
American football 83
American Museum of the Moving Image 67, **75**
American Museum of Natural History 67, **73**
American Park **124**
AMS Chelsea Bowl 90
Amtrak 161
Amy Downs 8, 102
Anandamali 12
Angel 10
Angelica Kitchen 29, **123**
Angelika Film Center 139
Angel's Share 30, **132**
Anna 27
Anna Sui 16, **95**
Annex Flea Market 38, **109**
Anthology Film Archives 139
Anthropologie 16
Antik 12
Antique Boutique 21, **97**
Apartment 48 38
APC 95
Apollo Theatre 144
Aquagrill 18
aquarium 86
Aquavit 49, **116**
Arlene Grocery 143
Arthur Ashe Stadium 83
Artie's New York Delicatessen 57, **115**
Asia de Cuba **128**
Asia Society 159
Astor Restaurant & Lounge 23
Astor Wines & Spirits 108
Astroland Amusement Park 90
Astroturf 64
Atlantic Theater Company 137
Atsuro Tayama 16
Australian consulate 164
Auto 38, **104**
Avalon 35
Aveda 18, 103
Avenue 57
Avenue A shopping 93
Avenue A Sushi 29
Avery Fisher Hall 140
Avis 163, 164
Avodah Jewish Services Corp 166
Avon Center 88

B
B & H Photo-Video **107**
B-Bar & Grill 23, **118**
Babbo 34, **118**
Baby Jupiter 10, **128**
babysitting 164
Bagels by the Park 64
bags **102**
Bah'ai Center 166
Baktun **133**, 135
Balducci's 34, **108**
Balthazar 23, **118**
BAM's Next Wave Festival 141, 142
Bamboozle Studio 60
Banana Republic 43, **99**
banks 164
Baptist Church 166
Bar d'O 35, **128–129**
Bar 89 19, **130**
Bar Odeon 13
Bar Pitti 34, **126**
Bar Six 34
Baraza 30, **128**
Barbara Gladstone 82
BargeMusic 141
Barnes & Noble 43, **106**, 142
Barney Greengrass 57, **115**
Barney's Co-Op 38
Barney's New York 52, **94**
bars **128–132**, 164
Chelsea & the Meatpacking District **40**
children in 164
East Village **29–30**
gay bars 132
Gramercy Park & the Flatiron District **45**
Harlem & the Heights **60–61**
Lower East Side & Chinatown **10**
Midtown **49–50**
Nolita & Noho **24**
Soho **19**
sports bars **130**
tipping 167
Tribeca **14**
Upper East Side **54–55**
Upper West Side **58**
West Village **35**
baseball 83
basketball 83
baths 88
Battery Park 67, 85
Bayard's **116**
Bayou 60
beaches 85
Beacon Theater 143
Beau Gosse 33
beauty stores **103**
beauty treatments 89
Bebe 43
Bed & Breakfast On The Park 157
Bed Bath and Beyond **104**
Behrle 13
Bell Atlantic Jazz Festival 144, 147
Bellevue Bar 49
Bemelman's Bar 55
Bereket 10
Bergdorf Goodman 46, **94**
Bessie Schonberg Theater 142
Best Cellars **108**
Betsey Johnson 15, **97**
bicycles 163
Bicycles Plus 163
Big Apple Greeter 67
Big Cup 69
Big Drop 16
Big Nick's Burger 57, **120**
Big Onion Walking Tours 67
Bigelow Pharmacy 33, **103**
Bike New York: The Great Five Boro Bike Tour 148
Bikes in the City 163
Birdland 144
Black & White 30
Black Star Lounge **134**
Blades East & West 163
Bleecker Bob's Golden Oldies **107**
Bleecker Street shopping 93
Bleecker Street Records 34
Bliss 88
Bliss Spa 18, **103**
Bloomingdale's 52, **94**
Blue 27

Blue Bar 50, **132**
Blue Note 143
Blue Ribbon 18, **126**
Blue Skirt 27
Blue Water Grill 43
boat tours 67
Body Adorned 89
body & soul 88–89
Body & Soul @ Vinyl 135
body art 89
Bond 07 22, **102**
Bond St 23, 24, **118**
Bongo 40
book shops **106**
Books of Wonder 87
Borders Books and Music **106**
Botanica 24, **128**
Bottino 39
The Bottom Line 143
Bouley Bakery 13, **116**
Bowery Ballroom 143
bowling 90
Bowlmor Lanes 90
Box Tree 155
boxing 83
The Brasserie 48
Bright Food Shop 40
Brighton Beach 65, 85, 111
Brisas del Caribe 19
Broadway shopping 93
Broadway Inn 157
Bronx 7
Bronx Zoo 67, 86
Brooklyn 62–65
Brooklyn Academy of Music (BAM) 140, 142
Brooklyn Ale House 63
Brooklyn Botanical Gardens 67, 85
Brooklyn Bridge 67, 68
Brooklyn Heights 7
Brooklyn Heights Promenade 70
Brooklyn Moon Café 63–64, 143
Brooklyn Museum of Art 67, **79–80**
Brooks Bros **99**
Brownies 143
Bryant Park 67, 85
films 139
Bryant Park Grill & Café 48
Bubble Lounge 14, **130**
Bubby's 13
Buddhism 166
Budget car hire 163
Buffa's Delicatessen 24
Built By Wendy 22
Burberry 47
bureaux de change 164
buses 162
airport 158, 159, 160
tours 67
Butta Cup Lounge 64

C
C & M Gallery 82
cabaret 137–138
cabs see car services; taxis
Café Boulud 54, **116**
Café Carlyle 55, 137
Café con Leche 57
Café des Artistes 57, **114**
Café Gitane 24
Café Habana 24
Café Lalo 57
Café Largo 60–61
Café Noir 19
Café Restaurant Volna 65
Café Spice 35
cafés & diners 166
Chelsea & the Meatpacking District **39–40**
East Village **29**
Gramercy Park & the Flatiron District **44**
Harlem & the Heights **60**
Internet cafés 145
Lower East Side & Chinatown **9–10**
Midtown **49**
Nolita & Noho **24**
Soho **19**
Tribeca **13**
Upper East Side **54**
Upper West Side **57**
West Village **35**
Cafeteria 39, **118**
Calle Ocho 57, **122**

Calvin Klein 53, **95**
Calypso St Barths 22, **97–98**
Campagna Home Shop 43
Canadian consulate 164
Canal Jean Co 17, **100**
Canal Street shopping 93
Candela 44
Canteen 18
Capsouto Frères 13, **124**
car services 158–159, 160, 163
Carapan 88
Carino 54
Carlton Arms 154
Carlyle 151
Carnegie Hall 140
Caroline's on Broadway 138
Carroll Gardens 64–65
cars, driving in New York 163
Cartier 47
Casa 34
Casa La Femme 18
Casa Mexicana 10
Casablanca 155
Casimir 28
Casio Baby G-Shock 17
Catherine 16, **98**
Catholic Church 166
CBGB 143
CDs, records & tapes **107–108**
Celebrate Brooklyn 144
Cello 54
Central Park 67, 84, 87
Central Park Summerstage 147
Central Park Wildlife Center 67, 86
Centro Fly **135**
Century 21 **100**
chain stores 99
Chanel 47
Chanterelle 13
Chase 50, **132**
Chase Manhattan 164
Chelsea & the Meatpacking District **37–41**, 111
shopping 93
Chelsea Garden Store 38
Chelsea Hotel 151
Chelsea International Hostel 154
Chelsea Market 38, **109**
Chequepoint USA 164
Cherry 9, **100**
chess 90
Chess Forum 90
Chez Brigitte 35
Chez Es Saada 28
Chicago BLUES 144
Chicama 43–44, **122**
children 86–87, 164
on subways and buses 160
Children's Museum of the Arts 67, 86
Children's Museum of Manhattan 67, **86**
Chinatown see Lower East Side & Chinatown
Chinatown Ice Cream Factory 10
Chinese emporiums 9
Chinese New Year 148
Chloé 53
Cho Dang Gol 48, **122**
Christian Dior 47
Christian Louboutin 54, **101**
Christopher Street shopping 93
Chrome Hearts 53
Chrysler Building 67, 68
Chumley's 35
Ciel Rouge 40, **129**
Cine-Noir Film Society 139
cinema 139–140
Circle Line at Pier 83 67
Circuit City 43
City Bakery 44
City Center 137, 141, 144
City Hall 67, 68
Citypass 67
Claremont Riding Academy 84
Clay 23
Clearview's Ziegfeld 139
Clementine 35
The Cloisters 67, **78–79**
clothes, size conversions 164
Club Monaco 43, **99**
clubs **133–135**

Chelsea & the
  Meatpacking District 40
Coney Island & Brighton
  Beach 65
East Village 29–30
Lower East Side &
  Chinatown 10
Nolita & Noho 24
Soho 19
Tribeca 14
West Village 35
CO Encore Worldwide 139
Cobblestones 42
The Cock 30, 132, 135
Coffee Shop 44
Coliseum Books 47
Colony Records 107
Columbus Avenue,
  shopping 93
Columbus Circle Market 109
Columbus Day Parade 148
Columbus Flea Market 109
comedy 138
Comedy Cellar 138
Comfort Diner 54, 95
Comic Strip Live 138
Comme des Garçons 37, 95
Commune 44
Coney Island & Brighton
  Beach 65, 85, 90
Coney Island Hip 143
consulates 164
conversion chart 164
Coogan's 61, 130
Cooler 143
Cooper Hewitt, National
  Design Museum 67, 76
  museum store 105
Copacabana 144
Copeland's 60, 114
Corner Bistro 35, 120
Cort Theater 136
Costume National 16, 95
Country Café 18
Country Inn The City 157
courier services 163
Courtney Washington 63
Cowgirl Hall of Fame 86
Crate & Barrel 47
credit cards 164
Creed 22, 103
Crunch 88
currency 164
Curry in a Hurry 44
customs 164
cycling 163
Cynthia Rowley 15, 98

D
Daffy's 43, 100
Dakota Building 67, 69
Danal 28
dance 90
  ballet 141–142
  dance studios 88
Dance Ritual @ Vinyl 134
Dance Theater of Harlem
  142
Dance Theater Workshop
  142
Dancetracks 28, 107
Dangerfield's 138
Daniel 54, 117
Danube 13
Daryl K 22, 27, 98
dates 164
Dave's New York 38
DDC. Lab 9
Dean & Deluca 17, 108
debit cards 164
Decibel 30, 131
dentists 165
department stores 94
Devachan 89
Dia Center for the Arts
  67, 80
Dick's 30, 132
Diesel 53, 95
Diner 63
diners see cafés & diners
Direct Drive @ Baktun 135
disabled visitors 165
  on subways and buses 160
Disco Rama 107
discount stores 100
Disney Store 47, 102
Dive Bar 58
DKNY 53, 95
DL Cerney 13, 95
DL Lab 9
Do Hwa 35
Dojo's 29

Dok Suni 28
Dolce & Gabbana 53, 95
Dom 17
Domsey's Warehouse
  Outlet 63
Don Giovanni 48
Don Hills 135
Don't Tell Mama 138
Dosa 9
Double Happiness 24
Drinkland 30
Drip 57
'Dropping the Ball' 148
DT-UT 54
DUMBO 7
duty free 165
Dylan Prime 14

E
E 7th Street shopping 93
E 9th Street shopping 93
Each and Them 100
Ear Wax 62
East Village 26–31, 111
Easter Sunday Parade 148
Easy Star Reggae Tuesdays
  @ Black Star Lounge 134
Eclectic Home 38
Eddie Bauer 99
Edison Hotel 154–155
8 Ball Records 107
Eight Mile Creek 23
8th Street shopping 93
Eighty Eights 138
Eileen Fisher 27
Eisenberg Sandwich Shop
  44
El Cid 39
El Museo del Barrio 67, 77
El Rey del Sol 39
El Sombrero 10
Elaine's 54, 129
electricity 165
electronics shops 107
The Elephant 28
Eleven Madison Park 43, 118
Eli's Bread at The Vinegar
  Factory 108–109
Ellen's Stardust Diner 86
Ellis Island (Museum of
  Immigration) 67, 71
email 165
emergencies 165
Emilio Pucci 53
Empire Diner 39–40, 119
Empire State Building 67,
  68, 70, 72
Emporio Armani 42, 53,
  95–96, 98
Enchanted Forest 87
Enid's 63
Enterprise 163
entertainment 136–145
entry requirements 167
Esca 48
ESPN Zone 130
Ess-a-Bagel 49, 115
Etherea 28
Etro 53
Evangelical Church 166
Evelyn Lounge 58
events 147–148
Exodus Industrial Sport 63
Express 99
eyewear 102

F
F&B 40
FAB 208 27, 103
Face Stockholm 57, 103
Fairways 57
Fall Café 64
The Fan Club 43
Fanelli 18
FAO Schwarz 47, 87
fashion shops 95–99
  Chelsea & the
    Meatpacking District
    37–38
  East Village 27
  Gramercy Park & the
    Flatiron District 42–43
  Harlem & the Heights
    59–60
  Lower East Side &
    Chinatown 8–9
  Nolita & Noho 21–23
  Soho 15–17
  Tribeca 13
  Upper East Side 52–53
  Upper West Side 56–57
  West Village 32–33
Fat Beats 34, 107
Fat Cat Billiards 90
Feast of San Gennaro 147

Feinstein's at the Regency
  55, 129, 137
Felissimo 47, 105
Fendi 47, 98
ferries 160
festivals
  cinema 140
  classical music 141
  dance 142
  music 144
  theatre 137
Fez 24, 143
Fifth Avenue shopping 93
57th Street shopping 93
film see cinema
Film Forum 139
Filth Mart 27
Find Outlet 22, 100
Finyl Vinyl 28
FireBird Café 137
Firefighter's Friend 22
First 28, 126
First Wok 54
Fishs Eddy 43, 104
fitness studios 88
Fitzpatrick 155
Five Points 23
Flatiron Building 67, 68
Flatiron District see
  Gramercy Park & the
  Flatiron District
Flavors 44
Fleet Bank 164
Flor de Sol 13
Florent 39, 114
Flor's Kitchen 29
Foley & Corinna 9, 100
food stores 108–109
Foot Locker 102
Footlight Records 28, 107
Forbidden Planet 28, 106
Fort Greene 63–64, 111
Four Seasons 152
4W Circle of Art 63
Foxy @ The Cock 135
Fragile 9
Fragments 17, 102
Franklin 150
Franklin Street
  shopping 93
Fred Astaire Dance Studio
  88
Frédéric Fekkai 55
French Connection 99
French Institute 139
French Roast 34
Fresh 53
Fressen 39, 118–119
Frick Collection 67
  concerts 140–141
Frida's Closet 64
Fun 133

G
G 40
Gabriela's 57
Gagosian Gallery 82
The Galaxy 45
galleries 81–82
  see also museums
  Ace Gallery 81
  American Fine Arts 81
  Barbara Gladstone 82
  C & M Gallery 82
  Deitch Projects 81
  Gagosian Gallery 82
  Hirschl & Adler 82
  Janet Borden 81
  John Weber 82
  Kennedy Galleries 82
  Knoedler & Company 82
  Larry Gagosian 81
  Marlborough Gallery 82
  Mary Boone 82
  Matthew Marks Gallery 82
  Metro Pictures 82
  PaceWildenstein 82
  Pat Hearn 82
  Paula Cooper 82
  Phyllis Kind 81
  Robert Miller 82
  Salander-O'Reilly 82
  303 Gallery 82
  Tony Shafrazi Gallery 81
  Wildenstein & Co 82
games & activities 90–91
Gap 47, 99
Garden of Eden 108
Garment District 7
gas stations 163
Gateway Bus Tours Inc 67
Gay and Lesbian Pride Day
  147
gay bars 132
Gemini Lounge 134–135

Generation Records 107
Gershwin 156
Giant Step @ Shine 134
gift stores 105–106
Givenchy 53
Godiva Chocolatier 47
Goethe House 139
Good World Bar & Grill
  10, 131
Gotham Bar and Grill 35, 117
Gotham Book Mart 106
Gotham Comedy Club 138
Gourmet Garage 17, 108
Grace 13
Gracious Home 53, 104
Gramercy Park & the
  Flatiron District 41
Gramercy Park Hotel 156
Gramercy Tavern 43, 115
Grand Bar 19, 130
Grand Central Station 67,
  68, 72
Grand Sichuan 10
Grand Street shopping 93
Grange Hall 34, 126
Gray Line 67
Gray Line Airport Shuttle
  158, 159
Great Jones Café 24
Great Shanghai 10
Greatest Bar on Earth 130
Greenwich Village
  Halloween Parade 148
Gregg Wolf 27
Grimaldi's 120
The Grocery 64
Grove Street Playhouse 87
Gucci 47, 96
Guernica 30
Guess? 99
Guggenheim Museum
  Soho 67, 75
  see also Solomon R
  Guggenheim Museum
Guinness Fleadh 144
Guastavino's 49

H
H 27
H & M 47, 99
Habib's Place 29
hair care 89
Halcyon 62
Halo 35, 128
Hammerstein Ballroom
  143
Hangawi 48
Harlem & the Heights
  59–61, 111
The Harlem Collective 59
Harlem Spirituals 67
Harlem Week 147
Harry Cipriani 54, 130
Hassidic New York 67
hats 102
Haveli 29
Hedra Prue 22
Heights see Harlem &
  the Heights
Helen's Place 64
Hell 40, 128
Hell's Kitchen 7
Helmut Lang 17, 96
help & advice lines 165
Henri Bendel 47
Henrietta Hudson 35
Herban Kitchen 19
Here 87
Hermès 47
Hertz 163
Hirschl & Adler 82
Hispanic Day Parade
  147–148
HMV 47, 107
Hogs & Heifers 40
Hold Everything 38
holidays, public 166
Holy Basil 29
Home 34
Home Boy of Harlem 60
Hong Kong Egg Cake Co 10
Honmura An 18
Hostelling International
  New York 156
Hotel Beacon 154
Hotel Élysée 150
Hotel of the Rising Star 22
Hotel 17 156
Hotel Venus 17, 96
Hotel Wales 150
Hotels 149–157, 165
  children in 164
Housing Works Thrift Shop
  38, 100

index

Houston Street
shopping 93
Howard Kaplan Antiques 33
Hudson 156
Hungarian Pastry Shop 60

I
I Trulli 44
Ice Bar 14
ice hockey 83
ice-skating 91
Ideya 18
Idlewild 10
If Soho New York 16, **96**
Il Bagatto 28, **119**
Il Buco 23, **119**
IMAX 87
immigration 165
Imperial Theater 136
Ina **100**
The Independent 13
Indigo 35
Indochine 23
The Inn at Irving Place 157
'Ino 35, **120**
insurance 165
interiors stores **104–105**
Chelsea & the
Meatpacking District **38**
East Village **27**
Gramercy Park & the
Flatiron District **43**
Harlem & the Heights
59–60
Lower East Side &
Chinatown **9**
Midtown **47**
Soho **35**
Tribeca **12**
West Village **33**
Intermix 42–43
International Center of
Photography (ICP) 67, **80**
Internet 145, 165
Intrepid Sea Air Space
Museum 67, 86–87
Iridium 144
Irish consulate 164
Irish Rep 137
Irving Plaza 13
Isabel Toledo Lab 42
Isamu Noguchi Garden
Museum 67, **80**
Isay's Leather 65
Isla 34
Island Burgers & Shakes
49, **120**
Issey Miyake Pleats Please
16, **98**
It's a Mod, Mod World 27

J
J & R Music & Computer
World **107**
J Crew 43, 99
J Sisters **89**
Jackson Hole 54, **120**
Jamin Puech 22, 102
Janet Borden 81
Janet Russo 22, **98**
Japan Society 139
Japas 55 50
Japonica 35, **122**
Jazz at Lincoln Center 144
Jazz Record Center 38, **107**
Jean Claude 18–19
Jean Cocteau Repertory
Theater 137
Jean Georges 57, **117**
Jeannette Lang 33, **98**
Jefferson Market 34
Jeffrey 38, **94**
Jerry's 19, **114**
Jerry's Men's Hair Styling
Salon 89
jewellery 102
Jewish Museum 67, **77**
Jill Anderson 27
Jimmy Choo 47, **101**
Jimmy's Bronx Café 144
Jimmy's Corner **130**
Jing Fong 10
Jivamukti 89
Joan & David **101**
Joanie's 44
Joe Jr's 40, **119**
Joe's Bar 30
Joe's Pub 24, **129**
cabaret 138
music 144
Joe's Shanghai 10, **122**
John F Kennedy Airport
158–159
John Weber 82
JoJo 54

Jonathan Adler 17, **104**
Jones Beach 85
Jones Diner 24
Joseph 53
Josie's 57
Joyce Theater 142
Juan Anon 9
Judy's Chelsea 138
Juilliard Theater 140
Jules 28
Juniors **119**
Junk 62
Junno's 35
Juno's **101**
Jutta Neumann 27, **101**
JVC Jazz Festival 144, 147

K
K-Mart **99**
Kaarta Imports 60
Kasia's 63
Katayone Adeli 22
Kate Spade 17, **102**
Kate's Paperie 33
Katz's Deli 9, **115**
Keens Steakhouse 48
Kelley & Ping 19
Kelly Christie 102
Kennedy Galleries 82
Kenneth Cole 43, **101**
Keur 'n' Dye 63
KGB 30, 131
Kiehl's 26, **103**
Kim's Video & Music 28, **107**
King Juan Carlos I Center 139
Kirna Zabête 16, **98**
Kitano New York 155
Kitchen Arts & Letters **106**
Kitchen Club 23, 141
Kitchenette 17
'Knicks' Basketball Season
148
Knitting Factory 14, 143
Knoedler & Company 82
Krispy Kreme 60
Kush 10, 131

L
L Café 63
La Bonne Soupe 48, **124**
La Casa de Vida Natural 88
La Guardia Airport 160
La Lunchonette 39
La Maison Moderne 28
Lafayette Street
shopping 93
Lakeside Lounge 30, **143**
Lakruwana 48
Language 22
Larchmont Hotel 156
Larry Gagosian 81
Las Venus 9, 104
Latin Quarter 144
Latin Tribe @ Gemini
Lounge 134–135
Layla 13
Le Bernardin 49, **117**
Le Corset 17
Le Gamin 40
Le Jardin Bistrot 23, **124**
Le Tableau 28
Lee's Mardi Gras 38
left luggage 165
Lei Bar 30, **131**
Lenox Lounge 60
Lenox Room 54
Leo House 156
Leshko's 29
Lespinasse 49, **117**
Lexington Avenue,
shopping 93
Lexington Candy Shop 54
Liberty Helicopters 67
Liberty Science Center
67, 87
Lighting the Rockefeller
Center Christmas Tree 148
Limelight **133**
limos 91, 158–159, 160
Lincoln Center Festival 137,
141, 143
Ling 89
Lips 91
Liquor Store 14
listings magazines 145
Little Italy 7
Lively Set 33
Living Room 143
Loehmann's 38, **100**
Lola 44
Lombardi's 23, **121**
Londel's 61
Long Island Rail Road (LIRR)
161

Los Dos Rancheros
Mexicanos 49
lost property 165
Lot 61 40
lottery 91
Lotus Club 10
Louie 16
Louis Vuitton 17
Lowell 155
Lower East Side &
Chinatown **8–11**, 111
Lower East Side Gardens
85
Lower East Side Tenement
Museum 67, **76**
Lower Manhattan 7
Lucian Blue 63
Lucien 28
Lucky Cheng's 29, 91
Lucky Strike 18
Lucky Wang 9
Ludlow Street shopping 93
Luna Lounge 138, 143
Lunt-Fontanne Theater 136
Lupa 34, **126–127**
Lush 14, **130**

M
M&I 65
M&R 24
M.A.C. 18, **103**
Macy's 47, **94**
Macy's Fourth of July
Fireworks 147
Macy's Thanksgiving Day
Parade 148
Madison Avenue,
shopping 93
Madison Square Garden
83, 143
Main Street Ephemera/
Paper Collectibles 64
Majestic Theater 136
Malachy's Donegal Inn 58
Malcolm Shabazz Harlem
Market 60, **109**
Malia Mills 22
Malibu 156
Manhattan 7
Manhattan Portage 27, **102**
Manhattan Theater Club 137
Mannes College of Music
140
Manolo Blahnik 47, **101**
Mansfield 150
Marc Jacobs 16, **98**
Mare Chiaro 24, 131
Margie Tsai 22
Mark Garrison Salon 89
Mark Montana 27
Mark Schwartz 22, **101**
markets **109**
Marlborough Gallery 82
Marquis Theater 136
Mars 29
Mart 125 60
Martin Beck Theater 136
Martin Luther King Jr Day
148
Mary Adams 8
Mary Boone 82
Marylou's 35
Matthew Marks Gallery 82
Max 28
Max & Roebling 62
Max Fish 10, **131**, 143
Maxilla & Mandible 57
Mayle 22
Mayrose 44
Me & Ro 22, **102**
Meadowlands Sports
Complex 83
measurements 165
Meatpacking District see
Chelsea & the
Meatpacking District
media 145
medical care 166
medicines 166
Meigas 18
Mekka 29
MeKong 23
Memorial Day Parade 148
men's fashion shops **97**
Meow Mix 10, **129**, 143
Mercer Hotel 152
Mercer Kitchen 18, **119**
Mercury Lounge 143
Merkin Concert Hall 140
Mermaid Day Parade 147
Mesa Grill 43, **122**, 124
MetLife Building 67, 69
Metrazur 50
Metro Bike 163

Metro-North Railroad 161
Metro Pictures 82
MetroCards 160
Metropolis 27
Metropolitan Museum of
Art 67, **73–74**
concerts 140
museum store **105**
Metropolitan Opera House
140, 141
Mexican Radio 23
Mezze 49
Michael Jordan's The
Steakhouse 48, **121**
Midnight Footrace in
Central Park 148
Midsummer Swing Series
144
Midtown 46–51, 111
Milano's 24
Miss Ann's 63
Miss Saigon 54
Missoni 53
Mrs Stahl's Knishery 65
Mitzi E Newhouse Theater
137
Miu Miu 16, **99**
Modell's **102**
MoMa's New Directors/
New Films Festival 140
Monteleone's 64
Montrachet 13
Moomba 35
Moondance Diner 19
Morgan Library 67, **77**
Morgane Le Fay 16, **99**
Morgans 152–153
Mormons 166
Morris-Jumel Mansion
Museum 67, **76–77**
Moschino 53
Moshood 63
Moss 17, **104**
Mostly Mozart Festival 141
Moustache 35
MUNY (Music Under
New York) 161
Murder Ink 106
Murray & Penny Show @
The Slipper Room 134
Murray Hill 7
Murray's Cheese Shop **108**
Museum for African Art 67,
77–78
Museum of American Folk
Art 67, **79**
Museum Mile 7
Museum of Modern Art
(MoMA) 67, **74**
cinema 139
museum store **105**
New Directors/New
Films Festival 140
Museum of Television and
Radio 91
Museums 66–67, **71**, **73–81**
for children 86
museum stores **105–106**
music 143–144
ballet 141–142
CDs, records & tapes
107–108
classical music & opera
140–141
Muslims 166
Mxplyzyk 38

N
Nancy Whiskey Pub 14, **131**
Nassau Coliseum 83
Nathan's Famous
Restaurant 65
National Black Theatre 143
National Museum of the
American Indian 67, **78**
Naughty & Nice 56
Navy Yard 7
NBA Store 47
Nederlander Theater 136
Negril 39
Nell's **133**, 144
New Amsterdam Theater
136
New City Bar & Grill 63
New Festival 140
New Jersey Transit 161
New Museum of
Contemporary Art 67, **80**
New Victory Theater 87
New Wonton Garden 10
New York Airport Service
158, 160
New York Aquarium 86
New York Botanical
Gardens 67, **75**

New York City Ballet 141
New York City Marathon 148
New York Film Festival 140, 147
New York Hall of Science 67, **75**
New-York Historical Society 67, **79**
New York Noodle Town 10
New York Palace 152
New York Philharmonic & Metropolitan Opera in the Park 147
New York Public Library 67, **71**, 142
New York State Theater 140, 141
New York Underground Film Festival 140, 148
New York Youth Theater 87
New Zealand consulate 164
Newark Airport 159
newspapers 167
Next Door Nobu 13
Nha Trang 10
Nice Price SSS **100**
Nicole Farhi 53
Nicole Miller 15
Night Café 58
nightlife, getting your bearings **110–111**
Niketown 47, **102**
9 & Co 101
Nine West 101
92nd Street Y 140, 142
Nobody Beats the Wiz 17
Nobu 13, 117
Nocturne 53
Noho *see Nolita & Noho*
Nolita & Noho 21–25, 111
Nougatine 57
Nova USA 9, **97**
NowBar 35, **135**
Nuyorican Poets Café 142, 144
Nylon Squid 21
Nyonya 23
NYU Cantor Film Center 139

O
O Padeiro 40, 127
Oak Room 138
Obaa Koryoe 60
The Odeon 13, **115**, 124
Odessa 30, 65
Off Soho Suites 154
office & business centres 166
Old Devil Moon 29, **121**
Old Navy 38, **99**
Olive & Bette 56, **99**
Olympia Trails Bus Company 159
Omni Berkshire Place 155
Once upon a Tart 19
105 Stanton 9
125th Street shopping 93
169 Bar 10
One 51 50
Only Hearts 56
Opaline 135
Open Center 89
opera 140
opticians 166
Orange Chicken 12
Orchard Bar 10, **128**
Orchard Street shopping 93
Orchard Street Market 109
O'Reilley's Pub 50
Oriental Dress Company 9
Oriental Gifts 9
Original Levi's Store 100
Osaka Health Center 89
Oscar Wilde Memorial Bookstore 34
Oser 12
Other Music **107**
Otto Tootsi Plohound 17, **100**
Out of the Closet 53, **100**
Oyster Bar 48, **115**
Oznot's Dish 63

P
PaceWildenstein 82
Palace Theater 136
Pall Mall Antiques 33
Pampa 57, **121**
Papaya King 54
Paragon 43
Paramount 153
Parasail NYC 91
Paris Theatre 139
Park Avenue Country Club **130**

Park View at the Boathouse 124–125
parking 163
parks 84–85
Pastis 33, 119
Pat Hearn 82
Patch 155, 8
PATH 161
Patois 64
Patria 44, **123**
Patricia Field 32–33
Paul Smith 42, **97**
Paul Taylor Dance Company 141
Paula Cooper 82
Payard Patisserie & Bistro 54, **127**
Payless 101
Pearl Oyster Bar 35
Pearl River Mart 9, **105**
Pearson's Texas Barbecue **121**
Peasant 23
Penang 11
Peninsula 152
Penny Whistle Toys 87
Pepe Rosso 19, **121**
Pepolino 13
Performing Garage 137
Periyali 44
Perk's **144**
Peter Luger Steakhouse 63, **121**
Pete's Tavern 45
Petit Peton 33, **101**
Petite Abeille 50
Philip's Candy Store 65
Philosophy di Alberta Ferretti 16
photography 166
Phyllis Kind 81
Pickwick Pub 50
Pierre 152
Pink Pussycat Boutique 33
Pisces 28, **127**
PJ Hanley's 64
The Place 34
Plan-eat Thailand 63
Plaza 151
Plaza Athénée 152
Pleasure Chest 33
Pó 34, **127**
poetry 142–143
Poetry Project at St Mark's 142
Poets House 142
police 166
Polo Ralph Lauren 53, **96**
Polo Sport 17, 53
Pommes Frites 29
Pop Shop 22
Portico Bed & Bath 17
postal services 166
Potion Lounge 58
Pottery Barn **104**
Pour House 63, **132**
Power Pilates 88–89
Prada 47, 53, **96**
Prada Sport 17, **96**
Primorski 65
Prospect Park 67, 85
Prune 28, **127**
PS1 Museum of Contemporary Art 67, **81**
PS 44 Market 109
PS 122 Theater 137, 142
PS 183 Market 109
public holidays 166
Public Theater 137
Puerto Rican Day Parade 147

Q
Quad 139
Quakers 166
Queens 7
Queens Museum of Art 67, **75**
Quench 64
Quilted Corner 27
Quilty's 18, **125**

R
R 62
radio 145
Radio City Music Hall 67, 69
Radio Perfecto 28
Radio Shack **107**
Rags A Go Go 27
Rain 57
Rainbow Room 70
Rangers Ice Hockey Season 148
Raoul's 19, **130**
Rasputin 70
Raymond Dragon 38
Recon 9

Record Explosion **107**
Red Cat 39
Red Hook 7
Red Tape 27
Reebok Sports Club 91
Refinery 64
Regents 50, **132**
religion 166
Rent-a-Wreck 163
Republic 44
Restaurant 147 39, 40
Restaurant Week 147
restaurants 114–127, 166
 brunch **124**
 burgers **120**
 Carroll Gardens 64
 Chelsea & the Meatpacking District 39
 for children 86, 164
 Coney Island & Brighton Beach 65
 East Village 28–29
 eat-in delis **115**
 Fort Greene 63–64
 Gramercy Park & the Flatiron District 43–44
 Harlem & the Heights 60
 Lower East Side & Chinatown 9–10
 Midtown 48–49
 Nolita & Noho 23
 Soho 18–19
 tipping 167
 Tribeca 13
 Upper East Side 54
 Upper West Side 57
 vegetarian 123
 West Village 34–35
Resurrection 22, 27, 100
Revolution 89
Rhône 40
Rialto 23, 24, **120**
Rice 23
Richart 47
Ricky's 18, **103**
Riverside Church Observatory 70
Rizzoli 47, **106**
Robert Marc 102
Robert Miller 82
Robert Moses State Park 85
Roberto Cavalli 53
Rockaway Beach 85
Rockefeller Center 67, 69
Rocking Horse Café Mexicano 40
Rockport 17, **101**
roller blades 163
Rooftop Sculpture Garden 70
Roosevelt Island 7
Roosevelt Island Tramway 70
Roseland 143
Rosemarie's 13, **125**
Roxy 91
Royale Theater 136
Royalton 153
Ruby's Old Thyme Bar 65
Rudy's 49, **132**
Russ & Daughters 9
Russian Samovar 50, **131**
Russian Tea Room 48

S
S J South & Sons 14
Sacco 101
safety 166
St Dymphna's 29
St Ignatius Loyola, concerts 141
St John the Divine 67, 69 concerts 141
St Mark's Bookshop 106
St Mark's Place shopping 93
St Nick's Pub 59, 60
St Patrick's Cathedral 67, 69
St Patrick's Day Parade 148
St Regis 152
Saints 58
Saks Fifth Avenue 46–47, **94**
Salander-O'Reilly 82
sales tax 166
Sapphire **134**
Sarah Samoiloff 21
Savoia 23
Savoy 23
Say it Loud @ Opaline 135
Scheme 59
Schomberg Center for Research in Black Culture 67, **81**
Scoop 16, **99**
Screaming Mimi's 22, **100**

Screening Room 13, **125** films 139
SEA Cambodian 63
Sea Lane Bakery 65
Sean 17, **97**
Searle 53
Sears & Robot 27
Second Avenue Deli 29, **115**
Second Stage 137
Selia Yang 27
Selima Optique 17, **102**
Sephora 18, **103**
Serena 40, 134
Serendipity 3 86
Service Station 89
7A 29, **124**
71 Clinton Fresh Food 10, **126**
Shabby Chic 17, **105**
Shack Inc 10
Shakespeare & Co 106
Shakespeare in the Park 137, 147
Shanghai Tang 52–53, **96**
Sharper Image 107
Shea Stadium 83
Shelburne Murray Hill 154
Shelter @ Vinyl 135
Shi 22, **106**
Shine **133**, 134
shoe shops 101
 Gramercy Park & the Flatiron District 43
 Midtown 47
 Nolita & Noho 22
 Soho 17
 Upper East Side 53–54
 West Village 32–33
shopping 92–109, 166–167
 accessories 102
 beauty 103
 books 106
 Carroll Gardens 64
 CDs, records & tapes 107–108
 chain stores 99
 Chelsea & the Meatpacking District 37–38
 children's stores 87
 Coney Island & Brighton Beach 65
 department stores 94
 discount stores 100
 East Village 26–28
 electronics 107
 fashion 95–99
 food stores 108–109
 Fort Greene 63
 getting your bearings 92–93
 gift & museum stores 105–106
 Gramercy Park & the Flatiron District 42–43
 Harlem & the Heights 59–60
 interiors 104–105
 Lower East Side & Chinatown 8–9
 markets 109
 Midtown 46–47
 Nolita & Noho 21–22
 shoes 101
 Soho 15–18
 theme stores 100
 Tribeca 12–13
 Upper East Side 52–54
 Upper West Side 56–57
 vintage fashion 100
 West Village 32–33
 Williamsburg 62–63
Shout @ 13 135
Shu Uemura 18, **103**
Shubert Theater 136
Siberia 49, **132**
Sideshows by the Seashore 90
Sigerson Morrison 22, **101**
sights 66–82
 getting your bearings 66–67
Sixth Avenue shopping 93
Skate City 91
Sleaze Factor @ Sapphire 134
Slice of Harlem 60
Slipper Room 10, **134**
Smalls Underground 143
Smith Limousine Service 91
Smoke 58
smoking 167
SOB 143
Soba-ya 29
Soho 15–20, 111
Soho Antique Fair Collectables Market 109

Soho Grand 153
Soho Sanctuary 88
Soho Steak 18–19
Solomon R Guggenheim Museum 67, 74
   museum store 105
Sony Lincoln Square 139
Sony Style 47, 102
Sony Wonder Technology Lab 87
Sophie's 29
Sorelle Firenze 13
Soup Kiosk 19
Soup Kitchen International 49
Southgate Tower Suite Hotel 154
Spa 30, 133
Spanish Harlem 7
Spartina 13, 125
spas 88
Splash 45
sport
   games & activities 90–91
   spectator sports 83
   sports bars 130
   sports gear 102
Spring Festival 148
Spring Lounge 24
Spring Street Market 109
Squeezebox @ Don Hills 135
Stacia New York 64
Staten Island 7
Staten Island Ferry 70
Statue of Liberty 67, 69, 71–72
Steinberg & Sons 22
Stella Dallas 33, 100
Stéphane Kélian 53, 101
Steve Madden 17, 101
Steven Alan 16–17, 96
Stinger Club 63, 129
The Strand 28, 106
Strawberry Fields 67, 69
Street Smarts 67
Structure 99
students 167
Studio 54 136
Studio Museum Gift Shop 60
Studio Museum of Harlem 67, 81
Stussy 17
Suarez 47
Subliminal Sessions @ Centro Fly 135
suburban trains 161
Subway 70
Subway Inn 55
subways 161
Sugar Shack 61
Summerstage 144
Super Shuttle 158, 159
Supper Club 90, 144
Supreme 22
Sur 64
Surya 35, 123
Sway 19
Swedish Marionette Theater 87
Sweet & Vicious 24, 128
Sweet Basil 143
Sweet Melissa 64
Swine on Nine 50, 131
Swing 46 Jazz & Supper Club 90
Sylvia's 60, 124
Symphony Space 144

T
Tabla 43, 123
Tabla 35
Takahachi 29, 123
Takashimaya 47, 94
Taqueria de Mexico 23
Tatiana Café 65
tax, sales 166
Tax Free Week 148
taxis 162
   airports 158, 159, 160
   tipping 167
Tea & Sympathy 35, 121
The Tea Box 49
Teddy's 63
telephoning 167
television 91, 145
Temple Records 28
tennis 83
Xth Ave Lounge 50
Tenth Street Baths & Health Club 88
Teresa's 29
The Terrace 60
Teuscher 47
TG-170 8, 99
Thailand Restaurant 10
Theater District 7, 111
   theater 136–137
   for children 87
Theatreworks/USA 87
theme stores 102
   13, 153
Thomas Cook 164
303 Gallery 82
357 19, 130
Three Cups 29
Three Lives & Company 34, 106
Throb 28
Tiffany's 47
Tillie's of Brooklyn 64
time 167
Time Hotel 153
Times Square 70, 90
Timtoum 9, 100
tipping 167
Titou 34
Tocca 16
Tod's 54, 101
Tokio 7 27, 100
Tokyo Joe 27
Tom of Finland 37–38
Tompkins Square Books 28
Tom's Restaurant 60, 119
Tonic club 10, 129, 143
The Tonic restaurant 39
Tony Shafrazi Gallery 81
Top of The Tower 50, 70, 130
Torch 10, 138
Tossed 44
TOTEM 12, 105
tourist information 167
tours 67
Tower Books 106
Tower Flea Market 109
Tower Records 47, 107
Town Hall 144
Toys in Babeland 9
Tracey Feith 22, 99
trains 161
Trannie Chaser @ NowBar 135
transport 158–163
Trattoria dell'Arte 48, 115
travellers' cheques 164
Tribeca 12–14, 111
Tribeca Blues 14

Tribeca Grand Hotel 153
Tribeca Grill 13
Tribes Gallery 142–143
Trinity Church, concerts 141
Troy 17, 106
Trufaux 16, 99
Trump Tower 67, 70
TSE 53
TSE Surface 22
Tunnel 133
Tuscan Square 49
'21' Club 48, 116
27 Standard 44
Twilo 133–134, 135
Twilo @ Twilo 135
2A 30
Two Boots 29, 86
   films 139
288 24

U
Ugly Luggage 62
UN Building 67, 70
UN Delegates' Dining Room 48–49
Uncle Pho 64
Union Pacific 44, 125
Union Square Café 43, 116
Union Square Market 109
Untitled 33, 96–97
Upper East Side 52–55
Upper Manhattan 7
Upper West Side 56–58, 111
US Open Tennis Tournament 147

V
Va Tutto! 23
Valentino 53
Vegetarian Paradise 3 10
Velvet 24
Velveteen @ Serena 134
Veniero's 29
Vera Cruz 63
Verbena 44, 125
Veritas 44, 127
Versace 47, 53, 97
Veruka 19
View Lounge 70
views 70
Village 35
Village Chess Shop 33
Village Idiot 40
Village Vanguard 143
Vinnie's Tampon Case 9
Vinny's of Carroll Gardens 64
vintage fashion 100
Vinyl 134, 135
Vinylmania 34
Virgil's Real BBQ 48
Virgin Megastore 47, 107
visas 167
Vivienne Tam 15–16
Vivienne Westwood 16, 97
Void 19, 131, 139
Von 24
Vynl Diner 49

W
W 18th and W 19th Streets, shopping 93
W 25th and W 26th Streets shopping 93
W 28th Street shopping 93
W 47th Street shopping 93
W New York 153

Waldorf Astoria 151
Walkers 31
walking tours 67
Walter Kerr Theater 136
Walter Reade Theater 139
Warner Bros Studio Store 47, 102
Washington Heights 111
Washington Square Hotel 157
Washington Square Music Festival 147
Waterloo 34, 120
weather 167
websites 145
Webster Hall 143
Weill Recital Hall 140
Welcome to the Johnsons 10
West Broadway shopping 93
West Indian-American Day Carnival 147
West Village 32–36, 111
Western Union 164
Westside Theater 137
Wet Bar 50
Wetlands 144
Whiskey Blue 50
Whiskey Park 50
Whitney Museum of American Art 67, 75
Wigstock 147
Wildenstein & Co 82
Williams-Sonoma 38, 105
Williamsburg 62–63
Wilson's 138
Winnie's 10, 129
Winter Garden 144
Women's Film Festival 140
Wonder Bar 30, 132
Woolworth Building 67, 70
Working Class 13
World Trade Center 67, 70
   music festival 144
   Observation Deck 70
Wyeth 12

X
X-Large 22
XOXO 99
XS New York 91

Y
Yaffa Café 29
Yama 44
Yankee Stadium 83
Yankees & Mets Baseball Season 148
yellow cabs 162
Yohji Yamamoto 17, 97
Yonah Schimmel's Knishery 9
Yorkville 7
Yves Saint Laurent Rive Gauche 17, 97

Z
Zabar's 57, 109
Zao 9
Zapatas Manoletas 61
Zara 17, 99
Zen Palate 44, 123
Zero 22
Zona 17, 105
zoos 86

↓ shopping index

accessories 102
   see also eyewear; hats; jewellery; shoes
Bond 07 22
Chrome Hearts 53
Lucky Wang 9
Pop Shop 22
Ugly Luggage 62
Vinnie's Tampon Case 9
antiques
   see also vintage furniture
Howard Kaplan Antiques 33
Pall Mall Antiques 33
Soho Antique Fair Collectibles Market 109
art 81–82
bags 102
Fendi 47
Jamin Puech 22, 102
Jutta Neumann 27

Kate Spade 17, 102
Louis Vuitton 17
Manhattan Portage 27, 102
Refinery 64
Teuscher 47
Suarez 47
beauty supplies 103
Aveda 18, 103
Bigelow Pharmacy 33, 103
Bliss Spa 18, 103
Creed 22, 103
Demeter 26–27
Face Stockholm 57, 103
Frédéric Fekkai 54
Fresh 53
Kiehl's 26, 103
M.A.C. 18, 103
Ricky's 18, 103
Sephora 18, 103
Shu Uemura 18, 103
books 106
A Different Light 38, 106

A Photographer's Place 106
Barnes & Noble 43, 106
Books of Wonder 87
Borders Books and Music 106
Coliseum Books 47
Forbidden Planet 28, 106
Gotham Book Mart 106
Kitchen Arts & Letters 106
Murder Ink 106
Oscar Wilde Memorial Bookstore 34
Rizzoli 47, 106
St Mark's Bookshop 106
Shakespeare & Co 106
The Strand 28, 106
Three Lives & Company 34, 106
Tompkins Square Books 28
Tower Books 106

CDs, records & tapes 107
A Different Light 38
Academy CDs & Records 43, 107
Bleecker Bob's Golden Oldies 107
Bleecker Street Records 34
Borders Books and Music 106
Colony Records 107
Dancetracks 28, 107
Disco Rama 107
Ear Wax 62
8 Ball Records 107
Etherea 28
Fat Beats 34, 107
Finyl Vinyl 28
Footlight Records 28, 107
Generation Records 107
HMV 47, 107
J & R Music & Computer

World 107
Jazz Record Center 38, 107
Jeffrey 38, 94
Kim's Video & Music 28, 107
Other Music 107
Record Explosion 107
Temple Records 28
Throb 28
Tower Records 47, 107
Vinylmania 34
Virgin Megastore 47, 107
chain stores 99
Banana Republic 43, 99
Bebe 43
Brooks Bros 99
Club Monaco 99
Eddie Bauer 99
Express 99
French Connection 99
Gap 47, 99
Guess? 99
H & M 47, 99
J Crew 43, 99
K-Mart 99
Old Navy 38, 99
Structure 99
XOXO 99
Zara 17, 99
Chinese emporiums
Oriental Dress Company 9
Oriental Gifts 9
Pearl River Mart 9, 105
clubwear
Air Market 27
Hotel Venus 33
L'Impasse 33
Mary Adams 8
consignment stores
Tokio 7 125, 100
Tokyo Joe 27
cosmetics
see beauty supplies
department stores 94
Barney's New York 52, 94
Bergdorf Goodman 46, 94
Bloomingdale's 94
Felissimo 47
Henri Bendel 47
Jeffrey 94
Macy's 47, 94
Saks Fifth Avenue
46–47, 94
Takashimaya 47, 94
designer clothes 95–99
see also consignment
stores; menswear;
vintage clothes
À Détacher 21
Alpana Bawa 16
Anna 27
Anna Sui 16, 95
Antique Boutique 21, 97
APC 25
Atsuro Tayama 16
Behrle 13
Betsey Johnson 15, 97
Big Drop 16
Blue 27
Blue Skirt 22
Built By Wendy 22
Burberry 47
Calvin Klein 53, 95
Calypso St Barths
22, 97–98
Catherine 16, 98
Chanel 47
Chloé 53
Christian Dior 47
Comme des Garçons 37, 95
Costume National 16, 95
Cynthia Rowley 15, 98
Daryl K 22, 27, 98
DDC.Lab 9
DKNY 53, 95
DL Cerney 13, 95
Dolce & Gabbana 53, 95
Dosa 16
Eileen Fisher 27
Emporio Armani 42, 53,
95–96
Etro 95
Fendi 98
Find Outlet 22, 100
Fragile 9
Frida's Closet 64
Givenchy 53
Gucci 47, 95
Hedra Prue 22
Helmut Lang 95
If Soho New York 16, 96
Intermix 42–43
Isabel Toledo Lab 42
Issey Miyake Pleats
Please 16, 98
Janet Russo 22, 98

Jeannette Lang 33, 98
Jeffrey 38, 94
Jill Anderson 27
Joseph 53
Juan Anon 9
Katayone Adeli 22
Kirna Zabète 16, 98
Language 22
Louie 9
Marc Jacobs 16, 98
Margie Tsai 9
Mark Montana 27
Max & Roebling 62
Mayle 22
Missoni 53
Miu Miu 16, 99
Morgane Le Fay 16, 99
Moschino 53
Nicole Farhi 53
Nicole Miller 15
Nova USA 9, 97
Nylon Squid 21
Olive & Bette 56, 99
105 Stanton 9
Patch 155 8
Patricia Field 32–33
Paul Smith 42
Philosophy di Alberta
Ferretti 16
Polo Ralph Lauren 53, 96
Prada 47, 53, 96
Red Tape 27
Roberto Cavalli 53
Scheme 9
Scoop 16, 99
Selia Yang 27
Shack Inc 13
Shanghai Tang 52–53, 98
Sorelle Firenze 13
Stacia New York 64
Steven Alan 16, 96
Tocca 16
Tracey Feith 22, 99
TSE 53
TSE Surface 22
Untitled 33, 96–97
Valentino 53
Versace 47, 53, 97
Vivienne Tam 15–16
Vivienne Westwood 16, 97
Yohji Yamamoto 17, 97
Zao 9
Zero 22
discount stores 100
Century 21 100
Daffy's 43, 100
Find Outlet 22, 100
Loehmann's 38, 100
Nice Price SSS 100
drink
Astor Wines & Spirits 108
Best Cellars 108
electronics 107
B & H Photo-Video 107
Circuit City 43
J & R Music & Computer
World 107
Nobody Beats the Wiz 107
Radio Shack 107
Sharper Image 107
erotica
Naughty & Nice 56
Pink Pussycat Boutique 9
Pleasure Chest 33
Toys in Babeland 9
eyewear 102
Robert Marc 102
Selima Optique 17, 102
fabrics
Kaarta Imports 60
fashion see chain stores;
clubwear; designer
clothes; discount stores;
flagship stores;
menswear; streetwear;
vintage clothes
flagship stores 47
Burberry 47
Chanel 47
Christian Dior 47
Gap 47
Gucci 47
H & M 47
Hermès 47
Prada 47
Versace 47
flowers & plants
Chelsea Garden Store 38
Union Square Market 109
food 107–108
Balducci's 34, 108
Chelsea Market 38
Dean & Deluca 17, 108
Eli's Bread at The Vinegar

Factory 108–109
Fairways 57
Garden of Eden 108
Godiva Chocolatier 47
Gourmet Garage 17, 108
Jefferson Market 34
M&I 65
Mrs Stahl's Knishery 65
Murray's Cheese Shop 108
Odessa 65
Philip's Candy Store 65
Richart 47
Russ & Daughters 108
Sea Lane Bakery 65
Teuscher 47
Zabar's 57, 109
furniture
see also antiques; interiors;
vintage furniture
Amalgamated Home 33
Anandamali 12
Crate & Barrel 47
H 27
Las Venus 9, 104
TOTEM 12, 105
Wyeth 12
Zona 17, 105
gift stores 105–106
see also museum stores
Alphaville 33
Felissimo 105
Isay's Leather 65
Main Street Ephemera/
Paper Collectibles 64
Pearl River Mart 105
Sears & Robot 27
Shi 106
Troy 17, 106
hats 102
Amy Downs 8, 102
Kelly Christie 102
health & beauty see beauty
home furnishings see
furniture; interiors
interiors 104–105
ABC Carpet & Home 43,
104
Ad-Hoc Software 17, 104
African Paradise 60
Amalgamated Hardware
33
Amalgamated Home 33
Antik 12
Apartment 48 38
Astroturf 64
Auto 38, 104
Bed Bath and Beyond 104
Campagna Home Shop 43
Cobblestones 27
Dom 17
Eclectic Home 38
Fishs Eddy 43, 104
Gracious Home 53, 104
H 27
Hold Everything 38
It's a Mod, Mod World 27
Jonathan Adler 17, 104
La Maison Moderne 38
Las Venus 104
Moss 17, 104
Mxyplyzyk 38
Orange Chicken 12
Oser 12
Portico Bed & Bath 17
Pottery Barn 104
Quilted Corner 27
Shabby Chic 17, 105
Shi 22
TOTEM 12, 105
Williams-Sonoma 38, 105
Wyeth 12
Zona 17, 105
jewellery 102
Bamboozle Studio 60
Bond 07 102
Cartier 47
Fragments 17, 102
Gregg Wolf 27
Home Boy of Harlem 60
Me & Ro 22, 102
Sarah Samoiloff 27
Tiffany's 47
lingerie
Le Corset 17
Nocturne 53
Only Hearts 56
Toys in Babeland 9
magazines
Barnes & Noble 43, 106
Forbidden Planet 28, 106
Tower Books 106
markets 109
Annex Flea Market
38, 109
Chelsea Market 38, 109

Columbus Circle Market
109
Columbus Flea Market
109
Malcolm Shabazz Harlem
Market 60, 109
Mart 125, 60
Orchard Street Market 109
PS 44 Market 109
PS 183 Market 109
Soho Antique Fair
Collectibles Market 109
Spring Street Market 109
Tower Flea Market 109
Union Square Market 109
menswear 97
Alpana Bawa 16
Beau Gosse 33
Helmut Lang 17, 98
Hotel of the Rising Star 22
Lee's Mardi Gras 38
Nova USA 9, 97
Paul Smith 97
Raymond Dragon 38
Recon 9
Savoia 27
Sean 17, 97
Steinberg & Sons 27
Steven Alan Menswear 17
Tom of Finland 37–38
Yves Saint Laurent Rive
Gauche 17
museum stores 105
Cooper-Hewitt, National
Museum of Design Store
105
Guggenheim Museum
Store 105
Metropolitan Museum of
Art Store 105
Museum of Modern Art
Store 105
Studio Museum Gift
Shop 60
newspapers
Barnes & Noble 43, 106
Tower Books 106
secondhand clothes see
vintage clothes
shoes 101
Christian Louboutin 54, 101
Jamin Puech 22
Jimmy Choo 47, 101
Joan & David 101
Juno's 101
Jutta Neumann 27, 101
Kenneth Cole 43
Kirna Zabète 16, 98
Manolo Blahnik 47, 101
Mark Schwartz 101
9 & Co 101
Nine West 101
Otto Tootsi Plohound
17, 101
Payless 101
Petit Peton 33, 101
Rockport 17, 101
Sacco 101
Sigerson Morrison 22, 101
Stéphane Kélian 53, 101
Steve Madden 17, 101
Tod's 54, 101
sports gear 102
Foot Locker 102
Modell's 102
Paragon 43
sportswear
Club Monaco 43
Malia Mills 22
Polo Sport 17, 53
Prada Sport 17, 96
Reebok Sports Club 57
Stussy 17
Supreme 22
stationery
Kate's Paperie 33
streetwear
see also chain stores
Anthropologie 16
Barney's Co-Op 38
Canal Jean Co 17, 100
Courtney Washington 63
Dave's New York 38
Diesel 53, 95
Emilio Pucci 53
Exodus Industrial Sport
63
4W Circle of Art 63
The Harlem Collective 59
Hotel Venus 17
Moshood 63
Searle 53
Trufaux 16, 99
Working Class 13
X-Large 22

index

theme stores 102
Disney Store 47, 102
FAO Schwarz 47, 87
Firefighter's Friend 22
Maxilla & Mandible 57
NBA Store 47
Niketown 47, 102
Original Levi's Store 102
Sony Style 47, 102
Village Chess Shop 33
Warner Bros Studio Store 47, 102

thrift stores
Filth Mart 27
Housing Works Thrift Shop 38, 100
Out of the Closet 53

toys
Enchanted Forest 87
FAO Schwarz 47, 87
Penny Whistle Toys 87

vintage clothes 100
see also consignment stores

Allan & Suzi 56
Canal Jean Co 17, 100
Cherry 9, 100
Domsey's Warehouse Outlet 63
Each and Them 100
FAB 208 27
The Fan Club 43
Foley & Corinna 9, 100
Ina 100
Metropolis 27
Out of the Closet 100

Rags A Go Go 27
Resurrection 22, 27, 100
Screaming Mimi's 22, 100
Stella Dallas 33, 100
Timtoum 9, 100

vintage furniture
Junk 62
Las Venus 9
Lively Set 33
R 62

watches
Casio Baby G-Shock 17

↓ eating index

African/Caribbean
Africa 60
Brisas del Caribe 19
Ideya 18
Keur 'n' Dye 63
Mekka 29
Negril 39
Obaa Koryoe 60

American *see also burgers; diners; Mexican; soul food; steaks & grills*
Alison on Dominick Street 18
Alley's End 39
Astor Restaurant & Lounge 23
B-Bar & Grill 118
Blue Ribbon 18, 126
Bouley Bakery 13, 116
Bryant Park Grill & Café 48
Cafeteria 39
Candela 44
Commune 44
Copeland's 60, 114
Cowgirl Hall of Fame 86
Danal 28
Eleven Madison Park 43, 118
First 28, 126
Five Points 23
Fressen 39, 118–119
Gotham Bar and Grill 35, 117
Grace 13
Gramercy Tavern 43, 115
Grange Hall 34, 126
The Grocery 64
Home 34
The Independent 13
Indigo 35
Jean Georges 57, 117
Joanie's 44
Lenox Room 54
Lucian Blue 63
Mercer Kitchen 18, 119
Mesa Grill 43, 122, 124
Miss Ann's 63
Nathan's Famous Restaurant 65
New City Bar & Grill 63
The Odeon 13, 115, 124
Old Devil Moon 29, 121
Park View at the Boathouse 124–125
Prune 28, 127
Quilty's 18, 125
Red Cat 39
Restaurant 147 39
Savoy 23
Screening Room 13, 125
Serendipity 3 86
71 Clinton Fresh Food 10, 126
Tabla 43, 123
The Tonic 39
Torch 10
Tribeca Grill 13
'21' Club 48, 116
Two Boots 29
Union Square Café 43, 116
Verbena 44, 125
Veritas 44, 127

Australian
Eight Mile Creek 23

Austrian
Danube 13

bagels
Bagels by the Park 64
Barney Greengrass 57
Ess-a-Bagel 49, 115
Russ & Daughters 9–10
Yonah Schimmel's Knishery 9

bar/restaurants
Baby Jupiter 10, 128
Bar 89 130
Bar Odeon 13

Baraza 30, 128
Bongo 40
Bubble Lounge 130
Café Largo 60–61
Chumley's 129
Clementine 35
Dylan Prime 14
Elaine's 129
Enid's 63
Good World Bar & Grill 131
Grand Bar 130
The Greatest Bar on Earth 130
Guernica 30
Halo 35, 128
Harry Cipriani 130
Japas 55, 50
Joe's Pub 129
Junno's 35
Lot 61 40
Lucian Blue 63
Lush 130
Malachy's Donegal Inn 58
Metrazur 50
Nancy Whiskey Pub 131
Odessa 30
PJ Hanley's 64
Primorski 65
Regents 50, 132
Rudy's 49, 132
The Russian Samovar 131
S J South & Sons 14
St Dymphna's 29
Sugar Shack 61
Swine on Nine 131
357 130
Tonic 10, 129
Top of the Tower 130
Winnie's 129
Winter Garden 65

Belgian
Markt 39
Petite Abeille 40
Pommes Frites 29
Waterloo 34, 120

bistros
Alley's End 39
Balthazar 23, 118
The Brasserie 48
Canteen 18
Casimir 28
Corner Bistro 35, 120
Guastavino's 49
Indigo 35
Jules 28
La Bonne Soupe 48, 124
Le Jardin Bistrot 23, 124
Le Tableau 3
Lucien 28
Lucky Strike 18
Montrachet 13
New City Bar & Grill 63
The Odeon 13, 115, 124
Pastis 39, 119
Patois 64
Payard Patisserie & Bistro 54, 127
Village 35

breakfast & brunch 124
Mesa Grill 43, 122, 124
The Odeon 13, 115, 124
7A 29, 124
Sylvia's 60, 124

burgers 120
Big Nick's Burger 57, 120
Corner Bistro 35, 120
Fanelli 18
Island Burgers & Shakes 49, 120
Jackson Hole 54, 120
Rialto 23, 120
Walkers 13

cafés *see also bistros; diners; teas*
ABC Parlour 44
Big Cup 40
Brooklyn Moon Café 63–64

Bryant Park Grill & Café 48
Café con Leche 57
Café Gitane 24
Café Habana 24
Café Lalo 57
Café Restaurant Volna 65
Cafeteria 118
Chez Brigitte 35
City Bakery 44
Coffee Shop 44
Dojo's 29
Drip 57
DT-UT 54
Eisenberg Sandwich Shop 44
F&B 40
Fall Café 64
Flavors 44
Great Jones Café 24
Habib's Place 29
Halcyon 64
Herban Kitchen 19
Hungarian Pastry Shop 60
Joe Jr's 40, 119
Kelley & Ping 19
Krispy Kreme 10
L Café 63
Le Gamin 40
Lexington Candy Shop 54
Lotus Club 10
Mezze 49
Monteleone's 64
Nougatine 57
Once upon a Tart 19
Papaya King 54
Payard Patisserie & Bistro 54, 127
Pepe Rosso 19, 121
Republic 44
Soup Kiosk 19
Soup Kitchen International 49
Sweet Melissa 64
Tatiana Café 65
Tea & Sympathy 35, 121
Tillie's of Brooklyn 64
Tossed 44
Tuscan Square 49
Veniero's 29
Yaffa Café 29

Cambodian
SEA Cambodian 63

Chinese
First Wok 54
Grand Sichuan 10
Great Shanghai 10
Hong Kong Egg Cake Co 10
Jing Fong 10
Joe's Shanghai 10, 122
New Wonton Garden 10
New York Noodle Town 10

delicatessens 115
Artie's New York Delicatessen 57, 115
Balducci's 34
Barney Greengrass 57, 115
Buffa's Delicatessen 24
Ess-a-Bagel 115
Jefferson Market 34
Katz's Deli 115
Second Avenue Deli 115

diners *see also bistros; cafés*
Bubby's 13
Comfort Diner 54, 120
Diner 63
Ellen's Stardust Diner 86
Empire Diner 39–40, 119
Jerry's 19, 114
Jones Diner 24
Juniors 19
Kitchenette 13
Mayrose 44
Moondance Diner 19
Old Devil Moon 29, 121
Tom's Restaurant 60, 119

Vynl Diner 49

East European
Kasia's 63
Leshko's 29
Russian Tea Room 48
Teresa's 9

French
Alison on Dominick Street 18
Avenue 57
Balthazar 23, 118
Bar Six 34
Bayard's 116
Café Boulud 54, 116
Café des Artistes 57, 101
Capsouto Frères 13, 124
Casimir 28
Cello 54
Chanterelle 13
Country Café 18
Daniel 54, 117
Diner 63
Eleven Madison Park 43, 118
Florent 39, 114
French Roast 34
Jean Claude 18–19
Jean Georges 57, 117
JoJo 54
Jules 28
Kitchen Club 23
La Bonne Soupe 48, 124
La Lunchonette 39
Le Bernardin 49, 117
Le Jardin Bistrot 23, 124
Lespinasse 48, 117
Lucien 28
Mercer Kitchen 18, 119
Montrachet 13
New City Bar & Grill 63
Patois 64
Payard Patisserie & Bistro 54, 127
The Terrace 60
Titou 34
Village 35

global
Asia de Cuba 48
Bright Food Shop 40
Café Boulud 54, 116
Lola 44
Radio Perfecto 28
27 Standard 44
UN Delegates' Dining Room 48–49
Union Pacific 44, 125

Greek *see also Mediterranean*
Periyali 44

ice cream
Chinatown Ice Cream Factory 10
Monteleone's 64

Indian
Café Spice 35
Curry in a Hurry 44
Haveli 29
Surya 35, 123
Tabla 43, 123

Internet cafés 145
Cyber Café 145
Internet café 145
Void 145

Irish
St Dymphna's 29

Italian *see also pasta; pizzas*
Babbo 34, 118
Bar Pitti 34, 126
Bottino 39
Carino 54
Don Giovanni 48
Esca 48
Helen's Place 64
I Trulli 43
Il Bagatto 28, 119
Il Buco 23, 119
'Ino 35, 120

index

174

Lombardi's 23, **121**
Lupa 34, **126–127**
Max 28
Monteleone's 64
Peasant 23
Pó 34, **127**
Rosemarie's 13, **125**
Three of Cups 29
Trattoria dell'Arte 48, **115**
Two Boots 29
Va Tutto! 23
Vinny's of Carroll Gardens 64
Japanese
Avenue A Sushi 29
Bond St 23, 24, **118**
Japonica 35, **122**
Next Door Nobu 13
Nobu 13, **117**
Soba-ya 29
Taka 35
Takahachi 29, **123**
Yama 44
Jewish see also delicatessens
Russ & Daughters 9–10
Yonah Schimmel's Knishery 9
Korean
Cho Dang Gol 48, **122**
Clay 23
Do Hwa 35
Dok Suni 28
Hangawi 48
Latin American see also Mexican; South American
Malaysian
Nyonya 23
Penang 18
Mediterranean see also French; Greek; Italian; Portuguese; Spanish
Acquario 23, **126**
Danal 28
Five Points 23
Mezze 49
The Place 34

Red Cat 39
Rice 23
Spartina 13, **125**
Mexican
Casa Mexicana 10
El Rey del Sol 39
El Sombrero 10
Gabriela's 57
Los Dos Rancheros Mexicanos 49
Mesa Grill 43, 122, 124
Mexican Radio 23
Rocking Horse Café Mexicano 40
Taqueria de Mexico 35
Vera Cruz 63
Middle Eastern
Casa La Femme 18
Habib's Place 29
Layla 13
Moustache 35
Oznot's Dish 63
Moroccan
Bar Six 34
Chez Es Saada 28
Country Café 18
Oriental
see also Cambodian; Chinese; Japanese; Korean; Thai; Vietnamese
American Park **124**
The Elephant 28
Honmura An 18
Lucky Cheng's 29, 91
Rice 23
Zen Palate 44, **123**
outdoor tables
American Park **124**
Bar Pitti 34, **126**
Bottino 39
Bryant Park Grill & Café 48
Park View at the Boathouse **124–125**
Radio Perfecto 28
Rialto 23
7A 29, **124**

Tatiana Café 65
Verbena 44, **125**
Yaffa Café 29
pasta
Babbo 34, **118**
Pepe Rosso 19, **121**
Pepolino 13
pizzas
Grimaldi's **120**
Lombardi's 13, **121**
Slice of Harlem 60
Two Boots 86
Portuguese
O Padeiro 40, **127**
Scandinavian
Aquavit 49, **116**
seafood
Acquario 23, **126**
Aquagrill 18
Blue Water Grill 43
Cello 54
Esca 48
Ideya 18
Le Bernardin 49, **117**
Oyster Bar 48, **115**
Pearl Oyster Bar 35
Periyali 48
Pisces 28, **127**
Surya 35, **123**
Union Pacific 44, **125**
soul food
Bayou 60
Copeland's 60, **114**
Jerry's 19, **114**
Sugar Shack 61
Sylvia's 60, **124**
South American see also Mexican
Calle Ocho 57, **122**
Casa 34
Chicama 43–44, **122**
Flor's Kitchen 29
Ideya 18
Isla 34
Pampa 57, **121**
Patria 44, **123**
Sur 64

Spanish
El Cid 39
Flor de Sol 13
Meigas 18
Sri Lankan
Lakruwana 48
steaks & grills 121
B-Bar & Grill 23
Keens Steakhouse 48
Michael Jordan's The Steakhouse 24, **121**
Pearson's Texas Barbecue **121**
Peter Luger Steakhouse 63, **121**
Soho Steak 18–19
Sur 64
Virgil's Real BBQ 48
teas
Payard Patisserie & Bistro 54, **127**
Tea & Sympathy 35, **121**
The Tea Box 49
Thai
Holy Basil 29
Plan-eat Thailand 63
Rain 57
Thailand Restaurant 10
Turkish
Bereket 10
vegan
Josie's 57
Zen Palate 44, **123**
vegetarian 123
Angelica Kitchen 29, **123**
Josie's 57
Vegetarian Paradise 3 10
Zen Palate 44, **123**
Vietnamese
Indochine 23
MeKong 23
Miss Saigon 54
Nha Trang 10
Rain 57
Uncle Pho 64

175

index

↓ acknowledgements

No part of this text may be reproduced, stored in a retrieval system, or transmitted in any form or by any means, electronic, mechanical, photocopying, recording or otherwise, without the prior written permission of the copyright owner.

This book is sold subject to the condition that it shall not, by way of trade or otherwise, be lent, resold, hired out or otherwise circulated without the publisher's prior written consent in any form of binding or cover other than in that which it is published and without a similar condition, including this condition being imposed upon the subsequent purchaser.

Conceived, edited & designed by
Virgin Publishing Ltd
London w6 9ha
Tel: 020 7386 3300

Project Editor: Naomi Peck
Designer: Lisa Kosky
DTP Designer: Ingrid Vienings
Editorial Assistant: Claire Fogg
Design & editorial assistance: Cooling Brown, Michael Ellis, Sarah Handy (NYCVB, London), Anthony Limerick, Irene Lyford, Ella Milroy, Sally Prideaux, Annie Reid, Jane Simmonds, Clare Tomlinson, Fiona Wild, Trond Wilhelmsen, Simon Winstone
Series Editor: Georgina Matthews
Consultant: Eve Claxton
Researcher: Katya Rogers
Proof reader: Stewart Wild
Index: Hilary Bird
Jacket concept: Debi Ani

Cartographic editor: Dominic Beddow
Cartographer: Jethro Lennox
Draughtsman Ltd, London
020 8960 1602 | Email: mail@magneticnorth.net

Photography: Benoit Peverelli

Reproduced by Colourwise
Printed by Jarrold Book Printers

Features in this guide were written and researched by:
Transport: Katya Rogers | **Getting Your Bearings (areas):** Katya Rogers | **Area write-ups:** Eve Claxton (introductions), Eve Claxton, Michael Dolan, C Leggett (shopping), Angela Tribelli (bars), Julie Besonen (restaurants) | **Brooklyn:** Alfred Gingold, Helen Rogan | **Landmarks:** Katya Rogers | **Sights, Museums and Galleries:** Karen Robinovitz,

Walter Robinson, Katya Rogers | **Sport and Kids:** Anngel Delaney | **Parks & Beaches:** Katya Rogers | **Body & Soul** and **Game for a Laugh:** Karen Robinovitz | **Shops:** Julie Besonen, Eve Claxton, C Leggett, Denise Maher, Karen Robinovitz | **Restaurants:** Julie Besonen, Karen Robinovitz, Kate Sekules | **Bars:** Angela Tribelli | **Entertainment:** Michael Atkinson (cinema), Dan Bova (comedy), Lorie Caval (clubs), Viven Goldman (music & poetry), Scott Jolley (cabaret), Ann Midgette (dance, opera & classical music, theatre), Katya Rogers (media and events) | **Hotels:** Monica Forrestall | **Practical:** Katya Rogers.

Acknowledgements and credits:
Virgin Publishing Ltd would like to thank all galleries, museums, shops, restaurants, bars and other establishments who provided photographs. Photo credits (t=top; b=bottom): Sara Matthews 34; Todd Eberle 37b; Antoine Bootz for Felissimo 47b; Enrico Ferorelli 73t; Fred George 73b; Ellen Labenski 75; Sara Moy 76; John Berens 80; Linda Farwell 86; Laurence Galud 88. New York subway and bus maps were reproduced with the permission of MTA New York City Transit.

Revised edition 2000
Project Editor: Naomi Peck
Assistant Editor: Alex Arfi
Design & editorial assistance: Cooling Brown, Anthony Limerick, Georgina Matthews, Sally Prideaux, Sylvia Tombesi-Walton, Clare Tomlinson, Ingrid Vienings, Jane Webber, Trond Wilhelmsen
Entries in this updated edition were revised, written and researched by: Eve Claxton, Lorie Caval, Denise Maher, Katya Rogers, Diana Shafter

Great care has been taken with this guide to be as accurate and up-to-date as possible, but details such as addresses, telephone numbers, opening hours, prices and travel information are liable to change. The publishers cannot accept responsibility for any consequences arising from the use of this book. We would be delighted to receive any corrections and suggestions for inclusion in the next edition.

Please write to or email:
Virgin Travel Guides
Virgin Publishing Ltd
Thames Wharf Studios
Rainville Road
London w6 9ha
Fax: 020 7386 3360
Email: travel@virgin-pub.co.uk

⊙ key to symbols

☎ telephone number
▯ fax
e email
w worldwide web
❶ hot tips
♘ good points
♞ bad points
◑ opening times
♿ wheelchair access
(phone to check details)
▯ shop
☕ restaurant/café *or*
food available
▯ bar/pub
☆ live entertainments
☞ hotel
▣ (admission) price
◷ frequency/times
↗ picture arrow
▱ map reference
▰ several branches
(phone to check details)

▭ **credit cards**
AE = American Express
DC = Diners Club
MC = Mastercard
V = Visa
all = AE/DC/MC/V
are accepted

★ recommended
(featured in
listings section)

transport

Ⓜ subway
▱ city bus/coach
▬ shuttle bus
▭ cabs
✕ airport
⤜ ferry/cruise boat pier
🄿 parking
↕ uptown/downtown service
↔ crosstown service
③ highway
95 US interstate

key to area maps

 white streets = streets
with lots of shops,
restaurants, bars etc

 grey block =
important building

sights, museums, galleries & parks

👁 don't miss
▣ recorded information line
☞ guided tours
🎧 audio guides
8 kids' activities/age group
◐ sports & activities
▰ roller blading
▰ ice skating
♞ horse riding
🚻 restroom

restaurants & cafés, bars & clubs

♠ capacity
⤴ smoking allowed
▤ air conditioning
✿ outdoor area/garden
➴ live music
Ⓥ good vegetarian selection
Ⓡ reservation recommended
⑤ set menu
○ happy hour
● DJs
◔ satellite/cable TV
👔 dress code
▯ small venue
▮ mid-sized venue
▮ large venue
◖ open during the day,
usually at weekends
$ cheap (main courses under
$10 excluding taxes)
$$ moderate (main courses
$10–$20 excluding taxes)
$$$ expensive (main courses
over $20 excluding taxes)

hotels

♠ number of beds
▱ breakfast included
▤ air conditioning
24 24-hour room service
≋ swimming pool
↔ fitness facilities
✎ business facilities
✿ outdoor area/garden

shops

$ cheap
$$ moderate
$$$ expensive